## PRESIDENT'S SPECIAL REVIEW BOARD
New Executive Office Building - Room 5221
Washington, D.C. 20506
202-456-2566

JOHN TOWER
*Chairman*

EDMUND MUSKIE

BRENT SCOWCROFT

RHETT DAWSON
*Director*

W. CLARK MCFADDEN III
*General Counsel*

The Honorable Ronald W. Reagan
The President of the United States
Washington, D.C. 20500

Dear Mr. President:

We respectfully submit to you the Report of the Special
Review Board. This Report is the product of our study of the
National Security Council, its operation and its staff.

For the last three months, we have reviewed the evolution of
the NSC system since its creation forty years ago. We had
extensive discussions with almost every current and former senior
official involved in national security affairs. Case studies
from several Administrations were also conducted to inform our
judgments.

At your direction, we also focused on the Iran/Contra matter
and sought to follow your injunction that "all the facts come
out." We attempted to do this as fairly as we knew how so that
lessons for the future could be learned.

The Report is based in large part on information and
documentation provided to us by U.S. departments and agencies and
interviews of current and former officials. We relied upon
others in the Executive Branch to conduct the search for
materials or information we requested. In general, we received a
positive response to our inquiries from every agency, including
the White House, although the Independent Counsel and the Federal
Bureau of Investigation responded negatively to our request for
material. We found that the individuals from agencies that
appeared before us generally did so in a forthcoming manner.

The portions of this Report that recite facts were reviewed
by appropriate agency representatives in order to identify
classified material. This was done to enable you to make the
Report public. These representatives performed this security

review without regard for domestic political consequences. No material was deleted on the grounds that it might prove embarrassing to your Administration. There was, however, some information that we concluded had to remain in the classified domain. The appropriate Congressional committees may find this information of use.

While the publication of the material in this Report may be troublesome to some in the short term, we believe that, over time, the nation will clearly benefit by your decision to commission this review. We commend this Report to you and to future Presidents in the hope that it will enhance the effectiveness of the National Security Council.

We are honored to have had the opportunity to serve on this Board.

Sincerely,

Edmund S. Muskie          John Tower          Brent Scowcroft

A
# 𝔑𝔢𝔴 𝔜𝔬𝔯𝔨 𝔗𝔦𝔪𝔢𝔰
SPECIAL

# THE TOWER COMMISSION REPORT

## THE FULL TEXT OF THE
## PRESIDENT'S SPECIAL
## REVIEW BOARD

JOHN TOWER, Chairman
EDMUND MUSKIE and
BRENT SCOWCROFT, members

Introduction by
R. W. APPLE, JR.
Chief Washington Correspondent of
The New York Times

BANTAM    Times
BOOKS     BOOKS

Joint Publication of Bantam Books, Inc.
and Times Books, Inc.

THE TOWER COMMISSION REPORT

First printing / February 1987

This book is co-published in the United States by Bantam Books, Inc., and by Times Books, a division of Random House, Inc., New York, and simultaneously in Canada by Bantam Books, Inc., and Random House of Canada Limited, Toronto.

Material reprinted from The New York Times copyright © 1987, The New York Company. All rights reserved.

ISBN 0-553-26968-2

*Published simultaneously in the United States and Canada*

PRINTED IN THE UNITED STATES OF AMERICA
KR 0 9 8 7 6 5 4 3 2 1

# Table of Contents

# Introduction

John F. Kennedy was assassinated. Lyndon B. Johnson was shouldered into retirement by massive disenchantment with the war in Vietnam. Richard M. Nixon was sunk by Watergate, resigning in the face of probable impeachment. Gerald R. Ford was doomed by his pardon of his predecessor. Jimmy Carter ran aground on the shoals of Iran.

Five presidents. Five presidencies prematurely terminated.

For almost six years, Ronald Wilson Reagan seemed destined to break the string, seemed, indeed, to be one of those rare politicians blessed with the ability, so admired by Machiavelli, to identify himself with the national purpose. But then came the series of events for which no one has been able to devise a more euphonious name than the Iran-contra affair. Their revelation shook the President's grip on the nation and shook the President himself. And now comes the report of the special review board named by the President to decide what went wrong and what to do about it. That report, scathing in its import if not in its language, forms the body of this book. It may, in retrospect, be seen as the watershed of the Reagan presidency.

The pages you are about to read stand apart from past appraisals of Reagan and his era. We used to be told that the failures in Washington in his time were not his failures; his were the successes of rekindling in the American people confidence in themselves, in their country, in their political institutions, in their historical purpose and righteousness. Rambo America was America rampant—too materialistic, too self-obsessed, too superficial, critics said, but nevertheless a forceful presence once again on the grand stage of global power.

But as the report makes clear, the Iran-contra affair constituted a pair of grievous missteps: first, the covert sale of arms to Iran at a time when official American policy continued to call for the isolation of Ayatollah Khomeini and all his works, and second, the diversion of some of the profits to the Nicaraguan rebels at a time when Congress had ruled out direct or indirect American governmental aid.

Iran-contra is not Watergate, and it seems highly unlikely, as this is written, that it will force Ronald Reagan from office. But it has profoundly affected relations between the United States and its friends as well as its foes. It has crippled the Reagan presidency, perhaps paralyzed it. It has changed the way that the American public and the world look at this President, perhaps forever. No more poignant testimony on that point could be adduced than that of Newt Gingrich, the conservative Representative from Atlanta, one of that band of true believers for whom Reagan represented the realization of long-frustrated dreams: "He will never again be the Reagan he was before he blew it. He is not going to regain our trust and our faith easily."

In the months after the disclosure of the broad outlines of the scandal, bits and pieces of the story leaked out. The President and his associates tried several times to "cauterize the wound," as one of them put it, with a singular lack of success. Inevitably, the investigations began—one by the Senate intelligence committee; two by select committees of the Congress; one by a special prosecutor, Lawrence E. Walsh, and the one by the special review board, which was charged specifically with studying what went wrong in the National Security Council, the President's own foreign-policy staff apparatus, which under the leadership of Robert C. McFarlane and then Vice Adm. John M. Poindexter appears to have run wild, with an obscure, zealous Marine Lieutenant Colonel named Oliver L. North making key foreign-policy decisions for the mightiest nation in the free world.

The report of the review board is a first draft, as it were, prepared without the testimony of a number of key figures —Admiral Poindexter, Colonel North, and General Richard V. Secord, a key intermediary—whose accounts are expected to become available later if, as anticipated, they are granted limited immunity from prosecution. The board itself concedes that "the whole matter cannot be fully explained," that some aspects remain an enigma.

Nonetheless, the report represents not only the first detailed official look at the matter, but also a major political event in itself. It is given weight by the reputation of the men who signed it: former Senator John Tower, Republican of Texas, a conservative with special expertise in national security, who was the board's chairman; former Senator and former Secretary of State Edmund S. Muskie, Democrat of Maine, a onetime Presidential candidate known for his probity and level-headedness, and Brent Scowcroft, a retired Air Force general who served several Republican presidents as a key foreign-policy adviser. It is given weight by the fact that the President asked for it to be compiled. And it is given weight by its compellingly sober tone.

The report is particularly harsh on the men surrounding the President, men that he chose and on whom he relied heavily, in keeping with the loose style of management that has served him so well, first in Sacramento and then in the White House. It gives poor marks not only to Robert McFarlane, Admiral Poindexter and Colonel North, not only to Secretary of State George P. Shultz and Defense Secretary Caspar W. Weinberger and William J. Casey, the former Director of Central Intelligence, but also to Donald T. Regan, the autocratic chief of staff, almost certainly ending his government career. These men, the report argues, gave the President bad advice and failed to grasp "the serious political and legal risks" involved in the whole undertaking.

More important, the board painted a picture of Ronald Reagan very different from that the world had become accustomed to in the last six years. No trace here of the lopsided smile, the easy wave, the confident mien that carried him through every past crisis; this portrait is of a man confused, distracted, so remote that he failed utterly to control the implementation of his vision of an initiative that would free American hostages and re-establish American influence in Iran, with all of its present and future strategic importance. At times, in fact, the report makes the President sound like the inhabitant of a never-never land of imaginary policies.

"The President," it says, "appears to have proceeded with a concept of the initiative that was not accurately reflected in the reality of the operation. The President did not seem to be aware of the way in which the operation was implemented and the full consequences of U. S. participation . . . He did not force his policy to undergo the most critical review of which the National Security Council participants and the process were capable. At no time did he insist upon accountability and performance review. Had the President chosen to drive the NSC system, the outcome could well have been different . . . The President's priority in the Iran initiative was the release of U. S. hostages. But setting priorities is not enough when it comes to sensitive and risky initiatives that directly affect U. S. security. He must ensure that the content and tactics of an initiative match his priorities and objectives. He must insist upon accountability. For it is the President who must take the responsibility for the NSC system and deal with the consequences."

Senator Tower was blunt when he answered the questions of reporters a few minutes after the report was released. He summed up his conclusions this way: "I believe the President was poorly advised and poorly served. I think that he should have followed up more and monitored this operation more closely. I think he was not aware of a lot of things that were going on and the way the operation was structured and who was involved in it. He very clearly didn't understand all of that." Senator Muskie added, in his pithy way: "The policy was a wrong policy, and it was the President's policy."

His buoyancy conspicuously absent, Reagan had little to say in a brief public statement just before the board held its press conference, except for a pledge to "do whatever is necessary to enact the proper reforms and to meet the challenges ahead." The problem with that was that all three members of the board made it plain that they considered this a policy blunder caused not by institutions but by individuals.

The report exonerates the President of complicity in any

attempt to cover up the blunder. "The board," it says, "is convinced that the President does indeed want the full story to be told." But the report strongly suggests that at various times McFarlane, Regan, Poindexter and North all made misleading statements and tried to "distance" Reagan from the entire controversy.

One of the more vivid examples of deception recounted in the report involves Admiral Poindexter and Colonel North. The marine officer, according to the report, recounted in an internal message how he had misinformed a Congressional committee about his role in directing covert aid to the Nicaraguan rebels, and his boss, the admiral, replied, "Well done." The board also found notes of key meetings missing; General Scowcroft said he considered the lack of written records appalling and added, "It may be that some went into the shredder, but we can't prove it."

The report describes the President's shifting account of whether or not he approved the arms sales to Iran as early as August, 1985, as McFarlane testified. Reagan told the board on Jan. 26 that he had done so, on Feb. 11 that he had not done so and in a letter of Feb. 20 that "I don't remember—period." He said in the letter that "I'm afraid that I let myself be influenced by others' recollections, not my own," in his earlier answers. The board concluded that the President, "most likely" did approve, just as McFarlane said he did.

Reagan has always insisted that he did not try to trade arms for hostages, but the report thoroughly rebuts that assertion. "Whatever the intent," it says, "almost from the beginning the initiative became, in fact, a series of arms-for-hostages deals . . . As arms-for-hostages trades, they could not help but create an incentive for further hostage-taking . . . The arms-for-hostages trades rewarded a regime that clearly supported terrorism and hostage-taking . . . They raised questions as to whether U.S. policy statements could be relied upon . . . A pattern of successive bargained exchanges of arms and hostages was quickly established. While release of all the hostages continued to be promised, in fact the hostages came out singly if at all. This sad history is powerful evidence, that of why the United States should never have become involved in the arms transfers."

"The Iran initiative ran directly counter to the Administration's own policies on terrorism, the Iran/Iraq war and military support to Iran," the report concludes. "This inconsistency was never resolved, nor were the consequences of this inconsistency fully considered and provided for. The result taken as a whole was a U. S. policy that worked against itself . . . an unprofessional and, in substantial part, unsatisfactory operation."

In other words, it was an inept policy, poorly implemented.

The report pictures a National Security Council led by reckless cowboys, off on their own on a wild ride, taking direct operational control of matters that are the customary province of more sober agencies such as the C. I. A., the State Department and the Defense Department. In this instance, the report says, a kind of parallel government came into being, operating in secret, paying scant heed to laws, deceiving Congress and avoiding oversight of any kind. Poindexter and North, the report adds, "functioned largely outside the orbit of the U.S. government," acting through a shadowy network of Americans, Israelis and Iranians, some of whom were considered most unreliable by other senior United States officials.

On some other questions, the board ran into what it called murky, unfathomable situations. The report says that it is not certain whether laws were violated—deciding that issue will be the job of Special Prosecutor Walsh and, ultimately, the courts—but does say that the President's aides willfully ignored legal restraints. The report also says that while some of the same problems as plagued the Iran initiative also beset the Contra support efforts, the board's information on that subject is far less comprehensive. The Senate and House select committees are expected to concentrate heavily on Contra aid.

In its futile efforts to trace the diversion of money from the arms deal, the board stumbled upon a vast network of private assistance to the Contras being run out of the Security Council offices in apparent defiance of a Congressional ban. This discovery, which Tower described as a spur to the entire investigation, also awaits further exploration by the other official inquiries into the Iran-contra affair.

But it is not any individual finding in the report that seemed most likely to damage Ronald Reagan's ability to function as a vigorous and effective President for the last

23 months of his term and to cloud his place in history. It is instead the almost pathetic picture of a man wholly out of touch with a central episode in his presidency. It is the cumulative impact of page after page of careful, unemotional description of experts unconsulted, of policies unevaluated, of records unkept, of questions unasked, of operations concealed by senior public servants even from one another—and of a policy so convoluted and incomprehensible that some of the charts illustrating individual transactions look like Rube Goldberg cartoons, full of arrows, boxes, circles, numbers and labels.

This is not a portrait of venality. It is a portrait of ineptitude verging on incompetence. It is a portrait not of inadequate institutions but of stumbling, short-sighted stewardship of the national trust at a moment of crisis, from the President on down, which may be why the board chose as the epigraph for its narrative a line from the Latin poet Juvenal. It can be freely translated as "Who shall guard the guardians themselves?"

by R. W. Apple Jr.
Chief Washington Correspondent
*The New York Times*

# The Findings: A Summary

*Former Secretary of State Edmund S. Muskie, speaking at a news conference in Washington at which the Tower commission's report was made public, offered a summary of the report's findings, which were unanimously adopted.*

- The Iran initiative was handled almost casually and through informal channels, always, apparently, with an expectation that the process would end with the next arms-for-hostages exchange. And of course it did not. It was subjected neither to the general procedures for interagency consideration and review of policy nor the procedures for covert operations.

- The opportunity for a full hearing before the President was inadequate.

- Interagency consideration of the initiative was limited to the Cabinet level and inadequate at that. It was never examined at the staff level where expertise on the situation in Iran, the difficulties of dealing with terrorists and the mechanisms of conducting diplomatic openings may have made a difference.

- Intelligence analysis could also have provided an independent evaluation of the Israeli proposals, a systematic vetting of those engaged as intermediaries and a thorough examination of the effects of the initiative on the balance in the Iran-Iraq war.

- Insufficient attention was given to the implications of the N.S.C. staff having operational control of the initiative rather than the C.I.A.

- Concern for preserving the secrecy of the initiative provided an excuse for abandoning sound process.

- The informality of the initiative meant that it lacked a formal institutional record and informed analysis. The result was that we were too often dependent on mere recollection instead of a clear and complete record.

- The implementation of the initiative was never subjected to a rigorous review at appropriate times in this long 18-month history.

- The N.S.C. system will not work unless the President makes it work. After all, this system was created to serve the President of the United States in ways of his choosing. By his actions, by his leadership, the President, therefore, determines the quality of its performance.

- The President did not force his policy to undergo the most critical review of which the N.S.C. participants and the process were capable.

- The board found a strong consensus among N.S.C. participants that the President's priority in the Iran initiative was the release of U.S. hostages. But setting priorities is not enough when it comes to sensitive and risky initiatives that directly affect U.S. national security. For it is the President who must take responsibility for the N.S.C. system and deal with the consequences.

- President Reagan's personal management style places an especially heavy responsibility on his key advisers. Knowing his style, they should have been particularly mindful of the need for special attention to the measures in which this arms sales initiative developed and proceeded. On this score, neither the national security adviser Robert C. McFarlane and Vice Adm. John M. Poindexter nor the other N.S.C. principals deserve high marks.

- The national security adviser failed in his responsibility to see that an orderly process was observed.

- The chief of staff Donald T. Regan also shares in this responsibility. More than almost any chief of staff of recent memory, he asserted personal control over the White House staff and sought to extend his control to the national security adviser. He, as much as anyone, should have insisted that an orderly process be observed. In addition, he especially should have insured that plans were made for handling any public disclosure of the initiative.

- Given the importance of the initiative, Secretary Shultz and Secretary Weinberger, while indicating their opposition, distanced themselves from the march of events.

- There is no evidence that (C.I.A.) Director Casey made clear to the President that Lieutenant Colonel North, rather than the C.I.A., was running the operation. The President does not recall ever being informed of this fact. Indeed, Director Casey should have gone further and pressed for operational responsibility to be transferred to the C.I.A.

# The Tower Commission
Report

*Part I*

# Introduction to the Tower Commission Report

In November, 1986, it was disclosed that the United States had, in August, 1985, and subsequently, participated in secret dealings with Iran involving the sale of military equipment. There appeared to be a linkage between these dealings and efforts to obtain the release of U.S. citizens held hostage in Lebanon by terrorists believed to be closely associated with the Iranian regime. After the initial story broke, the Attorney General announced that proceeds from the arms transfers may have been diverted to assist U.S.-backed rebel forces in Nicaragua, known as Contras. This possibility enlarged the controversy and added questions not only of policy and propriety but also violations of law.

These disclosures became the focus of substantial public attention. The secret arms transfers appeared to run directly counter to declared U.S. policies. The United States had announced a policy of neutrality in the six-year old Iran/Iraq war and had proclaimed an embargo on arms sales to Iran. It had worked actively to isolate Iran and other regimes known to give aid and comfort to terrorists. It had declared that it would not pay ransom to hostage-takers.

Public concern was not limited to the issues of policy, however. Questions arose as to the propriety of certain actions taken by the National Security Council staff and the manner in which the decision to transfer arms to Iran had been made. Congress was never informed. A variety of intermediaries, both private and governmental, some with motives open to question, had central roles. The NSC staff rather than the CIA seemed to be running the opera-

1

tion. The President appeared to be unaware of key elements of the operation. The controversy threatened a crisis of confidence in the manner in which national security decisions are made and the role played by the NSC staff.

It was this latter set of concerns that prompted the President to establish this Special Review Board on December 1, 1986. The President directed the Board to examine the proper role of the National Security Council staff in national security operations, including the arms transfers to Iran. The President made clear that he wanted "all the facts to come out."

The Board was not, however, called upon to assess individual culpability or be the final arbiter of the facts. These tasks have been properly left to others. Indeed, the short deadline set by the President for completion of the Board's work and its limited resources precluded a separate and thorough field investigation. Instead, the Board has examined the events surrounding the transfer of arms to Iran as a principal case study in evaluating the operation of the National Security Council in general and the role of the NSC staff in particular.

The President gave the Board a broad charter. It was directed to conduct "a comprehensive study of the future role and procedures of the National Security Council (NSC) staff in the development, coordination, oversight, and conduct of foreign and national security policy."[1]

It has been forty years since the enactment of the National Security Act of 1947 and the creation of the National Security Council. Since that time the NSC staff has grown in importance and the Assistant to the President for National Security Affairs has emerged as a key player in national security decision-making. This is the first Presidential Commission to have as its sole responsibility a comprehensive review of how these institutions have performed. We believe that, quite aside from the circumstances which brought about the Board's creation, such a review was overdue.

The Board divided its work into three major inquiries: the circumstances surrounding the Iran/Contra matter, other case studies that might reveal strengths and weaknesses in the operation of the National Security Council system under stress, and the manner in which that system has served eight different Presidents since its inception in 1947.

At Appendix B is a narrative of the information obtained from documents and interviews regarding the arms sales to Iran. The narrative is necessarily incomplete. As of the date of this report, some key witnesses had refused to testify before any forum. Important documents located in other countries had yet to be released, and important witnesses in other countries were not available. But the appended narrative tells much of the story. Although more information will undoubtedly come to light, the record thus far developed provides a sufficient basis for evaluating the process by which these events came about.

During the Board's work, it received evidence concerning the role of the NSC staff in support of the Contras during the period that such support was either barred or restricted by Congress. The Board had neither the time nor the resources to make a systematic inquiry into this area. Notwithstanding, substantial evidence came before the Board. A narrative of that evidence is contained at Appendix C.

The Board found that the issues raised by the Iran/Contra matter are in most instances not new. Every Administration has faced similar issues, although arising in different factual contexts. The Board examined in some detail the performance of the National Security Council system in 12 different crises dating back to the Truman Administration.[2] Former government officials participating in many of these crises were interviewed. This learning provided a broad historical perspective to the issues before the Board.

Those who expect from us a radical prescription for wholesale change may be disappointed. Not all major problems—and Iran/Contra has been a major one—can be solved simply by rearranging organizational blocks or passing new laws.

In addition, it is important to emphasize that the President is responsible for the national security policy of the United States. In the development and execution of that policy, the President is the decision-maker. He is not obliged to consult with or seek approval from anyone in the Executive Branch. The structure and procedures of the National Security Council system should be designed to give the President every assistance in discharging these heavy responsibilities. It is not possible to make a system immune from error without paralyzing its capacity to act.

At its senior levels, the National Security Council is primarily the interaction of people. We have examined with care its operation in the Iran/Contra matter and have set out in considerable detail mistakes of omission, commission, judgment, and perspective. We believe that this record and analysis can warn future Presidents, members of the National Security Council, and National Security Advisors of the potential pitfalls they face even when they are operating with what they consider the best of motives. We would hope that this record would be carefully read and its lessons fully absorbed by all aspirants to senior positions in the National Security Council system.

This report will serve another purpose. In preparing it, we contacted every living past President, three former Vice Presidents, and every living Secretary of State, Secretary of Defense, National Security Advisor, most Directors of Central Intelligence, and several Chairmen of the Joint Chiefs of Staff to solicit their views. We sought to learn how well, in their experience, the system had operated or, in the case of past Presidents, how well it served them. We asked all former participants how they would change the system to make it more useful to the President.[3]

Our review validates the current National Security Council system. That system has been utilized by different Presidents in very different ways, in accordance with their individual work habits and philosophical predilections. On occasion over the years it has functioned with real brilliance; at other times serious mistakes have been made. The problems we examined in the case of Iran/Contra caused us deep concern. But their solution does not lie in revamping the National Security Council system.

That system is properly the President's creature. It must be left flexible to be molded by the President into the form most useful to him. Otherwise it will become either an obstacle to the President, and a source of frustration; or an institutional irrelevance, as the President fashions informal structures more to his liking.

Having said that, there are certain functions which need to be performed in some way for any President. What we have tried to do is to distill from the wisdom of those who

4

have participated in the National Security Council system over the past forty years the essence of these functions and the manner in which that system can be operated so as to minimize the likelihood of major error without destroying the creative impulses of the President.

## Part II

# Organizing for National Security

Ours is a government of checks and balances, of shared power and responsibility. The Constitution places the President and the Congress in dynamic tension. They both cooperate and compete in the making of national policy.

National security is no exception. The Constitution gives both the President and the Congress an important role. The Congress is critical in formulating national policies and in marshalling the resources to carry them out. But those resources—the nation's military personnel, its diplomats, its intelligence capability—are lodged in the Executive Branch. As Chief Executive and Commander-in-Chief, and with broad authority in the area of foreign affairs, it is the President who is empowered to act for the nation and protect its interests.

## A. The National Security Council

The present organization of the Executive Branch for national security matters was established by the National Security Act of 1947. That Act created the National Security Council. As now constituted, its statutory members are the President, Vice President, Secretary of State, and Secretary of Defense. The President is the head of the National Security Council.

Presidents have from time to time invited the heads of other departments or agencies to attend National Security Council meetings or to participate as de facto members. These have included the Director of Central Intelligence (the "DCI") and the Chairman of the Joint Chiefs of Staff (the "CJCS"). The President (or, in his absence, his designee) presides.

The National Security Council deals with the most vital issues in the nation's national security policy. It is this body that discusses recent developments in arms control and the Strategic Defense Initiative; that discussed whether or not to bomb the Cambodia mainland after the *Mayaguez* was captured; that debated the timetable for the U.S. withdrawal from Vietnam; and that considered the risky and daring attempt to rescue U.S. hostages in Iran in 1980. The National Security Council deals with issues that are difficult, complex, and often secret. Decisions are often required in hours rather than weeks. Advice must be given under great stress and with imperfect information.

The National Security Council is not a decision-making body. Although its other members hold official positions in the Government, when meeting as the National Security Council they sit as advisors to the President. This is clear from the language of the 1947 Act:

> "The function of the Council shall be to advise the President with respect to the integration of domestic, foreign, and military policies relating to the national security so as to enable the military services and the other departments and agencies of the Government to cooperate more effectively in matters involving the national security."

The National Security Council has from its inception been a highly personal instrument. Every President has turned for advice to those individuals and institutions whose judgment he has valued and trusted. For some Presidents, such as President Eisenhower, the National Security Council served as a primary forum for obtaining advice on national security matters. Other Presidents, such as President Kennedy, relied on more informal groupings of advisors, often including some but not all of the Council members.

One official summarized the way the system has been adjusted by different Presidents:

> "The NSC is going to be pretty well what a President wants it to be and what he determines it should be. Kennedy—and these are some exaggerations and gen-

eralities of course—with an anti-organizational bias, disestablished all [the Eisenhower created] committees and put a tight group in the White House totally attuned to his philosophic approach * * *. Johnson didn't change that very much, except certain difficulties began to develop in the informality which was [otherwise] characterized by speed, unity of purpose, precision * * *. So it had great efficiency and responsiveness. The difficulties began to develop in * * * the informality of the thing."

The Nixon Administration saw a return to the use of the National Security Council as a principal forum for national security advice. This pattern was continued by President Ford and President Carter, and in large measure by President Reagan.

Regardless of the frequency of its use, the NSC has remained a strictly advisory body. Each President has kept the burden of decision for himself, in accordance with his Constitutional responsibilities.

# B. The Assistant to the President for National Security Affairs

Although closely associated with the National Security Council in the public mind, the Assistant to the President for National Security Affairs is not one of its members. Indeed, no mention of this position is made in the National Security Act of 1947.

The position was created by President Eisenhower in 1953. Although its precise title has varied, the position has come to be known (somewhat misleadingly) as the National Security Advisor.

Under President Eisenhower, the holder of this position served as the principal executive officer of the Council, setting the agenda, briefing the President on Council matters, and supervising the staff. He was not a policy advocate.

It was not until President Kennedy, with McGeorge Bundy in the role, that the position took on its current form. Bundy emerged as an important personal advisor to the President on national security affairs. This introduced an element of direct competition into Bundy's relationship with the members of the National Security Council. Although President Johnson changed the title of the position to simply "Special Assistant," in the hands of Walt Rostow it continued to play an important role.

President Nixon relied heavily on his National Security Advisor, maintaining and even enhancing its prominence. In that position, Henry Kissinger became a key spokesman for the President's national security policies both to the U.S. press and to foreign governments. President Nixon used him to negotiate on behalf of the United States with Vietnam, China, the Soviet Union, and other countries. The roles of spokesman and negotiator had traditionally been the province of the Secretary of State, not of the National Security Advisor. The emerging tension between the two positions was only resolved when Kissinger assumed them both.

Under President Ford, Lt Gen Brent Scowcroft became National Security Advisor, with Henry Kissinger remaining as Secretary of State. The National Security Advisor exercised major responsibility for coordinating for the President the advice of his NSC principals and overseeing the process of policy development and implementation within the Executive Branch.

President Carter returned in large part to the early Kissinger model, with a resulting increase in tensions with the Secretary of State. President Carter wanted to take the lead in matters of foreign policy, and used his National Security Advisor as a source of information, ideas, and new initiatives.

The role of the National Security Advisor, like the role of the NSC itself, has in large measure been a function of the operating style of the President. Notwithstanding, the National Security Advisor has come to perform, to a greater or lesser extent, certain functions which appear essential to the effective discharge of the President's responsibilities in national security affairs.

• He is an "honest broker" for the NSC process. He assures that issues are clearly presented to the President; that all reasonable options, together with an analysis of their disadvantages and risks, are brought to his attention; and that the views of the President's other principal advisors are accurately conveyed.

- He provides advice from the President's vantage point, unalloyed by institutional responsibilities and biases. Unlike the Secretaries of State or Defense, who have substantial organizations for which they are responsible, the President is the National Security Advisor's only constituency.
- He monitors the actions taken by the executive departments in implementing the President's national security policies. He asks the question whether these actions are consistent with Presidential decisions and whether, over time, the underlying policies continue to serve U.S. interests.
- He has a special role in crisis management. This has resulted from the need for prompt and coordinated action under Presidential control, often with secrecy being essential.
- He reaches out for new ideas and initiatives that will give substance to broad Presidential objectives for national security.
- He keeps the President informed about international developments and developments in the Congress and the Executive Branch that affect the President's policies and priorities.

But the National Security Advisor remains the creature of the President. The position will be largely what he wants it to be. This presents any President with a series of dilemmas.

- The President must surround himself with people he trusts and to whom he can speak in confidence. To this end, the National Security Advisor, unlike the Secretaries of State and Defense, is not subject to confirmation by the Senate and does not testify before Congress. But the more the President relies on the National Security Advisor for advice, especially to the exclusion of his Cabinet officials, the greater will be the unease with this arrangement.
- As the "honest broker" of the NSC process, the National Security Advisor must ensure that the different and often conflicting views of the NSC principals are pre-

sented fairly to the President. But as an independent advisor to the President, he must provide his own judgment. To the extent that the National Security Advisor becomes a strong advocate for a particular point of view, his role as "honest broker" may be compromised and the President's access to the unedited views of the NSC principals may be impaired.

- The Secretaries of State and Defense, and the Director of Central Intelligence, head agencies of government that have specific statutory responsibilities and are subject to Congressional oversight for the implementation of U.S. national security policy. To the extent that the National Security Advisor assumes operational responsibilities, whether by negotiating with foreign governments or becoming heavily involved in military or intelligence operations, the legitimacy of that role and his authority to perform it may be challenged.

- The more the National Security Advisor becomes an "operator" in implementing policy, the less will he be able objectively to review that implementation—and whether the underlying policy continues to serve the interests of the President and the nation.

- The Secretary of State has traditionally been the President's spokesman on matters of national security and foreign affairs. To the extent that the National Security Advisor speaks publicly on these matters or meets with representatives of foreign governments, the result may be confusion as to what is the President's policy.

## C. The NSC Staff

At the time it established the National Security Council, Congress authorized a staff headed by an Executive Secretary appointed by the President. Initially quite small, the NSC staff expanded substantially under President Eisenhower.

During the Eisenhower Administration, the NSC staff assumed two important functions: coordinating the executive departments in the development of national policy (through the NSC Planning Board) and overseeing the implementation of that policy (through the Operations Coordination Board). A systematic effort was made to coordi-

11

nate policy development and its implementation by the various agencies through an elaborate set of committees. The system worked fairly well in bringing together for the President the views of the other NSC principals. But it has been criticized as biased toward reaching consensus among these principals rather than developing options for Presidential decision. By the end of his second term, President Eisenhower himself had reached the conclusion that a highly competent individual and a small staff could perform the needed functions in a better way. Such a change was made by President Kennedy.

Under President Kennedy, a number of the functions of the NSC staff were eliminated and its size was sharply reduced. The Planning and Operations Coordinating Boards were abolished. Policy development and policy implementation were assigned to individual Cabinet officers, responsible directly to the President. By late 1962 the staff was only 12 professionals, serving largely as an independent source of ideas and information to the President. The system was lean and responsive, but frequently suffered from a lack of coordination. The Johnson Administration followed much the same pattern.

The Nixon Administration returned to a model more like Eisenhower's but with something of the informality of the Kennedy/Johnson staffs. The Eisenhower system had emphasized coordination; the Kennedy-Johnson system tilted to innovation and the generation of new ideas. The Nixon system emphasized both. The objective was not inter-departmental consensus but the generation of policy options for Presidential decision, and then ensuring that those decision were carried out. The staff grew to 50 professionals in 1970 and became a major factor in the national security decision-making process. This approach was largely continued under President Ford.

The NSC staff retained an important role under President Carter. While continuing to have responsibility for coordinating policy among the various executive agencies, President Carter particularly looked to the NSC staff as a personal source of independent advice. President Carter felt the need to have a group loyal only to him from which to launch his own initiatives and to move a vast and lethargic government. During his time in office, President Carter reduced the size of the professional staff to 35, feeling that a smaller group could do the job and would have a closer relationship to him.

What emerges from this history is an NSC staff used by each President in a way that reflected his individual preferences and working style. Over time, it has developed an important role within the Executive Branch of coordinating policy review, preparing issues for Presidential decision, and monitoring implementation. But it has remained the President's creature, molded as he sees fit, to serve as his personal staff for national security affairs. For this reason, it has generally operated out of the public view and has not been subject to direct oversight by the Congress.

## D. The Interagency Committee System

The National Security Council has frequently been supported by committees made up of representatives of the relevant national security departments and agencies. These committees analyze issues prior to consideration by the Council. There are generally several levels of committees. At the top level, officials from each agency (at the Deputy Secretary or Under Secretary level) meet to provide a senior level policy review. These senior-level committees are in turn supported by more junior interagency groups (usually at the Assistant Secretary level). These in turn may oversee staff level working groups that prepare detailed analysis of important issues.

Administrations have differed in the extent to which they have used these interagency committees. President Kennedy placed little stock in them. The Nixon and Carter Administrations, by contrast, made much use of them.

## E. The Reagan Model

President Reagan entered office with a strong commitment to cabinet government. His principal advisors on national security affairs were to be the Secretaries of State and Defense, and to a lesser extent the Director of Central Intelligence. The position of the National Security Advisor was initially downgraded in both status and access to the President. Over the next six years, five different people held that position.

The Administration's first National Security Advisor, Richard Allen, reported to the President through the senior White House staff. Consequently, the NSC staff assumed a reduced role. Mr. Allen believed that the Secretary of State had primacy in the field of foreign policy. He viewed the job of the National Security Advisor as that of a policy coordinator.

President Reagan initially declared that the National Security Council would be the principal forum for consideration of national security issues. To support the work of the Council, President Reagan established an interagency committee system headed by three Senior Interagency Groups (or "SIGs"), one each for foreign policy, defense policy, and intelligence. They were chaired by the Secretary of State, the Secretary of Defense, and the Director of Central Intelligence, respectively.

Over time, the Administration's original conception of the role of the National Security Advisor changed. William Clark, who succeeded Richard Allen in 1982, was a longtime associate of the President and dealt directly with him. Robert McFarlane, who replaced Judge Clark in 1983, although personally less close to the President, continued to have direct access to him. The same was true for VADM John Poindexter, who was appointed to the position in December, 1985.

President Reagan appointed several additional members to his National Security Council and allowed staff attendance at meetings. The resultant size of the meetings led the President to turn increasingly to a smaller group (called the National Security Planning Group or "NSPG"). Attendance at its meetings was more restricted but included the statutory principals of the NSC. The NSPG was supported by the SIGs, and new SIGs were occasionally created to deal with particular issues. These were frequently chaired by the National Security Advisor. But generally the SIGs and many of their subsidiary groups (called Interagency Groups or "IGs") fell into disuse.

As a supplement to the normal NSC process, the Reagan Administration adopted comprehensive procedures for covert actions. These are contained in a classified document, NSDD-159, establishing the process for deciding, implementing, monitoring, and reviewing covert activities.

# F. The Problem of Covert Operations

Covert activities place a great strain on the process of decision in a free society. Disclosure of even the existence of the operation could threaten its effectiveness and risk embarrassment to the Government. As a result, there is strong pressure to withhold information, to limit knowledge of the operation to a minimum number of people.

These pressures come into play with great force when covert activities are undertaken in an effort to obtain the release of U.S. citizens held hostage abroad. Because of the legitimate human concern all Presidents have felt over the fate of such hostages, our national pride as a powerful country with a tradition of protecting its citizens abroad, and the great attention paid by the news media to hostage situations, the pressures on any President to take action to free hostages are enormous. Frequently to be effective, this action must necessarily be covert. Disclosure would directly threaten the lives of the hostages as well as those willing to contemplate their release.

Since covert arms sales to Iran played such a central role in the creation of this Board, it has focused its attention in large measure on the role of the NSC staff where covert activity is involved. This is not to denigrate, however, the importance of other decisions taken by the government. In those areas as well the National Security Council and its staff play a critical role. But in many respects the best test of a system is its performance under stress. The conditions of greatest stress are often found in the crucible of covert activities.

*Part III*

# Arms Transfers to Iran, Diversion, and Support for the Contras

The Iran/Contra matter has been and, in some respects, still is an enigma. For three months the Board sought to learn the facts, and still the whole matter cannot be fully explained. The general outlines of the story are clear. The story is set out here as we now know it.

Given the President's injunction that he wanted "all the facts to come out," the Board sought to include all relevant materials. The Board tried to be faithful to the testimony and documents that came before it. This Board was not established, however, as an investigative body nor was it to determine matters of criminal culpability. Rather, the Board was established to gather the facts, to place them in their proper historical context, and to make recommendations about what corrective steps might be taken.

The limits of time, resources, and legal authority were handicaps but not unreasonable ones.

The Board had no authority to subpoena documents, compel testimony, swear witnesses, or grant immunity.

But these limitations did not prevent the Board from assembling sufficient information to form a basis for its fundamental judgments. The Board received a vast quantity of documents and interviewed over 80 witnesses. The Board requested all affected departments and agencies to provide all documents relevant to the Board's inquiry. The Board relied upon these agencies to conduct thorough searches for all relevant materials in their possession. In addition, the Board reviewed the results and relevant portions of working files from both the CIA and Department of the Army Inspectors General reports.

Several individuals declined our request to appear before the Board: VADM John Poindexter; General Richard Secord, USAF Ret.; LtCol Oliver North; LtCol Robert Earl; Mr. Albert Hakim; and Miss Fawn Hall. The Board requested that the President exercise his powers as Commander-in-Chief and order VADM Poindexter and LtCol North to appear. The President declined.[1]

Despite the refusal of VADM Poindexter and LtCol North to appear, the Board's access to other sources of information filled much of this gap. The FBI provided documents taken from the files of the National Security Advisor and relevant NSC staff members, including messages from the PROF system[2] between VADM Poindexter and LtCol North. The PROF messages were conversations by computer, written at the time events occurred and presumed by the writers to be protected from disclosure. In this sense, they provide a first-hand, contemporaneous account of events.

In the closing days of the Board's inquiry, we gained access to a considerable number of additional exchanges on PROFs between VADM Poindexter, LtCol North, and Mr. McFarlane.

The Board had access to another contemporaneous record of events. The President keeps a diary in which he chronicles, in long hand, key events that occurred during the day. President Reagan reviewed his notes and, at the Board's request, culled from them the relevant notes he had made on particular dates requested by the Board. The Board was permitted to review but not to retain a typewritten copy of these diary entries.

No one interviewed by the Board seemed able to provide a unified account of the events in August independent of calendars or meeting notes. In the lives of these particularly busy individuals this should not be surprising. This lack of a total and accurate recall may suggest an equally important point: when these events occurred, they were not treated by many of the participants as sufficiently important.

Those that are present at meetings or privy to conversations will retain different impressions of what occurred. That certainly happened here. Many of these events occurred almost two years ago, and memories fade. There is also the chance that, for whatever reason, individuals concealed evidence or deliberately misled the Board. In any event, the Board's mandate was not to resolve conflicts among various recollections but to attempt to ascertain the essential facts as they affect conclusions about the national security process.

The Independent Counsel at various points denied the Board access to some materials in which he had established an interest. The Government of Israel was asked to make certain individuals available in any way that would be convenient to them. They declined to do so. They agreed to answer written interrogatories. We dispatched those to the Government of Israel but no response has, as yet, been received.

The first section of this Part III summarizes the evidence before the Board concerning the arms transfers to Iran. A more detailed narrative of this evidence is set out in Appendix B.

The second section summarizes the evidence before the Board concerning a diversion of funds from the arms sales to the support of the Contras fighting in Nicaragua.

The third section summarizes the evidence accumulated by the Board concerning the role of the NSC staff in the support of the Contras during the period that support from the U.S. government was either barred or restricted by Congress. A more detailed narrative of this evidence is set out in Appendix C.

# Section A: The Arms Transfers to Iran

Two persistent concerns lay behind U.S. participation in arms transfers to Iran.

First, the U.S. government anxiously sought the release of seven U.S. citizens abducted in Beirut, Lebanon, in seven separate incidents between March 7, 1984, and June 9, 1985. One of those abducted was William Buckley, CIA station chief in Beirut, seized on March 16, 1984. Available intelligence suggested that most, if not all, of the Americans were held hostage by members of Hezballah, a fundamentalist Shiite terrorist group with links to the regime of the Ayatollah Khomeini.

Second, the U.S. government had a latent and unresolved interest in establishing ties to Iran. Few in the U.S. government doubted Iran's strategic importance or the risk of Soviet meddling in the succession crisis that might follow the death of Khomeini. For this reason, some in the U.S. government were convinced that efforts should be made to open potential channels to Iran.

Arms transfers ultimately appeared to offer a means to achieve both the release of the hostages and a strategic opening to Iran.

The formulation, development, and implementation of the Iran initiative passed through seven distinct stages. Each is analyzed in this section of the report. For the purposes of the Board's mandate, the critical questions for each stage are: What was U.S. policy? How were decisions made? What action was authorized and by whom? How was this action carried out? What happened as a result?

## Stage 1: The NSC Staff Seeks a New Look at U.S. Policy on Iran

The Shah of Iran was overthrown on January 16, 1979, ending an intimate, twenty-five year relationship between the United States and Iran. Mutual hostility and tension characterized U.S. relations with the regime of the Ayatollah Khomeini, which, after some months, succeeded the Shah's rule. On November 4, 1979, radical Iranian elements seized the U.S. embassy in Tehran and held its staff hostage. The United States responded by blocking the transfer of all property of the Iranian government, imposing a trade embargo, freezing all other Iranian assets, and breaking diplomatic relations. In addition, the United States imposed an embargo on all arms shipments to Iran, including arms that had been purchased under the Shah but not yet delivered.

On January 19, 1981, many of these restrictions were lifted, as part of the agreement that led to the release of the embassy staff. However, this did not extend to the embargo on arms transfers. Iraq had attacked Iran on September 22, 1980. The United States had adopted a policy of neutrality and refused to ship arms to either side. The result was a continuation of the arms embargo against Iran.

The Reagan Administration had adopted a tough line

against terrorism. In particular, the United States adamantly opposed making any concessions to terrorists in exchange for the release of hostages—whether by paying ransom, releasing prisoners, changing policies, or otherwise. Some time in July of 1982, the United States became aware of evidence suggesting that Iran was supporting terrorist groups, including groups engaged in hostage-taking. On January 20, 1984, the Secretary of State designated Iran a sponsor of international terrorism.[3] Thereafter, the United States actively pressured its allies not to ship arms to Iran, both because of its sponsorship of international terrorism and its continuation of the war with Iraq.

*The NSC Staff Initiates a Reevaluation.* By early 1984, Robert McFarlane, the National Security Advisor, and members of the NSC staff, had become concerned about future U.S. policy toward Iran. They feared that the death of Khomeini would touch off a succession struggle which would hold important consequences for U.S. interests. They believed that the United States lacked a strategy and capability for dealing with this prospect.

Initially, Mr. McFarlane tried to use the formal interagency policy process to address this issue. On August 31, 1984, he requested an interagency study of U.S. relations with Iran after Khomeini. On October 19, 1984, the State Department sent Mr. McFarlane the interagency response to his request. It concluded that the United States had "no influential contacts" within the Iranian government or Iranian political groups. The study suggested little that the United States could do to establish such contacts. Separately, in a letter dated December 11, 1984, to Mr. McFarlane's deputy, VADM John Poindexter, the CIA professed only a limited capability to influence events in Iran over the near term.

*The Reevaluation Yields No New Ideas.* Howard Teicher, one of the NSC staff members involved, told the Board that the interagency effort failed to identify any new ideas for significantly expanding U.S. influence in Iran. It resulted in no change in U.S. policy. The U.S. government continued aggressively to discourage arms transfers by other nations to Iran under a program called "Operation Staunch."

# Stage 2: The NSC Staff Tries a Second Time

Mr. Teicher, Donald Fortier, and perhaps other NSC staff members were unhappy with the result of the interagency effort. They placed a high priority on fashioning a strategy for acquiring influence and checking the Soviets in Iran. Graham Fuller, then the National Intelligence Officer for the Near East and South Asia, told the Board that in early 1985 the U.S. intelligence community began to believe that serious factional fighting could break out in Iran even before Khomeini died. This change in the community's assessment provided a second opportunity for a policy review.

*The NSC Staff Suggests Limited Arms Sales.* Mr. Teicher, and to a lesser extent Mr. Fortier, worked closely with CIA officials to prepare an update of a previous "Special National Intelligence Estimate" (or "SNIE") on Iran. Dated May 20, 1985, the update portrayed the Soviets as well positioned to take advantage of chaos inside Iran. The United States, by contrast, was unlikely to be able directly to influence events. Our European and other allies could, however, provide a valuable presence to help protect Western interests. The update concluded that the degree to which these allies "can fill a military gap for Iran will be a critical measure of the West's ability to blunt Soviet influence."

On June 11, 1985, Mr. Fortier and Mr. Teicher submitted to Mr. McFarlane a draft Presidential decision document (a National Security Decision Directive or "NSDD") drawing on the intelligence update. The draft set out immediate and long-term U.S. goals and listed specific steps to achieve them. First on the list was to "[e]ncourage Western allies and friends to help Iran meet its import requirements * * * includ[ing] provision of selected military equipment * * *."

The memorandum from Mr. Fortier and Mr. Teicher transmitting the draft NSDD to Mr. McFarlane suggested that "[b]ecause of the political and bureaucratic sensitivities," Mr. McFarlane should provide copies of the NSDD only to Secretary of State Shultz and Secretary of Defense Weinberger. "Whether to proceed with a restricted SIG [Senior Interagency Group], NSPG [National Security

Planning Group], or other forum [for consideration of the draft] would depend on their reactions."

Mr. McFarlane circulated the draft on June 17, 1985, to Secretary Shultz, Secretary Weinberger, and Director of Central Intelligence Casey. His transmittal memorandum requested that further distribution remain limited to lessen the risk of leaks. In letters to Mr. McFarlane dated June 29, 1985, and July 16, 1985, respectively, both Secretary Shultz and Secretary Weinberger objected sharply to the suggestion that the United States should permit or encourage transfers of Western arms to Iran. By contrast, in his reply of July 18, 1985, Director Casey "strongly endorse[d]" the thrust of the draft NSDD and particularly its emphasis on the need to take "concrete and timely steps to enhance U.S. leverage." He did not specifically address the issue of arms sales.

*The Suggestion Dies.* Mr. Teicher told the Board that the strong objections from Secretary Shultz and Secretary Weinberger apparently killed the draft NSDD. In mid-August he was told to "stand down" on the effort. The draft was never submitted to the President for his consideration or signature.

The abandonment of the draft NSDD marked the end of efforts by Mr. McFarlane and the NSC staff to use the formal interagency policy process to obtain an explicit change in U.S. policy toward Iran. From this point on, the matter moved along a different track.

## Stage 3: The Israelis Provide a Vehicle

While the NSC staff was seeking a reexamination of U.S. policy toward Iran, several staff members were growing ever more concerned about the hostage issue. On June 14, 1985, TWA flight 847 was hijacked enroute from Athens to Rome, with 135 U.S. citizens aboard. It was not until June 29 that all the hostages were released. One U.S. citizen was executed. The event dominated the news in the United States and dramatized the hostage issue. Frustration at the lack of progress in freeing the hostages in Beirut grew perceptibly within the U.S. government, especially in the face of pleas to the President for action by the families of the hostages. In the summer of 1985, a vehicle appeared that offered the prospect of progress both on the release of the hostages and a strategic opening to Iran.

Israel had long-standing interests in a relationship with Iran and in promoting its arms export industry. Arms sales to Iran could further both objectives. It also offered a means of strengthening Iran against Israel's old adversary, Iraq. Much of Israel's military equipment came originally from the United States, however. For both legal and political reasons, Israel felt a need for U.S. approval of, or at least acquiescence in, any arms sales to Iran. In addition, elements in Israel undoubtedly wanted the United States involved for its own sake so as to distance the United States from the Arab world and ultimately to establish Israel as the only real strategic partner of the United States in the region.

Iran badly wanted what Israel could provide. The United States had been the primary source of arms for the Shah, but U.S. shipments to Iran were now barred by the embargo. Iran desperately wanted U.S.-origin TOW and HAWK missiles,[4] in order to counter Iraq's chief areas of superiority—armor and air forces. Since Israel had these weapons in its inventory, it was an alternative source of supply. Israel was more than willing to provide these weapons to Iran, but only if the United States approved the transfer and would agree to replace the weapons.

Iranian interest in these weapons was widely known among those connected with the arms trade. These included Manucher Ghorbanifar, an Iranian businessman living in France, and Adolph Schwimmer and Yaacov Nimrodi, private Israeli arms dealers with contacts throughout the Middle East including Israel. Since September, 1984, Mr. Schwimmer had also been a consultant to then-Prime Minister of Israel Shimon Peres. In a series of meetings beginning in January, 1985, these men had discussed using arms sales to obtain the release of the U.S. citizens held hostage in Beirut and to open a strategic dialogue with Iran. Some of those meetings included Amiram Nir, since September, 1984, an advisor to Prime Minister Peres on counterterrorism. Also involved was Saudi businessman Adnan Khashoggi, a man well-connected in the Middle East and enjoying a special relationship with key Israeli officials. All these men subsequently played a role in the brokering of the arms deals that later did occur.

23

These men believed that the United States, Israel, and Iran, though with different interests, were susceptible to a relationship of convenience involving arms, hostages, and the opening of a channel to Iran. The catalyst that brought this relationship into being was the proffering by Israel of a channel for the United States in establishing contacts with Iran.

*An Opening to Iran.* On the 4th or 5th of May, 1985, Michael Ledeen, an NSC staff consultant, with the knowledge of Mr. McFarlane, went to Israel and met with Prime Minister Peres. Mr. Ledeen told the Board that he asked about the state of Israeli intelligence on Iran and whether Israel would be willing to share its intelligence with the United States. Two months later, the United States received the first of three separate requests regarding Iran from the Israeli government. The first two occurred in July, 1985.

(i) *The July Requests.* On July 3, 1985, David Kimche, the Director General of the Israeli Foreign Ministry, met at the White House with Mr. McFarlane. Mr. McFarlane told the Board that Mr. Kimche asked the position of the U.S. government toward engaging in a political discourse with Iranian officials. He recalled Mr. Kimche as saying that these Iranian officials had conveyed to Israel their interest in a discourse with the United States. Contact was to be handled through an intermediary (later disclosed to be Mr. Ghorbanifar) who was represented as having good connections to Iranian officials.

This was not the first time that Mr. Ghorbanifar had come to the attention of the U.S. government. The CIA knew of Mr. Ghorbanifar and had a history of contacts with him. CIA's first contact with Ghorbanifar was through a European intelligence service in January 1980. From the beginning, CIA found it "difficult to filter out the bravado and exaggeration from what actually happened." Other intelligence services had similar experiences with Mr. Ghorbanifar. By September of 1980, CIA decided to drop efforts at recruiting Ghorbanifar. It considered him neither reliable nor trustworthy. In addition, Theodore Shackley, a former CIA official, had met Mr. Ghorbanifar in Hamburg, West Germany, between November 19–21, 1984. Mr. Ghorbanifar at that time suggested payment of a cash ransom for the hostages in Beirut, with himself as middleman. This proposal, contained in a memorandum prepared by Mr. Shackley dated November 22, 1984, apparently reached the State Department where it elicited no interest. A memorandum from Mr. Shackley dated June 7, 1985, containing a later suggestion by Mr. Ghorbanifar that the ransom involve terms "other than money," also drew no response. At the time of his meeting with Mr. Kimche, Mr. McFarlane apparently did not know this background or even that Mr. Ghorbanifar was the intermediary Mr. Kimche had in mind. He learned this later in the month from Mr. Ledeen.

Mr. McFarlane told the Board that Mr. Kimche told him the Iranians understood that they would have to demonstrate their "bona fides" and that the Iranians believed they could influence Hezballah to release the hostages in Beirut. But Mr. McFarlane also recalled Mr. Kimche expressing the view that ultimately the Iranians would need something to show for the dialogue, and that this would "probably" be weapons.

Mr. McFarlane testified that he informed the President of his conversation with Mr. Kimche within three or four days after the meeting, shortly before the President entered the hospital for his cancer operation. Mr. McFarlane also stated that on July 13, 1985, he briefed Secretary Shultz, Secretary Weinberger, and Director Casey in separate conversations. Mr. McFarlane told the Board that the President was interested in the proposal and said that he believed we should explore it. Mr. McFarlane said this may have occurred in the first week of July, before the President entered the hospital.

On July 13, 1985, Mr. McFarlane apparently received a second request, this time brought by an emissary directly from Israeli Prime Minister Peres. The "emissary" was Mr. Schwimmer, who delivered the request to Mr. McFarlane through Mr. Ledeen. The emissary carried word of a recent meeting with Mr. Ghorbanifar and another Iranian in which the Iranians had said that others inside Iran were interested in more extensive relations with the West, and particularly, the United States. The Iranians reportedly said that their contacts in Iran could achieve the release of the seven Americans held in Lebanon but in exchange sought 100 TOW missiles from Israel. This was to be part of a "larger purpose" of opening a "private dialogue" on

25

U.S./Iranian relations. The emissary asked for a prompt response. Mr. McFarlane stated that he passed the President's decision to David Kimche by telephone.

On July 14, 1985, Mr. McFarlane cabled this proposal to Secretary Shultz, who was traveling in Asia. Mr. McFarlane recommended a tentative show of interest in a dialogue but with no commitment to the arms exchange. He asked for Secretary Shultz's guidance and indicated he would "abide fully" by the Secretary's decision. By return cable on the same day, Secretary Shultz agreed to "a tentative show of interest without commitment." He said this was consistent with U.S. policy of "maintaining contact with people who might eventually provide information or help in freeing hostages." Secretary Shultz advised Mr. McFarlane to "handle this probe personally" but asked that he stay in close contact.

White House Chief of Staff Regan told the Board that he and Mr. McFarlane met with the President on this issue in the hospital a few days after the President's cancer operation on July 13. Mr. Regan told the Board that the matter was discussed for 20 to 25 minutes, with the President asking quite a few questions. He recalled the President then saying "yes, go ahead. Open it up."

In his meeting with the Board on February 11, 1987, the President said he had no recollection of a meeting in the hospital in July with Mr. McFarlane and that he had no notes that would show such a meeting.

(ii) *The August Request.* On August 2, 1985, Mr. McFarlane again met at the White House with Mr. Kimche. According to Mr. McFarlane, Mr. Kimche said that the Iranians had asked whether the United States would supply arms to Iran. Mr. McFarlane recalled responding that he thought not. He told the Board that Mr. Kimche then asked what the U.S. reaction would be if Israel shipped weapons to Iran, and whether the United States would sell replacements "whether it's HAWKs or TOWs or whatever else." Mr. McFarlane recalled telling Mr. Kimche he would "get you our position."

What followed is quite murky.

Most NSC principals apparently had an opportunity to discuss this request with the President in and around the first two weeks of August. There clearly was a series of meetings with one or more of the principals in attendance.

In addition, a number of the participants seem to recall a single meeting at which all the principals were present. White House records, however, show no meetings of the NSC principals in August scheduled for the purpose of discussing this issue. Other evidence suggests that there were meetings of the NSC principals in August at which this issue could have been discussed.

It is also unclear what exactly was under consideration at this time. No analytical paper was prepared for the August discussions and no formal minutes of any of the discussions were made.

Mr. McFarlane said that Mr. Kimche made a special proposal that 100 TOWs to Iran would establish good faith and result in the release of all the hostages. Mr. McFarlane told the Board that he discussed this proposal with the President several times and, on at least one occasion, with all the "full" members of the NSC. Within days after the meeting, the President communicated his decision to Mr. McFarlane by telephone. He said the President decided that, if Israel chose to transfer arms to Iran, in modest amounts not enough to change the military balance and not including major weapon systems, then it could buy replacements from the United States. Mr. McFarlane said that the President also indicated that the United States was interested in a political meeting with the Iranians. Mr. McFarlane said he reminded the President of the opposition expressed by Secretary Shultz and Secretary Weinberger, but that the President said he wanted to go ahead —that he, the President, would take "all the heat for that."

Mr. McFarlane told the Board that he subsequently conveyed the President's decision to Mr. Kimche. He said that he emphasized to Mr. Kimche that the U.S. purpose was a political agenda with Iran, not an exchange of arms for hostages. Mr. McFarlane told the Board that he also conveyed this decision to the NSC principals.

Secretary Shultz told the Board that on August 6, 1985, during one of his regularly scheduled meetings with the President, he discussed with the President a proposal for the transfer of 100 TOW missiles from Israel. The Iranians were for their part to produce the release of four or more hostages. Secretary Shultz told the Board that he opposed the arms sales at the meeting with the President. He said that Mr. McFarlane was present at this meeting. Secretary

Shultz did not recall a telephone call from Mr. McFarlane regarding a decision by the President.

Secretary Weinberger recalled a meeting with the President at his residence after the President's return from the hospital. He told the Board that he argued forcefully against arms transfers to Iran, as did George Shultz. He said he thought that the President agreed that the idea should not be pursued.

Mr. Regan also recalled an August meeting with the President. He told the Board that the President expressed concern with any one-for-one swap of arms for hostages and indicated "we should go slow on this but develop the contact." Mr. Regan also told the Board that in early September, Mr. McFarlane informed the President that Israel had sold arms to the Iranians and hoped to get some hostages out. Mr. Regan stated that the President was "upset" at the news and that Mr. McFarlane explained that the Israelis had "simply taken it upon themselves to do this." Mr. Regan said that after some discussion, the President decided to "leave it alone."

In his meeting with the Board on January 26, 1987, the President said that sometime in August he approved the shipment of arms by Israel to Iran. He was uncertain as to the precise date. The President also said that he approved replenishment of any arms transferred by Israel to Iran. Mr. McFarlane's testimony of January 16, 1986, before the Senate Foreign Relations Committee, which the President embraced, takes the same position. This portion of Mr. McFarlane's testimony was specifically highlighted on the copy of testimony given by the President to the Board.

In his meeting with the Board on February 11, the President said that he and Mr. Regan had gone over the matter a number of times and that Mr. Regan had a firm recollection that the President had not authorized the August shipment in advance. The President said he did not recall authorizing the August shipment in advance. He noted that very possibly, the transfer was brought to him as already completed. He said that subsequently there were arms shipments he authorized that may have had to do with replenishment, and that this approval for replenishment could have taken place in September. The President stated that he had been "surprised" that the Israelis had shipped arms to Iran, and that this fact caused the President to conclude that he had not approved the transfer in advance.

In a subsequent letter to the Board received on February 20, 1987, the President wrote: "In trying to recall events that happened eighteen months ago I'm afraid that I let myself be influenced by others' recollections, not my own . . .

". . . I have no personal notes or records to help my recollection on this matter. The only honest answer is to state that try as I might, I cannot recall anything whatsoever about whether I approved replenishment of Israeli stocks around August of 1985. My answer therefore and the simple truth is, 'I don't remember—period.'"

The Board tried to resolve the question of whether the President gave prior approval to Israel's transfer of arms to Iran. We could not do so conclusively.

We believe that an Israeli request for approval of such a transfer was discussed before the President in early August. We believe that Secretary Shultz and Secretary Weinberger expressed at times vigorous opposition to the proposal. The President agreed to replenish Israeli stocks. We are persuaded that he most likely provided this approval prior to the first shipment by Israel.

In coming to this conclusion, it is of paramount importance that the President never opposed the idea of Israel transferring arms to Iran. Indeed, four months after the August shipment, the President authorized the United States government to undertake directly the very same operation that Israel had proposed. Even if Mr. McFarlane did not have the President's explicit prior approval, he clearly had his full support.

*A Hostage Comes Out.* On August 30, 1985, Israel delivered 100 TOWs to Iran. A subsequent delivery of 408 more TOWs occurred on September 14, 1985.[5] On September 15, 1985, Reverend Benjamin Weir was released by his captors.

Mr. Ghorbanifar told the Board that the 100 TOWs were not linked to a hostage release. They were to evidence U.S. seriousness in reestablishing relations with Iran. The next step was to be the delivery of 400 more TOWs, for which

Iran was to free a hostage. The goal was to establish a new relationship between the two countries, which would include a pledge by Iran of no further terrorist acts against the United States or its citizens by those under Iran's control.

Mr. McFarlane said that he received a telephone call from Mr. Kimche informing him of Rev. Weir's impending release about a week before it occurred. LtCol North, the NSC staff officer with responsibility for terrorism policy, made arrangements for receiving and debriefing Rev. Weir.

Although it appears that Israel and the United States expected the release of the remaining hostages to accompany or follow the release of Rev. Weir, this did not occur.

## Stage 4: The Initiative Appears to Founder

The United States had only a supporting role in the August and September deliveries to iran. Israel managed the operation. The next three months saw an increasing U.S. role.

A number of important developments regarding the Iran initiative occurred between September and December, 1985. However, it proved difficult for the Board to establish precisely what happened during this period. This is in part because the period was one of great activity for the President, the NSC principals, and Mr. McFarlane. Issues that seemed to be both more important and more urgent than the Iran initiative clearly preoccupied them.

Mr. McFarlane described the foreign policy agenda for the period. The Soviet foreign minister visited Washington. Preparations for the Geneva Summit with General Secretary Gorbachev were under way; this included four Presidential speeches on arms control, human rights, regional issues, and U.S./Soviet bilateral relations. The President delivered an address to the United Nations on the occasion of its 40th Anniversary. The President met with twelve to fifteen heads of State in New York and Washington. In the middle of this hectic schedule, on October 7, 1985, the Achille Lauro was seized by four Palestinian hijackers.

*An Arms for Hostages Deal.* On October 8, 1985, LtCol

North's calendar indicated that he met with Mr. Ledeen, Mr. Schwimmer, Mr. Nimrodi, and Mr. Ghorbanifar (using the alias of Nicholas Kralis). Other meetings may have occurred. There is little evidence of what exactly went on in these meetings. All that is known for sure is that shortly after those meetings, David Kimche advanced a third proposal.

Mr. Kimche met with Mr. McFarlane and LtCol North on November 9, 1985. John McMahon, the Deputy Director of Central Intelligence, told the Board that Mr. McFarlane spoke with him on November 14. Mr. McFarlane told Mr. McMahon that Mr. Kimche had indicated that the Israelis planned to provide some arms to moderates in Iran who would oppose Khomeini. Mr. McFarlane suggested that the Israelis interpreted the Presidential authorization as an open charter for further arms shipments as long as the shipments were modest and did not alter the military balance between Iran and Iraq. Indeed, he did not recall any specific request by Israel in the late fall. He did, however, remember that early in November, Yitzhak Rabin, Israel's Defense Minister, asked whether U.S. policy would still permit Israel to buy replacements from the U.S. for arms it transferred to Iran. Mr. McFarlane confirmed that it would, although he indicated U.S. reservations about any trade of arms for hostages. They asked nothing further.

In a message to VADM Poindexter on November 20, 1985, LtCol North described the following plan. The Israelis were to deliver 80 HAWK missiles to a staging area in a third country, at noon on Friday, November 22. These were to be loaded aboard three chartered aircraft, which would take off at two hour intervals for Tabriz, Iran. Once launch of the first aircraft had been confirmed by Mr. Ghorbanifar, directions would be given to release the five U.S. citizens held hostage in Beirut. No aircraft was to land in Tabriz until all the hostages had been delivered to the U.S. embassy in Beirut. Israel would deliver forty additional HAWKs at a later time. The Iranians would commit to seeing that there were no further hostages seized.

Secretary Shultz told the Board that Mr. McFarlane told him on November 18, 1985, about a plan that would produce the release of the hostages on Thursday, November 21. Secretary Shultz told the Board he told Mr. McFarlane that had he known of it earlier, he would have stopped it.

31

He nonetheless expressed the hope to Mr. McFarlane that the hostages would be released. It is not clear what other NSC principals, if any, were told in advance about the plan.

Secretary Shultz said he told an associate on November 22 that "Bud says he's cleared with the President" on the plan. Chief of Staff Regan told the Board that the President was informed in advance of the Israeli HAWK shipment but was not asked to approve it. He said that Mr. McFarlane told the President early in the month on the margins of his briefings for the Geneva Summit to expect that a shipment of missiles would come from Israel through a third country to Iran, and that the hostages would come out.

In his first meeting with the Board on January 16, 1987, the President said he did not remember how the November shipment came about. The President said he objected to the shipment, and that, as a result of that objection, the shipment was returned to Israel.

In his second meeting with the Board on February 11, 1987, the President stated that both he and Mr. Regan agreed that they cannot remember any meeting or conversation in general about a HAWK shipment. The President said he did not remember anything about a call-back of the HAWKs.

Nonetheless, that the United States would sell replacement HAWKs to Israel seems to have been assumed at least by VADM Poindexter from the start. LtCol North informed VADM Poindexter on November 20, 1985, that "IAW [in accordance with] your instructions I have told their [Israel's] agent that we will sell them 120 items [HAWKs] at a price that they can meet."

*Failure.* In contrast to the August TOW shipment, the United States became directly involved in the November transfer of the HAWK missiles. Sometime on November 17 or 18, 1985, while Mr. McFarlane was in Geneva for the November summit, Mr. Rabin called Mr. McFarlane to say that a problem had arisen. Mr. McFarlane referred the matter to LtCol North.

North signed a letter for Mr. McFarlane dated November 19, 1985, requesting Richard Secord, a retired U.S. Air Force general officer, to proceed to a foreign country, to arrange for the transfer of "sensitive material" being shipped from Israel. That day Mr. Secord made arrangements for transshipment of the Israeli HAWKs.

But late in the day on November 21, these arrangements began to fall apart. The foreign government denied landing clearance to the aircraft bringing the HAWKs from Israel. LtCol North contacted Duane Clarridge of the CIA for assistance in obtaining the required landing clearance. When the CIA's efforts failed, LtCol North asked Mr. Clarridge to find a reliable commercial carrier to substitute for the Israeli flight. Mr. Clarridge put Mr. Secord in contact with a carrier that was a CIA proprietary.

The plan went awry again on November 22, when Mr. Schwimmer allowed the lease to expire on the three aircraft they had chartered to take the HAWKs to Tabriz. Mr. Secord was able to provide an aircraft for this leg of the journey, however. The CIA arranged for overflight rights over a third country. On November 25 the aircraft left a European country. Delivery was three days late, however, and the aircraft carried only 18 HAWKs. Contrary to LtCol North's description of this plan, the aircraft delivered the HAWKs before the release of any hostages. In fact, no hostages were ever released as a result of this delivery.

Not only were just 18 of the initial shipment of HAWKs delivered, the HAWKs did not meet Iranian military requirements. In addition, they bore Israeli markings. Mr. Ghorbanifar told the Board that this caused great unhappiness in Iran and had disastrous consequences for the emerging relationship. Ultimately the Iranians returned 17 of the HAWKs to Israel. The eighteenth had been test-fired at an Iraqi aircraft flying over Kharg Island to determine the missile's effectiveness.

When Deputy Director McMahon learned of the CIA role in the shipment some three or four days after the fact, he directed the CIA General Counsel to prepare a Covert Action Finding[6] providing Presidential authorization for the CIA's past support and any future support to the Iran initiative. A Finding was drafted and delivered to VADM Poindexter, but the evidence strongly suggests it was never signed by the President.

## Stage 5: The United States Sells Directly to Iran

On November 30, 1985, Mr. McFarlane resigned as National Security Advisor. VADM Poindexter was named National Security Advisor on December 4. That same day, LtCol North raised with VADM Poindexter a new proposal for an arms-for-hostages deal. It involved the transfer of 3,300 Israeli TOWs and 50 Israeli HAWKs in exchange for release of all the hostages. The arms were to be delivered in five installments, spread over a 24-hour period. Each installment was to result in the release of one or two hostages, so that in the end all five U.S. citizens held in Beirut and a French hostage would be freed.[7] If any installment did not result in a hostage release, all deliveries would stop.

*An Attempt to Break the Arms/Hostages Link.* This proposal was considered at a meeting with the President on December 7 in the White House residence. The President, Secretary Shultz, Secretary Weinberger, Mr. Regan, Mr. McMahon, Mr. McFarlane, and VADM Poindexter attended. Secretary Shultz described the meeting as the first "formal meeting" on the Iran initiative where the participants were informed in advance of the subject and had time to prepare. Mr. McFarlane said that the participants reviewed the history of the program. However, no analytical paper was circulated for discussion at the meeting; the Board was not able to acquire any minutes of this meeting. State Department notes of Secretary Shultz's contemporaneous report of a conversation he had with VADM Poindexter on December 5 indicate that VADM Poindexter asked that Secretary Shultz's calendar not show the meeting.

Recollections of the meeting are quite diverse. In his meeting with the Board on January 26, 1987, the President said he recalled discussing a complex Iranian proposal for weapons delivered by the Israelis in installments prior to the release of the hostages. The President said that Secretary Shultz and Secretary Weinberger objected to the plan, and that this was the first time he "noted down" their disapproval. The President said that the discussion at the meeting produced a stalemate.

Secretary Weinberger told the Board he argued strongly against the complicated arms and hostages plan, and that

34

he was joined in his opposition by Secretary Shultz. Mr. Regan told the Board that he supported the plan. But notes written that day by the President and State Department notes of Secretary Shultz's contemporaneous report of the meeting indicate that Mr. Regan joined Secretary Shultz and Secretary Weinberger in opposing the plan. Whatever disagreements were expressed at the meeting, a consensus emerged that Mr. McFarlane should go to London and deliver a message to the Iranians.

No written Presidential decision resulted from the meeting. Immediately after the meeting, Mr. McFarlane left for London to meet with Mr. Ghorbanifar and others to discuss the plan. There is no evidence that Mr. McFarlane was given any written instructions for the trip.

Mr. McFarlane's message at the London meeting was that, while the United States wanted the U.S. hostages released, and would be interested in better relations with Iran, it was making no offer of arms. According to a memorandum written by LtCol North, Mr. Ghorbanifar refused to transmit this message to his Iranian contacts, reportedly stating that to do so would endanger the lives of the hostages. There appears to be no formal record of the London meeting.

Mr. McFarlane reported the results of his trip directly to the President at a meeting held in the Oval Office on December 10. Once again, no analytical paper was distributed in advance, no minutes were kept, and no formal Presidential decision resulted. The President, Secretary Weinberger, Director Casey, Chief of Staff Regan, and VADM Poindexter were present. Secretary Weinberger has no recollection of the meeting though Mr. McFarlane recalled that the Secretary asserted his opposition to the operation. Secretary Shultz was in Europe, but his staff reported to him on the meeting apparently after talking to VADM Poindexter.

Mr. McFarlane reported that an impasse in the talks developed when he refused to discuss the transfer of arms to Iran. Mr. McFarlane also told the Board he recommended against any further dealings with Mr. Ghorbanifar or these arms transfers and left government thinking the initiative had been discontinued.

The President also noted on December 9 that Mr. McFarlane had returned from London. He had met with an

Iranian agent described as "a devious character." The President noted that the Iranian agent had said that Mr. McFarlane's message would kill the hostages. The President told the Board at the meeting on December 10, Mr. McFarlane expressed no confidence in the Iranian intermediary he met in London [Mr. Ghorbanifar]. The President noted that Mr. McFarlane recommended rejection of the latest plan.[8] The President said he agreed. "I had to."

Mr. Regan told the Board that at the meeting the President said the United States should try something else or abandon the whole project. Mr. Regan also said that the President noted that it would be another Christmas with hostages still in Beirut, and that he [the President] was looking powerless and inept because he was unable to do anything to get the hostages out.

Director Casey prepared a memorandum of the meeting dated the same day (December 10). It states that the President "argued mildly" for letting the Israelis sell the equipment but without any commitment from the United States other than replenishment. It reports that the President was concerned that terminating the ongoing discussions could lead to early action against the hostages. Director Casey ended the memorandum by saying that as the meeting broke up: "I had the idea that the President had not entirely given up on encouraging the Israelis to carry on with the Iranians. I suspect he would be willing to run the risk and take the heat in the future if this will lead to springing the hostages."

*The Arms/Hostages Link Reestablished.* The President was clearly quite concerned about the hostages. Mr. McFarlane told the Board that the President inquired almost daily about the welfare of the hostages. Chief of Staff Regan is reported to have told reporters on November 14, 1986, that "the President brings up the hostages at about 90 percent of his briefings." Mr. Regan is reported to have said that each morning at the daily intelligence briefing, the President asked VADM Poindexter: "John, anything new on the hostages?"

The premise of the McFarlane December 7 trip had been to try to break the arms/hostage link. However, on December 9, LtCol North submitted to VADM Poindexter a memorandum proposing direct U.S. deliveries of arms to Iran in exchange for release of the hostages, using Mr.

Secord to control Mr. Ghorbanifar and the delivery operation. The December 9 memorandum raises at least a question as to whether LtCol North, who accompanied Mr. McFarlane to the London meeting, fully supported the thrust of McFarlane's instructions in his own conversations in London with Mr. Ghorbanifar and others.

During the rest of December, LtCol North, Mr. Ghorbanifar, Mr. Ledeen, Mr. Secord, and Mr. Nir met variously among themselves. Again we know little of the proceedings. It is not clear who took the lead in developing the arms-for-hostages proposal that was soon presented by the Israelis. It is clear, however, that on January 2, 1986, Mr. Nir advanced a proposal just when the initiative seemed to be dying.

Mr. Nir met with VADM Poindexter in his office on January 2. Secretary Shultz recalls being told by VADM Poindexter that Mr. Nir proposed an exchange of certain Hezballah prisoners held by Israeli-supported Lebanese Christian forces, together with 3000 Israeli TOWs, for the release of the U.S. citizens held hostage in Beirut. On January 7, 1986, this proposal was discussed with the President at a meeting, probably held in the Oval Office, attended by the Vice President, Secretary Shultz, Secretary Weinberger, Attorney General Meese, Director Casey, Mr. Regan, and VADM Poindexter. Although the President apparently did not make a decision at this meeting, several of the participants recall leaving the meeting persuaded that he supported the proposal. Secretary Shultz told the Board that the President, the Vice-President, Mr. Casey, Mr. Meese, Mr. Regan, and VADM Poindexter "all had one opinion and I had a different one and Cap shared it."

At his meeting with the Board on January 26, 1987, the President said he approved a convoluted plan whereby Israel would free 20 Hezballah prisoners, Israel would sell TOW missiles to Iran, the five U.S. citizens in Beirut would be freed, and the kidnappings would stop. A draft Covert Action Finding had already been signed by the President the day before the meeting on January 6, 1986. Mr. Regan told the Board that the draft Finding may have been signed in error. The President did not recall signing the January 6 draft.

The President told the Board that he had several times asked for assurances that shipments to Iran would not alter

37

the military balance with Iraq. He did not indicate when this occurred but stated that he received such assurances. The President also said he was warned by Secretary Shultz that the arms sales would undercut U.S. efforts to discourage arms sales by its allies to Iran.

The President did not amplify those remarks in his meeting with the Board on February 11. He did add, however, that no one ever discussed with him the provision of intelligence to Iran.

On January 17, a second draft Finding was submitted to the President. It was identical to the January 6 Finding but with the addition of the words "and third parties" to the first sentence.

The President told the Board that he signed the Finding on January 17. It was presented to him under cover of a memorandum from VADM Poindexter of the same date. The President said he was briefed on the contents of the memorandum but stated that he did not read it. This is reflected in VADM Poindexter's handwritten note on the memorandum. That note also indicates that the Vice President, Mr. Regan, and Donald Fortier were present for the briefing.

Although the draft Finding was virtually identical to that signed by the President on January 6, the cover memorandum signaled a major change in the Iran initiative. Rather than accepting the arrangement suggested by Mr. Nir, the memorandum proposed that the CIA purchase 4000 TOWs from DoD and, after receiving payment, transfer them directly to Iran. Israel would still "make the necessary arrangements" for the transaction.

This was an important change. The United States became a direct supplier of arms to Iran. The President told the Board that he understood the plan in this way. That day, President Reagan wrote in his diary: "I agreed to sell TOWs to Iran."

It is important to note, however, that this decision was made at a meeting at which neither Secretary Shultz, Secretary Weinberger, nor Director Casey were present. Although Secretary Weinberger and Director Casey had been present at a meeting with Attorney General Meese, General Counsel Sporkin, and VADM Poindexter the preceding day to review the draft Finding, the new U.S. role does not appear in the text of the Finding. Attorney General Meese told the Board he did not recall any discussion of the implications of this change. Secretary Weinberger told the Board he had no recollection of attending the meeting.

The President made the point to the Board that arms were not given to Iran but sold, and that the purpose was to improve the stature within Iran of particular elements seeking ties to the Iranian military. The President distinguished between selling to someone believed to be able to exert influence with respect to the hostages and dealing directly with kidnappers. The President told the Board that only the latter would "make it pay" to take hostages.

The President told the Board that he had not been advised at any time during this period how the plan would be implemented. He said he thought that Israeli government officials would be involved. He assumed that the U.S. side would be on its guard against people such as Mr. McFarlane had met in London in early December. He indicated that Director Casey had not suggested to him at any time that the CIA assume operational responsibility for the initiative, nor was he advised of the downside risks if the NSC staff ran the operation. He recalls understanding at the time that he had a right to defer notice to Congress, and being concerned that any leaks would result in the death of those with whom the United States sought to deal in Iran.

The January 17 Finding was apparently not given or shown to key NSC principals. In particular, Secretary Shultz, Secretary Weinberger, and Mr. Regan stated that they did not see the signed Finding until after the Iran initiative became public. The Finding marked, however, a major step toward increasingly direct U.S. participation in, and control over, the Iran initiative.

## Stage 6: The NSC Staff Manages the Operation

In the months that followed the signing of the January 17th Finding, LtCol North forwarded to VADM Poindexter a number of operational plans for achieving the release of all the hostages. Each plan involved a direct link between the release of hostages and the sale of arms. LtCol North, with the knowledge of VADM Poindexter and the support of selected individuals at CIA, directly managed a network of private individuals in carrying out these plans. None of the plans, however, achieved their common objective—the release of all the hostages.

*Plans for "Operation Recovery."* The plan described in the cover memorandum to the January 17 Finding called for Israel to arrange for the sale of 4000 U.S. TOW missiles to Iran. The memorandum stated that both sides had agreed that the hostages would be released "immediately" upon commencement of the operation. It provided, however, that if all the hostages were not released after the first shipment of 1000 TOWs, further transfers would cease.

At this point elements of the CIA assumed a much more direct role in the operation. On January 18, 1986, VADM Poindexter and LtCol North met with Clair George, Deputy Director of Operations at CIA, Stanley Sporkin, CIA General Counsel and one of the primary authors of the January 17 Finding, the Chief of the Near East Division with the Operations Directorate at CIA. They began planning the execution of the plan. Because of an NSC request for clearance of Mr. Ghorbanifar, on January 11, 1986, the CIA had administered a polygraph test to Mr. Ghorbanifar during a visit to Washington. Although he failed the test, and despite the unsatisfactory results of the program to date, Mr. Ghorbanifar continued to serve as intermediary. A CIA official recalls Director Casey concurring in this decision.

On January 24, LtCol North sent to VADM Poindexter a lengthy memorandum containing a notional timeline for "Operation Recovery." The complex plan was to commence January 24 and conclude February 25. It called for the United States to provide intelligence data to Iran. Thereafter, Mr. Ghorbanifar was to transfer funds for the purchase of 1000 TOWs to an Israeli account at Credit Suisse Bank in Geneva, Switzerland. It provided that these funds would be transfered to an account in the same bank controlled by Mr. Secord; that $6 million of that amount would be transferred to a CIA account in that bank; and that the CIA would then wire the $6 million to a U.S. Department of Defense account in the United States.[9] The 1000 TOWs would then be transferred from the DoD to the CIA.

Mr. Secord and his associates, rather than the CIA, had the more substantial operational role. He would arrange for the shipment of the TOWs to Eilat, Israel. From there, an Israeli 707, flown by a crew provided by Mr. Secord, would deliver the TOWs to Bandar Abbas, Iran. On the return flight, the aircraft would stop in Tehran to pick up the HAWK missiles delivered in November of 1985 but later rejected by Iran. The plan anticipated that the next day (February 9) all U.S. citizens held hostage in Beirut would be released to the U.S. embassy there. Thereafter, 3000 more TOWs would be delivered. The plan anticipated that Khomeini would step down on February 11, 1985, the fifth anniversary of the founding of the Islamic Republic.[10]

Mr. Ghorbanifar's recollection of the terms of the arrangements are radically different. Mr. Ghorbanifar stated adamantly that the 1000 TOWs were to reestablish U.S. good faith after the disasterous November shipment of HAWK missiles. Mr. Ghorbanifar said there was no agreement that the U.S. hostages would be released as a result of the sale.

On February 18, the first 500 TOWs were delivered to Bandar Abbas, and the HAWK missiles were brought out. On February 24–27, LtCol North, a CIA official, Mr. Secord, Mr. Nir, and Mr. Albert Hakim (a business associate of Mr. Secord) held a series of meetings in Frankfurt, Germany with Mr. Ghorbanifar and other Iranians to review the details of the operation. On February 27, the second 500 TOWs were delivered to Bandar Abbas. Although a hostage release and a later meeting between senior U.S. and Iranian officials had been agreed upon at the Frankfurt meeting, the plan fell through. No hostages were released and the meeting failed to materialize until much later.

Although the cover memorandum to the January 17 Finding stated that further arms transfers would cease if all the hostages were not released after delivery of the first 1000 TOWs, the United States continued to pursue the initiative and arranged for another delivery of arms two months later.

*Authorization for "Operation Recovery."* LtCol North appears to have kept VADM Poindexter fully advised of the progress of Operation Recovery. Director Casey also appears to have been kept informed both by LtCol North

41

and by a CIA official. Both LtCol North and VADM Poindexter were in touch with Mr. McFarlane. In a message to LtCol North on February 27, 1986, Mr. McFarlane noted that he had just received a note from VADM Poindexter asking whether Mr. McFarlane could undertake the senior level meeting with the Iranians and indicating that "the President is on board." Mr. Regan told the Board that the President authorized the shipment of 1000 TOWs during one of VADM Poindexter's morning briefings to the President.

Secretary Shultz told the Board that on February 28, 1986, VADM Poindexter informed him the hostages would be released the following week. Secretary Shultz said VADM Poindexter reported nothing about arms. VADM Poindexter said that the Iranians wanted a high-level dialogue covering issues other than hostages, and that the White House had chosen Mr. McFarlane for the mission.

*Preparation for the May Trip.* Preparation for a meeting between Mr. McFarlane and senior Iranian officials began shortly after LtCol North's return from Frankfurt on February 27. That same day, VADM Poindexter met with Director Casey, Mr. George, and another CIA official to discuss plans for the meeting. On March 5, 1986, George Cave joined the group. He was a retired CIA officer who since retirement had served as a full-time paid consultant to the agency. He was a Farsi speaker and an expert on Iran.

LtCol North, Mr. Cave, and a CIA official met with Mr. Ghorbanifar in Paris on March 8, 1986. LtCol North reported on this conversation to Mr. McFarlane on March 10. He said he told Mr. Ghorbanifar that the United States remained interested in a meeting with senior Iranian officials as long as the hostages were released during or before the meeting. He said he briefed Mr. Ghorbanifar on the Soviet threat to Iran using intelligence supplied by Mr. Robert Gates, then the CIA Deputy Director for Intelligence. Mr. Ghorbanifar responded by presenting a list of 240 different types of spare parts, in various quantities, needed by Iran for its HAWK missile units. He also emphasized the importance of an advance meeting in Tehran to prepare for the meeting with Mr. McFarlane. This advance meeting would establish the agenda and who should participate from the Iranian side.

While further discussion occurred over the next month, it resulted in little progress. On April 3, 1986, Mr. Ghorbanifar arrived in Washington, D.C. He met with LtCol North, Mr. Allen, Mr. Cave, and another CIA official between April 3–4. In a message to Mr. McFarlane on April 7, 1986, LtCol North indicated that, at the request of VADM Poindexter, he had prepared a paper for "our boss" laying out the arrangements agreed upon at the meeting.

An unsigned, undated memorandum was found in LtCol North's files entitled "Release of American Hostages in Beirut."[11] It appears to have been prepared in early April.

In an interview with Attorney General Meese on November 23, 1986, LtCol North said he prepared this memorandum between April 4–7. Although in a form for transmittal by VADM Poindexter to the President, LtCol North indicated that he did not believe the President had approved the memorandum.

The memorandum provided for the following sequence of events:

—On April 9, the CIA would commence procuring $3.641 million worth of parts for HAWK missile units.

—On April 18, a private U.S. aircraft would load the parts and fly them to an Israeli airfield. The parts would then be transferred to an Israeli military aircraft with false markings.

—On April 19, Mr. McFarlane, LtCol North, Mr. Teicher, Mr. Cave, and a CIA official would board a CIA aircraft in Frankfurt en route to Tehran.

—On April 20, they would meet with a delegation of senior Iranian officials. Seven hours later, the U.S. hostages would be released in Beirut. Fifteen hours later, the Israeli military aircraft with the HAWK missile parts would land in Bandar Abbas, Iran.

That schedule was not met. On April 16, 1986, LtCol North wrote VADM Poindexter seeking approval for a meeting with Mr. Ghorbanifar in Frankfurt on April 18. In his reply of the same date, VADM Poindexter approved the trip but insisted that there be no delivery of parts until all the hostages had been freed. He expressly ruled out half shipments before release. "It is either all or nothing." He

43

authorized LtCol North to tell Mr. Ghorbanifar: "The President is getting very annoyed at their continual stalling." On April 21, VADM Poindexter sent a message to Mr. McFarlane informing him of this position.

The Frankfurt meeting was not held. On May 6, 1986, LtCol North and Mr. Cave met with Mr. Ghorbanifar in London. Mr. Ghorbanifar promised a meeting with senior Iranian officials but asked that the U.S. delegation bring all the HAWK spare parts with them. Mr. Cave recalls the Americans agreeing that one-quarter of the spare parts would accompany the delegation. Notwithstanding, LtCol North informed VADM Poindexter on May 8: "I believe we have succeeded. * * * Release of hostages set for week of 19 May in sequence you have specified."

On May 22, 1986, LtCol North submitted the final operating plan for the trip to VADM Poindexter. It provided that the McFarlane delegation would arrive in Tehran on May 25, 1986. The next day (but no later than May 28), the hostages would be released. One hour later, an Israeli 707 carrying the balance of the spare parts would leave Tel Aviv for Tehran.

*Authorization for the May Trip.* On May 3, 1986, while at the Tokyo economic summit, Secretary Shultz received word from the U.S. Ambassador to London that Mr. Khashoggi, Mr. Ghorbanifar, and Mr. Nir had sought to interest a British businessman in the shipment of spare parts and weapons to Iran. That same day, Secretary Shultz expressed his concern about any such transaction to Mr. Regan. Secretary Shultz told the Board that Mr. Regan said he was alarmed and would talk to the President. Secretary Shultz said he talked later to VADM Poindexter and was told that "that was not our deal." He recalls being told soon thereafter by both VADM Poindexter and Director Casey that the operation had ended and the people involved had been told to "stand down." The Tokyo Summit closed with a statement from all the heads of state strongly reaffirming their condemnation of international terrorism in all its forms.

Rodney McDaniel noted that during the national security briefing on May 12, 1986, VADM Poindexter discussed with the President the hostages and Mr. McFarlane's forthcoming trip.[12] The notes indicate that the President directed that the press not be told about the trip. On May 15,

1986, Mr. McDaniel's notes indicate that the President authorized Mr. McFarlane's secret mission to Iran and the Terms of Reference for that trip. Those notes indicate that the trip was discussed again with the President on May 21.

On May 17, LtCol North "strongly urged" that VADM Poindexter include Secretary Shultz and Secretary Weinberger along with Director Casey in a "quiet" meeting with the President and Mr. McFarlane to review the proposed trip. VADM Poindexter responded, "I don't want a meeting with RR, Shultz and Weinberger."

*The May Trip to Tehran.* LtCol North noted in a message to VADM Poindexter on May 19 that CIA was providing "comms, beacons, and documentation for the party." All the other logistics had been arranged through Mr. Secord "or affiliates." Mr. McFarlane, along with LtCol North, Mr. Cave, and a CIA official, left the United States on May 23. Mr. Nir had pressed to be included in the delegation. The Chief of the Near East Division in the CIA operations directorate told the Board that this request was initially rejected, and that position was transmitted by the White House to Israeli Prime Minister Peres who appealed it. He said that ultimately, the decision was left to Mr. McFarlane, who decided to let Mr. Nir join the group. Mr. Ghorbanifar recalls that in meetings with Iranian officials, Mr. Nir was always presented as an American.

On May 25 the delegation arrived in Tehran. Without the prior knowledge to Mr. McFarlane, the aircraft carried one pallet of HAWK spare parts. The delegation was not met by any senior Iranian officials. No hostages were released. Because of this, a second plane carrying the rest of the HAWK spare parts was ordered not to come to Tehran. Two days of talks proved fruitless. The Iranians initially raised demands for additional concessions, but later appeared to abandon them. Mr. McFarlane demanded the prior release of all hostages and the Iranians insisted on the immediate delivery of all HAWK spare parts. On May 27, Mr. McFarlane demanded the release of the hostages by 6:30 a.m. the next day. When no hostages were released, Mr. McFarlane and his party departed, but not before the pallet of HAWK spare parts had been removed from their aircraft by the Iranians.

In a report to VADM Poindexter on May 26, Mr. McFarlane stated: "The incompetence of the Iranian government to do business requires a rethinking on our part of why there have been so many frustrating failures to deliver on their part."

Mr. Ghorbanifar placed blame for the failure of the May trip squarely on the United States. Mr. Ghorbanifar said that he had proposed that he and LtCol North go to Tehran first to prepare the way. But after Mr. Ghorbanifar had made all the arrangements, LtCol North advised that VADM Poindexter had disapproved the trip. The failure to hold this preparatory meeting may have resulted in substantial misunderstanding between the two sides as to just what would occur and be discussed at the meeting with Mr. McFarlane. Mr. Ghorbanifar stated that the Iranians failed to meet Mr. McFarlane's plane because it arrived three hours ahead of schedule. Mr. Ghorbanifar also claimed that the delegation did meet with a senior-level foreign policy advisor.

The Board found evidence that LtCol North, Mr. Cave, Mr. Allen, and another CIA official knew as early as mid-April that if all the HAWK spare parts were not delivered with the delegation, then only one U.S. hostage would be released. Mr. McFarlane may not have been advised of this. While in Tehran, he insisted upon the release of all U.S. hostages prior to more than the token delivery of HAWK spare parts. This was apparently his and VADM Poindexter's understanding of the agreed arrangements. This led Mr. McFarlane to refuse an even better Iranian offer than the one LtCol North and his associates had reason to expect: two hostages immediately and the remaining two after delivery of the rest of the spare parts.

Notes made by Mr. McDaniel indicate that on May 27 the President received a report on the McFarlane trip. Those notes also indicate that Mr. McFarlane reported on his trip in person to the President on May 29. The notes indicate that the Vice President, Mr. Regan, VADM Poindexter, Mr. Teicher, and LtCol North also attended. Mr. McFarlane told the Board, and the notes confirm, that he told the President that the program ought to be discontinued. It was his view that while political meetings might be considered, there should be no weapons transfers.

*A Hostage Comes Out.* Mr. McDaniel's notes indicate that on June 20, 1986, the President decided that no further meeting with the Iranians would be held until the

46

release of the hostages. Early in July, LtCol North called Charles Allen, a CIA official, and asked him to take over the day-to-day contact with Mr. Nir. LtCol North wrote in a memorandum to VADM Poindexter about this same time that he believed he had "lost face" because of his failure to obtain the release of an American hostage. Mr. Allen recalled that Mr. Nir was alarmed at losing direct contact with LtCol North. Mr. Allen told the Board that as a result, Mr. Nir worked closely with Mr. Ghorbanifar to obtain the release of an American hostage.

Notes made by the NSC Executive Secretary indicate that on July 18, VADM Poindexter informed the President of the latest communications with the Iranian interlocutors. On July 21, LtCol North, Mr. Cave, and Mr. Nir met with Mr. Ghorbanifar in London. They discussed the release of the hostages in exchange for the HAWK spare parts that remained undelivered from the May mission to Tehran. On July 26, Father Lawrence Jenco was released.

VADM Poindexter briefed the President on the Jenco release that same day over a secure telephone. He used a memorandum prepared by LtCol North that claimed the release was "undoubtedly" a result of Mr. McFarlane's trip in May and the continuing contacts thereafter. A July 26, 1986 memorandum to VADM Poindexter from Director Casey reached the same conclusion.

In a memorandum to VADM Poindexter dated July 29, 1986, LtCol North recommended that the President approve the immediate shipment of the rest of the HAWK spare parts and a follow-up meeting with the Iranians in Europe. Notes of the NSC Executive Secretary indicate that the President approved this proposal on July 30. Additional spare parts were delivered to Tehran on August 3.

## Stage 7: The Second Channel Is Opened But the Initiative Leaks

From the start, U.S. officials had stressed to Mr. Ghorbanifar that Iran must use its influence to discourage further acts of terrorism directed against the United States and its citizens. Whether as a result of those efforts or for some other reason, from June 9, 1985, until September 9, 1986, no U.S. citizen was seized in Lebanon.[13] But on September 9, 1986, terrorists seized Frank Reed, a U.S. educator at the Lebanese International School. Two more U.S. citizens, Joseph Cicippio and Edward Tracey, were taken hostage on September 12 and October 21.

The McFarlane mission to Tehran marked the high-water mark of U.S. efforts to deal with Iran through Mr. Ghorbanifar. For a year he had been at the center of the relationship. That year had been marked by great confusion, broken promises, and increasing frustration on the U.S. side. LtCol North and other U.S. officials apparently blamed these problems more on Mr. Ghorbanifar than on Iran. The release of Rev. Jenco did little to mitigate their unhappiness.

Sometime in July, 1986, an Iranian living in London proposed to Mr. Hakim a second Iranian channel—the relative of a powerful Iranian official. On July 25, Mr. Cave went to London to discuss this possibility. On August 26, 1986, Mr. Secord and Mr. Hakim met with the second channel and other Iranians in London. The Iranians said they were aware of the McFarlane visit, the Israeli connection, and Mr. Ghorbanifar's role. They referred to Mr. Ghorbanifar as a "crook." Notes taken by Mr. McDaniel indicate that the President was briefed about the second channel on September 9, 1986.

LtCol North, Mr. Cave, and a CIA official met with the second channel and two other Iranians in Washington between September 19 and 21, 1986. The two sides discussed the Soviet threat, cooperation in support of the Afghan resistance, and improved relations between the United States and Iran. The bulk of the time, however, was spent discussing the "obstacle" of the hostages and Iran's urgent need (within two months) for both intelligence and weapons to be used in offensive operations against Iraq. LtCol North reviewed a list of military equipment and agreed "in principle" to provide that equipment, subject to the constraints of what was available within the United States or obtainable from abroad. The parties discussed the establishment of a secret eight-man U.S.-Iranian commission to work on future relations. Finally, LtCol North told the Iranians that unless contact came from North, Richard Secord, or George Cave, "there is no official message from the United States." Notes by Mr. McDaniel indicate that on September 23, the President was briefed on recent discussions with the second channel.

On October 5–7, 1986, LtCol North, Mr. Cave, and Mr. Secord met with the second channel in Frankfurt, Germany. They carried a Bible for the Iranians inscribed by the President on October 3. During the meeting, LtCol North misrepresented his access to the President and attributed to the President things the President never said.

In presenting the Bible, LtCol North related the following story to the Iranians:

"We inside our Government had an enormous debate, a very angry debate inside our government over whether or not my president should authorize me to say "We accept the Islamic Revolution of Iran as a fact * * *." He [the President] went off one whole weekend and prayed about what the answer should be and he came back almost a year ago with that passage I gave you that he wrote in front of the Bible I gave you. And he said to me, "This is a promise that God gave to Abraham. Who am I to say that we should not do this?"

In reality, the idea of the Bible and the choice of the inscription were contained in an October 2, 1986, memorandum from LtCol North to VADM Poindexter. The Bible was to be exchanged for a Koran at the October 5–7 meeting. VADM Poindexter approved the idea and the president inscribed the Bible the next morning. The President told the Board that he did inscribe the Bible because VADM Poindexter told him this was a favorite passage with one of the people with whom the U.S. was dealing in Iran. The President said he made the inscription to show the recipient that he was "getting through."

At two points during the October 5–7 Frankfurt meetings, LtCol North told two stories of private discussions with the President at Camp David. The first had the President saying that he wanted an end to the Iran/Iraq war on terms acceptable to Iran. The second had the President saying that the Gulf states had to be convinced that it was Saddam Husain of Iraq that was "causing the problem."

When pressed by the Iranians for an explicit statement of what the United States means by "an honorable victory" for Iran, LtCol North replied: "We also recognize that Saddam Husain must go."

The President emphasized to the Board that these statements are an "absolute fiction" and that there were no meetings as LtCol North describes. In addition, Mr. McDaniel noted that on October 3, 1986, the President reaffirmed that the United States wanted neither Iran or Iraq to win the war.

At the October 5–7 meeting, LtCol North laid out a seven-step proposal for the provision of weapons and other items in exchange for Iranian influence to secure the release of all remaining U.S. hostages, the body of William Buckley, a debrief by his captors, and the release of John Pattis, a United States citizen whom the Iranians had arrested on spying charges several months earlier. The Iranians presented a six-point counter-proposal that, in part, promised the release of one hostage following receipt of additional HAWK parts and a timetable for future delivery of intelligence information. The Iranians made clear that they could not secure the release of all the hostages. Mr. Cave recalls that the Iranians proposed exchanging 500 TOWs for the release of two hostages. He stated that the U.S. side agreed.

A second meeting was held in Frankfurt on October 26–28 at which the parties finalized the payment and delivery schedule for the TOWs. At that meeting, the parties apparently discussed a nine-point U.S. agenda with Iran. That agenda included delivery by the U.S. of the 500 TOWs, an unspecified number of HAWKs, discussion of the 17 Da'Wa prisoners held by Kuwait, additional arms including 1000 more TOWs, and military intelligence. In exchange the Iranians promised release of one and perhaps two U.S. citizens held hostage in Beirut and "further efforts to create the condition for release of other hostages."

At a meeting between representatives of the State Department and the second channel on December 13, 1986, the Iranian said that both sides had agreed to this nine-point agenda. The Board found no evidence that LtCol North had authority to agree to such an agenda. Secretary Shultz told the Board that he informed the President the next day. He said that the President was "stricken" and could not believe anything like this had been discussed. Of particular concern was the point that the United States had consistently given strong support to Kuwait in resisting terrorist demands for the release of the Da'Wa prisoners.

At the October 26–28 meeting, the Iranian participants said the story of the McFarlane mission to Tehran had been published in a small Hezbollah newspaper in Baalbek, Lebanon. The article was based on a series of leaflets distributed in Tehran on 15 or 16 October.

Mr. Regan recalls the President authorizing the shipment of 500 TOWs on October 29, 1986.

Because of a delay in the transfer of funds the TOWs actually delivered to Iran on October 29, 1986, were Israeli TOWs. The 500 U.S. TOWs were provided to Israel as replacements on November 7.

On November 2, hostage David Jacobsen was released. The next day, a pro-Syrian Beirut magazine published the story of the McFarlane mission. On November 4, Majlis Speaker Rafsanjani publicly announced the mission.

The President, VADM Poindexter, and LtCol North hoped that more hostages would be released. Notes taken by the NSC Executive Secretary indicate that on November 7, 1986, the President decided not to respond to questions on this subject for fear of jeopardizing the remaining hostages. No further hostages were released.

Mr. Ghorbanifar told the Board that the switch to the second channel was a major error. He claimed that he had involved all three major lines or factions within the government of Iran in the initiative, and that the second channel involved only the Rafsanjani faction thus stimulating friction among the factions and leading to the leak of the story to embarrass Rafsanjani. In addition, the price offered to this faction was lower ($8000 per TOW) than the price charged for the earlier TOW deliveries ($10,000 per TOW).

# Section B: Contra Diversion

Sizable sums of money generated by the arms sales to Iran remain unaccounted for. Determining whether these funds from the sale of arms to Iran were diverted to support the Contras proved to be extremely difficult. VADM Poindexter, LtCol North, Israeli participants, and other key witnesses refused to appear before the Board, and records for relevant bank accounts maintained in Switzerland and elsewhere could not be obtained by the Board.

Notwithstanding, there was considerable evidence before the Board of a diversion to support the Contras. But the Board had no hard proof.

Early in 1986, the need to find funds for the support of the Contras was desperate. At the same time, the idea of diverting funds from the arms sales to Iran surfaced. Attorney General Meese told the Board that VADM Poindexter and LtCol North both told him that a diversion had occurred.

*Money was Available.* Israel made three arms deliveries to Iran in 1985. One of these was the November shipment of HAWK missiles. After the November deal collapsed, 17 of the 18 HAWK missiles were returned to Israel and available evidence suggests that all of the money for that shipment was returned or credited to Iran. In the case of the TOW shipments in August and September 1985, the price charged to Iran by Israel was far in excess of what Israel paid the U.S. Department of Defense to replenish the arms it delivered. This excess amount was roughly $3 million for the August/September TOW shipments. Nothing is known by the Board about the disposition of those funds.

The United States directly managed four arms deliveries in 1986. In each case, the purchase money was deposited in Swiss bank accounts held in the name of Lake Resources and under the control of Richard Secord. Again, the price charged to Iran was far in excess of what was paid to the Department of Defense for the arms. The excess amounts totaled almost $20 million for the four deliveries: $6.3 million for the February shipment of TOWs, $8.5 million for the May and August shipments of HAWK parts, and $5 million for the October shipment of TOWs.[14]

Most of these monies remain unaccounted for. Mr. Khashoggi and other investors claim they are still owed $10 million from these transactions.

*The Contras Desperately Needed Funds.* In January, 1986, the President requested $100 million in military aid to the Contras. The request revived the often bitter Congressional debate over whether the United States should support the Contras. The obligational authority for the $27 million in humanitarian aid to the Contras approved by the Congress in 1985 would expire on March 31, 1986. LtCol North, who had primary NSC staff responsibility for matters relating to the Contras, became increasingly concerned. While anticipating Congressional approval of the President's January 1 request, LtCol North feared the Contras would run out of funds before then. On April 22, 1986, he wrote Mr. Fortier: "[T]he picture is dismal unless a new source of 'bridge' funding can be identified * * *. We need to explore this problem urgently or there won't be a force to help when the Congress finally acts."

*A Diversion was Suggested.* It is unclear who first suggested the idea of diverting funds from the arms sales to Iran to support the Contras. The evidence suggests that the idea surfaced early in 1986.

Attorney General Meese told the Board that during his interview with LtCol North on November 23, 1986, North indicated that the idea surfaced during a discussion with Mr. Nir in January, 1986, about ways Israel could help the Contras. LtCol North recalled the Israeli official suggesting that the "residuals" from the Iran arms sales be transferred to the Contras. Contemporaneous Justice Department notes of the November interview indicate that LtCol North said the diversion was an Israeli idea; that the Israelis wanted to be helpful.

Mr. Ghorbanifar told the Board that he had a conversation with LtCol North and Mr. Secord sometime in February of 1986 concerning arrangements for the upcoming delivery of 1000 TOW missiles to Iran. He said that LtCol North and Mr. Secord were extremely worried about a shortfall in funding for the Contras. Mr. Ghorbanifar said that LtCol North asked him if the Iranians would pay $10,000 per TOW missile, instead of $6,500. When told that Iran would pay that price, Mr. Ghorbanifar said LtCol North was greatly relieved—"he was a changed man."

In a memorandum of a meeting with Mr. Ghorbanifar in Paris on March 7–8, George Cave reported that Mr. Ghorbanifar, in an aside, "proposed that we use profits from these deals and others to fund support to the rebels in Afghanistan. We could do the same with Nicaragua."

Before the Board, Mr. Cave said that neither he nor Mr. Ghorbanifar made any mention of diversion.

*North and Poindexter Said Diversion Occurred.* Attorney General Meese told the Board that during his interview with LtCol North on November 23, 1986, North said that $3 to $4 million was diverted to the support of the Contras after the February shipment of TOW missiles and that more (though how much LtCol North was not sure) was diverted after the May shipment of HAWK parts. Contemporaneous Justice Department staff notes of that interview indicate that LtCol North said that the Israelis handled the money and that he gave them the numbers of three accounts opened in Switzerland by Adolpho Calero, a Contra leader. The notes also indicate that LtCol North said there was no money for the Contras as a result of the shipment in October, 1986. By then Congressional funding had resumed.

Mr. McFarlane testified that while standing on the tarmac at a Tel Aviv airport after the trip to Tehran in May of 1986, LtCol North told him not to be too downhearted because "this government is availing itself of part of the money [from the Iran initiative] for application to Central America." Assistant Secretary of Defense Richard Armitage told the Board that North told him sometime in November of 1986 that: "it's going to be just fine * * * as soon as everyone knows that * * * the Ayatollah is helping us with the Contras."

*Authorization.* It is unclear whether LtCol North ever sought or received prior approval of any diversion of funds to the support of the Contras. LtCol North prepared in early April an unsigned memorandum entitled "Release of American Hostages in Beirut," which sought Presidential approval for what became Mr. McFarlane's May trip to Tehran. In that memo, LtCol North stated that $12 million in "residual" funds from the transaction would "be used to purchase critically needed supplies for the Nicaraguan Democratic Resistance Forces." No evidence has emerged to suggest that this memorandum was ever placed before VADM Poindexter, the President, or any other U.S. official.

As a general matter, LtCol North kept VADM Poindexter exhaustively informed about his activities with respect to the Iran initiative. Although the Board did not find a specific communication from LtCol North to VADM Poindexter on the diversion question, VADM Poindexter said that he knew that a diversion had occurred. Mr. Regan told the Board that he asked VADM Poindexter on November 24, 1986, if he knew of LtCol North's role in a diversion of funds to support the Contras. VADM Poindexter replied that, "I had a feeling that something bad was going on, but I didn't investigate it and I didn't do a thing about it. * * * I really didn't want to know. I was so damned mad at Tip O'Neill for the way he was dragging the Contras around I didn't want to know what, if anything, was going on. I should have, but I didn't." Attorney General Meese told the Board that after talking to LtCol North, he asked VADM Poindexter what he knew about the diversion. "He said that he did know about it * * * Ollie North had given him enough hints that he knew what was going on, but he didn't want to look further into it. But that he in fact did generally know that money had gone to the Contras as a result of the Iran shipment."

The President said he had no knowledge of the diversion prior to his conversation with Attorney General Meese on November 25, 1986. No evidence has come to light to suggest otherwise. Contemporaneous Justice Department staff notes of LtCol North's interview with Attorney General Meese on November 23, 1986, show North telling the Attorney General that only he, Mr. McFarlane, and VADM Poindexter were aware of the diversion.

# Section C: The NSC Staff and Support for the Contras

Inquiry into the arms sale to Iran and the possible diversion of funds to the Contras disclosed evidence of substantial NSC staff involvement in a related area; private support for the Contras during the period that support from the U.S. Government was either banned or restricted by Congress.

There are similarities in the two cases. Indeed, the NSC staff's role in support for the Contras set the stage for its subsequent role in the Iran initiative. In both, LtCol North, with the acquiescence of the National Security Advisor, was deeply involved in the operational details of a covert program. He relied heavily on private U.S. citizens and foreigners to carry out key operational tasks. Some of the same individuals were involved in both. When Israeli plans for the November HAWK shipment began to unravel, LtCol North turned to the private network that was already in place to run the Contra support operation. This network, under the direction of Mr. Secord, undertook increasing responsibility for the Iran initiative. Neither program was subjected to rigorous and periodic inter-agency overview. In neither case was Congress informed. In the case of Contra support, Congress may have been actively misled.

These two operations also differ in several key aspects. While Iran policy was the subject of strong disagreement within the Executive Branch, the President's emphatic support for the Contras provoked an often bitter debate with the Congress. The result was an intense political struggle between the President and the Congress over how to define U.S. policy toward Nicaragua. Congress sought to restrict the President's ability to implement his policy. What emerged was a highly ambiguous legal environment.

On December 21, 1982, Congress passed the first "Boland amendment" prohibiting the Department of Defense and the Central Intelligence Agency from spending funds to overthrow Nicaragua or provoke conflict between Nicaragua and Honduras. The following year, $24 million was authorized for the Contras. On October 3, 1984, Congress cut off all funding for the Contras and prohibited DoD, CIA, and any other agency or entity "involved in intelligence activities" from directly or indirectly supporting military operations in Nicaragua.

The 1984 prohibition was subject to conflicting interpretation. On the one hand, several of its Congressional supporters believed that the legislation covered the activities of the NSC staff. On the other hand, it appears that LtCol North and VADM Poindexter received legal advice from the President's Intelligence Oversight Board that the restrictions on lethal assistance to the Contras did not cover the NSC staff.

Confusion only increased. In December 1985 Congress approved classified amounts of funds to the Contras for "communications" and "advice." The authorization was subject, however, to a classified annex negotiated by the Senate and House intelligence committees. An exchange of letters, initiated the day the law passed, evidences the extreme difficulty even the Chairmen of the two committees had in deciding what the annex permitted or proscribed.

The support for the Contras differs from the Iranian

initiative in some other important respects. First, the activities undertaken by LtCol North with respect to the Contras, unlike in the Iranian case, were in support of the declared policy of at least the Executive. Second, the President may never have authorized or, indeed, even been apprised of what the NSC staff was doing. The President never issued a Covert Action Finding or any other formal decision authorizing NSC staff activities in support of the Contras. Third, the NSC staff's role in support of the Contras was not in derogation of the CIA's role because, CIA involvement was expressly barred by statute.

The Board had neither the time nor the resources to conduct a full inquiry into the role of the NSC staff in the support of the Contras that was commensurate with its work on the Iran arms sales. As a consequence, the evidence assembled by the Board was somewhat anecdotal and disconnected. The most significant evidence is summarized in this Section C. A fuller treatment is contained in Appendix C.

*The Bid for Private Funding.* Because of Congressional restrictions, the Executive Branch turned to private sources to sustain the Contras militarily. In 1985 and 1986, Mr. McFarlane and the NSC staff repeatedly denied any direct involvement in efforts to obtain funds from these sources. Yet evidence before the Board suggests that LtCol North was well aware of these efforts and played a role in coordinating them. The extent of that role remains unclear.

In a memorandum to Mr. McFarlane dated April 11, 1985, LtCol North expressed concern that remaining Contra funds would soon be insufficient. He advised that efforts be made to seek $15 to $20 million in additional funds from the current donors which will "allow the force to grow to 30–35,000." The exact purpose to which these private funds were to be put was unambiguous. A number of memoranda from LtCol North make clear that the funds were for munitions and lethal aid.

Asked by the Board about the source of such funds, Mr. McFarlane provided a written response that indicated that "without solicitation" a foreign official offered $1 million a month from what he described as "personal funds." At Mr. McFarlane's request, LtCol North provided the numbers of a Contra bank account in Miami. Mr. McFarlane wrote that in 1985, the foreign official doubled his contribution to $2 million a month, a fact confirmed by two other U.S. officials.

Contributions appear to have been channeled through a series of non-profit organizations that LtCol North apparently had a hand in organizing. A diagram found in LtCol North's safe links some of these organizations to bank accounts controlled by Richard Secord and others known to be involved in purchasing and shipping arms to the Contras.

Other documents and evidence suggest that private contributions for the Contras were eventually funnelled into "Project Democracy,"[15] a term apparently used by LtCol North to describe a network of secret bank accounts and individuals involved in Contra resupply and other activities. In a message to VADM Poindexter dated July 15, 1986, LtCol North decribed "Project Democracy" assets as worth over $4.5 million. They included six aircraft, warehouses, supplies, maintenance facilities, ships, boats, leased houses, vehicles, ordnance, munitions, communications equipment, and a 6520-foot runway. The runway was in fact a secret airfield in Costa Rica. LtCol North indicated in a memorandum dated September 30, 1986, that the airfield was used for direct resupply of the Contras from July 1985 to February 1986, and thereafter as the primary abort base for damaged aircraft.

On September 9, 1986, following Costa Rica's decision to close the airfield, LtCol North received word that the Costa Rican government was planning to call a press conference to announce the existence of the airfield. The same day, LtCol North informed VADM Poindexter that he had held a conference call with then U.S. Ambassador to Costa Rica, Louis Tambs, and Assistant Secretary Elliott Abrams to discuss the potential public revelation of the airfield. All three participants confirm the conference. North said that they had decided North would call Costa Rican President Arias and tell him if the press conference went forward the U.S. would cancel $80 million in promised A.I.D. assistance and Arias' upcoming visit with President Reagan. North added that both Ambassador Tambs and Assistant Secretary Abrams reinforced this message with Arias. VADM Poindexter replied: "You did the right thing, but let's try to keep it quiet."

Assistant Secretary Abrams and Ambassador Tambs told the Board that the conference call took place, but only Tambs was instructed to call Arias and that no threat to withhold U.S. assistance was made. They each doubted that North ever called the President of Costa Rica on this matter. The Costa Rican Government later announced the discovery and closure of the airfield.

*Coordinating the Resupply Operation.* The CIA Headquarters instructed its field stations to "cease and desist" with action which can be construed to be providing any type of support either direct or indirect to the various entities with whom we dealt under the program. The Chief of the CIA Central American Task Force added that in other respects the interagency process on Central America was in disarray in October 1984 and that "it was Ollie North who then moved into that void and was the focal point for the Administration on Central American policy until fall 1985."

As early as April 1985, LtCol North maintained detailed records of expenditures for Contra military equipment, supplies, and operations. On April 11, 1985, LtCol North sent a memorandum to Mr. McFarlane describing two sealifts and two airlifts "[a]s of April 9, 1985." The memorandum set out the kind of munition purchased, the quantity, and in some instances the cost. LtCol North also noted that from July 1984 to April 9, 1985: "$17,145,594 has been expended for arms, munitions, combat operations, and support activities."

Evidence suggests that at least by November 1985, LtCol North had assumed a direct operational role, coordinating logistical arrangements to ship privately purchased arms to the Contras. In a note to Poindexter on November 22, 1985, he described a prospective delivery as "our first direct flight (of ammo) to the resistance field [in] Nicaragua." This shipment was delayed when Mr. Secord was asked to use the aircraft instead to deliver the 18 HAWK missiles to Iran in November, 1985.

In 1986, North established a private secure communications network. North received 15 encryption devices from the National Security Agency from January to March 1986, provided in support of his counter-terrorist activities. One was provided to Mr. Secord and another, through a private citizen, to a CIA field officer posted in Central America.

Through this mechanism, North coordinated the resupply of the Contras with military equipment apparently purchased with funds provided by the network of private benefactors. The messages to LtCol North from Mr. Secord and the CIA officer: (a) asked him to direct where and when to make Contra munitions drops; (b) informed him of arms requirements; and (c) apprised him of payments, balances, and deficits.

At least nine arms shipments were coordinated through this channel from March through June, 1986. The CIA field officer in Costa Rica outlined his involvement in the resupply network and described the shipments: "This was all lethal. Benefactors only sent lethal stuff." The CIA officer added that the private benefactor operation was, according to his understanding, controlled by LtCol North.

Mr. Secord was in charge of arranging the actual deliveries, using at least in part Southern Air Transport ("SAT"). Assistant Commissioner William Rosenblatt told the Board that LtCol North contacted him after a SAT C–123 aircraft crashed in Nicaragua, prompting a Customs investigation. North told him that the Customs investigation was focused on "good guys" who committed "no crimes." The Customs Service then narrowed the investigation to the specific aircraft involved in the crash rather than on the activities of the whole company. U.S. Customs Commissioner William von Rabb said that LtCol North had previously contacted him to complain that Custom's agents were conducting an investigation involving a Maule aircraft. A former CIA officer in Central America said that at least one Maule aircraft was used in support of the Contra forces. Mr. Rosenblatt and Mr. von Rabb told the Board that LtCol North never asked them to close out their investigations. The Board obtained evidence that at least one Maule aircraft was used in Contra military operations. This evidence was referred to the Independent Counsel.

*Authorization.* The evidence before the Board contained no record that LtCol North's role to support the Contras was formally authorized. It appears, however, that LtCol North did keep the National Security Advisor informed, first Mr. McFarlane and then VADM Poindexter. It is not clear to what extent other NSC principals or their departments were informed. On May 15, 1986, VADM Poindexter cautioned North: "From now on, I don't want you to talk to anybody else, including Casey, except me about any of your operational roles."

The President told the Board on January 26, 1987, that he did not know that the NSC staff was engaged in helping the Contras. The Board is aware of no evidence to suggest that the President was aware of LtCol North's activities.

## Part IV

# What Was Wrong

The arms transfers to Iran and the activities of the NSC staff in support of the Contras are case studies in the perils of policy pursued outside the constraints of orderly process.

The Iran initiative ran directly counter to the Administration's own policies on terrorism, the Iran/Iraq war, and military support to Iran. This inconsistency was never resolved, nor were the consequences of this inconsistency fully considered and provided for. The result taken as a whole was a U.S. policy that worked against itself.

The Board believes that failure to deal adequately with these contradictions resulted in large part from the flaws in the manner in which decisions were made. Established procedures for making national security decisions were ignored. Reviews of the initiative by all the NSC principals were too infrequent. The initiatives were not adequately vetted below the cabinet level. Intelligence resources were underutilized. Applicable legal constraints were not adequately addressed. The whole matter was handled too informally, without adequate written records of what had been considered, discussed, and decided.

This pattern persisted in the implementation of the Iran initiative. The NSC staff assumed direct operational control. The initiative fell within the traditional jurisdictions of the Departments of State, Defense, and CIA. Yet these agencies were largely ignored. Great reliance was placed on a network of private operators and intermediaries. How the initiative was to be carried out never received adequate attention from the NSC principals or a tough working-level review. No periodic evaluation of the progress of the initiative was ever conducted. The result was an unprofessional and, in substantial part, unsatisfactory operation.

In all of this process, Congress was never notified.

As noted in Part III, the record of the role of the NSC staff in support of the Contras is much less complete. Nonetheless, what is known suggests that many of the same problems plagued that effort as well.

The first section of this Part IV discusses the flaws in the process by which conflicting policies were considered, decisions were made, and the initiatives were implemented.

The second section discusses the responsibility of the NSC principals and other key national security officials for the manner in which these initiatives were handled.

The third section discusses the special problem posed by the role of the Israelis.

The fourth section of this Part IV outlines the Board's conclusions about the management of the initial public presentation of the facts of the Iran initiative.

# A. A Flawed Process

*1. Contradictory Policies Were Pursued.*—The arms sales to Iran and the NSC support for the Contras demonstrate the risks involved when highly controversial initiatives are pursued covertly.

*Arms Transfers to Iran.*—The initiative to Iran was a covert operation directly at odds with important and well-publicized policies of the Executive Branch. But the initiative itself embodied a fundamental contradiction. Two objectives were apparent from the outset: a strategic opening to Iran, and release of the U.S. citizens held hostage in Lebanon. The sale of arms to Iran appeared to provide a means to achieve both these objectives. It also played into the hands of those who had other interests—some of them personal financial gain—in engaging the United States in an arms deal with Iran.

In fact, the sale of arms was not equally appropriate for achieving both these objectives. Arms were what Iran wanted. If all the United States sought was to free the hostages, then an arms-for-hostages deal could achieve the immediate objectives of both sides. But if the U.S. objective was a broader strategic relationship, then the sale of arms should have been contingent upon first putting into place the elements of that relationship. An arms-for-hostages deal in this context could become counter-productive to achieving this broader strategic objective. In addition, release of the hostages would require exerting influence with Hezballah, which could involve the most radical elements of the Iranian regime. The kind of strategic opening sought by the United States, however, involved what were regarded as more moderate elements.

The U.S. officials involved in the initiative appeared to have held three distinct views. For some, the principal motivation seemed consistently a strategic opening to Iran. For others, the strategic opening became a rationale for using arms sales to obtain the release of the hostages. For still others, the initiative appeared clearly as an arms-for-hostages deal from first to last.

Whatever the intent, almost from the beginning the initiative became in fact a series of arms-for-hostages deals. The shipment of arms in November, 1985, was directly tied to a hostage release. Indeed, the August/September transfer may have been nothing more than an arms-for-hostages trade. By July 14, 1985, a specific proposal for the sale of 100 TOWs to Iran in exchange for Iranian efforts to secure the release of all the hostages had been transmitted to the White House and discussed with the President. What actually occurred, at least so far as the September shipment was concerned, involved a direct link of arms and a hostage.

The initiative continued to be described in terms of its broader strategic relationship. But those elements never really materialized. While a high-level meeting among senior U.S. and Iranian officials continued to be a subject of discussion, it never occurred. Although Mr. McFarlane went to Tehran in May of 1986, the promised high-level Iranians never appeared. In discussions among U.S. officials, the focus seemed to be on the prospects for obtaining release of the hostages, not on a strategic relationship. Even if one accepts the explanation that arms and hostages represented only "bona fides" of seriousness of purpose for each side, that had clearly been established, one way or another, by the September exchange.

It is true that, strictly speaking, arms were not exchanged for the hostages. The arms were sold for cash; and to Iran, rather than the terrorists holding the hostages. Iran clearly wanted to buy the arms, however, and time and time again U.S. willingness to sell was directly conditioned upon the release of hostages. Although Iran might claim that it did not itself hold the hostages, the whole arrangement was premised on Iran's ability to secure their release.

While the United States was seeking the release of the hostages in this way, it was vigorously pursuing policies that were dramatically opposed to such efforts. The Reagan Administration in particular had come into office declaring a firm stand against terrorism, which it continued to maintain. In December of 1985, the Administration completed a major study under the chairmanship of the Vice President. It resulted in a vigorous reaffirmation of U.S. opposition to terrorism in all its forms and a vow of total war on terrorism whatever its source. The Administration continued to pressure U.S. allies not to sell arms to Iran and not to make concessions to terrorists.

No serious effort was made to reconcile the inconsistency between these policies and the Iran initiative. No effort was made systematically to address the consequences of this inconsistency—the effect on U.S. policy when, as it inevitably would, the Iran initiative became known.

The Board believes that a strategic opening to Iran may have been in the national interest but that the United States never should have been a party to the arms transfers. As arms-for-hostages trades, they could not help but create an incentive for further hostage-taking. As a violation of the U.S. arms embargo, they could only remove inhibitions on other nations from selling arms to Iran. This threatened to upset the military balance between Iran and Iraq, with consequent jeopardy to the Gulf States and the interests of the West in that region. The arms-for-hostages trades rewarded a regime that clearly supported terrorism and hostage-taking. They increased the risk that the United States would be perceived, especially in the Arab world, as a creature of Israel. They suggested to other U.S. allies and friends in the region that the United States had shifted its policy in favor of Iran. They raised questions as to whether U.S. policy statements could be relied upon.

As the arms-for-hostages proposal first came to the

United States, it clearly was tempting. The sale of just 100 TOWs was to produce the release of all seven Americans held in Lebanon. Even had the offer been genuine, it would have been unsound. But it was not genuine. The 100 TOWs did not produce seven hostages. Very quickly the price went up, and the arrangements became protracted. A pattern of successive bargained exchanges of arms and hostages was quickly established. While release of all the hostages continued to be promised, in fact the hostages came out singly if at all. This sad history is powerful evidence of why the United States should never have become involved in the arms transfers.

*NCS Staff Support for the Contras.*—The activities of the NSC staff in support of the Contras sought to achieve an important objective of the Administration's foreign policy. The President had publicly and emphatically declared his support for the Nicaragua resistance. That brought his policy in direct conflict with that of the Congress, at least during the period that direct or indirect support of military operations in Nicaragua was barred.

Although the evidence before the Board is limited, no serious effort appears to have been made to come to grips with the risks to the President of direct NSC support for the Contras in the face of these Congressional restrictions. Even if it could be argued that these restrictions did not technically apply to the NSC staff, these activities presented great political risk to the President. The appearance of the President's personal staff doing what Congress had forbade other agencies to do could, once disclosed, only touch off a firestorm in the Congress and threaten the Administration's whole policy on the Contras.

*2. The Decision-making Process Was Flawed.*—Because the arms sales to Iran and the NSC support for the Contras occurred in settings of such controversy, one would expect that the decisions to undertake these activities would have been made only after intense and thorough consideration. In fact, a far different picture emerges.

*Arms Transfers to Iran.*—The Iran initiative was handled almost casually and through informal channels, always apparently with an expectation that the process would end with the next arms-for-hostages exchange. It was subjected neither to the general procedures for interagency consideration and review of policy issues nor the more restrictive procedures set out in NSDD 159 for handling covert operations. This had a number of consequences.

*(i) The Opportunity for a Full Hearing before the President Was Inadequate.*—In the last half of 1985, the Israelis made three separate proposals to the United States with respect to the Iran initiative (two in July and one in August). In addition, Israel made three separate deliveries of arms to Iran, one each in August, September, and November. Yet prior to December 7, 1985, there was at most one meeting of the NSC principals, a meeting which several participants recall taking place on August 6. There is no dispute that full meetings of the principals did occur on December 7, 1985, and on January 7, 1986. But the proposal to shift to direct U.S. arms sales to Iran appears not to have been discussed until later. It was considered by the President at a meeting on January 17 which only the Vice President, Mr. Regan, Mr. Fortier, and VADM Poindexter attended. Thereafter, the only senior-level review the Iran initiative received was during one or another of the President's daily national security briefings. These were routinely attended only by the President, the Vice President, Mr. Regan, and VADM Poindexter. There was no subsequent collective consideration of the Iran initiative by the NSC principals before it became public 11 months later.

This was not sufficient for a matter as important and consequential as the Iran initiative. Two or three cabinet-level reviews in a period of 17 months was not enough. The meeting on December 7 came late in the day, after the pattern of arms-for-hostages exchanges had become well established. The January 7 meeting had earmarks of a meeting held after a decision had already been made. Indeed, a draft Covert Action Finding authorizing the initiative had been signed by the President, though perhaps inadvertently, the previous day.

At each significant step in the Iran initiative, deliberations among the NSC principals in the presence of the President should have been virtually automatic. This was not and should not have been a formal requirement, something prescribed by statute. Rather, it should have been something the NSC principals desired as a means of ensuring an optimal environment for Presidential judgment. The meetings should have been preceded by consideration by the NSC principals of staff papers prepared according to the procedures applicable to covert actions. These should have reviewed the history of the initiative, analyzed the issues then presented, developed a range of realistic options, presented the odds of success and the costs of failure, and addressed questions of implementation and execution. Had this been done, the objectives of the Iran initiative might have been clarified and alternatives to the sale of arms might have been identified.

*(ii) The Initiative Was Never Subjected to a Rigorous Review below the Cabinet Level.*—Because of the obsession with secrecy, interagency consideration of the initiative was limited to the cabinet level. With the exception of the NSC staff and, after January 17, 1986, a handful of CIA officials, the rest of the executive departments and agencies were largely excluded.

As a consequence, the initiative was never vetted at the staff level. This deprived those responsible for the initiative of considerable expertise—on the situation in Iran; on the difficulties of dealing with terrorists; on the mechanics of conducting a diplomatic opening. It also kept the plan from receiving a tough, critical review.

Moreover, the initiative did not receive a policy review below cabinet level. Careful consideration at the Deputy/Under Secretary level might have exposed the confusion in U.S. objectives and clarified the risks of using arms as an instrument of policy in this instance.

The vetting process would also have ensured better use of U.S. intelligence. As it was, the intelligence input into the decision process was clearly inadequate. First, no independent evaluation of the Israeli proposals offered in July and August appears to have been sought or offered by U.S. intelligence agencies. The Israelis represented that they for some time had had contacts with elements in Iran. The prospects for an opening to Iran depended heavily on these contacts, yet no systematic assessment appears to have been made by U.S. intelligence agencies of the reliability and motivations of these contacts, and the identity and objectives of the elements in Iran that the opening was supposed to reach. Neither was any systematic assessment made of the motivation of the Israelis.

Second, neither Mr. Ghorbanifar nor the second channel seem to have been subjected to a systematic intelligence vetting before they were engaged as intermediaries. Mr. Ghorbanifar had been known to the CIA for some time and the agency had substantial doubts as to his reliability and truthfulness. Yet the agency did not volunteer that information or inquire about the identity of the intermediary if his name was unknown. Conversely, no early request for a name check was made of the CIA, and it was not until January 11, 1986, that the agency gave Mr. Ghorbanifar a new polygraph, which he failed. Notwithstanding this situation, with the signing of the January 17 Finding, the United States took control of the initiative and became even more directly involved with Mr. Ghorbanifar. The issues raised by the polygraph results do not appear to have been systematically addressed. In similar fashion, no prior intelligence check appears to have been made on the second channel.

Third, although the President recalled being assured that the arms sales to Iran would not alter the military balance with Iran, the Board could find no evidence that the President was ever briefed on this subject. The question of the impact of any intelligence shared with the Iranians does not appear to have been brought to the President's attention.

A thorough vetting would have included consideration of the legal implications of the initiative. There appeared little effort to face squarely the legal restrictions and notification requirements applicable to the operation. At several points, other agencies raised questions about violations of law or regulations. These concerns were dismissed without, it appears, investigating them with the benefit of legal counsel.

Finally, insufficient attention was given to the implications of implementation. The implementation of the initiative raised a number of issues: should the NSC staff rather than the CIA have had operational control; what were the implications of Israeli involvement; how reliable were the Iranian and various other private intermediaries; what were the implications of the use of Mr. Secord's private network of operatives; what were the implications for the military balance in the region; was operational security adequate. Nowhere do these issues appear to have been sufficiently addressed.

The concern for preserving the secrecy of the initiative

provided an excuse for abandoning sound process. Yet the initiative was known to a variety of persons with diverse interests and ambitions—Israelis, Iranians, various arms dealers and business intermediaries, and LtCol North's network of private operatives. While concern for secrecy would have justified limiting the circle of persons knowledgeable about the initiative, in this case it was drawn too tightly. As a consequence, important advice and counsel were lost.

In January of 1985, the President had adopted procedures for striking the proper balance between secrecy and the need for consultation on sensitive programs. These covered the institution, implementation, and review of covert operations. In the case of the Iran initiative, these procedures were almost totally ignored.

The only staff work the President apparently reviewed in connection with the Iran initiative was prepared by NSC staff members, under the direction of the National Security Advisor. These were, of course, the principal proponents of the initiative. A portion of this staff work was reviewed by the Board. It was frequently striking in its failure to present the record of past efforts—particularly past failures. Alternative ways of achieving U.S. objectives —other than yet another arms-for-hostages deal—were not discussed. Frequently it neither adequately presented the risks involved in pursuing the initiative nor the full force of the dissenting views of other NSC principals. On balance, it did not serve the President well.

*(iii) The Process Was Too Informal.*—The whole decision process was too informal. Even when meetings among NSC principals did occur, often there was no prior notice of the agenda. No formal written minutes seem to have been kept. Decisions subsequently taken by the President were not formally recorded. An exception was the January 17 Finding, but even this was apparently not circulated or shown to key U.S. officials.

The effect of this informality was that the initiative lacked a formal institutional record. This precluded the participants from undertaking the more informed analysis and reflection that is afforded by a written record, as opposed to mere recollection. It made it difficult to determine where the initiative stood, and to learn lessons from the record that could guide future action. This lack of an

70

institutional record permitted specific proposals for arms-for-hostages exchanges to be presented in a vacuum, without reference to the results of past proposals. Had a searching and thorough review of the Iran initiative been undertaken at any stage in the process, it would have been extremely difficult to conduct. The Board can attest first hand to the problem of conducting a review in the absence of such records. Indeed, the exposition in the wake of public revelation suffered the most.

*NSC Staff Support for the Contras.*—It is not clear how LtCol North first became involved in activities in direct support of the Contras during the period of the Congressional ban. The Board did not have before it much evidence on this point. In the evidence that the Board did have, there is no suggestion at any point of any discussion of LtCol North's activities with the President in any forum. There also does not appear to have been any interagency review of LtCol North's activities at any level.

This latter point is not surprising given the Congressional restrictions under which the other relevant agencies were operating. But the NSC staff apparently did not compensate for the lack of any interagency review with its own internal vetting of these activities. LtCol North apparently worked largely in isolation, keeping first Mr. McFarlane and then VADM Poindexter informed.

The lack of adequate vetting is particularly evident on the question of the legality of LtCol North's activities. The Board did not make a judgment on the legal issues raised by his activities in support of the Contras. Nevertheless, some things can be said.

If these activities were illegal, obviously they should not have been conducted. If there was any doubt on the matter, systematic legal advice should have been obtained. The political cost to the President of illegal action by the NSC staff was particularly high, both because the NSC staff is the personal staff of the President and because of the history of serious conflict with the Congress over the issue of Contra support. For these reasons, the President should have been kept apprised of any review of the legality of LtCol North's activities.

Legal advice was apparently obtained from the President's Intelligence Oversight Board. Without passing on the quality of that advice, it is an odd source. It would be one thing for the Intelligence Oversight Board to review the legal advice provided by some other agency. It is another for the Intelligence Oversight Board to be originating legal advice of its own. That is a function more appropriate for the NSC staff's own legal counsel.[1]

3. *Implementation Was Unprofessional.*—The manner in which the Iran initiative was implemented and LtCol North undertook to support the Contras are very similar. This is in large part because the same cast of characters was involved. In both cases the operations were unprofessional, although the Board has much less evidence with respect to LtCol North's Contra activities.

*Arms Transfers to Iran.*—With the signing of the January 17 Finding, the Iran initiative became a U.S. operation run by the NSC staff. LtCol North made most of the significant operational decisions. He conducted the operation through Mr. Secord and his associates, a network of private individuals already involved in the Contra resupply operation. To this was added a handful of selected individuals from the CIA.

But the CIA support was limited. Two CIA officials, though often at meetings, had a relatively limited role. One served as the point man for LtCol North in providing logistics and financial arrangements. The other (Mr. Allen) served as a contact between LtCol North and the intelligence community. By contrast, George Cave actually played a significant and expanding role. However, Clair George, Deputy Director for Operations at CIA, told the Board: "George was paid by me and on the paper was working for me. But I think in the heat of the battle, * * * George was working for Oliver North."

Because so few people from the departments and agencies were told of the initiative, LtCol North cut himself off from resources and expertise from within the government. He relied instead on a number of private intermediaries, businessmen and other financial brokers, private operators, and Iranians hostile to the United States. Some of these were individuals with questionable credentials and potentially large personal financial interests in the transactions. This made the transactions unnecessarily complicated and invited kick-backs and payoffs. This arrangement also dramatically increased the risks that the initiative would leak. Yet no provision was made for such an eventuality. Further, the use of Mr. Secord's private network in the Iran initiative linked those operators with the resupply of the Contras, threatening exposure of both operations if either became public.

The result was a very unprofessional operation.

Mr. Secord undertook in November, 1985, to arrange landing clearance for the Israeli flight bringing the HAWK missiles into a third-country staging area. The arrangements fell apart. A CIA field officer attributed this failure to the amateurish way in which Mr. Secord and his associates approached officials in the government from which landing clearance was needed. If Mr. Ghorbanifar is to be believed, the mission of Mr. McFarlane to Tehran was undertaken without any advance work, and with distinctly different expectations on the part of the two sides. This could have contributed to its failure.

But there were much more serious errors. Without adequate study and consideration, intelligence was passed to the Iranians of potentially major significance to the Iran/Iraq war. At the meeting with the second channel on October 5–7, 1986, LtCol North misrepresented his access to the President. He told Mr. Ghorbanifar stories of conversations with the President which were wholly fanciful. He suggested without authority a shift in U.S. policy adverse to Iraq in general and Saddam Husain in particular. Finally, in the nine-point agenda discussed on October 26–28, he committed the United States, without authorization, to a position contrary to well established U.S. policy on the prisoners held by Kuwait.

The conduct of the negotiators with Mr. Ghorbanifar and the second channel were handled in a way that revealed obvious inexperience. The discussions were too casual for dealings with intermediaries to a regime so hostile to U.S. interests. The U.S. hand was repeatedly tipped and unskillfully played. The arrangements failed to guarantee that the U.S. obtained its hostages in exchange for the arms. Repeatedly, LtCol North permitted arms to be delivered without the release of a single captive.

The implementation of the initiative was never subjected to a rigorous review. LtCol North appears to have kept VADM Poindexter fully informed of his activities. In addition, VADM Poindexter, LtCol North, and the CIA officials involved apparently apprised Director Casey of

73

many of the operational details. But LtCol North and his operation functioned largely outside the orbit of the U.S. Government. Their activities were not subject to critical reviews of any kind.

After the initial hostage release in September, 1985, it was over 10 months before another hostage was released. This despite recurring promises of the release of all the hostages and four intervening arms shipments. Beginning with the November shipment, the United States increasingly took over the operation of the initiative. In January, 1986, it decided to transfer arms directly to Iran.

Any of these developments could have served as a useful occasion for a systematic reconsideration of the initiative. Indeed, at least one of the schemes contained a provision for reconsideration if the initial assumptions proved to be invalid. They did, but the reconsideration never took place. It was the responsibility of the National Security Advisor and the responsible officers on the NSC staff to call for such a review. But they were too involved in the initiative both as advocates and as implementors. This made it less likely that they would initiate the kind of review and reconsideration that should have been undertaken.

*NSC Staff Support for the Contras.*—As already noted, the NSC activities in support of the Contras and its role in the Iran initiative were of a piece. In the former, there was an added element of LtCol North's intervention in the customs investigation of the crash of the SAT aircraft. Here, too, selected CIA officials reported directly to LtCol North. The limited evidence before the Board suggested that the activities in support of the Contras involved unprofessionalism much like that in the Iran operation.

*(iv) Congress Was Never Notified.*—Congress was not apprised either of the Iran initiative or of the NSC staff's activities in support of the Contras.

In the case of Iran, because release of the hostages was expected within a short time after the delivery of equipment, and because public disclosure could have destroyed the operation and perhaps endangered the hostages, it could be argued that it was justifiable to defer notification of Congress prior to the first shipment of arms to Iran. The plan apparently was to inform Congress immediately after the hostages were safely in U.S. hands. But after the first delivery failed to release all the hostages, and as one hostage release plan was replaced by another, Congress certainly should have been informed. This could have been done during a period when no specific hostage release plan was in execution. Consultation with Congress could have been useful to the President, for it might have given him some sense of how the public would react to the initiative. It also might have influenced his decision to continue to pursue it.

*(v) Legal Issues.*—In addition to conflicting with several fundamental U.S. policies, selling arms to Iran raised far-reaching legal questions. How it dealt with these is important to an evaluation of the Iran initiative.

*Arms Transfers to Iran.*—It was not part of the Board's mandate to consider issues of law as they may pertain to individuals or detailed aspects of the Iran initiative. Instead, the Board focused on the legal basis for the arms transfers to Iran and how issues of law were addressed in the NSC process.

The Arms Export Control Act, the principal U.S. statute governing arms sales abroad, makes it unlawful to export arms without a license. Exports of arms by U.S. government agencies, however, do not require a license if they are otherwise authorized by law. Criminal penalties—fines and imprisonment—are provided for willful violations.

The initial arms transfers in the Iran initiative involved the sale and shipment by Israel of U.S.-origin missiles. The usual way for such international retransfer of arms to be authorized under U.S. law is pursuant to the Arms Export Control Act. This Act requires that the President consent to any transfers by another country of arms exported under the Act and imposes three conditions before such Presidential consent may be given:

(a) the United States would itself transfer the arms in question to the recipient country;

(b) a commitment in writing has been obtained from the recipient country against unauthorized retransfer of significant arms, such as missiles; and

(c) a prior written certification regarding the retransfer is submitted to the Congress if the defense equipment, such as missiles, has an acquisition cost of 14 million dollars or more. 22 U.S.C. 2753 (a), (d).

In addition, the Act generally imposes restrictions on which countries are eligible to receive U.S. arms and on the purposes for which arms may be sold.[2]

The other possible avenue whereby government arms transfers to Iran may be authorized by law would be in connection with intelligence operations conducted under the National Security Act. This Act requires that the Director of Central Intelligence and the heads of other intelligence agencies keep the two Congressional intelligence committees "fully and currently informed" of all intelligence activities under their responsibility. 50 U.S.C. 413. Where prior notice of significant intelligence activities is not given, the intelligence committees are to be informed "in a timely fashion." In addition, the so called Hughes-Ryan Amendment to the Foreign Assistance Act requires that "significant anticipated intelligence activities" may not be conducted by the CIA unless and until the President finds that "each such operation is important to the national security of the United States." 22 U.S.C. 2422.

When the Israelis began transferring arms to Iran in August, 1985, they were not acting on their own. U.S. officials had knowledge about the essential elements of the proposed shipments. The United States shared some common purpose in the transfers and received a benefit from them—the release of a hostage. Most importantly, Mr. McFarlane communicated prior U.S. approval to the Israelis for the shipments, including an undertaking for replenishment. But for this U.S. approval, the transactions may not have gone forward. In short, the United States was an essential participant in the arms transfers to Iran that occurred in 1985.

Whether this U.S. involvement in the arms transfers by the Israelis was lawful depends fundamentally upon whether the President approved the transactions before they occurred. In the absence of Presidential approval, there does not appear to be any authority in this case for the United States to engage in the transfer of arms or consent to the transfer by another country. The arms transfers to Iran in 1985 and hence the Iran initiative itself would have proceeded contrary to U.S. law.

The Attorney General reached a similar judgment with respect to the activities of the CIA in facilitating the November, 1985 shipment by the Israelis of HAWK missiles.

In a letter to the Board,[3] the Attorney General concluded that with respect to the CIA assistance, "a finding under the Hughes-Ryan Amendment would be required."[4]

The Board was unable to reach a conclusive judgment about whether the 1985 shipments of arms to Iran were approved in advance by the President. On balance the Board believes that it is plausible to conclude that he did approve them in advance.

Yet even if the President in some sense consented to or approved the transactions, a serious question of law remains. It is not clear that the form of the approval was sufficient for purposes of either the Arms Export Control Act or the Hughes-Ryan Amendment. The consent did not meet the conditions of the Arms Export Control Act, especially in the absence of a prior written commitment from the Iranians regarding unauthorized retransfer.

Under the National Security Act, it is not clear that mere oral approval by the President would qualify as a Presidential finding that the initiative was vital to the national security interests of the United States. The approval was never reduced to writing. It appears to have been conveyed to only one person. The President himself has no memory of it. And there is contradictory evidence from the President's advisors about how the President responded when he learned of the arms shipments which the approval was to support. In addition, the requirement for Congressional notification was ignored. In these circumstances, even if the President approved of the transactions, it is difficult to conclude that his actions constituted adequate legal authority.

The legal requirements pertaining to the sale of arms to Iran are complex; the availability of legal authority, including that which may flow from the President's constitutional powers, is difficult to delineate. Definitive legal conclusions will also depend upon a variety of specific factual determinations that the Board has not attempted to resolve—for example, the specific content of any consent provided by the President, the authority under which the missiles were originally transferred to Israel, the knowledge and intentions of individuals, and the like. Nevertheless, it was sufficient for the Board's purposes to conclude that the legal underpinning of the Iran initiative during 1985 was at best highly questionable.

The Presidential Finding of January 17, 1986, formally approved the Iran initiative as a covert intelligence operation under the National Security Act. This ended the uncertainty about the legal status of the initiative and provided legal authority for the United States to transfer arms directly to Iran.

The National Security Act also requires notification of Congress of covert intelligence activities. If not done in advance, notification must be "in a timely fashion." The Presidential finding of January 17 directed that Congressional notification be withheld, and this decision appears to have never been reconsidered. While there was surely justification to suspend Congressional notification in advance of a particular transaction relating to a hostage release, the law would seem to require disclosure where, as in the Iran case, a pattern of relative inactivity occurs over an extended period. To do otherwise prevents the Congress from fulfilling its proper oversight responsibilities.

Throughout the Iran initiative, significant questions of law do not appear to have been adequately addressed. In the face of a sweeping statutory prohibition and explicit requirements relating to Presidential consent to arms transfers by third countries, there appears to have been at the outset in 1985 little attention, let alone systematic analysis, devoted to how Presidential actions would comply with U.S. law. The Board has found no evidence that an evaluation was ever done during the life of the operation to determine whether it continued to comply with the terms of the January 17 Presidential Finding. Similarly, when a new prohibition was added to the Arms Export Control Act in August of 1986 to prohibit exports to countries on the terrorism list (a list which contained Iran), no evaluation was made to determine whether this law affected authority to transfer arms to Iran in connection with intelligence operations under the National Security Act. This lack of legal vigilance markedly increased the chances that the initiative would proceed contrary to law.

*NSC Staff Support for the Contras.*—The NSC staff activities in support of the Contras were marked by the same uncertainty as to legal authority and insensitivity to legal issues as were present in the Iran initiative. The ambiguity of the law governing activities in support of the Contras presented a greater challenge than even the considerable complexity of laws governing arms transfers. Intense Congressional scrutiny with respect to the NSC staff activities relating to the Contras added to the potential costs of actions that pushed the limits of the law.

In this context, the NSC staff should have been particularly cautious, avoiding operational activity in this area and seeking legal counsel. The Board saw no signs of such restraint.

# B. Failure of Responsibility

The NSC system will not work unless the President makes it work. After all, this system was created to serve the President of the United States in ways of his choosing. By his actions, by his leadership, the President therefore determines the quality of its performance.

By his own account, as evidenced in his diary notes, and as conveyed to the Board by his principal advisors, President Reagan was deeply committed to securing the release of the hostages. It was this intense compassion for the hostages that appeared to motivate his steadfast support of the Iran initiative, even in the face of opposition from his Secretaries of State and Defense.

In his obvious commitment, the President appears to have proceeded with a concept of the initiative that was not accurately reflected in the reality of the operation. The President did not seem to be aware of the way in which the operation was implemented and the full consequences of U.S. participation.

The President's expressed concern for the safety of both the hostages and the Iranians who could have been at risk may have been conveyed in a manner so as to inhibit the full functioning of the system.

The President's management style is to put the principal responsibility for policy review and implementation on the shoulders of his advisors. Nevertheless, with such a complex, high-risk operation and so much at stake, the President should have ensured that the NSC system did not fail him. He did not force his policy to undergo the most critical review of which the NSC participants and the process were capable. At no time did he insist upon accountability and performance review. Had the President chosen to drive the NSC system, the outcome could well have been different. As it was, the most powerful features of the NSC system—providing comprehensive analysis, alternatives and follow-up—were not utilized.

The Board found a strong consensus among NSC participants that the President's priority in the Iran initiative was the release of U.S. hostages. But setting priorities is not enough when it comes to sensitive and risky initiatives that directly affect U.S. national security. He must ensure that the content and tactics of an initiative match his priorities and objectives. He must insist upon accountability. For it is the President who must take responsibility for the NSC system and deal with the consequences.

Beyond the President, the other NSC principals and the National Security Advisor must share in the responsibility for the NSC system.

President Reagan's personal management style places an especially heavy responsibility on his key advisors. Knowing his style, they should have been particularly mindful of the need for special attention to the manner in which this arms sale initiative developed and proceeded. On this score, neither the National Security Advisor nor the other NSC principals deserve high marks.

It is their obligation as members and advisors to the Council to ensure that the President is adequately served. The principal subordinates to the President must not be deterred from urging the President not to proceed on a highly questionable course of action even in the face of his strong conviction to the contrary.

In the case of the Iran initiative, the NSC process did not fail, it simply was largely ignored. The National Security Advisor and the NSC principals all had a duty to raise this issue and insist that orderly process be imposed. None of them did so.

All had the opportunity. While the National Security Advisor had the responsibility to see that an orderly process was observed, his failure to do so does not excuse the other NSC principals. It does not appear that any of the NSC principals called for more frequent consideration of the Iran initiative by the NSC principals in the presence of the President. None of the principals called for a serious vetting of the initiative by even a restricted group of disinterested individuals. The intelligence questions do not appear to have been raised, and legal considerations, while raised, were not pressed. No one seemed to have complained about the informality of the process. No one called for a thorough reexamination once the initiative did not meet expectations or the manner of execution changed. While one or another of the NSC principals suspected that something was amiss, none vigorously pursued the issue.

Mr. Regan also shares in this responsibility. More than almost any Chief of Staff of recent memory, he asserted personal control over the White House staff and sought to extend this control to the National Security Advisor. He was personally active in national security affairs and attended almost all of the relevant meetings regarding the Iran initiative. He, as much as anyone, should have insisted that an orderly process be observed. In addition, he especially should have ensured that plans were made for handling any public disclosure of the initiative. He must bear primary responsibility for the chaos that descended upon the White House when such disclosure did occur.

Mr. McFarlane appeared caught between a President who supported the initiative and the cabinet officers who strongly opposed it. While he made efforts to keep these cabinet officers informed, the Board heard complaints from some that he was not always successful. VADM Poindexter on several occasions apparently sought to exclude NSC principals other than the President from knowledge of the initiative. Indeed, on one or more occasions Secretary Shultz may have been actively misled by VADM Poindexter.

VADM Poindexter also failed grievously on the matter of Contra diversion. Evidence indicates that VADM Poindexter knew that a diversion occurred, yet he did not take the steps that were required given the gravity of that prospect. He apparently failed to appreciate or ignored the serious legal and political risks presented. His clear obligation was either to investigate the matter or take it to the President—or both. He did neither. Director Casey shared a similar responsibility. Evidence suggests that he received information about the possible diversion of funds to the Contras almost a month before the story broke. He, too, did not move promptly to raise the matter with the President. Yet his responsibility to do so was clear.

The NSC principals other than the President may be

somewhat excused by the insufficient attention on the part of the National Security Advisor to the need to keep all the principals fully informed. Given the importance of the issue and the sharp policy divergences involved, however, Secretary Shultz and Secretary Weinberger in particular distanced themselves from the march of events. Secretary Shultz specifically requested to be informed only as necessary to perform his job. Secretary Weinberger had access through intelligence to details about the operation. Their obligation was to give the President their full support and continued advice with respect to the program or, if they could not in conscience do that, to so inform the President. Instead, they simply distanced themselves from the program. They protected the record as to their own positions on this issue. They were not energetic in attempting to protect the President from the consequences of his personal commitment to freeing the hostages.

Director Casey appears to have been informed in considerable detail about the specifics of the Iranian operation. He appears to have acquiesced in and to have encouraged North's exercise of direct operational control over the operation. Because of the NSC staff's proximity to and close identification with the President, this increased the risks to the President if the initiative became public or the operation failed.

There is no evidence, however, that Director Casey explained this risk to the President or made clear to the President that LtCol North, rather than the CIA, was running the operation. The President does not recall ever being informed of this fact. Indeed, Director Casey should have gone further and pressed for operational responsibility to be transferred to the CIA.

Director Casey should have taken the lead in vetting the assumptions presented by the Israelis on which the program was based and in pressing for an early examination of the reliance upon Mr. Ghorbanifar and the second channel as intermediaries. He should also have assumed responsibility for checking out the other intermediaries involved in the operation. Finally, because Congressional restrictions on covert actions are both largely directed at and familiar to the CIA, Director Casey should have taken the lead in keeping the question of Congressional notification active.

Finally, Director Casey, and, to a lesser extent, Secretary Weinberger, should have taken it upon themselves to assess the effect of the transfer of arms and intelligence to Iran on the Iran/Iraq military balance, and to transmit that information to the President.

## C. The Role of the Israelis

Conversations with emissaries from the Government of Israel took place prior to the commencement of the initiative. It remains unclear whether the initial proposal to open the Ghorbanifar channel was an Israeli initiative, was brought on by the avarice of arms dealers, or came as a result of an American request for assistance. There is no doubt, however, that it was Israel that pressed Mr. Ghorbanifar on the United States. U.S. officials accepted Israeli assurances that they had had for some time an extensive dialogue that involved high-level Iranians, as well as their assurances of Mr. Ghorbanifar's bona fides. Thereafter, at critical points in the initiative, when doubts were expressed by critical U.S. participants, an Israeli emissary would arrive with encouragement, often a specific proposal, and pressure to stay with the Ghorbanifar channel.

From the record available to the Board, it is not possible to determine the role of key U.S. participants in prompting these Israeli interventions. There were active and ongoing consultations between LtCol North and officials of the Israeli government, specifically David Kimche and Amiram Nir. In addition, Mr. Schwimmer, Mr. Nimrodi, and Mr. Ledeen, also in frequent contact with LtCol North, had close ties with the government of Israel. It may be that the Israeli interventions were actively solicited by particular U.S. officials. Without the benefit of the views of the Israeli officials involved, it is hard to know the facts.

It is clear, however, that Israel had its own interests, some in direct conflict with those of the United States, in having the United States pursue the initiative. For this reason, it had an incentive to keep the initiative alive. It sought to do this by interventions with the NSC staff, the National Security Advisor, and the President. Although it may have received suggestions from LtCol North, Mr.

Ledeen, and others, it responded affirmatively to these suggestions by reason of its own interests.

Even if the Government of Israel actively worked to begin the initiative and to keep it going, the U.S. Government is responsible for its own decisions. Key participants in U.S. deliberations made the point that Israel's objectives and interests in this initiative were different from, and in some respects in conflict with, those of the United States. Although Israel dealt with those portions of the U.S. Government that it deemed were sympathetic to the initiative, there is nothing improper *per se* about this fact. U.S. decision-makers made their own decisions and must bear responsibility for the consequences.

# D. Aftermath—The Efforts To Tell the Story

From the first hint in late-October, 1986 that the McFarlane trip would soon become public, information on the Iran initiative and Contra activity cascaded into the press. The veiled hints of secret activities, random and indiscriminate disclosures of information from a variety of sources, both knowledgeable and otherwise, and conflicting statements by high-level officials presented a confusing picture to the American public. The Board recognized that conflicts among contemporaneous documents and statements raised concern about the management of the public presentation of facts on the Iran initiative. Though the Board reviewed some evidence[5] on events after the exposure, our ability to comment on these events remains limited.

The Board found evidence that immediately following the public disclosure, the President wanted to avoid providing too much specificity or detail out of concern for the hostages still held in Lebanon and those Iranians who had supported the initiative. In doing so, he did not, we believe, intend to mislead the American public or cover-up unlawful conduct. By at least November 20, the President took steps to ensure that all the facts would come out. From the President's request to Mr. Meese to look into the history of the initiative, to his appointment of this Board, to his request for an Independent Counsel, to his willingness to discuss this matter fully and to review his personal notes with us, the Board is convinced that the President does indeed want the full story to be told.

Those who prepared the President's supporting documentation did not appear, at least initially, to share in the President's ultimate wishes. Mr. McFarlane described for the Board the process used by the NSC staff to create a chronology that obscured essential facts. Mr. McFarlane contributed to the creation of this chronology which did not, he said, present "a full and completely accurate account" of the events and left ambiguous the President's role. This was, according to Mr. McFarlane, done to distance the President from the timing and nature of the President's authorization. He told the Board that he wrote a memorandum on November 18, which tried to, in his own words, "gild the President's motives." This version was incorporated into the chronology. Mr. McFarlane told the Board that he knew the account was "misleading, at least, and wrong, at worst." Mr. McFarlane told the Board that he did provide the Attorney General an accurate account of the President's role.

The Board found considerable reason to question the actions of LtCol North in the aftermath of the disclosure. The Board has no evidence to either confirm or refute that LtCol North destroyed documents on the initiative in an effort to conceal facts from threatened investigations. The Board found indications that LtCol North was involved in an effort, over time, to conceal or withhold important information. The files of LtCol North contained much of the historical documentation that the Board used to construct its narrative. Moreover, LtCol North was the primary U.S. government official involved in the details of the operation. The chronology he produced has many inaccuracies. These "histories" were to be the basis of the "full" story of the Iran initiative. These inaccuracies lend some evidence to the proposition that LtCol North, either on his own or at the behest of others, actively sought to conceal important information.

Out of concern for the protection of classified material, Director Casey and VADM Poindexter were to brief only the Congressional intelligence committees on the "full" story; the DCI before the Committees and VADM Poindexter in private sessions with the chairmen and vice-chairmen. The DCI and VADM Poindexter undertook to do this on November 21, 1986. It appears from the copy of the DCI's testimony and notes of VADM Poindexter's meetings, that they did not fully relate the nature of events as they had occurred. The result is an understandable perception that they were not forthcoming.

The Board is also concerned about various notes that appear to be missing. VADM Poindexter was the official note taker in some key meetings, yet no notes for the meetings can be found. The reason for the lack of such notes remains unknown to the Board. If they were written, they may contain very important information. We have no way of knowing if they exist.

## Part V

# Recommendations

"Not only \* \* \* is the Federal power over external affairs in origin and essential character different from that over internal affairs, but participation in the exercise of the power is significantly limited. In this vast external realm, with its important, complicated, delicate and manifold problems, the President alone has the power to speak or listen as a representative of the nation." *United States* v. *Curtiss-Wright Export Corp.*, 299 U.S. 304, 319 (1936).

Whereas the ultimate power to formulate domestic policy resides in the Congress, the primary responsibility for the formulation and implementation of national security policy falls on the President.

It is the President who is the usual source of innovation and responsiveness in this field. The departments and agencies—the Defense Department, State Department, and CIA bureaucracies—tend to resist policy change. Each has its own perspective based on long experience. The challenge for the President is to bring his perspective to bear on these bureaucracies for they are his instruments for executing national security policy, and he must work through them. His task is to provide them leadership and direction.

The National Security Act of 1947 and the system that has grown up under it affords the President special tools for carrying out this important role. These tools are the National Security Council, the National Security Advisor, and the NSC Staff. These are the means through which the creative impulses of the President are brought to bear on the permanent government. The National Security Act, and custom and practice, rightly give the President wide latitude in fashioning exactly how these means are used.

There is no magic formula which can be applied to the NSC structure and process to produce an optimal system. Because the system is the vehicle through which the President formulates and implements his national security policy, it must adapt to each individual President's style and management philosophy. This means that NSC structures and processes must be flexible, not rigid. Overprescription would, as discussed in Part II, either destroy the system or render it ineffective.

Nevertheless, this does not mean there can be no guidelines or recommendations that might improve the operation of the system, whatever the particular style of the incumbent President. We have reviewed the operation of the system over the past 40 years, through good times and bad. We have listened carefully to the views of all the living former Presidents as well as those of most of the participants in their own national security systems. With the strong caveat that flexibility and adaptability must be at the core, it is our judgment that the national security system seems to have worked best when it has in general operated along the lines set forth below.

*Organizing for National Security.* Because of the wide latitude in the National Security Act, the President bears a special responsibility for the effective performance of the NSC system. A President must at the outset provide guidelines to the members of the National Security Council, his National Security Advisor, and the National Security Council staff. These guidelines, to be effective, must include how they will relate to one another, what procedures will be followed, what the President expects of them. If his advisors are not performing as he likes, only the President can intervene.

The National Security Council principals other than the President participate on the Council in a unique capacity.[1] Although holding a seat by virtue of their official positions in the Administration, when they sit as members of the Council they sit not as cabinet secretaries or department heads but as advisors to the President. They are there not simply to advance or defend the particular positions of the departments or agencies they head but to give their best advice to the President. Their job—and their challenge—is

88

to see the issue from this perspective, not from the narrower interests of their respective bureaucracies.

The National Security Council is only advisory. It is the President alone who decides. When the NSC principals receive those decisions, they do so as heads of the appropriate departments or agencies. They are then responsible to see that the President's decisions are carried out by those organizations accurately and effectively.

This is an important point. The policy innovation and creativity of the President encounters a natural resistance from the executing departments. While this resistance is a source of frustration to every President, it is inherent in the design of the government. It is up to the politically appointed agency heads to ensure that the President's goals, designs, and policies are brought to bear on this permanent structure. Circumventing the departments, perhaps by using the National Security Advisor or the NSC Staff to execute policy, robs the President of the experience and capacity resident in the departments. The President must act largely through them, but the agency heads must ensure that they execute the President's policies in an expeditious and effective manner. It is not just the obligation of the National Security Advisor to see that the national security process is used. All of the NSC principals —and particularly the President—have that obligation.

This tension between the President and the Executive Departments is worked out through the national security process described in the opening sections of this report. It is through this process that the nation obtains both the best of the creativity of the President and the learning and expertise of the national security departments and agencies.

This process is extremely important to the President. His decisions will benefit from the advice and perspective of all the concerned departments and agencies. History offers numerous examples of this truth. President Kennedy, for example, did not have adequate consultation before entering upon the Bay of Pigs invasion, one of his greatest failures. He remedied this in time for the Cuban missile crisis, one of his greatest successes. Process will not always produce brilliant ideas, but history suggests it can at least help prevent bad ideas from becoming Presidential policy.

*The National Security Advisor.* It is the National Security Advisor who is primarily responsible for managing this process on a daily basis. The job requires skill, sensitivity, and integrity. It is his responsibility to ensure that matters submitted for consideration by the Council cover the full range of issues on which review is required; that those issues are fully analyzed; that a full range of options is considered; that the prospects and risks of each are examined; that all relevant intelligence and other information is available to the principals; that legal considerations are addressed; that difficulties in implementation are confronted. Usually, this can best be accomplished through interagency participation in the analysis of the issue and a preparatory policy review at the Deputy or Under Secretary level.

The National Security Advisor assumes these responsibilities not only with respect to the President but with respect to all the NSC principals. He must keep them informed of the President's thinking and decisions. They should have adequate notice and an agenda for all meetings. Decision papers should, if at all possible, be provided in advance.

The National Security Advisor must also ensure that adequate records are kept of NSC consultations and Presidential decisions. This is essential to avoid confusion among Presidential advisors and departmental staffs about what was actually decided and what is wanted. Those records are also essential for conducting a periodic review of a policy or initiative, and to learn from the past.

It is the responsibility of the National Security Advisor to monitor policy implementation and to ensure that policies are executed in conformity with the intent of the President's decision. Monitoring includes initiating periodic reassessments of a policy or operation, especially when changed circumstances suggest that the policy or operation no longer serves U.S. interests.

But the National Security Advisor does not simply manage the national security process. He is himself an important source of advice on national security matters to the President. He is not the President's only source of advice, but he is perhaps the one most able to see things from the President's perspective. He is unburdened by departmental responsibilities. The President is his only master. His advice is confidential. He is not subject to Senate confirmation and traditionally does not formally appear before Congressional committees.

To serve the President well, the National Security Advisor should present his own views, but he must at the same time represent the views of others fully and faithfully to the President. The system will not work well if the National Security Advisor does not have the trust of the NSC principals. He, therefore, must not use his proximity to the President to manipulate the process so as to produce his own position. He should not interpose himself between the President and the NSC principals. He should not seek to exclude the NSC principals from the decision process. Performing both these roles well is an essential, if not easy, task.

In order for the National Security Advisor to serve the President adequately, he must have direct access to the President. Unless he knows first hand the views of the President and is known to reflect them in his management of the NSC system, he will be ineffective. He should not report to the President through some other official. While the Chief of Staff or others can usefully interject domestic political considerations into national security deliberations, they should do so as additional advisors to the President.

Ideally, the National Security Advisor should not have a high public profile. He should not try to compete with the Secretary of State or the Secretary of Defense as the articulator of public policy. They, along with the President, should be the spokesmen for the policies of the Administration. While a "passion for anonymity" is perhaps too strong a term, the National Security Advisor should generally operate offstage.

The NSC principals of course must have direct access to the President, with whatever frequency the President feels is appropriate. But these individual meetings should not be used by the principal to seek decisions or otherwise circumvent the system in the absence of the other principals. In the same way, the National Security Advisor should not use his scheduled intelligence or other daily briefings of the President as an opportunity to seek Presidential decision on significant issues.

If the system is to operate well, the National Security

Advisor must promote cooperation rather than competition among himself and the other NSC principals. But the President is ultimately responsible for the operation of this system. If rancorous infighting develops among his principal national security functionaries, only he can deal with them. Public dispute over external policy by senior officials undermines the process of decision-making and narrows his options. It is the President's responsibility to ensure that it does not take place.

Finally, the National Security Advisor should focus on advice and management, not implementation and execution. Implementation is the responsibility and the strength of the departments and agencies. The National Security Advisor and the NSC Staff generally do not have the depth of resources for the conduct of operations. In addition, when they take on implementation responsibilities, they risk compromising their objectivity. They can no longer act as impartial overseers of the implementation, ensuring that Presidential guidance is followed, that policies are kept under review, and that the results are serving the President's policy and the national interest.

*The NSC Staff.* The NSC staff should be small, highly competent, and experienced in the making of public policy. Staff members should be drawn both from within and from outside government. Those from within government should come from the several departments and agencies concerned with national security matters. No particular department or agency should have a predominate role. A proper balance must be maintained between people from within and outside the government. Staff members should generally rotate with a stay of more than four years viewed as the exception.

A large number of staff action officers organized along essentially horizontal lines enhances the possibilities for poorly supervised and monitored activities by individual staff members. Such a system is made to order for energetic self-starters to take unauthorized initiatives. Clear vertical lines of control and authority, responsibility and accountability, are essential to good management.

One problem affecting the NSC staff is lack of institutional memory. This results from the understandable desire of a President to replace the staff in order to be sure it is responsive to him. Departments provide continuity that can help the Council, but the Council as an institution also needs some means to assure adequate records and memory. This was identified to the Board as a problem by many witnesses.

We recognize the problem and have identified a range of possibilities that a President might consider on this subject. One would be to create a small permanent executive secretariat. Another would be to have one person, the Executive Secretary, as a permanent position. Finally, a pattern of limited tenure and overlapping rotation could be used. Any of these would help reduce the problem of loss of institutional memory; none would be practical unless each succeeding President subscribed to it.

The guidelines for the role of the National Security Advisor also apply generally to the NSC staff. They should protect the process and thereby the President. Departments and agencies should not be excluded from participation in that process. The staff should not be implementors or operators and staff should keep a low profile with the press.

## Principal Recommendation

The model we have outlined above for the National Security Council system constitutes our first and most important recommendation. It includes guidelines that address virtually all of the deficiencies in procedure and practice that the Board encountered in the Iran/Contra affair as well as in other case studies of this and previous administrations.

We believe this model can enhance the performance of a President and his administration in the area of national security. It responds directly to President Reagan's mandate to describe the NSC system as it ought to be.

**The Board recommends that the proposed model be used by Presidents in their management of the national security system.**

# Specific Recommendations

In addition to its principal recommendation regarding the organization and functioning of the NSC system and roles to be played by the participants, the Board has a number of specific recommendations.

1. *The National Security Act of 1947.* The flaws of procedure and failures of responsibility revealed by our study do not suggest any inadequacies in the provisions of the National Security Act of 1947 that deal with the structure and operation of the NSC system. Forty years of experience under that Act demonstrate to the Board that it remains a fundamentally sound framework for national security decision-making. It strikes a balance between formal structure and flexibility adequate to permit each President to tailor the system to fit his needs.

As a general matter, the NSC Staff should not engage in the implementation of policy or the conduct of operations. This compromises their oversight role and usurps the responsibilities of the departments and agencies. But the inflexibility of a legislative restriction should be avoided. Terms such as "operation" and "implementation" are difficult to define, and a legislative proscription might preclude some future President from making a very constructive use of the NSC Staff.

Predisposition on sizing of the staff should be toward fewer rather than more. But a legislative restriction cannot foresee the requirements of future Presidents. Size is best left to the discretion of the President, with the admonition that the role of the NSC staff is to review, not to duplicate or replace, the work of the departments and agencies.

**We recommend that no substantive change be made in the provisions of the National Security Act dealing with the structure and operation of the NSC system.**

2. *Senate Confirmation of the National Security Advisor.* It has been suggested that the job of the National Security Advisor has become so important that its holder should be screened by the process of confirmation, and that once confirmed he should return frequently for ques-

tioning by the Congress. It is argued that this would improve the accountability of the National Security Advisor.

We hold a different view. The National Security Advisor does, and should continue, to serve only one master, and that is the President. Further, confirmation is inconsistent with the role the National Security Advisor should play. He should not decide, only advise. He should not engage in policy implementation or operations. He should serve the President, with no collateral and potentially diverting loyalties.

Confirmation would tend to institutionalize the natural tension that exists between the Secretary of State and the National Security Advisor. Questions would increasingly arise about who really speaks for the President in national security matters. Foreign governments could be confused or would be encouraged to engage in "forum shopping.".

Only one of the former government officials interviewed favored Senate confirmation of the National Security Advisor. While consultation with Congress received wide support, confirmation and formal questioning were opposed. Several suggested that if the National Security Advisor were to become a position subject to confirmation, it could induce the President to turn to other internal staff or to people outside government to play that role.

**We urge the Congress not to require Senate confirmation of the National Security Advisor.**

3. *The Interagency Process.* It is the National Security Advisor who has the greatest interest in making the national security process work, for it is this process by which the President obtains the information, background, and analysis he requires to make decisions and build support for his program. Most Presidents have set up interagency committees at both a staff and policy level to surface issues, develop options, and clarify choices. There has typically been a struggle for the chairmanships of these groups between the National Security Advisor and the NSC staff on the one hand, and the cabinet secretaries and department officials on the other.

Our review of the operation of the present system and that of other administrations where committee chairmen came from the departments has led us to the conclusion that the system generally operates better when the committees are chaired by the individual with the greatest stake in making the NSC system work.

**We recommend that the National Security Advisor chair the senior-level committees of the NSC system.**

4. *Covert Actions.* Policy formulation and implementation are usually managed by a team of experts led by policymaking generalists. Covert action requirements are no different, but there is a need to limit, sometimes severely, the number of individuals involved. The lives of many people may be at stake, as was the case in the attempt to rescue the hostages in Tehran. Premature disclosure might kill the idea in embryo, as could have been the case in the opening of relations with China. In such cases, there is a tendency to limit those involved to a small number of top officials. This practice tends to limit severely the expertise brought to bear on the problem and should be used very sparingly indeed.

The obsession with secrecy and preoccupation with leaks threaten to paralyze the government in its handling of covert operations. Unfortunately, the concern is not misplaced. The selective leak has become a principal means of waging bureaucratic warfare. Opponents of an operation kill it with a leak; supporters seek to build support through the same means.

We have witnessed over the past years a significant deterioration in the integrity of process. Rather than a means to obtain results more satisfactory than the position of any of the individual departments, it has frequently become something to be manipulated to reach a specific outcome. The leak becomes a primary instrument in that process.

This practice is destructive of orderly governance. It can only be reversed if the most senior officials take the lead. If senior decision-makers set a clear example and demand compliance, subordinates are more likely to conform.

Most recent administrations have had carefully drawn procedures for the consideration of covert activities. The Reagan Administration established such procedures in January, 1985, then promptly ignored them in their consideration of the Iran initiative.

We recommend that each administration formulate precise procedures for restricted consideration of covert action and that, once formulated, those procedures be strictly adhered to.

5. *The Role of the CIA.* Some aspects of the Iran arms sales raised broader questions in the minds of members of the Board regarding the role of CIA. The first deals with intelligence.

The NSC staff was actively involved in the preparation of the May 20, 1985, update to the Special National Intelligence Estimate on Iran. It is a matter for concern if this involvement and the strong views of NSC staff members were allowed to influence the intelligence judgments contained in the update. It is also of concern that the update contained the hint that the United States should change its existing policy and encourage its allies to provide arms to Iran. It is critical that the line between intelligence and advocacy of a particular policy be preserved if intelligence is to retain its integrity and perform its proper function. In this instance, the CIA came close enough to the line to warrant concern.

We emphasize to both the intelligence community and policymakers the importance of maintaining the integrity and objectivity of the intelligence process.

6. *Legal Counsel.* From time to time issues with important legal ramifications will come before the National Security Council. The Attorney General is currently a member of the Council by invitation and should be in a position to provide legal advice to the Council and the President. It is important that the Attorney General and his department be available to interagency deliberations.

The Justice Department, however, should not replace the role of counsel in the other departments. As the principal counsel on foreign affairs, the Legal Adviser to the Secretary of State should also be available to all the NSC participants.

Of all the NSC participants, it is the Assistant for National Security Affairs who seems to have had the least access to expert counsel familiar with his activities.

The Board recommends that the position of Legal Adviser to the NSC be enhanced in stature and in its role within the NSC staff.

7. *Secrecy and Congress.* There is a natural tension between the desire for secrecy and the need to consult Congress on covert operations. Presidents seem to become increasingly concerned about leaks of classified information as their administrations progress. They blame Congress disproportionately. Various cabinet officials from prior administrations indicated to the Board that they believe Congress bears no more blame than the Executive Branch.

However, the number of Members and staff involved in reviewing covert activities is large; it provides cause for concern and a convenient excuse for Presidents to avoid Congressional consultation.

We recommend that Congress consider replacing the existing Intelligence Committees of the respective Houses with a new joint committee with a restricted staff to oversee the intelligence community, patterned after the Joint Committee on Atomic Energy that existed until the mid-1970s.

8. *Privatizing National Security Policy.* Careful and limited use of people outside the U.S. Government may be very helpful in some unique cases. But this practice raises substantial questions. It can create conflict of interest problems. Private or foreign sources may have different policy interests or personal motives and may exploit their association with a U.S. government effort. Such involvement gives private and foreign sources potentially powerful leverage in the form of demands for return favors or even blackmail.

The U.S. has enormous resources invested in agencies and departments in order to conduct the government's business. In all but a very few cases, these can perform the functions needed. If not, then inquiry is required to find out why.

We recommend against having implementation and policy oversight dominated by intermediaries. We do not recommend barring limited use of private individuals to assist in United States diplomatic initiatives or in covert activities. We caution against use of such people except in very limited ways and under close observation and supervision.

## Epilogue

If but one of the major policy mistakes we examined had been avoided, the nation's history would bear one less scar, one less embarrassment, one less opportunity for opponents to reverse the principles this nation seeks to preserve and advance in the world.

As a collection, these recommendations are offered to those who will find themselves in situations similar to the ones we reviewed: under stress, with high stakes, given little time, using incomplete information, and troubled by premature disclosure. In such a state, modest improvements may yield surprising gains. This is our hope.

**THE WHITE HOUSE**

Office of the Press Secretary

For Immediate Release                    December 1, 1986

Executive Order 12575

**President's Special Review Board**

By the authority vested in me as President by the Constitution and laws of the United States of America, and in order to establish, in accordance with the Federal Advisory Committee Act, as amended (5 U.S.C. App. I), a Special Review Board to review activities of the National Security Council, it is hereby ordered as follows:

**Section 1.** *Establishment.* (a) There is established the President's Special Review Board on the future role of the National Security Council staff. The Board shall consist of three members appointed by the President from among persons with extensive experience in foreign policy and national security affairs.

(b) The President shall designate a Chairman from among the members of the Board.

**Sec. 2.** *Functions.* (a) The Board shall conduct a comprehensive study of the future role and procedures of the National Security Council (NSC) staff in the development, coordination, oversight, and conduct of foreign and national security policy; review the NSC staff's proper role in operational activities, especially extremely sensitive diplomatic, military, and intelligence missions; and provide recommendations to the President based upon its analysis of the manner in which foreign and national security policies established by the President have been implemented by the NSC staff.

(b) The Board shall submit its findings and recommendations to the President within 60 days of the date of this Order.

**Sec. 3.** *Administration.* (a) The heads of Executive departments, agencies, and independent instrumentalities, to the extent permitted by law, shall provide the Board, upon request, with such information as it may require for purposes of carrying out its functions.

(b) Members of the Board shall receive compensation for their work on the Board at the daily rate specified for GS-18 of the General Schedule. While engaged in the work of the Board, members appointed from among private citizens of the United States may be allowed travel expenses, including per diem in lieu of subsistence, as authorized by law for persons serving intermittently in the government service (5 U.S.C. 5701–5707).

(c) To the extent permitted by law and subject to the availability of appropriations, the Office of Administration, Executive Office of the President, shall provide the Board with such administrative services, funds, facilities, staff, and other support services as may be necessary for the performance of its functions.

**Sec. 4.** *General Provision.* The Board shall terminate 30 days after submitting its report to the President.

*Ronald Reagan*

THE WHITE HOUSE,
*December 1, 1986.*

# Note

In the following narrative, citations to the Board's record are indicated in parentheses. Where the citation is to a name, for example "(McFarlane (1) 6)", it means Robert C. McFarlane's first interview with the Board at page 6 of the transcript. The same page in Mr. McFarlane's second interview would be designated by "(McFarlane (2) 6)."

Representatives of those departments concerned with the national security of the United States reviewed the manuscript in order to declassify it. The criteria for deletions in the interests of the national security were: (1) protection of intelligence sources and methods; (2) protection of negotiations and relations with third countries; and (3) protection of life. The Board finds that these criteria have been reasonably applied.

# The Iran/Contra Affair: A Narrative

*Quis custodiet ipsos custodes.*
    —Juvenal, Satires, VI, 347

## Introduction

In 1985, the United States began a process that eventually included the shipment of advanced weapons unobtainable on the international arms market to Iran for cash and the freedom of Americans kidnapped and held hostage in Lebanon. Israel also sold such weapons to Iran, and the United States resupplied Israel, at least in part. In some instances, Iran apparently arranged for the release of American citizens, and perhaps nationals of other countries, kidnapped in Lebanon. These transactions involved American, Iranian, and Israeli middlemen, and occurred at a time when the public policy of the United States strongly deprecated arms shipments to Iran and ransoming hostages. Large sums changed hands. Large sums are unaccounted for, and may have been diverted to guerrilla groups in various countries, including the resistance in Nicaragua, or to middlemen.

A number of elements appear to have converged at the origin of these transactions. Without assigning priority, they include: (1) the strategic importance of Iran and concern of individuals in the United States government to restore something resembling normal relations with that country; (2) a long history of Russian and Soviet designs on Iran, and the perception that the Soviet invasion of Afghanistan represented an episode in this history; (3) evidence of Iranian influence with, and control over, groups engaging in terrorist acts against citizens and interests of the United States, its allies and friends; (4) Americans held hostage in Lebanon by such groups; (5) Iranian efforts to obtain advanced weapons for use against Iraq; (6) Israel's interest, for a number of reasons, in selling such weapons to Iran with the approval or acquiescence of the United States; (7) the perception by international arms dealers that the American concern about the future course of Iran and Americans held hostage, together with Iran's wish to buy weapons controlled by the United States, offered an opportunity for quick, sure profits.

## I. Background

On January 16, 1979, the Shah was overthrown, ending an intimate Iranian-American relationship over twenty-five years old. Mutual hostility and tension characterized American relations with the Khomeini government, which the seizure on November 4, 1979, of the American Embassy in Tehran intensified. From November 12 to 14, the United States adopted economic sanctions culminating in the decision on the 14th to "block" all Iranian government property and interests in the United States. Iranian oil could no longer be purchased, nor weapons shipped, even those previously purchased by Iran. (Order of 11/79, confirmed by Executive Order, 4/17/80) The United States broke diplomatic relations with Iran on April 7, 1980, and imposed further economic sanctions. Some six weeks after the Embassy seizure, the Soviet Union invaded Afghanistan. Since shortly thereafter, the United States and Iran have pursued compatible policies towards the Afghan resistance. On September 22, 1980, Iraq attacked Iran.

The hostage crisis begun November 4, 1979, continued until the end of the Carter Administration. At that time, direct, formal communications between Washington and Tehran resumed with the establishment, pursuant to the Algiers Accord of January 19, 1981, of the Iran-United States Claims Tribunal at the Hague in 1981. That agreement partially lifted economic sanctions, but the arms embargo was reinforced. In 1983, the United States helped bring to the attention of Tehran the threat inherent in the extensive infiltration of the government by the communist Tudeh Party and Soviet or pro-Soviet cadres in the country. Using this information, the Khomeini government took measures, including mass executions, that virtually eliminated the pro-Soviet infrastructure in Iran.

# A. Intellectual Threads in the NSC Staff: 1984

From the spring of 1982 through the summer of 1984, interagency groups attempted to formulate "a security strategy" for Southwest Asia. (Teicher 6–7) At the beginning of 1984, Geoffrey Kemp, Senior Director for Near East and South Asian Affairs on the staff of the National Security Council ("NSC") and the principal NSC staff officer responsible for the Persian Gulf, (id. at 6), wrote a memorandum to Robert C. McFarlane, Assistant to the President for National Security Affairs and head of the NSC staff, recommending that the Administration reevaluate its attitude towards Iran. He viewed the Khomeini government as a menace to American interests, and suggested a revival of covert operations against it. According to Kemp, Tehran's politics and policies enhanced Syria's standing among Arab states, and threatened western access to Persian Gulf oil. Khomeini's Iran was also believed to have engaged directly or indirectly, in terrorist acts against citizens and interests of the United States, its friends and allies. He reported that exiled Iranians, with whom he regularly communicated, hoped that, with foreign help, they might install a pro-Western government. Suggestions of divisions in the country and support from Saudi Arabia for the exiles encouraged Kemp to submit his proposal. (Kemp to McFarlane, 1/13/84)

Kemp prepared his memorandum during a period in which a number of foreign nationals living in Lebanon were kidnapped by groups known to have important ties to Iran. Further, the United States determined that Iran had played a role in hijackings and bombings, notably the bombings of the American Embassy and of the Marines barracks in Beirut on October 23, 1983. Evidence of Iranian complicity in such events caused the United States to designate Iran a sponsor of international terrorism and to impose additional controls on exports to Iran on January

104

23, 1984. Among those kidnapped after Kemp submitted his memorandum to McFarlane was William Buckley, CIA Chief of Station in Beirut, seized on March 16, 1984. Buckley eventually died in captivity.

On August 31, 1984, McFarlane formally requested an interagency analysis of American relations with Iran after Khomeini. (NSSD 5–84, 8/31/84; Teicher 7) According to the detailed interagency study completed in October 1984, Khomeini's death was probably a precondition to changes in Iranian policies and the realistic prospect of improved Iranian-American relations. The study, which incorporated the analysis of a Special National Intelligence Estimate ("SNIE") then in preparation on Iran, concluded that the possibility of resuming arms shipments to Iran depended on Iran's willingness to restore formal relations, which itself turned on Iran's perception of the importance of such shipments and the American perception of the impact of such shipments on the regional balance of power. (Enclosure to Hill to McFarlane, 10/19/84) The study conveyed an impression of relative American powerlessness to affect events in Iran, powerlessness that would continue indefinitely. (Id.)

The CIA reached a similar conclusion with regard to the utility of covert action in Iran to improve the United States position. The CIA Deputy Director of Operations considered the Marxist Mujaheddin E Khalq to be well organized, influenced by the Soviets, and likely to succeed Khomeini. (DDO to Poindexter, 12/11/84)

The State Department distilled these views into a draft National Security Decision Directive ("NSDD") at the end of 1984. This document would have directed the United States government to maintain and expand its capability to exploit opportunities that might arise in Iran, but reaffirmed, absent changes in the Iranian situation, existing policies. Thus, the draft NSDD would continue the policy of discouraging arms transfers to Iran. (Draft NSDD 5, in Hill to McFarlane, 12/14/84) Howard Teicher, Senior Director for Political-Military Affairs on the NSC staff, told the Board that these interagency efforts "produced no ideas which any of us involved considered to be of great value in terms of significantly affecting our posture in the region." (Teicher 8)

# B. Further 1984 Threads: Iran, Weapons, and Hostages

By the summer of 1984, Iranian purchasing agents were approaching international arms merchants with requests for TOW missiles. The Chief of the Near East Division of the CIA's Directorate of Operations ("C/NE") told the Board.

> We have in the DDO probably 30 to 40 requests per year from Iranians and Iranian exiles to provide us with very fancy intelligence, very important internal political insights, if we in return can arrange for the sale of a dozen Bell helicopter gunships or 1,000 TOW missiles or something else that is on the contraband list.

(C/NE (2) 98)

By November 1984, Iranians with connections to the Tehran government were indicating a connection between such weapons and the release of Americans kidnapped in Lebanon. Theodore Shackley, a former CIA officer, reported that, in meetings November 19–21, 1984, in Hamburg, West Germany, General Manucher Hashemi, former head of SAVAK's Department VIII (counterespionage), introduced him to Manuchehr Ghorbanifar. Hashemi said Ghorbanifar's contacts in Iran were "fantastic." ("American Hostages in Lebanon" at 2 (11/22/84)) Ghorbanifar was already known to the CIA, and the Agency did not have a favorable impression of his reliability or veracity. (Cave 3–5, 44; C/NE (2) *passim*) Shackley reported that Ghorbanifar had been a SAVAK agent, was known to be an international dealmaker, and, generally, an independent man, difficult to control. Ghorbanifar told Shackley that he and other Iranians wanted to help shape Iran's future policies and bring Tehran closer to the West.

He feared that Iran would become a Soviet satellite within the near term—three to five years—if he and people like General Hashemi did not do something to stem the tide. He rhetorically asked what can we do, for despite our ability to work with the "moderates" in

Iran, we can't get a meaningful dialogue with Washington. According to Ghorbanifar, it is President Reagan who has the destiny of the Iranian people in his hand. When at this juncture Ghorbanifar was asked if he had tried to open a dialogue with the Americans, he said, "We know the CIA in Frankfurt. They want to treat us like kleenex—use us for their purpose and then throw us out the window. We can't work with them as they are unreasonable and unprofessional. In fact, if you check on me with them, they will tell you I am unreasonable and undisciplined."

("American Hostages in Lebanon," *supra*, at 2)

To prove that he and Hashemi had influential contacts in Iran, Ghorbanifar suggested that Iran would be willing to trade some Soviet equipment captured in Iraq for TOW missiles. He further suggested the possibility of a cash ransom paid to Iran for the four Americans kidnapped in Lebanon (including Buckley), who, he said after making telephone calls, were alive. The transaction could be disguised by using Ghorbanifar as a middleman. Shackley reported that Ghorbanifar needed a response by December 7, 1984. According to Shackley, later that month, the State Department in effect replied: " 'thank you but we will work this problem out via other channels.' " ("American Hostages in Lebanon" at 1 (6/7/85).)[1]

# II. NSC Staff Diplomacy and Thinking: January–July 1985.

At the beginning of 1985, the Administration adopted new procedures for approving and coordinating covert actions. These were meticulously set forth in elaborate detail in a National Security Decision Directive signed by the President. They included comprehensive interagency evaluation of proposed covert actions, coordinated review of actions undertaken, and notification of Congress in accordance with statute. (NSDD 159, 1/18/85) The NSDD also specified that the President would approve in writing all covert action Findings made pursuant to section 501 of the National Security Act.

# A. The NSC Staff in Action

Early in 1985, the NSC staff undertook actions aimed at the least to improve the government's knowledge about Iran. Michael Ledeen, who, from November 1984 to December 1986, was an NSC consultant on terrorism and certain Middle East questions, including Iran, told the Board that the NSC staff regarded Iran as a strategically important place about which the United States had inadequate information. (Ledeen (1) 7–8) McFarlane was prepared in January to send Ledeen to Europe on a mission of inquiry. In this connection, Rear Admiral Poindexter, McFarlane's deputy, wrote a letter of introduction saying Ledeen "has the complete confidence of Bud McFarlane and myself." (Poindexter to Schurer, 1/4/85. *See also* McFarlane to Grossouvre, 1/4/85) In the early spring of 1985, Ledeen reported to McFarlane a discussion about Iran he had had with a European intelligence official who believed the situation there was more fluid than the United States government seemed to think. Ledeen's interlocutor suggested speaking to the Israelis as the best, quick way to learn about events in Iran. According to Ledeen, McFarlane

> suggested that I talk to Peres privately and ask him whether Israel had better information about Iran than we had, whether Israel had enough information about Iran, about Iranian terrorism, about Iran's role in international terrorism, all these various subjects, so that one could evaluate a rational policy and, if so, whether they would be willing to share that information with us.

(Ledeen (1) 8–9)[2]

Documents suggest a somewhat different origin and purpose for the trip. Donald Fortier, Special Assistant to the President and Senior Director for Political-Military Affairs, reported to McFarlane on April 9, that Ledeen told him on April 8 that McFarlane was prepared to approve Ledeen's travelling to Israel (apparently a previous trip had been cancelled) if Fortier, Covey, and Teicher approved. Fortier wondered if Ledeen had accurately represented McFarlane's view. Fortier, Covey, and Teicher disapproved of using Ledeen as the government's "primary channel for working the Iran issue with foreign governments, and we think you should probably should [sic] not provide a formal letter." (Fortier PROF note to McFarlane, 4/9/85, 10:22:14) On the other hand, they thought he could usefully carry two messages to Prime Minister Peres, whom Ledeen came to know when, as Secretary of State Haig's advisor, he had responsibility for dealing with the Socialist International. (Ledeen (1) 6)

1) the White House feels it is essential to begin to develop a more serious and coordinated strategy for dealing with the Iranian succession crisis—a crisis that is almost certain to turn on outside involvement of one kind or another; and 2) we would like his ideas on how we could cooperate more effectively. The last point is a hard one for us to ask our intelligence community to communicate, since we suspect they may be part of the problem. We don't think Mike should be the one to ask Peres for detailed operational information; he probably doesn't know, and even if he did, this should be reserved for official channels once we have arrived at ideas for restoring better cooperation.

(Fortier PROF note to McFarlane, 4/9/85, 10:22:14) On his own initiative, on April 9, Ledeen made arrangements to see Prime Minister Peres. Fortier and Teicher thought it wise for Teicher to sound out Nimrod Novik, the Prime Minister's Political Advisor, to see if Ledeen would be welcome. (Fortier PROF note to McFarlane, 4/9/85, 11:41:22) McFarlane approved the check with Novik. "If it turns up negative, simply tell Mike that the meeting is not sponsored by us and he should not so represent." (McFarlane PROF note to Fortier, 4/9/85, 12:45:22) He also wrote Fortier:

Yes I think it is entirely worthwhile to cooperate closely with Iran [sic: Israel] in our planning for Iranian succession. . . . As a separate matter I want to talk to Shultz so that he is not blindsided when Sam Lewis [Ambassador to Israel] reports—as he will surely find out—about Mike's wanderings.[3] So for the moment let's hold on the Ledeen aspect. I will get back to you. I do consider planning for the succfession [sic] to be one of our greatest failures and vulnerabilities so I am very glad you are turning to it.

(McFarlane PROF note to Fortier, 4/9/85, 11:22:47)

Ledeen traveled to Israel and met Prime Minister Peres on May 4 or 5, 1985. (Ledeen (1) 10) Ledeen told the Board that, "in essence," Prime Minister Peres

> said that while he thought their information was probably better than ours, he did not consider it satisfactory and he didn't feel that it was sufficient for them to base any kind of serious Iran policy, but that he agreed that it was an important matter and said that they would be happy to work with us to try to develop better information in all these areas—the internal Iranian situation, the Iran role in terror, general international terrorist questions and so forth.

> So he constituted a group of people outside the government, not government officials, to work with us to study the Iran question and the Iranian terrorist issue. The agreement was that each of us would try to find out what our respective governments knew about Iran. We would then sit down, compare notes, and see if possibly by putting them together we might be able to develop some kind of useful picture.

*(Id.* at 10–11)

In his second interview with the Board, Ledeen added that the Prime Minister

> was happy to work together to try to develop better information about Iran, but he, contrary to all these newspaper reports, which continue to drive me crazy and I don't know where they come from, there was no discussion of contacts with Iran, none. There was no discussion of hostages. And except for this one final point where he said we have received a request from the Iranian government to sell them this quantity of materiel, we will not do it without explicit American approval, will you please raise it with McFarlane when you get back to Washington and tell me shall we do it

or shall we not, there was no discussion of weapons or trade or relations or anything.

It was simply a discussion of what could be learned about Iran and how could we better work together to understand that situation.

* * *

[T]here was no discussion of policy at all between me and Peres. It was simply a discussion of information, and then hypothetically if there were information and they had policy recommendations to make, then okay. But we never got to them. It was purely a research trip.

(Ledeen (2) 10–11)

Shlomo Gazit, President of Ben Gurion University and a former chief of Israeli intelligence, led the Israeli team. Gazit still had good relations with Israeli intelligence and could direct both the military and Mossad to provide information. Ledeen did not know the other Israelis, but assumed that David Kimche, Director General of the Israeli Foreign Ministry, worked on this matter. (Ledeen (1) 11)

When Ledeen returned to Washington on May 13, he called Fortier with the news of "very positive feedback. [Ledeen] will brief me tomorrow on what that really means." (Fortier PROF note to Poindexter, 5/13/85, 18:12:20) According to Ledeen, during the May conversation, Prime Minister Peres also asked him to ask McFarlane if the United States would approve an arms shipment to Iran. Ledeen recalled that "[i]t was either ammunition for artillery pieces or some quantity of artillery pieces, but it had to do with artillery." (Ledeen (2) 13) Israel would not ship it to Iran "without explicit American approval." (Ledeen T–2) Ledeen said McFarlane subsequently authorized him to tell the Prime Minister "it's okay, but just that and nothing else." *(Id.)*

# B. Intellectual Formulations: The NSC and Intelligence Estimates

After Ledeen reported to McFarlane on the trip, McFarlane asked Fortier to direct the CIA to prepare a special intelligence estimate on Iran. (Ledeen (1) 11–12) Graham Fuller, National Intelligence Officer for Near East and South Asia, and Teicher participated in this effort. Fuller told the Board that he "regularly" saw Teicher who

> shared a lot of my feelings about our strategic bind vis a vis Iran. And there were others as well in Government, but Howard was the one I was most well aware of in that regard, who felt that we should at least be working towards [sic] an expanded policy towards Iran, expanded in the broadest sense, more than a purely negative one of no arms and slap down on terrorism. It was in fact that NSDD that in the end got nowhere that was part of the rationale for the estimate that we did in '85.

(Fuller 28–29)[4]

On May 17, 1985, Fuller submitted a five-page memorandum to William Casey, Director of Central Intelligence, entitled "Toward a Policy on Iran." Fuller began his analysis as follows:

> 1. The US faces a grim situation in developing a new policy toward [sic] Iran. Events are moving largely against our interests and we have few palatable alternatives. In bluntest form, the Khomeini regime is faltering and may be moving toward a moment of truth; we will soon see a struggle for succession. The US has almost no cards to play; the USSR has many. Iran has obviously concluded that whether they like Russia and Communism or not, the USSR is the country to come to terms with: the USSR can both hurt and help Iran more than the US can. Our urgent need is to develop a broad spectrum of policy moves designed to give us some leverage in the race for influence in Tehran.

(Fuller to DCI/DDCI, "Toward a Policy on Iran," 5/17/85)
Fuller then noted that the United States and Soviet Union
both supported Iraq, but for different reasons, and this
situation was inherently unstable. He wrote that both
countries "lack our preferred access to Iran. Whoever gets
there first is in a strong position to work towards [sic] the
exclusion of the other." *(Id.* at 1) Fuller reported that the
intelligence community monitored "Soviet progress toward developing significant leverage in Tehran," progress,
which, however uneven, merited a response given the
stakes. *(Id.)* He then analyzed American policy.

The United States had two attitudes towards Iran. First,
it was prepared to respond with force if Iran was involved
in a terrorist attack. Second, it strove to deny arms to Iran.
Fuller believed that these "twin pillars" were no longer
sensible because they were adopted to deal with a vacuum
in Iran and a strong Khomeini. These conditions no longer
existing, Fuller concluded, the policy pillars had become
entirely negative "and may now serve to facilitate *Soviet*
interests more than our own." *(Id.* at 2) While acknowledging the difficulty of formulating alternatives, he thought
that

> [i]t is imperative, however, that we perhaps think in
> terms of a bolder—and perhaps riskier policy which
> will at least ensure greater US voice in the unfolding
> situation. Right now—unless we are very lucky indeed
> —we stand to gain nothing, and lose more, in the
> outcome of developments in Iran, which are all out-
> side our control.

*(Id.* at 3)

"Nobody has any brilliant ideas about how to get us back
into Tehran," Fuller wrote, *(id.);* he then analysed a number of alternative courses, including helping Iraq to win
the war and encouraging friendly states to make arms
available to Iran as a means for gaining influence in Tehran. He noted that an Iraqi victory might lead to the establishment of an even more radical regime in Tehran. At-
tacking Iran's radical ally Libya would demonstrate our
resolve and, possibly, remove Qadhafi. Iran's other radical
ally, Syria, could only be pressured by Israel, which had no

wish for conflict at this time. He thought demonstrating to Iranians that we were not hostile by withdrawing our fleet from the Persian Gulf and making public statements about our friendly intentions, for example, might strengthen "Iranian moderates—and opportunists;" it also might produce derision in Tehran. The best course, he concluded, was to have friendly states sell arms that would not affect the strategic balance as a means of showing Tehran that it had alternatives to the Soviet Union. *(Id.* at 5) Were the Soviets to gain in Iran, we would have to strengthen our commitments to Turkey and Pakistan, as they are logical next Soviet targets. *(Id.* at 4) The Director of Central Intelligence provided a copy of this memorandum to the Secretary of State on June 4, 1985. (Note on routing sheet)

On May 20, 1985, the Intelligence Community circulated a revision of its SNIE of October 1984 on Iran (SNIE 34–84, *Iran: The Post Khomeini Era)* According to Fuller,

I think the [intelligence] community had very definitely felt that most of the Iranian regime perceived us as implacably hostile towards an Islamic republic in principle, and that maybe there were some gestures that could be made that would suggest that we were rather more sophisticated in our approach to it than simply that.

*(Id.* at 11)

The first SNIE and the update tried to predict Iran's course over the next six to twelve months, and acknowledged the difficulty that effort implied. Its conclusions were consistent with Fuller's earlier memo to the DCI. The Community expected Khomeini's health to continue to decline, and predicted that Iran would soon enter a period of instability, in part the result of the regime's declining popularity, the growth of private armies, and jockeying for political advantage by competing groups. One could confidently expect "serious instability" before Khomeini's death. Already the Community saw signs of opposition to the radicals among industrial workers. The prospects for the Communist left (the Tudeh Party and Mujahedin-e Khalq) were hard to estimate, but the Soviets were discreetly keeping their options open by allowing their East European allies to sell weapons to Iran while the

U.S.S.R. publicly supported Iraq. "Tehran's leadership seems to have concluded," the Community wrote, "that improvement of relations with the *USSR* is now essential to Iranian interests; any improvement of ties to the United States is not currently a policy option." *(Iran: Prospects for Near-Term Instability* at 5 (5/20/85) (to holders of SNIE 34–84)) Moscow would offer a number of incentives in return for Iran's ceasing to support the Afghan resistance. The United States currently lacked an ability to counter Soviet moves. As a whole, however, the West could take steps to improve its position.

> The United States is unlikely to be able to directly influence Iranian events, given its current lack of contact or presence in Iran. European states and other friendly states—including Turkey, Pakistan, China, Japan, and even Israel—can provide the next most valuable presence or entree in Iran to help protect Western interests. The degree to which some of these states can fill a military gap for Iran will be a critical measure of the West's ability to blunt Soviet influence. These states can also play a major role in the economic life of the country, lessening its isolation and providing alternatives to Soviet influence or that of the radical state.

*(Id.* at 12) According to Fuller, nothing in the May 1985 SNIE proved to be "highly controversial" in interagency deliberations. (Fuller 22)

Teicher told the Board that this estimate became the basis for a new draft NSDD on Iran. (Teicher 8–9) On May 28, Fortier wrote McFarlane:

> We spent the better part of the day working on the Iran NSSD [sic]. I have Dennis [?Ross, at that time an NSC consultant] here looking at the recent spate of Soviet activity and the levers we may have arising out of the war and other circumstances. I think we need about one more full day before we send up a draft for you and John [?Poindexter] to review. We also just got a bootleg copy of the draft SNIE. We worked closely with Graham Fuller on the approach, and I think it really is one of the best yet. Iran may come up in the

breakfast tomorrow. If pressed for action you can credibly promise paper within the next few days. I also think the Israeli option is one we have to pursue, even though we may have to pay a certain price for the help. I'm not sure though that we have the right interlocutor. Mike has a call into me now. His message is that he needs to see me urgently to follow up on his weekend conversation and to get a new plane ticket. Would appreciate guidance and substantive feedback. Thanks.

(Fortier PROF note to McFarlane, 5/28/85 18:52:14)

On June 11, 1985, Fortier and Teicher submitted to Mc-Farlane a draft NSDD on Iran that Teicher had worked on for much of May. They described it as

> provocative. It basically calls for a vigorous policy designed to block Soviet advances in the short-term while building our leverage in Iran and trying to restore the U.S. position which existed under the Shah over the longer-term. This would require a sharp departure from ongoing . . . measures, most notably the supply of Western military hardware, U.S. initiative to dialogue with Iranian leaders. . . .

> Because of the political and bureaucratic sensitivities, we believe that it would be best for you to provide a copy of the NSDD draft only to Shultz and Weinberger (eyes only) for their comments. Whether to proceed with a restricted SIG, NSPG or other forum would depend on their reactions.

(Fortier and Teicher to McFarlane, 6/11/85)

Teicher's draft NSDD, which had incorporated some comments of Vincent Cannistraro, Senior Director for Intelligence and the NSC staff member principally responsible for monitoring covert operations, set forth these points at length. Mirroring the analysis by Fuller, the NSDD defined immediate United States interests as:

(1) Preventing the disintegration of Iran, and preserving Iran as an independent buffer between the Soviet Union and the Persian Gulf;

(2) Limiting Soviet political opportunities in Iran, while positioning the United States to adjust to changes;

(3) Maintaining access to Persian Gulf oil and transit through the Gulf of Hormuz;

(4) Ending Iranian sponsorship of terrorism, and policy of destabilizing neighboring states; Longer-term goals were:

(1) Restoration of Iran's moderate and constructive role in the non-Communist political community, the Persian Gulf region, and "the world petroleum economy;"

(2) Continued Iranian resistance to Soviet expansion (in particular, in Afghanistan);

(3) An early end to the Iran-Iraq war without Soviet mediation or change in the regional balance of power;

(4) Elimination of Iranian human rights abuses;

(5) Movement toward the normalization of Iranian-American relations;

(6) Resolution of American legal and financial claims in the Hague tribunal;

(7) Iranian moderation on OPEC pricing policy.

To begin the process of reaching these goals, Teicher and Fortier recommended that the United States:

(1) Encourage Western allies and friends to help Iran meet its import requirements so as to reduce the attractiveness of Soviet assistance and trade offers, while demonstrating the value of correct relations with the West. This includes provision of selected military equipment as determined on a case-by-case basis.

(Draft NSDD, *U.S. Policy Toward [sic] Iran* at 1–2, 5–6, in McFarlane to Secretaries of State and Defense, 6/17/85)

(2) Cooperate with friendly intelligence services to improve ability to counter clandestine Soviet activities in Iran;

(3) Increase contacts with allies and friends on the Iranian situation and be ready to communicate through them to Iran;

(4) Establish links with, and provide support to, Iranian leaders who might be receptive to efforts to improve relations with the United States;

(5) Avoid actions that could alienate Iranian groups that might respond favorably to such efforts;

117

(6) Respond to Iranian supported terrorism with military action against terrorist infrastructures;

(7) Increase our Voice of America effort to discredit Moscow's Islamic credentials;

(8) Develop a ". . . plan" for supporting United States policy in various contingencies;

(9) Continue to encourage third party efforts to seek an end to the Iran-Iraq war. *(Id.)*

The Secretary of State responded to the draft NSDD on June 29, 1985. "The strategic importance of Iran and the value of reassessing our policy toward it are clear," he wrote. "The draft NSDD constructively and perceptively addresses a number of the key issues. I disagree, however, with one point in the analysis and one specific recommendation." (Comment on Draft NSDD, Shultz to McFarlane, 7/29/85) In his view,

> the draft NSDD appears to exaggerate current anti-regime sentiment and Soviet advantages over us in gaining influence. Most importantly, its proposal that we permit or encourage a flow of Western arms to Iran is contrary to our interest both in containing Khomeinism and in ending the excesses of this regime. We should not alter this aspect of our policy when groups with ties to Iran are holding US hostages in Lebanon. I, therefore, disagree with the suggestion that our efforts to reduce arms flows to Iran should be ended. If the NSDD is revised to reflect this concern, I would like to see the draft again before it is put in final form.

*(Id.)*

Secretary Shultz devoted the rest of his comments to further analysis of his reasons for opposing arms shipments to Iran and his disagreement with the NSDD's portrayal of Iran's relations with the Soviet Union. "The inherent limits on the Iranian-Soviet relationship are underplayed in the NSDD draft. Iranians have a deep historical mistrust of the USSR. The Iranian feelers to the Soviets are for arms and for limitations on Soviet arms supplies to Iraq; the Iranians do not seek a closer relationship." Any attempt at a closer relationship with the Soviet Union would encounter resistance. His comment further reminded McFarlane that, under the Shah, "Iranian-Soviet relations were closer and

118

more cooperative than they are now." *(Id.)* The Secretary had no objection to passing a message to the Speaker of the Iranian Majlis (Parliament) Rafsanjani while abroad expressing the United States interest in "correct" relations, and to encourage allies and friends to broaden their commercial relations with Iran. Such initiatives to diminish Iran's isolation should not undermine pressure to bring an end to the war and restrain arms flows. The comment concluded that this two track policy remained best. *(Id.)*

The Secretary of Defense submitted his reaction to the draft NSDD on July 16, 1985. He told the Board that his initial reaction was to write "absurd" in the margin. "I also added that this is roughly like inviting Qadhafi over for a cozy lunch." (Weinberger 5) While his formal comment noted his agreement

> with many of the major points in the paper, several of the proposed actions seem questionable. Moreover, it is extremely difficult to consider an explicit revision of our policy toward Iran as long as we continue to receive evidence of Iranian complicity in terrorist actions and planning against us. I do not believe, therefore, an NSDD should be issued in the proposed form.

(Weinberger to McFarlane, 7/16/85) The Secretary of Defense "fully" supported the short-term goal of blocking Soviet expansion into Iran.

> Under no circumstances, however, should we now ease our restriction on arms sales to Iran. Attempting to cut off arms while remaining neutral on sales to either belligerent is one of the few ways we have to protect our longer-range interests in both Iran and Iraq. A policy reversal would be seen as inexplicably inconsistent by those nations whom we have urged to refrain from such sales, and would likely lead to increased arms sales by them and a possible alteration of the strategic balance in favor of Iran while Khomeini is still the controlling influence. It would adversely affect our newly emerging relationship with Iraq.

Secretary Weinberger then enumerated those actions— improving intelligence gathering capabilities as recommended in the SNIE, establishing contacts with "moderates", whom intelligence might identify as favoring policies favorable to U.S. and Western interests; communicating our interest in correct relations through allies and friends while remaining neutral in the Iran-Iraq war; pressing the Khomeini government in public statements to mitigate its hostile policies, while encouraging opponents of those policies; and the like—he believed best calculated to achieve United States goals in the region. He concluded by reaffirming his support for present policies in face of Iran's "international lawlessness." He emphasized that "[c]hanges in policy and in conduct, therefore, must be initiated by a new Iranian government." The United States should encourage change, and support moderation and the development in the future of amicable relations. He did not think the program outlined in the draft NSDD served these goals. *(Id.)*

In contrast, the Director of Central Intelligence wrote McFarlane on July 18, 1985, that

> I strongly endorse the thrust of the draft NSDD on *U.S. Policy Toward Iran*, particularly its emphasis on the need to take concrete and timely steps to enhance U.S. leverage in order to ensure that the USSR is not the primary beneficiary of change and turmoil in this critical country. While I am broadly in agreement with its assessment of the current political situation, the NSDD needs to reflect more fully on the complex of Soviet motives and recent actions towards Iran and their implications for U.S. policy initiatives. . . .

(Casey to McFarlane, 7/19/85) The Director of Central Intelligence then enumerated what he considered to be substantial weaknesses in the intelligence analysis of the draft NSDD. *(Id.)*

Teicher told the Board that the reactions of the Secretaries of State and Defense brought inter-agency consideration of a new Iranian policy to "a standstill." (Teicher 13) Teicher sought guidance from Fortier, Poindexter, and "perhaps with McFarlane." *(Id.)* They asked him to see if the process had any other ideas. After discussing the matter with Richard Murphy, Assistant Secretary of State for Near East and South Asian Affairs, he concluded that

[i]t was clear there was no give and there really wasn't any more creativity.

I went back to Fortier and I said the only question is to do nothing, and hope that the situation doesn't create or lead to the negative dangerous situation that we see as a possibility, or present the President with a decision memorandum which lays out, in very clear terms, the different perspectives of his advisors and asks him to make a decision.

In the event, I was advised to do nothing and basically to stand down. I did not produce a draft decision memorandum for McFarlane to send to the President.

That was some time in August, about mid-August, 1985.

From that point on, until early March of 1986, I had no cognizance whatsoever of the other track that was taking place on Iran.

*(Id.* at 14)

# C. Events Keep the NSC's Ideas Alive: January-June 1985

Despite the criticisms of the Secretaries of State and Defense, the ideas embodied in the draft NSDD survived in action. This fact perhaps reflected the turbulent environment in which Teicher drafted the NSDD. A series of kidnappings occurred in Lebanon in 1985: on January 8, Jenco; on March 16, Anderson; on March 22, Fontaine and Carton, both French; on March 26, the British journalist Collett; on May 22, the Frenchmen Kaufmann and Seurat; on May 28, Jacobsen; on June 10, Sutherland. In the same period, meetings involving different members of the NSC staff took place with Israelis about Iran. The conversations became more systematic as time passed. Contemporaneous discussions among persons of various nationalities about Iranian-American relations also occurred. Together with violent events, especially including the hijacking of TWA Flight 847 in mid-June 1985, they formed part of the circumstances that seemed to have given life to the policies advocated by Fuller, Teicher, Fortier, McFarlane, and the Director of Central Intelligence.

In a series of meetings beginning in January 1985, Yaacov Nimrodi, an arms merchant and former Israeli Defense Attache in Tehran, Ghorbanifar, Amiram Nir, Advisor to Prime Minister Peres on Counterterrorism, and Adolph Schwimmer, a long-time arms merchant and, since September 1984, Special Advisor to Prime Minister Peres, considered Iran and the American hostages. They concluded that a plan to gain the release of the hostages and to "open up a dialogue with Iran" was realistic if they could obtain American support. Roy Furmark, a business associate of Adnan Khashoggi and participant in at least one of the meetings, told Charles Allen of the CIA that "profit was certainly a motive but that the group did see their efforts as leading toward stability in the region and the release of the hostages."[5] (DCI to Poindexter, undated but after October 22, 1986)

The Board also obtained rather cryptic evidence of a meeting in Cologne in late March involving Iranians, including probably the chief of the Iranian buying office, Dr. Shahabadi, a friend of Adnan Khashoggi. (Unsigned and undated note; Furmark 34)

Basic thrust of the meeting is that we wanted to open discussions with Iranian officials and we also wanted the hostages freed. Shabadi said that he would discuss this with Khameni'i and [a cleric] and come back out to see us at subsequent meeting this meeting never took place. However, there were two phone conversations with someone in Tehran who according to Zaheri was [a cleric]. In this case there were requests for weapons to show our bona fides. These were turned aside. They then tried to get boeing spare lkarts [parts]. Finally gave us a list of ten items of spare parts for a boeing. cast of characters was Zaheri, Shoja'i, ghorbanifar (no direct contact in his case) and Shahabadi. Zhaheri khad a falling out with Shoja'i over money. Zaheri finally gave up and returned to Houston. We determined that the Iranan side was only interesed in money.

(Original spelling and punctuation. Unsigned and undated note) In May, Shackley recalled discussing the hostage problem over lunch with Ledeen. Shackley told him about his report on his November 1984 meeting with Ghorbanifar. Shackley remembered that Ledeen asked for a copy of the report. Ledeen said people in the government were interested in investigating the hostage question, and asked if Shackley could "find out whatever that was as a channel, if it is still open." (Shackley 23)

On June 7, 1985, Shackley prepared a second report on "American Hostages in Lebanon." He gave it to Ledeen who passed it to LtCol Oliver North, the NSC staff officer responsible for counterterrorism. (Shackley 34; Ledeen (2) 5–6) Shackley reported that General Hashemi had taken soundings with Iranians on the possibility of arranging the freedom of Americans kidnapped in Lebanon. On June 1, Ghorbanifar told Hashemi that his Iranian friends had told him the following:

—Iranian authorities were flooded with proposals to help obtain the release of American hostages in Lebanon. As a result, they did not know who was who.

—Tehran was not interested in the humanitarian ploy that had been put forth by Ghorbanifar.[6]

—Tehran wanted the following:

(1) a dialogue with a responsible American who can identify what he represents;

(2) a discussion of a quid pro quo that involves items other money.

We told Ghorbanifar that we would pass on this commentary to "friends."

("American Hostages in Lebanon," 6/7/85)

# D. NSC Staff Activity: May–July 1985

On December 16, 1986, Secretary Shultz testified before the Senate Select Committee on Intelligence (closed session), and subsequently told the Board that, on May 30, Ambassador Lewis in Tel Aviv reported that Ledeen was on a "secret mission for the White House" and to ask if Secretary Shultz knew "what was going on."

> The answer was no. Ambassador Lewis said he had asked at the Israeli Ministry of Defense about Mr. Ledeen and had been told it was "too hot" to talk about, but that Defense Minister Rabin would tell me about it when he visited Washington.

(Shultz, 12/86, 4; SRB, 9)[7] When Secretary Shultz met Defense Minister Rabin on June 1, the Defense Minister mentioned neither Ledeen nor Iran. (Id. at 5) The Secretary further testified that an NSC staff member told a member of his staff that Ledeen had asked McFarlane for permission to follow up on his earlier trip to obtain intelligence about Iran, that McFarlane "was ambivalent, refused to give Mr. Ledeen a letter to Prime Minister Peres, but reportedly agreed to allow Mr. Ledeen to pursue the matter. We were told that Mr. Ledeen went to Israel and received a positive response to this proposition." (Id. at 4–5) On June 6, 1985, Poindexter informed Robert Kimmitt, at that time Executive Secretary of the NSC, that McFarlane had decided to cancel Ledeen's trip.

This activity concerned the Secretary of State. He told the Senate Select Committee on Intelligence that, on June 5, 1985, while he was in Lisbon, he

> sent a message to Mr. McFarlane complaining about Mr. Ledeen's contact with the Israelis, which had bypassed both Ambassador Lewis and myself. I said that

Israel's record of dealings with Iran indicates that Israel's agenda is not the same as ours, and an intelligence relationship with Israel concerning Iran might not be one upon which we could fully rely. I felt that "it could seriously skew our own perception and analysis of the Iranian scene. I said in my message to Mr. McFarlane, "I am mystified about the way this situation has been handled and am concerned that it contains the seeds of further embarrassment and serious error unless straightened out quickly."

On June 7, 1985, in Portugal, I received a message from Mr. McFarlane saying that he was "a little disappointed in my prejudgments", and that he had intended to tell me about the matter but had not had time to do so. He said "I am turning it off entirely . . ." Mr. McFarlane said that it had been an Israeli initiative and that Mr. Ledeen was acting "on his own hook."

(Shultz, 12/86, 5–6)

Also on June 7, North was working on various approaches to achieve the release of those Americans kidnapped in Lebanon. He submitted an action memorandum to McFarlane asking approval for two efforts aimed to secure the release of hostages. McFarlane approved both. Under the first, the United States would support efforts to find a private solution to the problem of the American and French hostages in Lebanon and the three Lebanese Da'Wa prisoners in Kuwait whose release the hostage holders demanded. "[T]he . . . operation will likely have produced results or failed by June 16, 1985," North wrote. The second plan involved the private ransoming of two hostages, including Buckley, for $2 million.[8] This operation would take "considerable time (contacts inside Lebanon, financial transactions, and rental of yacht/safehouse)"; thus, it was possible to undertake it at the same time as the private efforts were underway. (North to McFarlane, 6/7/85) To implement this proposal, North asked McFarlane to contact the Attorney General to secure the services of two officers of the Drug Enforcement Agency who would work with the NSC staff on this matter. McFarlane approved and wrote "North to follow up 6/10 w/AG." (Id.)

On June 14, 1985, two Lebanese men hijacked TWA flight 847, and directed the pilot to land at Beirut airport. There, the hijackers removed thirteen Americans from the plane and killed an American sailor. This episode absorbed the government until the surviving hostages were released on June 29. On June 17, the Director of Central Intelligence heard from his wartime friend, John Shaheen, that a Dr. Cyrus Hashemi, under indictment for attempting to sell arms to Iran, claimed to have discussed with the Iranian Foreign Ministry an exchange of hostages for the release of the Da'Wa prisoners in Kuwait, TOW missiles, and a nolle prosequi for Hashemi. (Casey to C/NE, 6/17/85) According to the CIA Inspector General, Israeli officials asked Ghorbanifar to use his influence in Tehran to obtain the release of hostages. (CIA/IG Chronology 2) On June 19, Iran sent the United States a message to the effect that Tehran wanted to do as much as it could to end the TWA crisis. (Teicher to McFarlane, 6/19/85) The United States responded on June 21 that "[i]t is the view of the United States that the government of Iran cannot escape its responsibilities . . . to help secure the release of the hostages. . . ." (DT 6/21/85 1828L)[9]

At the beginning of July, McFarlane and Ledeen had separate, but apparently related, meetings with Schwimmer and Kimche, respectively, in Washington. Ledeen told the Board that Kimche called him early in the month to ask him to meet Schwimmer. They met a week later (probably July 11; see note 10 *infra*). (Ledeen (1) 17) In his two interviews with the Board, Ledeen recalled Schwimmer reporting that he had recently met Ghorbanifar through Schwimmer's friend, Khashoggi. Ghorbanifar's knowledge of Iranian policies impressed the Israelis.

Ghorbanifar had for the first time given them what they considered to be a really solid picture, in detail, of the internal Iranian situation and the Iranian connection to international terrorism.

And in addition he had various proposals that he claimed to be representing on behalf of the Iranian government, who were high individuals inside the Iranian government, and they thought it was important that I should come and meet this person.

And I said [I] was planning to come to Israel anyway and that I would check with Bud [McFarlane] and if it was okay with Bud I would try to meet with him then. And I talked to Bud and he said fine.

(Ledeen (2) 17) Schwimmer, whom Ledeen described as one of Foreign Minister Peres' "close friends," knew about Ledeen's May conversation with the then-Prime Minister. *(Id.* at 19) "[A]s best as I can recall it at this point," Ledeen told the Board,

> I think that what happened was that Schwimmer described Ghorbanifar and he may have talked something about hostages also, that I went to Israel and met Ghorbanifar, where all of this took on real flesh, that Kimche then came back to Washington early in August and told Bud about it, and formulated the proposition, that Bud then discussed it with the President, and by the time I came back in the middle of August the President had approved it and I then communicated that decision to the Israelis.

And I'm quite sure that is the chronology.

General Scowcroft: Do you have any notion how this thing got transformed from a research project into an action program over a very short period of time and who made the transformation?

Mr. Ledeen: It is what I wrote in the Post, General. The Iranians came forward. Ghorbanifar came forward. Ghorbanifar is really the driving force behind this whole thing. I mean, one can speculate about Americans and Israelis, but it is clear that the guy really—I mean, these ideas did not come either from the Government of the United States or the Government of Israel or arms merchants. These ideas came from Ghorbanifar. He was the person who introduced them. He was the one who put them forward, and he was the one who claimed to have the capacity to achieve them.

So it happened because the Israelis were approached by Ghorbanifar as a way of getting to the United States, and I believe—I mean, one of the few things that I do believe that Khashoggi has said is what he said on that TV show with Barbara Walters, that he suggested to Ghorbanifar that the best way to get the Americans' attention was to go to the Israelis. That is the way he would think, and he was right, in fact, and it worked.

So that was the channel from Iran to the United States and that is how it happened, and I was the one who found myself in a room with them, that's all. It was an accident.

*(Id.* at 21–23)

Contemporaneously, Kimche also visited Washington. He met McFarlane on July 3. According to McFarlane, Kimche sought "the position of our government toward engaging in a political discourse with Iranian officials." (McFarlane (1) 6) Kimche thought the Iranians in question would ultimately need something, namely arms, to show for the discussions. "But," McFarlane told the Board in his first interview,

that was not a request [for arms] on July 3rd. He said that the Iranians understood that, because we had never seen them and had no basis for confidence that they were people of influence and authority, understood that they needed to demonstrate their own bona fides, and that they believed that they could influence the Hizaballah in Lebanon to release the hostages, and in fact went as far as to convey through him on July 3rd that they had three approaches, just in terms of formats, of where they might deliver the seven hostages, and sought our comment on which of these was preferable.

*(Id.* at 7–8) McFarlane took this message as an indication that Iranians understood that Iranian-American relations "couldn't prosper from our point of view for as long as people close to Iran and linked to them continued to hold hostages." *(Id.* at 8)

## III. The President, His Staff, and the Cabinet: July–August 1985.

In his first interview, McFarlane told the Board he then reported this conversation to the President before he entered the hospital for his cancer operation in the second week of July. He informed the Secretaries of State and Defense and the Director of Central Intelligence in separate conversations. He also said he visited with the President in hospital, and the Secretary of State "to discuss it in brief." (Id.) He told the President that Kimche's question was "what is your attitude toward engaging with Iran in a political agenda, period." (Id.) According to McFarlane, the President considered the question in a broad context, including Kimche's suggestion that eventually arms transfers would become an issue.

> And while it wasn't linked to the hostages, the President said, well, it seemed to him that the Middle East experience well beyond Iran is that elements to succeed ultimately to power do need to strengthen themselves, and that the currency of doing that is usually weapons. And he said the key element is not denying history, but deciding whether or not our doing that or somebody else doing that can be distinguished as a political matter of policy between the natural perception of people that weapons are going to people portrayed as terrorists. Iran is identified as a terrorist state. He said the key element is whether or not these people are indeed devoted to change and not just simply opportunists, self-serving radicals.

(Id. at 9)

In his meeting with the Board on February 11, 1987, the President said he had no recollection of a meeting in the hospital in July with McFarlane and that he had no notes that would show such a meeting. (R. Dawson & W.C. McFadden II, Memorandum for the Record, 2/9/87)

In his third interview with the Board, February 21, 1987, at the Bethesda National Naval Hospital, McFarlane recalled:

> I have felt since last November—and that is where we started—that it has been, I think, misleading, at least,

and wrong, at worst, for me to overly gild the President's motives for his decision in this, to portray them as mostly directed toward political outcomes.

The President acknowledged those and recognized that those were clearly important. However, by the tenor of his questioning, which was oriented toward the hostages and timing of the hostages, from his recurrent virtually daily questioning just about welfare and do we have anything new and so forth, it is very clear that his concerns here were for the return of the hostages.

Now maybe it's come to your attention that there was a meeting with the TWA 847 relatives and hostages on July 4 or 5, and the President stayed with Mrs. Reagan at Arlington Cemetery for an extra half hour or so going down and greeting each of the families there, and it was a very moving moment and it had an impact on him.

Within a day or so of that I brought to his attention this original proposal from Mr. Kimche, and the President's reaction was quite enthusiastic and somewhat perhaps excessively enthusiastic, given the many uncertainties involved. But it was expressive of his attitude on this issue from the beginning, and from the four, five, or six meetings we had in the next thirty days on it there weren't any inhibitions as persistently as well as the Secretary of State and Defense made them, and they were very well made.

But the President had no hesitancy about it at all, nor did he when he called me about it last week here in the hospital.

\* \* \*

Well, the recollection of my having briefed the President on Kimche's visit in the White House and his coming here and his reactions when here at the hospital, I briefed him on the new information received from Mr. Schwimmer, there is a vividness in my recollection that is documented datewise by the calendars that I have that the meetings were held in the image of being across the hall with Mr. Regan and the President, filling them in on this, and the President saying words to the effect that gee, that sounds pretty good.

The weapons issue is a problem, and our discussion of that, and he says: I guess we can't do the weapons or something like that ourselves, but isn't there a way that we can get at trying to keep this channel going or something like that.

Mr. Dawson: And that's tied in to the hostages at that point? It is clear that one of the purposes of this is not so much a strategic opening as you might have otherwise stated, but it is an attempt to get arms for hostages through the transfer from Israel to Iran?

Mr. McFarlane: Well, I think that was foremost in the President's mind.

Mr. Dawson: So if he didn't state to you in so many words, Bud, go ahead and do it, he clearly led you to believe from the outset that here was a chance to bring some hostages out through a third country?

Mr. McFarlane: It was unambiguously clear.

(McFarlane (3) 11–14)

On November 21, 1986, McFarlane wrote Poindexter that the President "was all for letting the Israelis do anything they wanted at the very first briefing in the hospital." (McFarlane PROF note to Poindexter, 11/21/86, 21:01)

Donald T. Regan, the President's Chief of Staff, recalled first learning of McFarlane's conversation with an Israeli about Iran while the President was in hospital, some two days after his operation. According to Regan, McFarlane wanted authority to enter discussions with the Iranians identified by the Israelis as having "reasonably good connections within Iran but who were on the outside." (Regan 4) Regan told the Board:

About the second day after the operation, I believe it was, we went out there—I can find the exact date if you don't have it—met with the President—he was in bed—and McFarlane told him that we had had a contact from Iranians whom he had reason to believe had reasonably good connections within Iran but who were on the outside, and this had come primarily as a result of Israeli connection with the Iranians.

At that time I didn't know their names, I now know them to be Ghorbanifar, Kimche, and the like, but at that time I didn't know the names.

And what McFarlane wanted was the President's authority to make this contact, to see if it could be developed and what it could lead to. There was a discussion of the importance of Iran as far as its strategic location . . . and the fact that it seemed worthwhile to McFarlane that this be pursued.

The President, after asking quite a few questions— and I would say the discussion lasted for perhaps 20, 25 minutes—assented and said yes, go ahead. Open it up.

(Regan 4–5) According to McFarlane, after this meeting, he then conveyed to Kimche the President's openness to a dialogue with Iran. (McFarlane (1) 9)

The Secretary of State testified before the House Foreign Affairs Committee that he first heard of this matter while flying between Perth and Canberra, Australia, on July 14, 1985. McFarlane reported that Kimche had met him secretly the week before,

and had asked him to confirm that the U.S. was in fact uninterested in pursuing the cooperation earlier proposed to Mr. Ledeen. Mr. McFarlane wrote that he had so confirmed. He then stated that an unnamed emissary had "today" reopened the issue on behalf of the Prime Minister.[10] The emissary said that in a recent meeting between Israelis and some Iranians, including Mr. Kimche, a Mr. Al Schwimmer, and Mr. Ghorbanifar, the Iranians had painted a pessimistic view of Iran. They allegedly said "their hope and that of what they portrayed as a significant cadre of the hierarchy was to develop a dialogue with the West," and emphatically with the United States. The Israelis had allegedly pressed "for some tangible show" of the Iranians' ability to deliver, and were purportedly told "that they could in the short term achieve the release of the seven Americans held in Lebanon." But, Mr. McFarlane repeated, in exchange the Iranians had said they would need to show "some gain" and sought specifically the delivery from Israel of 100 TOW missiles. "But they stated," Mr. McFarlane continued, "that the larger purpose would be the opening of the private dialogue with a high level American official and a sustained discussion of U.S.-Iranian relations."

Mr. McFarlane reviewed the "imponderable questions" raised by this proposal, including "our terrorism policy against negotiating with terrorists (notwithstanding the thin veil provided by Israel as the cut out on this specific matter)." He noted that our long term interest was in maintaining the possibility of renewed ties, and the importance of doing something soon about the seven hostages. He said: "We could make a tentative show of interest without commitment and see what happened or we could walk away. On balance I tend to favor going ahead." He said the emissary was leaving soon, asked for a prompt signal, and that he would "await and abide fully by your decisions."

I replied by a message to Mr. McFarlane that same day that "I agree with you that we should make a tentative show of interest without commitment. I do not think we could justify turning our backs on the prospect of gaining the release of the other seven hostages and perhaps developing an ability to renew ties with Iran under a more sensible regime—especially when presented to us through the Prime Minister of Israel."

This position—indicating a willingness to talk but no commitment to pay—was consistent with Administration policy of maintaining contact with people who might eventually provide information or help in freeing hostages. I pointed out, however, "the fraud that seems to accompany so many deals involving arms and Iran, and the complications arising from our 'blessing' an Israel-Iran relationship where Israel's interest and ours are not necessarily the same." I suggested that Mr. McFarlane should give the emissary "a positive but passive reply." That is, tell him that the U.S. "is receptive to the idea of a private dialogue involving a sustained discussion of U.S.-Iranian relations. In other words, we are willing to listen and seriously consider any statement on this topic that they might wish to initiate." I said I thought Mr. McFarlane should manage this probe personally, but that the two of us should discuss its sensitivity and the likelihood of disclosure after my return. I told him to tell the emissary "that you and I are in close contact and full agreement every step of the way; this is all the more important in view of the present lack of unity and full coordination on the Israeli side."

(Shultz, 12/86, 8–10; SRB, 17–20) On July 16, the Secretary saw an intelligence report, which indicated that Ghorbanifar, whose name McFarlane had mentioned, was " 'a talented fabricator.' " (Shultz, SRB, 20)

In the middle of July, Ledeen went to Israel on vacation and, toward the end of the month, attended a meeting with Ghorbanifar, Kimche, Schwimmer, and Nimrodi. "[T]o the best of my recollection," Ledeen said, this conversation,

is the first time that the subject of weapons and hostages was raised. They were raised in the context of the future relationship between the United States and Iran. They were not raised separately as a deal or an entity unto themselves because what Ghorbanifar had to say, in addition to this fairly enlightening picture of Iran that he presented us with, was that there were significant and powerful people within the government of Iran who were interested in improving relations with the United States. . . . [A]s part of the evolution of this relationship in a more positive direction Iran would undertake to make gestures of good faith and to demonstrate not only their willingness but their capacity to alter their policies in a direction which we would consider positive, and that at the same time they would like to see on the part of the United States a similar demonstration of willingness and capacity and that the only such gesture by the United States that would convince them simultaneously that the President was personally involved and committed to this policy and that the United States would act and exert its power in the world to do such things would be if the United States enabled Iran to obtain weapons which were at present unobtainable because of the American arms embargo, and that the sorts of gestures that the Iranian government would make to demonstrate its good faith and capacity included weighing in to try to obtain the release of hostages in Lebanon, but also other things, including statements by leaders of the government which we would see clearly were moving in that direction.

(Ledeen (1) 22–23) After the meeting, Ledeen, Kimche, Schwimmer, and Nimrodi decided that someone should report the conversation to McFarlane, which Kimche offered to do. (*Id.* at 24)

At the end of July, Furmark and Ghorbanifar met Yaacov Nimrodi, an arms merchant and former Israeli Defense Attache in Tehran, Amiram Nir, Advisor to Prime Minister Peres on counterterrorism, and Adolph Schwimmer, a long-time arms merchant and, since September 1984, Special Advisor to Prime Minister Peres, at one of Nimrodi's homes in Tel Aviv. (Furmark 40; Charles Allen reported that Furmark said Nir attended this meeting. C. Allen to DCI/DDCI, 10/17/86) Furmark, who was not within earshot of the conversation, possibly because the Israelis were concerned that Furmark might be a CIA agent, (Furmark at 41), provided only a sketchy account to the Board. He said that they discussed a program "to begin to open up relations between the U.S. and Iran." (*Id.* at 37) He heard no mention of hostages or arms, but did overhear a reference to "spare parts." (*Id.*) But he said,

> the U.S. had agreed, the Israelis had agreed, the Iranians had agreed to do some business, but nobody would trust each other. The Iranians would not pay for anything until they received and inspected the goods, because, I've heard on previous transactions involving even foodstuffs and stuff they would pay in advance and they opened up the crates and there were rocks in it. So they became very shell-shocked about paying in advance for anything.

And of course the Israelis would not send anything until they were paid in advance.

So now you had a stalemate. Khashoggi then said, well, I will trust the Iranians, I'll trust the Israelis, I'll trust the Americans, I'll put the money up.

So the first transaction I understand was a million dollar transaction which he deposited into a numbered account which the Israelis told him to put the money in. The financing operates like this: He puts a million dollars into an account, and then Ghorbanifar gives him what we will call a post-dated check for a million dollars in his account at Credit Suisse. And then after the shipment is made, the Iranians inspect the goods, and they then pay Ghorbanifar's account at Credit Suisse. Ghorbanifar tells Khashoggi the check is good, deposit it.

And that is how the financing was done all throughout.

*(Id.* at 5–6)

Furmark apparently told much the same story to Charles Allen, the CIA's National Intelligence Officer for Counterterrorism, and George Cave, a CIA annuitant and expert on Iran, who met with Furmark on October 16, 1986. Based on Furmark's account, Allen concluded that

[t]he idea of providing Iran with military equipment in exchange for American hostages—seen as a way of commencing a dialogue with Iran—also originated in the summer of 1985 and he along with Ghobanifar [sic], traveled to Tel Aviv in August 1985. . . . Subsequently, arms were delivered to Tehran in September 1985, a development that resulted in the release of Reverend Benjamin Weir.

(C. Allen to DCI/ DDCI, 10/17/86)

Kimche called McFarlane July 30 and saw him August 2. According to McFarlane, Kimche said that Rafsanjani, Musavi, the Prime Minister, and Khamenei, the President, had been preoccupied by domestic affairs for about a month, and, therefore, had not pursued the hostage or American issues during that period. Rafsanjani in particu-

lar had been dealing with "factional vulnerability." (Mc-
Farlane (1) 10) Now, Kimche said, they found it more difficult than they had thought to influence their friends in
Lebanon. The Iranians were "more concerned about the
bona fides of our side and specifically about whether or not
we would provide weapons right away, not for a threat, not
for expanding the war, but, as it was cast, for the expansion
of and consolidation of the faction with military elements,
of army elements specifically." *(Id.)* McFarlane informed
Kimche that he did not think it "wise or likely" that the
United States would transfer weapons to the Iranians, "because we had not dealt with these people. . . . [T]he notion of our giving weapons to people we did not know,
with the track record before us, was imprudent and I
thought politically silly." *(Id.* at 10–11) When Kimche
asked what the United States reaction would be if Israel
shipped weapons to Iran, McFarlane replied by asking
why Israel would.

> [I]n a nutshell, [Kimche] said: Well, we in Israel have
> our own interests. They are basically to ensure a stale-
> mate of the conflict with Iraq, but also to get the
> United States back into Iran, and that helps us if the
> United States' position in the Middle East is strength-
> ened; and separately, to reduce the Iranian support
> for terrorism, if that is feasible, is very much in our
> interest, and so we might very well do this as a matter
> of Israeli interest.

> But he said: I pose it for us doing that, because ulti-
> mately if we provide things we're going to have to
> come and buy other ones, and I need to know, are we
> going to be able to do that or not, whether it's Hawks
> or TOWs or whatever else.

> And I said: Well, that really isn't the issue. Israel has
> bought weapons from the United States for years and
> always will, and so you don't need to ask whether you
> can buy more weapons. It is a matter of whether or
> not the support of the idea of providing weapons to
> anybody in Iran is in policy terms sensible. But I will
> get you our position.

*(Id.* at 11)

# A. The Principals' Various Views: August 1985

In his meeting with the Board on January 26, 1987, the President said that sometime in August he approved the shipment of arms by Israel to Iran. He was uncertain as to the precise date. The President also said that he approved replenishment of any arms transferred by Israel to Iran. McFarlane's testimony of January 16, 1986, before the Senate Foreign Relations Committee, on which the President heavily relied, takes the same position. This portion of McFarlane's testimony was specifically highlighted on the copy of the testimony given by the President to the Board.

In his meeting with the Board on February 11, the President said that he and Regan had gone over the matter repeatedly and that Regan had a firm recollection that the President had not authorized the August shipment in advance. In response to a question from the Board, the President said he did not authorize the August shipment. He noted that very possibly, the transfer was brought to him as already completed. He said that subsequently there were arms shipments he authorized that may have had to do with replenishment, and that these could have taken place in September. A memorandum from Peter Wallison, White House Counsel, on which the President heavily relied, stated that the President had been "surprised" that the Israelis had shipped arms to Iran in September, and that this fact caused the President to conclude that he had not approved the transfer in advance.

On February 20, 1987, the President wrote Chairman Tower:

> In trying to recall events that happened eighteen months ago I'm afraid that I let myself be influenced by others' recollections, not my own.

\* \* \*

I have no personal notes or records to help my recollection on this matter. The only honest answer is to state that try as I might, I cannot recall anything whatsoever about whether I approved an Israeli sale in advance or whether I approved replenishment of Israeli stocks around August of 1985. My answer therefore and the simple truth is, "I don't remember—period."

In his first interview, McFarlane told the Board he reported to the President within two or three days of meeting Kimche on August 2. On McFarlane's recommendation, he told the Board, an informal National Security Planning Group ("NSPG") meeting occurred while the President was convalescing. The Secretaries of State and Defense, the Director of Central Intelligence, Admiral Poindexter, Regan, McFarlane, and possibly the Vice President attended. Neither the Vice President, nor McFarlane was certain about his attendance. (W.C. McFadden II, Memorandum for the Record, 12/29/86; McFarlane (1) 17) McFarlane remembered this meeting because the President was wearing pajamas. McFarlane recalled

a very active argument, really, for a good reason, about the wisdom of doing this and very sharp disagreements on the part of the Secretary of Defense, really, and to a lesser extent but emphatically by the Secretary of State, but for different reasons. . . . [T]he President had available to him very vivid, forceful, thorough expression of views of his Cabinet officers involved on this. And it was argued in policy terms, both the issue of a dialogue with Iran, the legitimacy of these people, the legal authorities for—this was not the United States doing something; it was Israel doing something, but nonetheless for involvement of U.S. weapons with U.S. endorsement, which is an important policy.

The legal ramifications, the political risks, the matter of Congressional oversight, and then basically the probabilities of, given all these factors, of this having any promise at all.

[A]t the end of it the President said, well, as he had

before, that his inclination was not to have any U.S.-owned weapons or our inventory involved in this, but that he believed that it was possible over time, if these people's standing and authority and intentions were reformist, if you will, that he could see the need to support them, and with weapons, although at the time he said, right now I'm inclined not to have any U.S. weapons involved, U.S.-owned, but if Israel, whose judgment on this is based on a track record of dealing with these people, believes that it is sensible to do it and does transfer weapons, then ultimately their wish to buy replacements we should honor and we should sell to them.

(McFarlane (1) 12–13)

Regarding hostages, McFarlane told the Board he tried faithfully to summarize Kimche's message:

that while the Iranians had told him to say that they understood they needed to demonstrate their bona fides and they thought the hostage release was the best evidence of that, and while the arms, the matter of arms, was ostensibly associated with the Iranians' perception of vulnerability, that you would be foolish not to recognize that, first of all, that may be just an artifice, deliberately to engage in a hostage for arms deal; and even if it isn't, if they are dealing in good faith, the perceptions of people of good will will be that that is the de facto condition.

The President understood that and he said: Well, you're right, the risks of misunderstanding are quite high, and the question is are these people valid interlocutories or not, dealing in good faith or not. And he says: We have no way of judging it, really, except the track record of the past seven years, and it is only this report, really, and other things, the corroborating work we have done, focused upon intelligence hard copy that had been provided by these Iranians to the Israelis and Israel and ultimately to us—that it was basically—an order of battle is the wrong word. It was the names of the leadership of the Iranian armed forces from about the battalion level up, and that is nothing novel, but identifying those who were disposed to support these elements and those who were not.

Separately, the complexion of the government in both the Prime Minister's office and the Foreign Minister's office; the Majlis, again identifying those were—well, they were identified in one, one [sic], two, or three lines or factions, basically extremists from left to right and where people stood on the political map.[11]

* * *

Well, all these things were considered by the President and, in a word, his decision was no U.S.-owned arms or U.S. transfers; if Israel chooses to do this and ultimately they seek replacements from us they can buy them from us; and yes, finally, we are interested in a political meeting with Iranians.

Well, I conveyed this to Mr. Kimche, and I was very precise in saying: The purpose here is a political agenda; the vulnerability and risk is a perception of something far different, which is arms for hostages.

(Id. at 14–16)

On January 16, 1987, McFarlane gave the Senate Foreign Relations Committee a somewhat different account from the one he had provided to the Board in his first interview. He said:

As I say, it began in July with the President convening each of the people on the Council, hearing their advice, not deciding, but thinking about it. Those same individuals meeting singly or in groups with him— again, the Secretary of State and Defense—and over time in the course of about a ten-day period, late July, early August, the President coming to a conclusion to authorize a specific authority for another country to do something. . . . The President viewed the decision as a decision to grant his approval for the actions of another government, although indeed ultimately that government would come to us again, Israel, to buy replacement arms. Now, he communicated that

141

to me, and when he did by telephone, I said to him, Mr. President, as you know, your Secretaries of State and Defense are opposed to this. He says, yes, I understand that, and provided his own explanation of the basis for his decision.

Then I notified the other National Security Council members, the Secretary of State and Defense and the others, and on those occasions heard once more the opposition of it from the Secretaries of State and Defense. And I encouraged them to be back in touch with the President, because you're quite right—the communications through channels that are not always open can lead to ambiguities and misunderstanding. And I know in at least one case, I believe the Secretary of State—perhaps more than once—after the decision, promptly though—reaffirmed his concerns about it, even though out of this country.

(McFarlane, 1/16/87, 18–19) The President's official schedule notes on August 6 meeting attended by the Vice President, the Secretary of Defense, the Chairman of the Joint Chiefs of Staff, the President's Chief of Staff, and McFarlane. (Ellen M. Jones, Presidential Diarist, to Jay B. Stephens, 1/24/87)

McFarlane told the Board on February 19, 1987:

[U]pon returning from the hospital, if you want to proceed in that direction, [the President] did convene his advisors, the members of the NSC, and discuss this matter.

As to when concretely he made his decision, I have to say, Mr. Chairman, I don't know and there is no written record of it. The basis on which I say that it had to have happened in the final week of July or the first week of August is, first of all, my own memory of the sequence of events and what we talked about in that period. And there are, and I think my schedule has been given to you, six meetings where he met with his NSC people, all or more than one, between July 22 and August 7, I believe.

Now on at least two occasions he discussed this matter

with more than me, with at least, on one occasion, with the Secretary of State and the Secretary of Defense, the DCI, the Vice President and Don Regan.

General Scowcroft: All together at once?

Mr. McFarlane: Yes. But my recollection is that there was disagreement on the matter and he did not make a decision at that meeting, and that only after a matter of days, but within two or three, did he call me directly and state that he had considered it and he wanted to go ahead and specifically that if Israel decided that it wanted to sell weapons to Iran that Israel could buy replacements from the United States.

Now I have to stress that I don't know, perhaps it has been minimized in the coverage of this so far, but at the meeting it is fair to say that though there was opposition by the Secretary of State and Defense that even those who favored it stressed the matter that what was being approved was something to be done by someone else—Israel—and not the United States.

And it was seen to be an authorization, a license if you will, for Israel to undertake a plan and that authority given to me on the telephone, and I shared in my recollection with the Secretary of State also by phone, and he expressed his opposition. And I encouraged him to be back in touch with the President on it, and I believe he was.

(McFarlane (2) 9–11)

McFarlane noted that "generally speaking the President would reach decisions only at the time of a meeting only if there was unanimity. Where there was disagreement it was his habit almost never to make the decision there but to wait and then convey it to me later on." *(Id.* at 16)

Regan remembered that the meeting was informal, without an agenda or briefing papers. It occurred in late July or early August, after the President returned from the hospital.

Bud [McFarlane] briefed at this and talked about the Israeli connection here and how the Israelis were dealing with the Iranians in an effort to secure the release of many Iranian Jews who were trapped in that country, and they were trying to get them out into Israel, and that the Israelis may have some type of arms sales going with the Iranians.

No specific mention that we would be asked to do that, although it was suggested at that time that we might have a chance of getting our hostages out through the Iranians. But the Iranians were sure to demand something in exchange for that, and it might be arms.

I recall at that time the President expressing concern over this one-for-one type of swap and not wanting to get into arms sales through people that he at this point did not have enough assurance from Bud that they were (a) reliable or (b) could deliver on anything, and that we should go slow on this but develop the contact.

(Regan 7–8)

The Secretary of Defense recalled a meeting at the President's residence after he returned from the hospital.

I argued very forcefully against the whole idea, saying that I didn't think it could work. I thought there were all kinds of risks, that the transfer of arms was obviously something we shouldn't even think about doing because we were urging every other country, and I had been urging [other countries] where we had found some transfers going, that this just shouldn't be done, that this would undercut everything we were going to do in the Mid East and everything else. George Shultz made many of the same points. My clear impression was that the idea was set aside, or finished, that that was the end of it. The President seemed to agree.

(Weinberger 6) The Secretary of Defense said Israeli arms transfers to Iran were not discussed. "It was all should we sell arms to Iran?" He recalled no discussion about resupplying Israel if it shipped arms to Iran, but noted that "McFarlane could have mentioned that the Israelis did this." (*Id.* at 7)

The Secretary of State testified on December 16, 1986, and subsequently told the Board that:

> On August 6, 1985 during one of my regular meetings with the President, at which Mr. McFarlane was also present, Mr. McFarlane said that he had again met with Mr. Kimche who reported that the Iranians and Israelis had held three meetings, during which the Iranians said Iran was in a shambles and a new government was inevitable. The military and the people, the Iranians reportedly said, were "still pro-American," and "want a dialogue with America." They also wanted arms from us, and wanted 100 TOW missiles from Israel. All would be totally deniable. The Iranians said they could produce four or more hostages and wanted a meeting somewhere. I stated my negative opinion fully. I do not recall the President having decided at that meeting to approve the Iranian offer. I noted then that Mr. McFarlane was pursuing the matter. I assumed this was on the basis we had discussed, with no commitments. Mr. McFarlane said that Foreign Minister Shamir had told Mr. Kimche that he wanted to know explicitly whether I was informed. At this point I felt that I was fully informed. As far as arms sales were concerned, I said in the meeting that it's a mistake. I said it had to be stopped.

(Shultz, 12/86, 11; SRB, 21–24)

# B. Post-Mortem

According to the NSC's Historical Chronology and the CIA Inspector General, Kimche called McFarlane on August 22 to ask about United States policy with regard to arms shipments to Iran. McFarlane

elevated the question to the President (and to the Secretaries of State and Defense, and the Director of Central Intelligence). The President stated that, while he could envision providing materiel support to moderate elements in Iran if all the Western hostages were freed, he could not approve any transfer of military materiel at that time-period. This position was conveyed to the Israeli diplomat.[12] *(Id.* at 43-45)

Regan told the Board that he called no discussion of the issue from August 6 until after Labor Day, 1985.

I don't recall anything further about this until after the President returned from the ranch, which would have been after Labor Day in '85. He had a long vacation then because they wanted him to take more time to rest from the operation.

At that time—again this was at a normal 9:30 meeting, not at a special meeting—McFarlane informed the President that indeed the Israelis had sold arms to the Iranians and that they hoped to get some of our hostages as well as some Jews from Iran out as a result of this. This would have been early September.

Now I recall at that meeting the President being upset at the fact that arms had been sold by the Israelis, American arms—and "upset" I think is the proper word; it wasn't real anger, but it was sort of, you know, well, why did they do that; how come we didn't know? That type of thing—and McFarlane explaining that the Israelis simply had taken it upon themselves to do this.

But the President at that time did not indicate that he wanted to make a big deal out of it. It was done. It had been done. There was a possibility of a hostage coming out. He decided to leave it alone, just accept the fact that it was done, leave it there.

I don't recall anything else happening, except I believe that Benjamin Weir did come out at that time, if I'm not mistaken, or shortly thereafter.

(Regan 8–9)

Secretary Shultz testified to the same effect on December 16, 1986, as did Secretary Weinberger. (Shultz, 12/86, 11; Weinberger 7) Ledeen told the Board that, when he returned to Washington in the middle of August and reported to McFarlane on his meetings in Israel, McFarlane said "that the President had decided to go ahead with the

146

test of the sort that Kimche had described—which is that we would authorize the Israelis to ship a quantity of weapons to Iran and we would see whether the Iranians followed through on their demonstrations of good faith and capacities and so forth." (Ledeen (1)27) According to information provided by the White House Counsel, the President spoke to McFarlane by telephone on August 23. Ledeen recalled that "all Bud said to me was the President has said that it's okay to tell them that. It's a go. And there wasn't any more detail than that." (*Id.* at 31) According to Ledeen, this statement meant that Israel had American approval to ship TOWs to Iran. (*Id.* at 32) Ledeen assumed it meant that the United States would resupply the Israelis for the TOWs.[13]

In any event, he conveyed this message to Kimche as his presumption. (*Id.* at 31) At the same time, Ledeen thought Secretary Shultz' displeasure with his trips "sounded like a simple standard turf irritation rather than anything substantive. It didn't seem to have anything to do with policy. There was no policy anyway." (*Id.* at 29)

On January 16, 1987, McFarlane recalled that

the President's approval came in August of 1985. The authority was that if Israel were to sell arms to Iran and ultimately came to the United States to replace them, that they could do that, so long as the quantity shipped and the character of the weapons wouldn't alter the complex of the situation in the war or contribute to terrorism.

(McFarlane, 1/16/87, 13)

In his third interview with the Board, McFarlane said:

I recall the President calling me and I while I couldn't give you verbatim quotes or near it, his point, his opening point was about that matter we discussed the other day, the hostages. Well, the matter was a very big matter and in terms of purposes and so forth, but it was expressive of the kind of motives that I think that lend some urgency to his call.

He called and said: I think we ought to get on with that. Let's go ahead with that. And that, frankly, was more the way the President dealt with an issue, as opposed to saying: well, I like Option 1, 2, 3 or 4. But I did then spell it out, and I said: Mr. President, what's involved here is the sale by Israel of weapons and ultimately them coming to us to buy replacements. And he says: Yes, I understand that. And I said: Do you understand, of course, now that George and Cap are very much opposed to this and they have very good reasons?

And he said: Yes, I do, but I draw a difference between our dealing with people that are not terrorists and shipping arms to terrorists. And I'm willing to defend that. And he even said something like: I will be glad to take all the heat for that.

But the point about the opposition from the Cabinet officers was made once more, and he said: Yes, I understand how they feel, but I want to go ahead with this.

(McFarlane (3) 17–18)

## IV. The NSC Staff, Arms, Hostages, and Finances

Whatever the President may or may not have decided on August 6, or subsequently, members of the NSC staff began in August 1985 to become involved in missions having to do with the shipment by Israel and the United States of advanced weapons to Iran and the release of American citizens kidnapped in Lebanon.

## A. The First Shipment of TOW Missiles: August–September 1985

While Ledeen's account is not altogether satisfactory on the point, and McFarlane did not mention the episode to the Board, when Ledeen reported on his August meetings in Israel, McFarlane apparently decided to establish secure telephone communication with Kimche. Ledeen flew to London on August 20, carrying an elementary code for Kimche, which he delivered the next day. (Ledeen (1) 28) Kimche gave Ledeen documents for McFarlane obtained from Ghorbanifar. At this or another meeting, Kimche explained that "in his experience with Iranians there was no way that Iran would deliver everything that it had promised, that whatever happened would be less than what they were promising, but that he thought that even something significantly less than what they had promised would still be significant and that he was basically positive about giving it a try." *(Id.* at 37)

In late August or early September, North, to whose office Ledeen was attached, *(id.* at 44), was directed to prepare "contingency plans for extracting hostages—hostage or hostages—from Lebanon." *(Id.* at 46)[14] On August 29 and 30, the NSC staff arranged for the State Department to issue a passport in the name of "William P. Goode" for North to use on "a sensitive operation to Europe in connection with our hostages in Lebanon." (North to McFarlane, 8/30/85; Martin to Platt, n.d.; McFarlane PROF note to Martin, 8/30/85, 17:40:38; Shultz, 12/86, 12) In addition, on August 31, 1985, Poindexter established a private method of interoffice computer communication with North, preventing normal screening by the Executive Secretary of the NSC. (Poindexter PROF note, "PRIVATE BLANK CHECK", to North, 8/31/85, 13:26:58) North asked Charles Allen, National Intelligence Officer for Counterterrorism, on September 12 to increase intelligence efforts against Iran and Lebanon, and informed him that Buckley might be released in the new few hours or days. (C. Allen 4–5; CIA/IG Chronology 3)

When the first information was received on September 13, Allen asked for

White House guidance on how th[is intelligence] should be disseminated. North, after consulting with National Security Advisor McFarlane, direct[ed] that dissemination be limited to Secretary Weinberger, the D[irector of] C[entral] I[ntelligence] (or Deputy Director McMahon), McFarlane, and himself. North [said] that McFarlane had directed that no copy be sent to the Secretary of State; and that he, McFarlane, would keep Secretary Shultz advised orally on the NSC project.

On August 30, 1985, Israel shipped 100 TOW missiles to Iran; on September 14, Israel shipped an additional 408 missiles. There is some evidence that this shipment was returned to Israel, in whole or in part, because it contained defective or otherwise unacceptable missiles, and that Israel replaced and reshipped the weapons. (Furmark 6–7) Ghorbanifar told the Board that he accompanied the shipment of 100 TOWs to Iran and that in exchange for these weapons, the Iranians gave a "guarantee" that they would neither engage in any "wrong-doing" nor support terrorism. (Ghorbanifar 46) Israel sold Iran 400 TOWs in exchange for Weir, Ghorbanifar recalled; when the plane arrived in Tabriz, eight extra TOWs were aboard. (Id. at 49; 100) Ledeen told the Board that he did "not believe that either we or they" saw the August and September shipments as two transactions. (Ledeen (2) 27–28)

In the second week of September, Kimche called McFarlane with the news that a hostage would be released, and that he expected all the hostages to be released soon. McFarlane probably relayed this message to the President, Vice President, Secretaries of State and Defense, Director of Central Intelligence, and Regan. (McFarlane (1) 18–19) The Director of Central Intelligence reportedly connected this release with diplomatic efforts in Damascus and Tehran aimed at resolving the hostage problem. (CIA/IG Chronology at 4; Casey to Shultz/McFarlane, 8/16/85; Sigur to McFarlane, 9/19/85) Reginald Bartholomew, the American Ambassador in Lebanon, reported on September 4 that "North was handling an operation that would lead to the release of all seven hostages. [A U.S.] team had been deployed to Beirut, we were told. Ambassador Bartholomew had been alerted directly by the NSC and would assist." (Shultz, 12/86, 12) The Director of Central Intelligence told his Deputy and Chief of Operations that "the Israelis were doing something and they believed as a part of the outcome of an affair the Israelis were in some of the hostages could be released," but that the Israelis did not want the CIA to be "notified." (George 3) Since 1984, the CIA had regarded Ghorbanifar as untrustworthy. (Cave 3–5)

Meanwhile, Ledeen met Ghorbanifar, Kimche, Nimrodi, and Schwimmer in Paris on September 4. Ledeen told the Board that

> [t]he bulk of this conversation was given over to the issue of future relations and future cooperation between the United States and Iran. And from time to time Ghorbanifar, Schwimmer and Nimrodi would sit down and start talking about hostages and weapons. And when this happened Kimche and I would go off and talk about the future of Iran and how we thought we were going.

(Ledeen (1) 44) According to Ledeen, Ghorbanifar predicted that Iranian leaders would soon give speeches in which they did not denounce the United States. After the speeches, Ghorbanifar called Ledeen to ask if he had seen them. Ledeen had not, but asked North to have the CIA find and translate them. Some weeks later, the CIA confirmed Ghorbanifar's account. Iranian leaders had attacked the Soviet Union. "So we were cheered by this. I was cheered by this." *(Id.* at 44–45)

On September 15, 1985, Reverend Weir, one of the Americans kidnapped in Lebanon, was freed. According to the CIA Inspector General, on September 16, the Director of Central Intelligence and Charles Allen discussed recent events, including Weir's release. The Director reported McFarlane's saying they were related to an NSC initiative. (CIA/IG Chronology at 4) Secretary Shultz testified that, on September 17, Ambassador Bartholomew reported that

> Mr. McFarlane had said the other hostages would be released in three batches, without publicity. But Weir had no information about the others, and in fact said he had been released only to bring pressure for the release of the Da'Wa prisoners. Bartholomew was pessimistic. He said four other hostages were reportedly in the Beirut area, possibly in the same place as Weir. . . . North was not in the area, but in Washington, D.C. Bartholomew said he knew "precious little about origins of this or who is involved. Bud has told me nothing of who else was involved." He was pessimistic about getting any more hostages.

Two months then passed during which, to my knowledge, the Department of State heard nothing more about any aspect of an operation involving arms for Iran.

(Shultz, 12/86, 12–13)

When Weir was released, McFarlane "learned of the transfer from Israel to Iran of 508 TOW missiles.[16] Well, I was concerned," he told the Board in his first interview, "frankly, because in concrete terms we, after a month's time, we Americans weren't dealing with Iran, Israel was, and so the central purpose from my point of view of the thing wasn't yet being fulfilled." (McFarlane (1) 20) Teicher told the Board that, although his involvement in this operation had ceased in August, after Weir was released, he became suspicious that the United States was trading arms to Iran for hostages. He queried North, who told him that he could say nothing about it, and McFarlane, who said the United States was not trading arms for hostages and that there was nothing more he could say. (Teicher 14–15)

(Historical Chronology 5-6)

At one of the President's 9:30 a.m. briefings in September (early in the month, according to Regan (Regan 8)), McFarlane reported that the Israelis had sold weapons to Iran, and a hostage had been released. McFarlane told the Board:

[W]hile I didn't know for certain because we had not negotiated with the Iranians, the appearance was surely there that weapons were transferred and one hostage was released, and so that certainly looked causal. And you would have to be a fool not to see that, whatever our intentions were, the reality was apparently arms for hostages.

And I said so to the President in the morning meeting, and it basically kind of validated what the Secretary of Defense and State had said before, and they expressed their concerns again on that score.

This is not an excuse, but it is I think mitigating. Recall

now that in this period from late September to November quite a number of things were happening in the government, and this was about number 12 on the agenda. I mean, you had the Soviet foreign minister in town, three other foreign heads of state, the preparation of four major presidential speeches to lay out the agenda for the summit, bilateral, regional issues, arms control issues, human rights issues, a visit to the United Nations by the President for a couple of days, meetings with 12 or 15 heads of government up there, and in the middle of that the Achille Lauro.

(McFarlane (1) 20–21)

As we have seen, Regan told the Board a somewhat different story.[17]

I don't recall anything else happening, except I believe that Benjamin Weir did come out at that time, if I'm not mistaken, or shortly thereafter.

\* \* \*

The only thing I can remember there [about the need to resupply Israel] is that there was talk that probably someday the Israelis will want us to replenish that, but no specific the Israelis have asked us to replace that at this time, no.

(Regan 9–10)

# B. Financing the Transaction

According to Furmark and Ghorbanifar, Khashoggi provided the bridge financing for the August and September shipments.[18] The Americans and Israelis had limited faith in the Iranians, and vice versa, so that deliveries would not be made before payment was received, and payment would not be made before weapons were delivered. (Ledeen (2) 25) Khashoggi broke the impasse by providing financing. (Furmark 5; D. St. John, Memorandum of Conversation with Adnan Khashoggi, 1/29/87) In August and September 1985, Khashoggi made two separate deposits in the amounts of $1 million and $4 million into a Swiss account designated by the Israelis; Ghorbanifar gave him two post-dated drafts for $1 and $4 million, drawn on his account at Credit Suisse, which Khashoggi would negotiate when the weapons were delivered, and Ghorbanifar had received payment from Iran. "[T]hat is how the financing was done all throughout." (Furmark 6) Khashoggi was repaid later than anticipated because the first shipment of TOWs included weapons unacceptable to Iran. *(Id.* at 6–7) According to Furmark, Khashoggi received no money in addition to principal for these payments; for the later transactions, he expected, and received until May 1986, a return of 20% above the principal amount to cover his expenses and provide a return to financiers who invested with him. *(Id.* at 31, 8)

Possibly in anticipation of this transaction, on August 27, 1985, the Central Bank of Iran (Bank Markazi) deposited $1,217,410 in the account of an Iranian official at Credit Suisse. This individual, an official in the Prime Minister's office, was responsible for arms procurement in Europe. On September 18, four days after the first successful shipment of TOWs, $5 million was deposited in the Iranian's account. On September 14, Ghorbanifar informed the holder of the Credit Suisse account that an aircraft would arrive at Tabriz that evening, and asked that a man on the plane be given a cheque and a list of weapons desired by Iran.

## V. United States Involvement Takes a New Form: October 1985–January 1986

The United States formally adopted a program to transfer advanced weapons to Iran in January 1986. That step culminated a process formed by, among other things, operations by various government bureaucracies and individuals, and the unending pressure created by the kidnappings in Lebanon, including hopes that just one more effort would bring the hostages home. Each individual, including the President, had his own perspective of the political and strategic significance of what he knew. These perspectives and pressures shaped the process of Presidential decision and the ultimate decision itself.

# A. Prelude to the Israeli Shipment of HAWK Missiles

According to Ledeen, North became obviously involved in operations connected with American hostages and relations with Iran at the time of the first Israeli shipment of TOWs. "[H]e was handling all the various intelligence operations that had been started to track this thing, and it was all coming through him."[19] (Ledeen (1) 51) On the other hand, North's office "was highly compartmentalized. [Ledeen] did not, until I was instructed by Bud to do so, I never told Ollie [North] what was going on, and Ollie never discussed what he was doing with me." *(Id.* at 57)

Ledeen's account of the September-October 1985 period is sketchy. For example, he told the Board that he introduced North and Schwimmer when Ghorbanifar, Schwimmer, and Nimrodi came to Washington in late October or early November. *(Id.* at 50) According to North's calendar, North had meetings on September 26 with Ledeen at 11:00 a.m. and Schwimmer at 11:30 a.m. On October 6, North asked the CIA to arrange for surveillance of Ghorbanifar and Nimrodi, whom he expected in Washington on the 7th. Such surveillance was put in place, and, on October 8, Ledeen, North, Nimrodi, Schwimmer, and one "Nicholas Kralis" (a Ghorbanifar alias) met at 9:00 a.m. in the Old Executive Office Building. (North calendar)

On October 1, 1985, Israel's air force bombed the PLO headquarters in Tunis, and on October 4, according to NSC staff chronologies prepared in November 1986, the Islamic Jihad announced the execution of Buckley in retaliation for the bombing.[20] The NSC staff chronologies state that "[t]his announcement led to a series of meetings in Europe among the U.S. (CIA and NSC), Israeli, and Iranian intermediaries." (Maximum Version 4; Historical Chronology 6) On October 7 the Italian ship *Achille Lauro* was hijacked by Palestinian terrorists.

Ledeen met Ghorbanifar, Kimche, Nimrodi (who was fluent in Farsi), and Schwimmer in September and October in Europe. (Ledeen (1) 46) In at least one such meeting, Ghorbanifar expressed the view that the arms and hostage matters, which engaged Schwimmer and Nimrodi particularly, should be dropped, and the prospective Iranian-American political relationship should be the focus of their energies. "[Ghorbanifar] said if we continue we shall become hostages to the hostages." *(Id.* at 47)

In his second interview, Ledeen told the Board that, in October, he told Schwimmer:

> if this kind of contact is going to continue it may be necessary at a certain point to have an account where there can be something for expenses for this person or persons like him. We may need an account for such things.
>
> And he said fine. I will do that. And he then opened an account at Credit Suisse and gave me the account number for this thing. I had no privileges on it. I couldn't sign for it. But he gave me the number. He said if at any point people want to put money in this, this is the thing which we have established for this purpose, if it would be necessary at a later date.
>
> I gave that number to Ollie [North].
>
> * * *
>
> I have no knowledge of that account ever being used for anything. I don't know of any money that ever went into it. But I recalled this when I was reading a newspaper story the other day which suggested that Ollie had inherited a structure of bank accounts in which there was already something there, into which money could flow, or through which money could flow, or something like that, and that reminded me that, hey, I remember that day they created that account.

(Ledeen (2) 41–42)

Ledeen reported these conversations to McFarlane and, in late October or early November 1985, when Ghorbanifar, Nimrodi, and Schwimmer came to Washington, he "urged that the hostage matter be dropped, and he [McFarlane] was in agreement with that." *(Id* at 50)

> So about a week afterwards I reported on this meeting to Bud, and I said again to him that I thought we

should shut down the hostage matter and pursue the political business. He said that no, he was inclined to shut down the whole thing, that he had a bad feeling about the whole matter. He didn't like it. . . . I appealed to him not to stop the whole thing but just to stop the hostage side of it. And he said, well, he would get back to me, and so off I went.

McFarlane told the Board in his second interview that Ledeen's memory was accurate.

As I speculated earlier, I was surprised by the move from 100 to at least 400 and by the release of only one. The President was pleased by the release of one and/or the continuation of the relationship. But that seemed to me a very clear evidence of bad faith, and I said so to Mr. Kimche, probably because I met with Mr. Ledeen, although I don't know that, but I made it very clear, and I think he's testified to the fact that I had a "bad feeling" about this program in October. And he expressed that, too, to the Israelis.

\* \* \*

Chairman Tower: Bud, do you remember any comment from the President after Weir was released? He made some rather critical comments of the Administration and of the President, characterizing Weir as being somewhat ungrateful for the efforts that were being made.

Mr. McFarlane: I don't recall that. I think it is very plausible to me that he would have been dismayed by the turn of events.

Mr. Dawson: Before we tie in this authorization to December let me now leave September for just one second and try to turn the authorization question, present it somewhat differently.

In the July, August and September time, in discussions that you had with the President did he ever exhibit any reluctance, opposition or disapproval or make any attempts to repudiate in your presence the transfer of arms by Israel to Iran?

Mr. McFarlane: No, he did not.

(McFarlane (2) 34–35)

After McFarlane gave his view of the August/September TOW shipment to Ledeen, the arms transfers to Iran took on a new dimension. The first Ledeen said he heard of it came in what he described as a "bizarre" call from Ghorbanifar. It was related, I [Ledeen]

> subsequently figured out, to the question of this shipment of additional weapons and Ghorbanifar called with a message from the Iranian Prime Minister to the President and asked me if I would transmit this.

> It was a message that said, grosso modo, we have been very patient with you people. We have behaved honorably with you people. We have done everything that we said we would have done, and now you are cheating us and making fun of us and so forth, and would you please do what you said you were going to do.

(Ledeen (1) 51–53) McFarlane being in Geneva with the President for the first Summit Meeting with General Secretary Gorbachev, Ledeen passed this message to Poindexter. It was Ledeen's "first and last" contact with Poindexter on this matter; Poindexter said "I was going to be taken off this matter, that people with more technical understanding or expertise were going to be" on it. *(Id.* at 53–54)

McFarlane told the Board that the episode mentioned by Ghorbanifar to Ledeen "was the first time that a U.S. government agency became involved in this matter, and it was the CIA." (McFarlane (1) 22) "[R]ight before I left for Geneva [for the Summit with Ghorbanifar]", Mr. McFarlane told the Board in his second interview, Israel Defense Minister Rabin saw McFarlane in Washington. "I believe that his [Rabin's] purpose in coming was simply to reconfirm that the President's authority for the original concept was still valid. We haven't changed our mind and I reconfirmed that that was the case. I don't recall that he said anything about any concrete intention in the short term to

158

do anything else." (McFarlane (2) 36) While he was in Geneva, Rabin called on an open line from New York to request assistance for a problem involving a transfer. McFarlane then called Poindexter and North and asked them to find out what the problem was. (McFarlane (1) 23) About a week earlier, on November 14, McFarlane had told the Director of Central Intelligence and John McMahon, his Deputy, "that Kimche was planning or had indicated that the Israelis planned to give some arms to moderates in Iran that would oppose Khomeini."[21] (J. McMahon 5) At that time, North was in London meeting Terry Waite and, separately, Ghorbanifar. (American Embassy, London, to North, 11/12/85; NSC Chronology of Events, dated 11/20/86)

Secretary Shultz testified before Congress and told the Board that McFarlane told him on November 18, 1985, in Geneva,

> that four hostages would be released on Thursday (November 21). He said that Israel would fly a plane with 100 Hawk missiles to [a third country], and transfer them to another aircraft. If the hostages were released, the airplane would fly to Iran; if not, it would fly to Israel. Israel would buy replacements for these missiles from the U.S., and would be paid by Iran. I complained to Mr. McFarlane that I had been informed so late that it was impossible to stop this operation. I nonetheless expressed my hope that the hostages would in fact be released.

(Shultz, 12/86, 13; 1/87, 23–24; SRB, 27–28)

# B. The Shipment of HAWKs: November 1985[22]

By letter dated November 19, 1985, which North signed with his own name "for" McFarlane, Secord was asked to play a role.

> Your discrete [sic?] assistance is again required in support of our national interest. At the earliest opportunity, please proceed to [a third country transit point],

and other locations as necessary in order to arrange for the transfer of sensitive materiel being shipped from Israel.

As in the past, you should exercise great caution that this activity does not become public knowledge. You should ensure that only those whose discretion is guaranteed are involved.

(McFarlane per North to Secord, 11/19/85)

The Board has obtained a number of operational reports sent by North to Poindexter by the Black Check private interoffice computer communication channel Poindexter had established on August 31. At about 9:30 p.m. on November 20, North wrote Poindexter:

The Israelis will deliver 80 Mod[ified] HAWKS to [a third country] at noon on Friday 22 Nov. These 80 will be loaded aboard three chartered aircraft, owned by a proprietary which will take off at two hour intervals for Tabriz. . . . Appropriate arrangements have been made with the proper [country name deleted] air control personnel. Once the aircraft have been launched, their departure will be confirmed by Agshari [Ghorbanifar] who will call [his contact in Tehran] who will call Niknam (DCM in Damascus) who will direct the IRG [Iranian Revolutionary Guard] commander in Beirut to collect the five rpt five Amcits from Hezballah and deliver them to the U.S. Embassy. There is also the possibility that they will hand over the French hostage who is very ill.

There is a requirement for 40 additional weaps of the same nomenclature for a total requirement of 120. $18M in payment for the first 80 has been deposited in the appropriate account. No acft will land in Tabriz until the AMCITS have been delivered to the embassy. The Iranians have also asked to order additional items in the future and have been told that they will be considered after this activity has succeeded. All transfer arrangements have been made by Dick Secord, who deserves a medal for his extraordinary short notice efforts.

160

Replenishment arrangements are being made through MOD [Ministry of Defense] purchasing office in NYC. There is, to say the least, considerable anxiety that we will somehow delay on their plan to purchase 120 of these weapons in the next few days. IAW [In accordance with] your instructions I have told their agent that we will sell them 120 items at a price they can meet. I have further told them that we will make no effort to move on their purchase LOA request until we have all five AMCITS safely delivered. In short, the pressure is on them.

\* \* \*

As soon as we have the release confirmed, we need to move quickly with Defense to provide the 120 missiles the Israelis want to buy. They are very concerned that they are degrading their defense capability, and in view of the Syrian shoot-down yesterday the PM has placed considerable pressure on both Rabin and Kimche for very prompt replacement. Both called several times today.

There is the distinct possibility that at the end of the week we will have five Americans home and the promise of no future hostage takings in exchange for selling the Israelis 120 Mod HAWKs. Despite the difficulty of making all this fit inside a 96-hour window, it isn't that bad a deal. . . . Warm regards. Recommend pass to RCM [McFarlane] after review. North.

(North PROF note to Poindexter, 11/20/85, 21:27:39) The remainder of the note concerned details about sending "a covert hostage debrief team to Wiesbaden." *(Id.)*

In the morning of November 21, North reported to Poindexter a call from Secord. The transit country's Defense Minister had assured Secord that the Prime Minister "had approved the xfer activity for Friday and that the FoMin is aware and supportive." As they were en route to Brussels, North suggested that McFarlane discreetly thank them for their help. (North PROF note to Poindexter, 11/21/85, 09:18:36. "Please pass to RCM as avail.") The operation began to unravel later that day.

Duane Clarridge, in 1985, Chief of the European Division of CIA's Directorate of Operations, told the Board that he first became involved during the evening of November 21. North called him for help in obtaining an over-flight clearance for an El Al 747. On the 22nd, Clarridge used CIA communications channels to help obtain the clearance. He had the impression that North was already "in touch with [the foreign] government at some level." (Clarridge 3) At this time, Charles Allen showed Clarridge reports indicating that the flight was part of an operation aimed at the liberation of hostages, but the CIA was permitted to reveal only that the flight had a humanitarian purpose. Clarridge informed the U.S. official trying to obtain flight clearance that he should be in touch with a man named "Copp", whom Clarridge was told was an alias for Secord. Despite the CIA's efforts, landing rights were denied. As a result, North asked for the name of a reliable charter airline. Given the shortage of time and the circumstances, CIA's air branch suggested the use of a proprietary. The proprietary was told to await a call; Clarridge suspects the caller was to be Copp. In any event, the airline was assured that the caller would have sufficient funds for the charter. (Id. at 2–6)

When the issue of a CIA proprietary airline was raised, Clarridge said, he became concerned about the propriety of CIA action. He asked Edward Juchniewicz, acting Deputy Director of Operations, whether he would approve the operation. He did. (Id. at 4–5) According to the CIA Inspector General, Juchniewicz remembered Clarridge alerting him that

North needed an aircraft to transport some unspecified material to Israel, and that North might call him about it. Juchniewicz remembers receiving a call at home that night from North, who said he understood that the Agency had an aircraft and asked whether it would be possible to charter it. Juchniewicz says he told North that the proprietary was a commercial venture and thus available for charter by anyone. He is certain that he did not give North the name of the proprietary, believing North already to be in possession of that information. Juchniewicz says he did not authorize the use of the proprietary to anyone, but acknowledges that his response could have been inter-

162

preted as approval. ([A CIA officer involved] recalls contacting Juchniewicz on or before the morning of 25 November to confirm that the project had been approved, and being given assurances that it had.)

(CIA/IG Chronology 7)

One of North's contemporaneous messages to Poindexter supports part of Clarridge's account. In the middle of the afternoon, November 22, North wrote that landing clearance still had not been obtained. "Despite the difficulties of the past 24 hours, all continue to believe that if RCM can get thru to the PM or FOMIN, that this can be done." (North PROF note to Poindexter, 11/22/85, 19:27:15 ("Status Report as of 1730")) North was considering three choices for continuing the operation: (1) chartering a new airline to pick up the cargo in Tel Aviv; (2) flying the three chartered aircraft to Tel Aviv, where the cargo would be loaded and the flight resumed; or (3) flying the three chartered aircraft to Tel Aviv, loading the cargo, and proceeding directly to Iran "w/o filing until airborne. . . ." *(Id.)* Everybody involved "(including Kimche)" believed the first option to be the best. North wrote that "Kimche urges that solution be found to matter this weekend to protect hostages and those who will deliver them." *(Id.)*

At 6:10 p.m., North had more news for Poindexter. McFarlane had contacted the Foreign Minister at 5:30; he agreed to permit an Israeli aircraft to land. In addition, North reported on the CIA's efforts:

Dewey [Clarridge] has arranged for a proprietary to work for Secord (Copp). Copp will charter two 707s in the name of LAKE Resources (our Swiss Co.) and have them p/u [pick up] the cargo and deliver it. . . . [T]he cargo will be xfered to the three Israeli chartered DC–8/55s for the flight to T[abriz]. Though I am sure Copp suspects, he does not know that the 707s belong to a proprietary. Clarridge deserves a medal— so does Copp.

Kimche (DK) has been told how screwed up his people are in planning something like this on such short notice. Not only was the 747 they planned to use a national airlines a/c [aircraft], but they only had it chartered for 14hrs. We have now taken charge of that

163

phase of the operation . . . to ensure flight clearance for the three DC–8s chartered by DK's boys. If all goes as we now hope, the cargo will be [at the staging area] by noon (local) and enroute [sic] to T shortly after dark. That means we can expect handovers (hopefully) Saturday night.

*(Id.* ("UPDATE AS OF 1810"))

North's optimism was a hope. He wrote Poindexter at 7:00 p.m. that Schwimmer had just reported that he had released the DC–8s, despite a call from North to Kimche to keep them on call. "Schwimmer released them to save $ and now does not think that they can be re-chartered before Monday." *(Id.* ("UPDATE AS OF 1900")) Secord kept the operation alive. He suggested using

one of our LAKE Resources A/C which was . . . to p/u a load of ammo for UNO. He will have the a/c repainted tonight and put into service nlt [no later than] noon Sat so that we can at least get this thing moving. So help me I have never seen anything so screwed up in my life. Will meet w/ Calero tonite to advise that the ammo will be several days late in arriving. Too bad, this was to be our first direct flight to the resistance field . . . inside Nicaragua. The ammo was already palletized w/ parachutes attached. Maybe we can do it on Weds or Thurs.

More as it becomes available. One hell of an operation.

*(Id.* ("UPDATE AS OF 1920"))[23]

Regan recalled that the President had been informed on the margins of his briefings for the Gorbachev meeting to expect that there is going to be a shipment of arms coming through [a third country] missiles, transshipped through Israel into Iran, and the hostages will come out.

(Regan 14–15)

# C. North's Plan to Free the Hostages

On December 4, in a long note to Poindexter, North reconstructed the story of the November shipment based on conversations with the participants, conveyed his view of the Iranian-Israeli-American situation at that time, and proposed a plan of action for the future.

The attempted transfer through [a third country] of 18 Hawk missiles went awry because the Iranians were in fact seeking a weapons system that would be capable of stopping Soviet reconnaissance flights along the Iranian/Soviet border and on the Iranian/Iraqi border.[24] Gorba [Ghorbanifar] rptd that these flights occur regularly and as deep as 40mi inside Iranian airspace. Because Schwimmer and Ledeen were unfamiliar with the operational parameters of the HAWK, they agreed to ship 120 weapons that were totally inadequate to meet the rqmts established by the Iranians. This delivery has created an atmosphere of extraordinary distrust on the part of the Iranians; [sic] in Kimche's view, because the credibility of the Gorba/[Iranian] mission has probably seriously been called into question.

Despite this perception (Gorba said numerous times that this whole thing was a "cheating game" on the part of the Israelis),[25] Copp & Kimche have been able to proceed with a renewed dialogue which still promises hope for achieving our three objectives:

—support for a pragmatic—army oriented faction which could take over in a change of government

—return of the five AMCIT hostages

—no more terrorism directed against U.S. personnel or interests.

From these ongoing discussions, which in two cases included Iranian military officers, Copp and Kimche conclude that the military situation in Iran is desperate. The Iranian descriptions of the state of their equipment, lack of competent management, inability to use much of the remaining U.S. materiel portends the real possibility of a military collapse (at least by the Army) in the near to mid-term. Thus, there is considerable pressure on the interlocutors in Europe to produce—quickly.

Given the relatively low level of competence on the part of the Iranians in Europe, and the fact that any supplies delivered will undoubtedly have to be examined by an Army or Air Force officer, it is very doubtful that a "single transaction" arrangement can be worked out with the parties in Tehran, no matter what is agreed to in Europe. In short, they have been "scammed" so many times in the past that the attitude of distrust is very high on their part. At the same time, in all discussions (including today's phone calls) they are desperate to conclude some kind of arrangement in the next 10 days and have even asked that the meeting scheduled for Saturday in London be advanced. Based on what we can conclude from intelligence in Beirut, we believe that they are very concerned that the hostages (the only Iranian leverage point besides the Jews in Iran) may be killed or captured/released by the Syrians, Druze, Phalange or Amal in the near future. Waite's contacts with the captors seems [sic] to corroborate this assessment. In short, time is very short for all parties concerned.

Finally, there is the matter of the longer term strategy for what we should be attempting to accomplish viz a viz [sic] the Iran-Iraq war and a more reasonable government in Iran. From my personal discussions with Kimche and Meron[26] it is apparent the [sic] the Israelis want: the war to continue at a stalemate, a more moderate Iranian government in the end and will somehow find a way to continue getting their people (Jews) out of Iran through some kind of barter arrangement. In that the first two of their goals are, it would seem, generally congruent w/ our interests, and their last a fact of life, we should probably be seeing the return of the AMCIT hostages as a subsidiary benefit—not the primary objective, though it may be a part of the necessary first steps in achieving the broader objectives. While Kimche, Meron, Copp and I all agree that there is a high degree of risk in pursuing the course we have started, we are now so far down the road that stopping what has been started could have even more serious repercussions. We all view the next steps as "confidence building" on the part of both sides. None of us have [sic] any illusions about the cast of characters we are dealing with on the other side. They are a primitive, unsophisticated group who are extraordinarily distrustful of the West in general and the Israelis/U.S. in particular. The have not the slightest idea of what is going on in our government or how our system works. Today for example, Gorba called Copp in absolute confusion over the fact that Rafsanjani had just received a letter from (of all people) Sen. Helms regarding the American Hostages. Since the Iranians are adamant that they not be publicly connected with the seizure, holding or release of the AMCITS, why, Gorba wanted to know, was Helms being brought into this "solution to the puzzle." Gorba reiterated that "[Vice President Bush] ought to have more control over the members of his parliament [sic]" than to allow them to confuse an already difficult problem. Dick told him the letter had nothing to do with what we are about, but Gorba did not seem convinced that this wasn't some sort of effort to embarass Iran.

Given this very unsophisticated view of things on their part and the distrust that the Iranians obviously feel, we believe that if we stop the current effort at this point and do not at least proceed with a "test" of the current relationship we:

—run the risk of never being able to establish a "foothold" for the longer term goals in that the people we are dealing with will be totally discredited at home; and

—incur the greater likelihood of reprisals against us for "leading them on." These reprisals could take the form of additional hostage seizures, execution of some/all of those now held, or both.

While the threat to carry out sanctions against us has not, to my knowledge, ever arisen (it certainly has not since Kimche/Copp/North have been directly engaged—and Michael never mentioned it), it is interesting to note that when Copp questioned the bona fides of Gorba and his cohorts as capable of delivering on their end of the arrangement, Gorba carefully noted that since these discussions began w/ Michael & Schwimmer, there has not been a single Islamic Jihad bomb threat, hijacking or kidnapping—and that there would be none of this "worked." D.K., Copp and I regard this to be at least one sign of confidence that this activity may yet prosper. There are some lesser indications of confidence in recent days:

—in response to Copp's demand for funds to be deposited in advance to defray operational costs, and what the Iranians were told were "purchases on the arms market" a total of $41M has been deposited;

—the 18 HAWKs delivered last week have been repackaged and are ready for return to origin on the next available flight;

—the parties in Europe continue to stress that their requirements are long-term and that they are anxious to get on with a longer range program of Israeli originated support which would include technical assistance w/ sophisticated hardware which is critically needed but deadlined (in this regard Gorba at one point noted that at times they have as few as 50 operational tanks and less than a dozen flyable aircraft).

With all of the above as a lengthy preamble describing two nearly frantic weeks w/ the Israelis & Iranians, the following proposal has evolved which the Iranians today said they wd like to discuss in detail on Saturday:

—The total "package" from the Israelis wd consist of 50 I HAWKs w/ PIP (product improvement package) and 3300 basic TOWs.

—Deliveries wd commence on or about 12 December as follows:

H-hr: 1 707 w/300 TOWs = 1 AMCIT

H + 10hrs: 1 707 (same A/C) w/300 TOWs = 1 AMCIT

H + 16hrs: 1 747 w/50 HAWKs & 400 TOWs + 2 AMCIT

H + 20 hrs: 1 707 w/300 TOWs = 1 AMCIT

H + 24hrs: 1 747 w/2000 TOWs = French Hostage

All involved on our side recognize that this does not meet one of the basic criteria established at the opening of this venture: a single transaction which would be preceded by a release of the hostages. However, given the points above regarding the mutual distrust in the dialogue, we all believe it is about the only way we get the overall process moving. Measures have been taken to reduce the chance for duplicity on the part of the Iranians and to preserve a measure of OP-SEC in carrying out the transaction. In the case of a double cross, one of the Iranians will be in the hands of assets we control throughout. One of them . . . has already suffered a serious (though apparently not fatal) heart attack after last week's HAWK transaction failed to produce results. The first two deliveries, via 707 freighters are relatively small and if they do not produce the desired outcomes, all else stops. All $ are now under our control.

OpSEC concerns are threefold: communications, deliveries enroute to Iran and replenishment of Israeli stocks. To solve the first problem an OPs Code is now in use by all parties. This code is similar to the one used to oversee deliveries to the Nicaraguan Resistance and has never been compromised. The delivery/flight planning security problem has been solved by a much more deliberate selection of aircraft and aircrews as well as a series of transient airfields which can be used enroute to the field controlled by the Iranian Army at Tabriz. Appropriate arrangements have also been made to ensure that the overflight . . . is not challenged. All A/C will be inspected by one of the Iranians at a transient location between Tel Aviv and Tabriz. Before the A/C actually crosses into Iranian airspace, the appropriate release(s) must occur. The last OPSEC concern, that of replenishing Israeli stocks is probably the most delicate issue. The quantity of TOWs requested represents [a significant proportion of] the Israeli PWR [prepositioned war reserves]. Meron and I are working w/ the Israeli purchasing office in NYC to ensure that the replenishment can be accomplished [as] quickly after December 12 as possible. All recognize that quantities such as those being discussed degrade Israeli readiness and that the items will need to be dispatched quickly in order to prelude disaffection and leaks. Meron has solved at least one of the problems in this regard by identifying a means of transferring the required cash to an IDF account which will allow cash (rather than FMS credit) purchases from the U.S.

In order to put this plan into action, Kimche, Copp, Schwimmer and Goode [North] plan to meet in London on Saturday morning to review all arrangements. If we are satisfied that all our assets (money, aircraft, aircrews, transit facilities, overflight arrangements and military equipment) are prepared, Copp and Kimche will meet at another hotel with Gorba and [an Iranian diplomat] to finalize the plan. Our side will then reconvene later in the evening at our hotel to review any last minute changes. I wd then call you (using the Ops code), transmit the agreed upon arrangements for approval and, if you concur, Kimche & Copp will meet again w/ the Iranians on Sunday a.m. to express our agreement with the plan. Copp & Goode wd return to the U.S. Sunday p.m. on separate flights. On the 11th, the day before the plan is to be executed, Copp will establish a CP [command post] . . . where he can monitor implementation and stop it at any point we desire. The secondary fields . . .

will be covered by Copp controlled assets who are not witting of the true origin, destination or contents of the A/C but who can "fix" things in a hurry if something goes wrong. . . .

Once in hand, the hostages will be flown to Larnaca on our Navy HH-53 where they will be picked up by a EUCOM C-141 and flown to Wiesbaden for debriefing. The debrief team will be staged at Wiesbaden 12 hours in advance, just as we did two weeks ago without notariety [sic]. Dewey [Clarridge] is the only other person fully witting of this. . . . The Israelis are in the same position. Dewey and I have been through the whole concept twice looking for holes and can find little that can be done to improve it given the "trust factor" with the Iranians. In that all parties involved have great interest in keeping this as quiet as possible, . . . we beleive [sic] it to be worth the risk. I have not confided in Dewey re the longer term goals we could/should hope to achieve. Thus, the only parties fully aware of all dimensions of what we are about are you and RCM [McFarlane].

I have given careful consideration to what you suggested re an RCM meeting with the Iranians in an effort to obtain release of the hostages before starting on an effort to undo the present regieme [sic] in Tehran. Like you and Bud, I find the idea of bartering over the lives of these poor men repugnant. Nonetheless, I believe that we are, at this point, barring unforseen [sic] developments in London or Tel Aviv, too far along with the Iranians to risk turning back now. If we do not at least make one more try at this point, we stand a good chance of condemning some or all to death and a renewed wave of Islamic Jihad terrorism. While the risks of proceeding are significant, the risks of not trying one last time are even greater.

(North PROF note to Poindexter, 12/04/85, 02:02:55)

# D. The President and His Advisors

In his first meeting with the Board on January 16, 1987, the President said he did not remember how the November shipment came about. The President said he objected to the shipment, and that, as a result of that objection, the shipment was returned to Israel. In his second meeting with the Board on February 11, 1987, the President stated that both he and Regan agreed that they cannot remember any meeting or conversation in general about a HAWK shipment. The President said he did not remember anything about a call-back of the HAWKs.

The Secretary of State testified:

November 21—the supposed release date—passed with no release.

On November 22, I was told by my staff that the release had slipped again, allegedly to get airspace clearance . . . . Also on that day, however, Ambassador Oakley—as these things happen, word kind of drifts around and your stuff, which you don't know whether it is right or wrong—Ambassador Oakley reported to us that he had heard from various sources that the hostages would be released that afternoon, in exchange for 120 HAWKS at $250,000 each—worth $30 million in all.

By this time we were back in Washington.

At a discussion in my presence on that day, [Mr. Michael Armacost] stated: "I don't like it. It's terrible."

I indicated my own apprehension. Deputy Secretary Whitehead noted: "We all feel uncomfortable." I replied: "Bud says he's cleared with the President." I regarded it as a $30 million weapons payoff.

On November 23, we heard again that no hostages were out, that the project had collapsed. I said, "It's over."

(Schultz, SRB, 28)

The President was informed "on the margins of his briefings for the Gorbachev meeting to expect that there is going to be a shipment of arms . . . missiles, transshipped through Israel into Iran, and the hostages will come out." (Regan 14) Around the time of the Geneva Summit, McFarlane told the President "that something had happened and the shipment didn't take place as originally scheduled." *(Id.* at 12) Regan recalled that the President had been "upset" about the September shipment. *(Id.* at 9) Regan explained McFarlane's belief that the President had authorized the transaction as follows: the President "hadn't raised Cain about the [first] Israeli shipment, so a second try might not be out of order. . . . Certainly there was nothing said to the President in advance, at least in my hearing, where it was said, now may we ship missiles to Iran through Israel. That was not asked of the President." *(Id.* at 14)

In his second interview with the Board, McFarlane expanded his first account.

I think it would be accurate to say that the President believed in August that he was approving the Israeli sale of modest levels of arms of a certain character, filling certain criteria, but that with that approval Israel could transfer or sell modest levels without further concrete approval.

Now as a separate but obviously related matter his concurrent expectation was that how that would be translated would be 100 TOWs. As far as the November shipment, then, I don't recall that having been a matter considered in Washington, raised to the President and decided. When I learned about it I did report it to the President and to the Secretary of State and to Mr. Regan in Geneva. I recall a conversation from Geneva with the Secretary of Defense, but I don't want to—I couldn't say beyond just the fact that it occurred because I always called him every day to debrief him on the meetings with Gorbachev, and so it might have been that.

But, at any rate, I raised it with the President, Mr. Regan. The routine in Geneva was that each morning before the prebriefing for the Gorbachev meetings he would have just a short meeting on other Presidential matters in his residence, and for that the Secretary of State and I and Mr. Regan would go to the chateau and meet with him for 15 minutes or so on non-summit issues, and that would have been where it would have been raised.

Then we left and walked over to the motorcade and on to the summit.

\* \* \*

Well, I wouldn't have reconfirmed it [the President's authorization] if I wasn't fully confident of it, and that could have been on the basis of what was a fairly routine reporting of any information that I had on this, that I would pass it on to the President and he would react to it, and his reaction was always well, cross your fingers or hope for the best, and keep me informed. But I was never to say at any point stop this or disapprove of it.

\* \* \*

General Scowcroft: But nobody talked to you about during the period from September through your learning of this shipment about the possibility of another shipment, about arrangements or anything like this before Rabin meets with you or the next day when he calls and says we're shipping something and we're in trouble?.

Mr. McFarlane: I have no concrete recollection of anything like that. I can imagine that meetings took place, but I don't know of any idea of a number of weapons to be sent over. I remember, for example, one time Mr. Ledeen conveying a concept—it was not a hard proposal—that the United States send Phoenix and one or two other kinds of precision guided systems, and it was out of the question. I said no.

But never any numerical kind of X day, Y weapons to Z place.

(McFarlane (2) 39–43)

# E. The First Draft of a "Finding": November 1985

When John McMahon, at that time Deputy Director of the CIA, heard that a CIA proprietary was involved in the November operation and that the Agency had asked foreign governments to grant overflight clearances for Israeli aircraft, he asked for a "Finding". Sending cables was one thing; shipments to Iran, whatever their character, was another. (Clarridge 9) In view of the arms embargo and other controls on trade, they smacked of an operation. (J. McMahon 5; Clarridge 9)

Under section 662 of the Foreign Assistance Act of 1961, as amended, 22 U.S.C. § 2422, the CIA may not use appropriated funds to conduct operations (other than to obtain "necessary intelligence") in foreign countries "unless and until the President finds that each such operation is important to the national security of the United States. Each such operation shall be considered a significant anticipated intelligence activity [covert operation] for the purpose of section 501 of the National Security Act of 1947." Section 501(b) of the National Security Act of 1947, as amended, 50 U.S.C. § 413, provides, in part, that, where prior notice of covert actions is not given to the House and Senate intelligence committees, the President "shall fully inform the intelligence committees in a timely fashion of intelligence operations in foreign countries, other than activities intended solely for obtaining necessary intelligence, for which prior notice was not given under subsection (a) and shall provide a statement of the reasons for not giving prior notice." NSDD 159 set forth procedures regarding implementation of these provisions, as well as for review of covert actions.

McMahon wrote on December 7, 1985, that, when he was informed about the CIA's involvement in the November shipment, he "went through the overhead pointing out that there was no way we could become involved in any implementation of this mission without a finding." (McMahon, "Memorandum for the Record," 12/7/85; J. McMahon 6) Juchniewicz first protested that "[w]e didn't do it; they came to us, and we told them we couldn't do it, so they asked us for the name of an airline, and we gave them the name of our proprietary." (J. McMahon 6) He explained that

> [w]hen General Secord visited the Agency he tried to get leads on airlines that might be available to move equipment to the Near East in a secure fashion. We told him we did not have any such airlift capability. However, Mr. Juchniewicz said it was pointed out to General Secord that there was a commercial airlift that might do it. . . . General Secord then took it from there and made arrangements for a flight on a strictly commercial basis.

(Memorandum for the Record, *supra.*) McMahon nonetheless directed operations officers to brief Stanley Sporkin, at that time General Counsel of the CIA, and prepare a Finding. McMahon told Sporkin to draft it to "cover retroactively the use of the Agency's proprietary." (J. McMahon 6; Memorandum for the Record, *supra)* Sporkin recalled thinking a Finding was prudent, but not required by law in this instance. (Sporkin 7–8) He included language ratifying prior acts by the CIA, and McMahon accepted it. *(Id.)*

Sporkin's draft Finding for the President provided:

> I have been briefed on the efforts being made by private parties to obtain the release of Americans held hostage in the Middle East, and hereby find that the following operations in foreign countries (including all support necessary to such operations) are important to the national security of the United States. Because of the extreme sensitivity of these operations, in the exercise of the President's constitutional authorities, I direct the Director of Central Intelligence not to brief the Congress of the United States, as provided for in

Section 501 of the National Security Act of 1947, as amended, until such time as I may direct otherwise.

*Description*

The provision of assistance by the Central Intelligence Agency to private parties in their attempt to obtain the release of Americans held hostage in the Middle East. Such assistance is to include the provision of transportation, communications, and other necessary support. As part of these efforts certain foreign material and munitions may be provided to the Government of Iran which is taking steps to facilitate the release of American hostages.

All prior actions taken by U.S. Government officials in furtherance of this effort are hereby ratified.

(Draft Finding enclosed in Casey to Poindexter, 11/26/85)

After speaking to Poindexter about his draft, the Director of Central Intelligence sent it to him on November 26, confirming that it "should go to the President for his signature and should not be passed around in any hands below our level." (Casey to Poindexter, 11/26/85)

Despite some testimony to the contrary, the President appears not to have signed this Finding. McMahon told the Board that his records showed that someone told him on December 5 that the President had signed. (J. McMahon 7; Memorandum for the Record, *supra*) Sporkin remembered that "[a]nother person who worked for me told me that at one point he was with Mr. North and Mr. North said: I want to give a message to Sporkin, that I've got a piece of paper that was signed, or some such thing as that." (Sporkin 8) In November 1986, North told the Attorney General that he never saw this draft. (Meese notes of interview with North, 11/22/86)

# F. December 1985: Bird's Eye View

At the beginning of December 1985, McFarlane resigned and Poindexter succeeded him as Assistant to the President for National Security Affairs. The next day, December 5, Poindexter told Secretary Shultz "the operation was at a decision point, and that he had set up a meeting for Saturday, December 7."[27] (Shultz, SRB, 29) According to notes of the Secretary's side of the conversation taken by the Secretary's Executive Assistant, Poindexter said there would be "[n]o calendar to show it." The Secretary of State "said the operation should be stopped; that I had been informed that Iran was playing a big role in Lebanon which even Syria could not influence. I told him: 'We are signalling to Iran that they can kidnap people for profit." *(Id.)* In the course of this "long phone call," *(id.* at 30), in which, according to notes by the Secretary's Executive Assistant, Poindexter gave Secretary Shultz more information than McFarlane ever had, Poindexter may have made use of a memorandum, dated December 5, 1985, apparently by North. Poindexter told the Secretary of State "that 3,300 TOWs and 60 HAWKs were being discussed." *(Id.)*

North's memorandum briefly summarized the history of the transactions with Iran through Weir's release and then described the current situation.

The Iranians have significant interest in continuing this process. They are under extraordinary military pressure from Iraq and are, by their own admission, subject to regular overflights of Iranian territory by Soviet aircraft. They currently have no capability to deal with this affront and find themselves in an increasingly desperate situation vis-a-vis Iraq. They have urged the Israelis, with whom they are in contact, to continue the process which resulted in the release of Benjamin Weir.

Our continuing efforts to achieve release of the hostages through diplomatic and other means have proven fruitless. There are numerous indications including reports from the special representative of the Archbishop of Canterbury, Terry Waite, that time is running out for the hostages. We are relatively confident of information that former Beirut Chief of Station, Bill Buckley, is dead. We also know, from Waite's November 14 visit to Beirut and a separate contact through Canada, that the other five hostages, Ander-

178

son, Jacobsen, Jenco, Kilburn, and Sutherland are still alive. Waite and others credibly report that those who hold the hostages are under immense political and military pressure from the Syrians, Druze, Phalange, and Amal and that there is the distinct possibility that our hostages as well as the French and British could be killed in the near future.

The Iranians, who have been in contact with the Israelis, are cognizant of the pressure being placed on the Hezballah surrogates in Lebanon and that it is entirely likely that the only leverage they will have over us (the hostages) may no longer be available in the near future. These Iranians, the same that arranged the release of Weir, have now proposed that in exchange for an immediate delivery of 3,300 TOW missiles and 50 Improved HAWK Surface-to-Air missiles from Israel, they will guarantee:

—The release of the five Americans and one of the French hostages still being held.

—No further acts [of] Shia fundamentalist terrorism (hijackings, bombings, kidnappings) directed against U.S. property or personnel.

There is considerable reason not to accept this proposal. It is contrary to our stated policy of not making concessions to terrorists or those who sponsor them. It is also possible that such an arrangement is a "double-cross" in that the Iranians can not or will not release the captives as agreed. Such an arrangement, bartering for the lives of innocent human beings, is repugnant. Finally, the quantities which the Iranians wish to purchase will significantly degrade Israeli stockpiles and require very prompt replenishment.

*U.S. Interests:* Notwithstanding the undesirable nature of such a transaction, it must be noted that the first two Israeli objectives are congruent with our own interests:

—A more moderate Iranian government is essential to stability in the Persian Gulf and MidEast.

—Such a change of government in Iran is most likely to come about as a consequence of a credible military establishment which is able to withstand the Iraqi onslought [sic] and deter Soviet adventurism/intimidation. The Iranian army (not the Revolutionary Guards) must be capable of at least stalemating the war.

—Shia fundamentalist terrorism is a serious threat to the United States which has long-term adverse consequences for our interests and we must endeavor to stop its spread.

—The return of the American hostages will relieve a major domestic and international liability —in addition to its obvious humanitarian aspect.

The first three of these goals may well be achievable— and the fourth accrued as a subsidiary benefit—by commencing the process of allowing the Israeli sales as proposed by the Iranian agents in Europe. It is unlikely, however, that we can proceed further toward the first three—and not at all on the hostage release unless we allow the process of delivery to begin.

Discussions toward this end have been proceeding among the Israelis, Iranians and a U.S. businessman acting privately on behalf of the USG for nearly three weeks. There are several indications of confidence that an arrangement can be consummated in the next 10 days which would result in the release of the hostages and commencement of a process leading toward the first three objectives above. The military situation in the Iran/Iraq war and the increasing pressure on the Hezballah in Lebanon both point toward immediate action. There is also, as the Iranian intermediaries pointedly noted last week, a complete absence of *any* Shia fundamentalist hijackings, assassinations, hostage seizures, or bombings since this dialogue began in September. While there have not been expressed or implied threats by the Iranians in these discussions, the Israeli and U.S. private citizen participants believe that if the current effort is not at least tried, we run the

ed the President. The problem, he felt, was that Mc-
[Fa]ne did not tell him the whole story.

[Th]e Secretary of Defense had a different recollection of
[the m]eeting, which he remembered as taking place in the
[Oval] Office.

[T]here was a quite specific, more detailed proposal
[th]at there had indeed been negotiations and discus-
[si]ons between somebody representing McFarlane's of-
[fi]ce and some Iranians who were reported to be
[m]oderates. I think at that meeting John McMahon was
[t]here. I'm not sure. Bill Casey may have been, or they
[b]oth may have been. But there were some adverse
comments passed about the veracity of the Iranians
involved, I think Ghorbanifar or some such name, but
a more formal presentation was now made by McFarlane about what could be accomplished with this and
points with respect to getting a better relationship
with Iran as well as hopes that they might have a
favorable effect on the release of the hostages.

Again, I opposed it very strongly and said I thought
really it was a terrible idea and that the transfer of
arms which was part of the plan which was to be done
to establish the good faith of the negotiators—I think I
made some comment about what about the good faith
of the Iranian negotiators, and why—went through a
whole catalogue of things which didn't require any
gift of prophecy as to what would happen if this became public. . . . [T]he advice I gave in this case was
as firm as I could do it, obviously not persuasive
enough but as persuasive as I could do it, that all kinds
of very unfortunate effects would result if this took
place, that we were pleading with a large number of
countries not to do this, that Jordan and Egypt regarded Iran as at least as much of a great Satan as they
regarded us, and that it would be a very bad thing in
every way to do, and that it wouldn't accomplish anything, and that they would undoubtedly continue to
milk us.

At this time again, the Israeli connection or the Israeli
support of such a transaction I guess is the better way
to put it, was advanced by McFarlane. And I said that

risk of abandoning both the longer term goals and the
likelihood of reprisals against us for "leading them
on." These reprisals would probably take the form of
additional hostage seizures, execution of some/all of
those now held, or both.

*Next Steps:* The Iranians, the Israelis, and our U.S.
businessman plan to meet in London on Saturday,
December 6 to discuss whether or not to proceed with
the sale of the TOWs and HAWKs. The Israeli government has informally told us that if they can be assured
of "prompt" resupply, they will sell the quantities requested from their prepositioned war reserve. 3,300
TOWs represents [sic] [a significant proportion] their
available supplies.

The U.S. businessman has arranged for the charter of
two non-U.S. registered aircraft for use in the deliveries. The total delivery would be conducted in 5
flights from Tel Aviv to Tabriz, Iran via interim airfields in Europe. . . . Each delivery is to result in the
release of a specified number of hostages. Arrangements for the interim airfields, overflight rights, and
flight plans have been made, some with the help of the
CIA. A communications code to preserve operational
security is available for use by all parties. All aircraft
would be inspected by an Iranian at one of the transient locations between Tel Aviv and Tabriz. The entire evolution is designed to be completed in a 24 hour
period. It can be stopped at any point if the Iranians
fail to deliver.

The greatest operational security concern is that of
replenishing Israeli stocks. The Israelis have identified
a means of transferring the Iranian provided funds to
an Israeli Defense Force (IDF) account, which will be
used for purchasing items not necessarily covered by
FMS. They will have to purchase the replenishment
items from the U.S. in FMS transaction from U.S.
stocks [sic]. Both the number of weapons and the size
of the cash transfer could draw attention. If a single
transaction is more than $14.9 M, we would normally
have to notify Congress. The Israelis are prepared to

justify the large quantity and urgency based on damage caused to the equipment in storage.

\* \* \*

If this process achieves the release of the hostages and proves the credibility of the Iranian contacts in Europe, Bud McFarlane would then step in to supervise achieving the longer range goals. Additional meetings with the Iranians would be arranged to further our objectives without requiring such large scale sales/deliveries by the Israelis.

Approval is now required for us to take the next steps on Saturday. After carefully considering the liabilities inherent in this plan, it would appear that we must make one last try or we will risk condemning some or all of the hostages to death and undergoing a renewed wave of Islamic Jihad terrorism. While the risks of proceeding are significant, the risks of not trying are even greater.

([North], "Special Project Re Iran," 12/5/85)

The President met his principal national security advisors on December 7 in his residence. The President, Secretaries of State and Defense, Deputy Director of the CIA, McFarlane, Poindexter, and the President's Chief of Staff attended. (Ellen M. Jones, Presidential Diarist, to Jay M. Stephens, 1/24/87 (information from the Presidential Calender, which apparently is called a Diary))

Recollections of the meeting vary. In his meeting with the Board on January 26, 1987, the President said he recalled discussing a complex Iranian proposal for weapons delivered by the Israelis in installments prior to the release of the hostages. The President said that Secretary Shultz and Secretary Weinberger objected to the plan, and that this was the first time he "noted down" their opposition. The President said that the discussion at the meeting produced a stalemate.

The Attorney General remembered attending; he did not think McFarlane was present, and thought that Fortier probably attended. (Meese 4) The subject of the meeting—

the Iran transactions—was announced in adv[ance] principals had time to prepare. (Shultz, SRB [31–3] 5) According to the Secretary of State,

Poindexter suggested that Mr. McFarlane c[on-] tact the Iranians in London to ask them to re[lease] hostages without getting equipment. If they [did] so, we, then, would be prepared for a better [relation-] ship with them.

I fully supported this proposal.

Vice Admiral Poindexter suggested that Mr. [McFar-] lane should be authorized to ask the British [to sell] arms to Israel [?Iran] if the Iranians rejected h[is] proposal. I opposed this idea. I said it was stil[l selling] arms, that it was a more complicated deal that w[ould] make us even more vulnerable. Other views [were] expressed.

No decision was made, however, at that meetin[g as] far as I could see. . . .

On December 7, Vice Admiral Poindexter told [me] privately that the project had fallen apart dur[ing] Thanksgiving week. That is thinking back to that [pe-] riod. He said he had recommended to the Presid[ent] that we disengage, but that the President did not w[ant] to.

I felt in the meeting that there were views oppos[ed,] some in favor, and the President didn't really tak[e a] position, but he seemed to, he was in favor of [the] project somehow or other. And, of course, by now [he] has said publicly that he was in favor of working at [the] Iranian operation and being willing to sell arms a[s a] signal, as he has now put it.

(Shultz, SRB, 31–32)

When the Secretary of State returned to his offic[e he] told his staff that Secretary Weinberger and Regan [had] strongly opposed the initiative. The Secretary of Defense spoke for thirty minutes. The Secretary told his staff he felt that he perhaps should have barged in earlier and con-

another of the problems that I thought with it was that doing anything of this kind and attempting to keep it on a clandestine basis would leave us open to blackmail of the very most elementary kind by the people who knew about it, that is, the Israelis and also Iranians, and that any time they weren't getting what they wanted, they could in one way or another, in Mideast fashion, go public with it and cause all kinds of problems with it, that there was no way that I ever felt I could talk with [moderate Arab States] again if we were supplying arms to [a] bitter enemy when we wouldn't supply arms to him et cetera, et cetera, just a whole series of arguments. George Shultz made some very strong arguments along the same line . . . A very strong, very persuasive argument. And again, my impression pretty clearly was that the President agreed that this couldn't be done, that it might be a good thing to achieve these objectives but it wouldn't work, and that this was not a good way to do it.

(Weinberger 9–12) Armitage remembered the Secretary of Defense saying that he and Secretary Shultz "thought they had 'strangled the baby in the cradle.' " (Armitage 6)

In his first interview with the Board, McFarlane recalled suggesting to the President on December 1 that the negotiations with the Iranians "seemed to be getting skewed towards arms going that way and hostages coming this way. . . . I thought we ought to seek a meeting directly with the Iranians and discontinue any kind of sponsorship of arms transfers." (McFarlane (1) 25) In this interview, McFarlane remembered the President's suggesting an NSC meeting to consider it. *(Id.)* At the meeting,

we went through the record of what had occurred since August in terms of Israeli transfers and the absence of meetings, and at consensus, the unanimous view of all of his advisors, the President decided: All right, you go to London, McFarlane, and you meet with the Iranians and make clear that we remain open to the political discourse, and here it is. And there were about four generic areas that we wanted to talk to Iran about, our disagreements and so forth.

And the second point is that we will not transfer nor encourage any other government to transfer weapons to them.

*(Id.* at 26)

McFarlane gave the Board a fuller account in his second interview.

[R]ight after the summit, after I got back from debriefing the Holy Father and Mitterand and Prime Minister Thatcher, we had some time to look at other things, and I didn't even come to the office. I went directly from London to Washington to California but had two days before the President got there to just kind of think through how things had gone, and they hadn't gone very well.

The idea originally of us getting in direct communication with Iranian officials hadn't happened, and instead this imperfect demonstration of bona fides had been imperfect, rather dramatically, and had become their priority, with a very clear lack of good faith, I thought. And I said to the President after thinking about it, and I went down to Santa Barbara and we talked, both about my resignation but then about the results of this program. And I believe it occurred in the Century Plaza Hotel on a morning.

And I said that it seems to me that we ought to try to reorient it to its original purpose, Mr. President, and that is for us to avoid dealing through intermediaries and to talk to Iranians directly, and he agreed with that. And he said convene the NSC—the Secretary of State and Defense—and let's talk it over when we get back. So that is what led me to then do two things— convene a meeting and tentatively ask Admiral Poindexter, I believe, to have a meeting with the Iranian intermediary set up in London.

So with that prelude a meeting was convened on December 7 of the NSC, and I would, I believe, have presided because I was still sitting in the chair. What I am saying now is based upon routine and not notes from it. But I always started off by briefing the issue.

Here we are today convened to talk about the Iranian program. Here is what has happened since the beginning and here is the return, the benefits and the liabilities of it, and the decision is what should we do or what should we do henceforth—continue as we have, change, or something else.

And then invite the comments of everybody around the table, usually start with the Secretary of State, then the Secretary of Defense, and around the table, and that would have led to the Director of the CIA, and any one of the other ad hoc members that happened to be present. Usually it was Mr. Regan.

And it was unanimous in the meeting that this really had gone badly off course and that we should yes, still be open to talking to Iranian officials, authorities, and have a concrete political agenda to describe. And we talked a little bit about that—our view of our interests in the area, how they were threatened by Iran, disagreements we had with them over terrorism and fundamentalists' crusade in the Middle East, and ultimately perhaps even some common interest—Afghanistan and elsewhere.

But because of how things had gone up until then we ought to also tell them that we were not going to transfer U.S. weapons, sell U.S. weapons. We were not going to allow or encourage anybody else to do so. And I don't recall anybody disagreeing with that at all.

The President wasn't terribly—didn't intervene in the meeting, as I recall, very much on one side or the other, but at the end said well, okay. That's what you should say. And I left that evening and was in London the next morning, and we took off from there.

(McFarlane (2) 45–47)

Regan's recollection is somewhat different. He recalled that, although McMahon, for example, was informally dressed,

the December meeting got to be more formal because McMahon, among others, raised the question of, you

187

know, what the hell are we doing here. Arms are being sent. Where is the formal authority? You know, what are we doing here? Is this going to be policy?

And as a result of that meeting and people expressing views which now are commonly known, such as State Department and Defense opposed to this. CIA was in favor. NSC was in favor. And I must say that I favored it. I won't deny that I favored keeping the channel open, if necessary selling a modest amount of arms, in order to make certain that we were having contacts with Iran and at the same time, if as a result of this they could influence the Hezballah, as they had in the case of Benjamin Weir, why not.

So I am not certain, but I think I probably also reflect for the most part the President's view on that.

(Regan 14–15)

John McMahon, who represented the CIA, recalled that "[t]here was no decision. We didn't walk away with any marching orders or any decision at that moment." The President asked questions about strengthening moderates in Iran by selling weapons. McMahon "pointed out that we had no knowledge of any moderates in Iran, that most of the moderates had been slaughtered when Khomeini took over." (J. McMahon 11–12) He noted that any weapons sold "would end up in the front, and that would be to the detriment of the Iran-Iraq balance." *(Id.* at 12) He did not know that McFarlane was about to leave for London. *(Id.)*

After the meeting, McFarlane went to London, where he joined North. North had traveled on December 6 to meet Kimche, Secord, and Schwimmer "to review all the arrangements" in connection with the plan North set forth in his note to Poindexter of December 4. (North *PROF* note to Poindexter, 12/4/85, 02:02:55) On December 8, before meeting with Ghorbanifar, and Nimrodi, McFarlane privately reported his instructions to Kimche. Kimche

was upset and he said: I think you're missing a big opportunity; that you have to have some patience; that these movements take time to consolidate; and these people are delivering to us important items, information basically; and that we see signs from our intelligence that they're making headway and beginning to lock up and arrest radical elements and put their own people in more responsible positions, and the gradual evidence of their growing influence and ability to act.

And I said: Well, we don't see that; and further, we think it is being skewed off in the wrong direction. So he said: Well, we disagree.

And we went ahead and met with this Mr. Ghorbanifar, and in the course of about three hours I covered my instructions. And he said: Well, I understand the political dialogue, and our people in Iran are very much open to that; and so, the point is that you are misunderstanding how much turmoil there is in Iran. There is quite a lot of conflict between the radical and centrist and traditionalist elements there, and it is just not going to succeed in getting my superiors to take much in the way of risk if they don't see that the United States is truly willing to demonstrate the political capital investment to do it.

And I said: I understand what you say; my instructions are these, and we are not going to transfer any more arms. Well, we had not and did not, but Israel had.[28]

In his second interview with the Board, McFarlane provided more detail than in his first:

Colonel North was already there, and I went alone, and I may have had—I think I was alone, and was met on arrival by Colonel North at Heathrow and we went in to the Hilton Hotel and I asked to get together with Mr. Kimche. And he said well, we will set that up right away, and we did, I believe, within an hour or so in the Hilton that morning.

And I had known him for a long time and then got right to the point and said that this was well-meaning, well-intentioned, but it hasn't turned out and the President has decided that it has to be reoriented very substantially and my instructions are to say that if they are open to dialogue, we are too, and if not so be it, but under no circumstances are we prepared to sell arms nor to allow anybody else to either.

And he rejoindered and said he thought that we should have more patience and try to keep this going.

Chairman Tower: So this was in effect going back to the August approval on our part, or the termination of the August approval?

Mr. McFarlane: Yes, sir.

Chairman Tower: I'm sorry to interrupt. Go ahead.

Mr. McFarlane: And Mr. Kimche said that while he could understand why we were disappointed that this was the nature of things in the Middle East and they couldn't always go as hoped, and we ought to keep going with it. And it was irreconcilable, really, and I said I'm sorry, we just—I have my instructions. And he told me the meeting, I think the meeting was for 3:00, I think, 2:00 or 3:00 in the afternoon, and we went on separately to the meeting.

And at the meeting, which was in a West End London apartment—and I don't know. I've seen reports that it was Mr. Schwimmer's apartment. I don't know that firsthand. But at the meeting I met with, from the Israeli side, again Mr. Kimche and Mr. Nimrodi. The only Iranian present, to my knowledge, was Mr. Ghorbanifar. And from the American side myself and Colonel North.

And it was about a three-hour meeting, as I recall. Colonel North was the notetaker. And I began my brief saying here is our experience or our view of the experience of the past three months or so, and our purposes are these, and they haven't been met, and we think that there has been bad faith on the Iranian side, and it calls into question two fundamentals from out point of view. Number one, is there good faith at all and whether or not there is, is there competence, is there real authority. Can you take decisions and change things?

Our conclusions are that we are open to a political dialogue, and I have developed that, to his great dismay, for about an hour. And I said that the President has decided that there can be no sale of U.S. weapons nor will we approve the sale by others of weapons.

And he replied in a kind of a cursory fashion, accepting that his superiors in Tehran were in fact interested in changing Iranian policy and forming a government with better relations with the West, but that I had to understand that their vulnerability was quite high and that they needed badly to maintain their own support from within the military and that the coin of that relationship and support and strength within Iran was the weapons.

And I listened to him talk for a half hour or so, and just in observing, as any human being does, to evaluate what kind of person this was, and by this time I had also after the Summit gotten a lot more information about him, but it was mostly from that meeting where it was very apparent that his agenda was buying weapons and his interest in our political agenda very superficial.

And though he purported or represented that his seniors were interested in that he personally obviously was not conversant with those things and had only a passing interest in them. And after hearing him out I said, well, I understand what you have said. I delivered my instructions. Please convey that to your government. And that's the end of it.

And I left and went back briefly to the Hilton to pick up some things and went on out to the airplane and took off.

Senator Muskie: Did Ghorbanifar express any concern about the quality of the arms shipment, the HAWKs?

Mr. McFarlane: That seems likely, Mr. Secretary. I think he complained about a lot of things that were foreign to me, but I think probably he did.

Chairman Tower: What kind of representations did he

make to you about the people that he was in liaison with in Iran or that he represented? Did he go into the matter of the three lines or factions with you at all in Iran? Or did he talk about one specific faction or group?

Mr. McFarlane: We had received intelligence on the political map of Tehran, so to speak, from two sources. We in the United States had received from the Israelis what they had received from the Iranians, and separately Mr. Ghorbanifar transferred to us his own product of intelligence that described, as you say, these three lines of political affiliation that were, call it, radical-center and conservative.

But that goes back to August, really, the original product, and in this meeting he did describe that the people with whom he was associated included basically those who were oriented toward a less extreme return to kind of a non-aligned position but normal trade and discourse with the West and retrenchment on this fundamentalist crusade, and recognized the isolation that it was producing, and did however have within it mullahs, some bazaaris and a substantial number of military leaders and people from outside the government like the bazaaris.

(McFarlane (2) 48–53)

Ghorbanifar provided the Board with his version of the December meeting. He said the meeting took place at Nimrodi's London home, with Kimche, Schwimmer, McFarlane, North, and Secord. Ghorbanifar described the meeting as an exchange of "tough" lectures.

McFarlane gave a lecture that we want to know the importance, strategic point of Iran, we know the people, we know we had bitter relations before, and so on and so on, and we want a better one.

I said what are you talking about? You just left a mess behind and you want something else? I was tough. I explained, I explained to him that what is the situation inside Iran between the rival groups, between the politicians, what is this mess, what the hell a problem has brought this one, this issue has presented to this big policy.

\* \* \*

I told him what the hell is this, what is the problem, you leave a mess behind, and if you want to continue this way, I said, just is better you cut off and don't put us, the blame on us, and by the fire on your side because then there will be fire back on your interests.

(Ghorbanifar 122–123) Ghorbanifar also remembered Nir saying that Ledeen, Schwimmer, Nimrodi, and Kimche no longer would participate in the negotiations or the transaction. *(Id.* at 120)

North returned from London on December 8. The next day, he submitted a memorandum to McFarlane and Poindexter summarizing the results of the London meetings and setting forth a new plan of action.

The meetings this weekend with the Israelis and Gorbanifahr [sic] were inconclusive. Gorbanifahr refused to return to Geneva with our message that no further deliveries would be undertaken until all the hostages were released. Gorbanifahr and the Israelis both believe that if he were to pass such a message to the Iranian Prime Minister or the Oil Minister (who provides funds for items delivered)—one or more of the hostages would be executed. Gorbanifahr noted that nine Hezballah leaders had been summoned to Tehran on Friday [December 6] and that, given the pressures inside Lebanon, all it would take for the hostages to be killed would be for Tehran to "stop saying no."

Much of what we decide to do in the days ahead depends upon whether or not we can trust Gorbanifahr. The Israelis believe him to be genuine. Gorbanifahr's earlier game plan delivered Reverend Weir. He has proposed that we "deliver something" so that he can retain credibility with the regime in Tehran. He even suggested that the weapons delivered be useful only to the Army or Air Force (not the Revolutionary Guards) and that they be "technically disabled." He urged that, if improved HAWKs were not feasible, to at least keep the door open by some kind of delivery between now and the end of the week. He said we must recognize that if TOWs are provided that they will probably go to the Revolutionary Guards.

The Israelis have willingly consented to "kick-back" arrangement which allows Israeli control over Gorbanifahr and Ayatollah Karami. Israel believes strongly in using any means to bridge into Iran. Their last three governments over a four year period have been consistent in this theme.

Whether we trust Gorbanifahr or not, he is irrefutably the deepest penetration we have yet achieved into the current Iranian Government. There is nothing in any of the [tailored intelligence reporting] which contradicts what he has told us or the Israelis over the past several months. Much of our ability to influence the course of events in achieving a more moderate Iranian Government depends on the validity of what Gorbanifahr has told us—and his credibility as one who can "deliver" on what the Iranians need. While it is possible that Gorbanifahr is doubling us or simply lining his own pockets, we have relatively little to lose in meeting his proposal; i.e., the Israelis start delivering TOWs and no hostages are recovered. On the other hand, a supply operation now could very well trigger results he claims.

The current situation is one in which information is incomplete, the motivation of the various participants uncertain, and our operational control tenuous in that we have had to deal exclusively through the Israelis. The near term risk to the hostages has undoubtedly been increased by Iranian "expectations" arising from earlier decisions to proceed with deliveries and by the increasing pressure against Hezballah in Lebanon. Terry Waite, our only access to events in Lebanon, readily admits that his influence is marginal at best. Waite shares our belief that the hostages are increasingly endangered and that one or more of them could well be executed by the end of the week.

Our greatest liability throughout has been lack of operational control over transactions with Gorbanifahr. The Israeli contact, Schwimmer, has arranged deliveries of items which were not requested by Gorbanifahr for the Iranian military. Further, the terms which he negotiated are disadvantageous to the IDF and our ability to replenish the Israelis. It was apparent, during the meeting with McFarlane, that Gorbanifahr preferred only to deliver items useful to the Iranian military—not the Revolutionary Guard. Despite admonishments to the contrary, Schwimmer had already arranged for the 3,300 TOWs as part of the next steps.

Schwimmer's arrangements would have exchanged the 3,300 TOWs for three hostages at a price which would not allow the IDF to recoup expenses, thus complicating our ability to replenish IDF stores. In short, most of the problems with this endeavor have arisen because we have been unable to exercise operational control over arrangements or their expected outcome. For example, at the meeting with McFarlane we learned for the first time that the Iranians want desperately to return the 18 basic HAWK missiles which are still in Tehran. All agree that we should only do so if the in-bound aircraft has something aboard which the Iranians want. At the end of the meeting it was agreed that we would "get back" to Gorbanifahr quickly as to our next steps. He departed for Geneva to brief the Iranian Oil Minister to the effect that "technical difficulties remain to be overcome before further deliveries can be scheduled."

The question which now must be asked is should we take a relatively small risk by allowing (encouraging) a small Israeli-originated delivery of TOWs and hope for the best or should we do nothing? If such a delivery were to take place, we would have to plan to replenish the Israeli stocks on a "routine" basis to avoid drawing attention.

If we are to prevent the death or more of the hostages in the near future, we appear to have four options available:

Accept Gorbanifahr/Schwimmer's game plan:

—Stretch any replenishment to Israel over several months making it routine.

—1,100 TOWs are maximum risk materielly [sic]. Cost and cover can be maintained by selling from stock to Israel over time.

—If hostages are recovered disclosure doesn't hurt much.

Raid and attempt rescue:

—If this option is pursued, then the military should be directed to execute by NLT next Saturday and talks with Gorbanifahr should be resumed in effort to hold Hezballah in check over the next 6 days.

Allow the Israelis to deliver 400–500 TOWs while picking up 18 HAWKs in effort to show good faith to both factions in Iran:

—This could cause Iran to deliver a hostage as sign of cooperation. It will also serve to boost Gorbanifahr's reputation.

—Israel could do this unilaterally and seek routine replacements.

—This gives U.S. more breathing time (maybe!).

Do nothing:

—Very dangerous since *U.S. has, in fact, pursued earlier Presidential decision* to play along with Gorbanifahr's plan. U.S. reversal now in midstream could ignite Iranian fire—hostages would be our minimum losses.

There is a fifth option which has not yet been discussed. We could, with an appropriate covert action Finding commence deliveries ourselves, using Secord as our conduit to control Gorbanifahr and delivery operations. This proposal has considerable merit in that we will reduce our vulnerabilities in the replenishment of Israeli stocks and can provide items like the Improved HAWK (PIP II) which the Iranian Air Force wants and the Israelis do not have. Finally, Secord can arrange for third country nationals to conduct a survey of ground and air military requirements which is what Gorbanifahr has been attempting to obtain from the Israelis for nearly three months.

(North to McFarlane/Poindexter, 12/9/85)

McFarlane reported to the President, the Secretary of Defense, the Director of Central Intelligence, Regan, and Poindexter on December 10. (Jones to Stephens, 1/24/87 (Presidential calendar); DCl to DDCI, 12/10/85) On his way to the NATO Ministerial Meeting in Brussels, the Secretary of State received a report of the meeting: "White House meeting this morning. The turn-off is complete (we think). McFarlane turned down in London. Ollie did paper saying this means hostages will die." (Shultz, SRB, 34)

The President told the Board on January 26, 1987, that McFarlane expressed no confidence in the Iranian intermediary he met in London (Ghorbanifar). The President said McFarlane recommended rejection of the latest Iranian plan. The President said he agreed. "I had to."

In a memorandum, dated December 10, 1985, the Director of Central Intelligence noted that McFarlane

did not have a good impression of Gorbanifehr [sic] and recommended that we not pursue the proposed relationship with him. He recommended that we pursue the relationship with others representing the moderate forces in the Iranian government, talking and listening to them on a purely intelligence basis but being alert to any action that might influence events in Iran.

2. Everybody supported this in our round-table discussion. Other options which Bud had suggested were to let the Israelis go ahead doing what they would probably do anyway, and hope we get some benefit, or to mount a rescue effort. The President argued mildly for letting the operation go ahead without any commitments from us except that we should ultimately fill

up the Israeli pipeline in any event, or the Congress will do it for us. He was afraid that terminating the ongoing discussions, as Bud had speculated they might, could lead to early action against the hostages. The trend of the succession of this was that it was a little disingenuous and would still bear the onus of having traded with the captors and provide an incentive for them to do some more kidnapping, which was the main burden of the argument against going forward on the program. The President felt that any ongoing contact would be justified and any charges that might be made later could be met and justified as an effort to influence future events in Iran. I did point out that there was historical precedent for this and that was always the rationale the Israelis had given us for their providing arms to Iran. . . .

4. As the meeting broke up, I had the idea that the President had not entirely given up on encouraging the Israelis to carry on with the Iranians. I suspect he would be willing to run the risk and take the heat in the future if this will lead to springing the hostages. It appears that Bud has the action.

(Casey to DDCI, 12/10/85)

In his first interview with the Board, McFarlane remembered that the meeting occurred on December 11, and that the Vice President and John McMahon (for the Director of Central Intelligence) attended.

I debriefed that I had carried out my instructions and came home. But I added, I said: Whatever may be the case in Iran, this fellow is a person of no integrity and I would not do any more business with him, the Iranian Ghorbanifar. And I left the government believing that it was discontinued.

(McFarlane (1) 28)

In his second interview, McFarlane added:

I believe, unlike the preparatory meeting on the seventh, this time Mr. Casey was there but the Secretary of State was not. And Mr. Regan and the Secretary of

Defense I recall specifically sitting opposite me in the Oval Office. And it was a short meeting, I think probably fifteen or twenty minutes, and I stated basically that I had carried out the instructions, that I had made the two points, and went through the specific content of our political agenda that we were prepared to talk about, and the second point on the unwillingness from our side to sell arms or authorize anybody else to do so, and that they acknowledged that they were prepared for this political dialogue but that it was unrealistic to assume that it could occur or make any headway without weapons, and that at that impasse the talks were broken off.

And then separately I provided kind of a commentary on my evaluation of Mr. Ghorbanifar, which was that he was not a trustworthy person and had a very different agenda from our own and was an unsatisfactory intermediary. And finally I believe I also said that it is conceivable some day that our original point, the political dialogue, they may come back to you on. I doubt it, but I recommend that you have nothing further to do with this person nor with these arms transfers.

And the President was rather pensive. At that point the Secretary of Defense kind of assertively made the point. He said, I agree with Bud that this program is a very ill-advised program and that we should have nothing further to do with it, and the President was still kind of reflective, nodding but not saying anything, as I recall it.

I think Mr. Casey was essentially passive but listening and said well, so be it or something accepting that kind of emerging consensus. And that was the end of it.

\* \* \*

General Scowcroft: In other words, you think what you said is let's stop this program and if the dialogue is going to come maybe they will get back to us, but clear termination of the program?

Mr. McFarlane: Yes, it is, General, and I say that not

only because I believe that was my reaction to the three months' experience of it but because as a practical matter I was leaving the government and I had real misgivings about this thing going on at all afterwards.

General Scowcroft: Do you remember Ollie North saying to you or writing a memo or anything saying this means the hostages will die?

Mr. McFarlane: No, I don't.

Senator Muskie: Or Ghorbanifar?

Mr. McFarlane: I hadn't thought about that, Mr. Secretary, although he was given to extravagant kinds of things. It wouldn't surprise me if he said that.

\* \* \*

[The President] was, however, of a mood that was not uncommon when he was uncomfortable with the situation, when in this case everyone else in the room seemed to be of one view and he didn't want to oppose that view. I don't recall his having been emphatic about an opposing point of view.

The President was always very hopeful, optimistic and on almost every issue, and I think on this one on that day, was disappointed that he hadn't turned out so far, but always looking for the bright side or the possibility that it could be salvaged. But concretely did he say anything by way of decision? I don't believe so.

And I drew my conclusion that well, Mr. Regan did say he agreed that it ought to be closed out, as I recall.

\* \* \*

I would characterize it as a recommendation on my part that there should be nothing more to do with this person, Ghorbanifar, that there be no further arms shipped whatsoever by anyone, that in my judgment that would lead to a complete discontinuation of any exchanges, finally that I could imagine someday they might come back and say all right, without any arms involved we are open to your political agenda, but that concretely don't do business with that person and don't sell any arms.

Chairman Tower: Well, was the suggestion that if there was to be a reopening of this that it would come from them?

Mr. McFarlane: That's right.

(McFarlane (2) 55–58)

Regan recalled that,

right after [McFarlane's] return there was a meeting with the President, and I believe Shultz, Weinberger and Casey were present, to discuss what further should be done. Bud led me to believe that this contact, while it wasn't as good as they had originally hoped and that it wasn't as productive a contact as they had hoped, and we weren't getting any hostages out, we weren't really meeting with the top side of the Iranian government. And, accordingly, something different had to be tried.

\* \* \*

The NSC were trying to make contacts through Ghorbanifar directly to a higher level within Iran. They were trying to establish better relations than just the people with whom they were meeting in Europe. This is one of the things that McFarlane brought back from his meeting. . . . [Despite his negative impression of Ghorbanifar, McFarlane stated] that we could and should make contacts at a different level, at a better level than Ghorbanifar.

\* \* \*

[T]he President urged that, as a matter of fact, that we try something else or abandon the whole project, because he wanted to keep it open not only for geopolitical reasons but also the fact that we weren't getting anywhere in getting more hostages out. And we were going to spend another Christmas with hostages there, and he is looking powerless and inept as President

201

because he's unable to do anything to get the hostages out.

(Regan 15, 31–32, 17) Weinberger did not remember this meeting. (Weinberger 14)

# G. The NSC Staff, the CIA, and Ghorbanifar: December 1985–January 1986

Some ten days after this meeting, Ghorbanifar visited Washington. (Ledeen (1) 7)[29] Ghorbanifar's visit was one of a number of meetings and conversations in December 1985 about which little is known. Early in the month, Ledeen told Clarridge and Charles Allen that he had important intelligence about Iranian-backed terrorism in Western Europe. He provided Ghorbanifar's name and telephone numbers to Allen, and said he had McFarlane's approval to pursue the matter. He told Allen Kimche was involved. (C. Allen 10; CIA/IG Chronology 11) The Director of Central Intelligence met Ledeen on December 19. On December 22 and 23, Ledeen and Ghorbanifar met the Chief of the CIA's Iran desk.

According to the CIA's report of the meeting Ledeen met this official alone, and reviewed his relationship with Ghorbanifar.

He said about a year ago, he (Ledeen) had gone to the former National Security Advisor Robert McFarlane to discuss the need for an Iran policy. Ledeen suggested to McFarlane that he be authorized to contact the Israeli Government to see what could be done in conjunction with them. McFarlane authorized this contact and shortly thereafter Ledeen met Prime Minister Peres. Ledeen added that Peres was very enthusiastic about working with Ledeen and the U.S. Government on the Iranian problem and told him about their contact with Subject [Ghorbanifar]. Two Israeli officials, David Kimche and Jacob Nimradi [sic], introduced Ledeen to Subject. Since then, he has seen Subject 20–30 times, often in conjunction with Kimche and Nimradi. It was from this contact that the operation developed to have the Israelis at our behest deliver to Iran 500 Tow [sic] missiles and, more recently, 18 Hawk missiles in exchange for the release of all the hostages held in Lebanon. Ledeen is convinced that the release of Reverend Weir was tied directly to the first shipment of missiles. Ledeen went on to say, however, that he never really expected the Iranians to deliver all the hostages given the "Iranian's merchant mentality."

—The delivery of the Hawk missiles has been an operational nightmare. There was a misunderstanding about the type of missiles the Iranians were seeking. They wanted a missile that could hit a target at seventy-thousand feet and already had Hawk missiles in their arsenal. What they thought they were going to get was a modified and advanced version of the Hawk. They are quite angry about the delivery of the missiles and have asked that they be removed from Iran as soon as possible. Their presence in Iran is politically troublesome to the Iranian hierarchy. They are now asking for Hercules or Phoenix missiles.

—Ledeen stated that at a recent high-level meeting which included the President, Secretary of State Schultz [sic] and Defense Secretary Weinberger a decision was made not to proceed with Ghorbanifar in an effort to release the hostages. Schultz and Weinberger reportedly were quite unhappy about this operation.

—As an aside, Ledeen noted they had purposely overcharged the Iranians and had used around $200,000 of these funds to support Subject's political contacts inside Iran. Later that same evening, Subject stated he was holding $40 million which the Iranians want returned.

—Ledeen is a fan of Subject and describes him as a "wonderful man. . . . [sic] almost too good to be true." He had asked Subject to come to the U.S. to meet with us in order to straighten out his credibility and to find a way to keep the relationship going with him. The number one item in this latter area is his proposed Libyan operation. Ledeen said that when he learned of our Burn Notice on Subject, he contacted him in an effort to have him explain situation (see Attachment A). He commented that Subject admitted lying to us, saying he could not reveal his source nor explain his relationship with senior Iranian officials. He felt we would not understand his relationship with the Iranian government. We suggested that perhaps a new polygraph would be useful given these latest revelations. He agreed to a polygraph to be conducted in the Hqs area on 6 January.

—In closing out this session, Ledeen made the point that any serious covert action operations directed against Iran using Ghorbanifar should be run out of the White House not CIA because "it will leak from Congress."

(Chief, NESA, to DCI, n.d.)

The meeting continued at 9 p.m. at Ledeen's house, with Ghorbanifar. Ghorbanifar discussed a three-man "Iranian hit team," operating in Europe with instructions to assassinate a number of Iranian ex-patriots. On December 23, Ghorbanifar again met the CIA official, and named his source about the assassins. This name provoked the comment:

*This is the same source who provided the false information last March concerning an alleged Iranian plan to assassinate Presidential candidates which did not hold up during Subject's polygraph.*

* * *

(Comment: Subject's reporting on this team [Iranian hit team] is very reminiscent of his previous terrorist reporting which, after investigation and polygraph, turned out to be fabricated. It is our feeling there are bits of valid information in Subject's reporting but he has embellished and projected his own feelings in presenting this information as hard fact. This has been a presistant [sic] problem throughout the four years we

204

have known him. His reporting has sometimes been useful but it is extremely difficult to separate the good from the bad information. It is hard to find in the file any instance where his reporting in fact resulted in a solid development.)

*(Id.)* The Chief of the Near East Division in CIA's Operations Directorate later said of him: "This is a guy who lies with zest." (C/NE (1) 48)

Ghorbanifar used the rest of the interview to discuss Iranian politics—he described political groupings as "Lines." He also provided information on Islamic Jihad, which preliminarily did not appear useful to the CIA, and his relations with Iranian leaders, especially an official in the Prime Minister's office. (Chief, NESA, to DCI, n.d.)

> —Subject said that because of the negotiations concerning the exchange of the hostages for missiles, there has not been a terrorist act directed against the USG since July. He implied that this might change now that the negotiations have broken off.

*(Id.)* Ghorbanifar, supported by Ledeen, then proposed a "sting" operation against Qadhafi—accepting $10 million to stage the disappearance of the Libyan opposition leader, al-Mugarieff.

Ghorbanifar planned to travel to London on December 24; he agreed to return for a polygraph test on January 5 or 6. The interview ended when, at 11 p.m., North "dropped by to say hello to Subject and to talk with him about the problem of retrieving the missiles from Iran. We departed at 2400 hours and it was arranged to get together on the afternoon of 23 December to discuss further some of his ideas." *(Id.)*

On December 23, North met Ledeen at the Madison Hotel at 2:30 p.m., (North calendar), where Ghorbanifar was staying under the alias Nicholas Kralis. (Chief, NESA, to DCI, n.d.) At 3:45 p.m. on the 23rd, North met Secord at the Hay Adams Hotel. (North calendar) Also on December 23, the Director of Central Intelligence sent the President a memorandum, including as the fifth paragraph:

The Iranian Gorbanifar [sic], who the NSC staff believes arranged to release Weir, turned up in Washington over the weekend. Ollie North put him in touch with us. He has 3 or 4 scenarios he would like to play out. He gave us information about 3 Iranians going into Hamburg as a hit team. We have verified their movement but not their purpose. It could be a deception to impress us. It is necessary to be careful in talking with Gorbanifar. Still, when our man talked to him on Saturday and asked him if he would take another polygraph he said he would. We think this is worth doing for what we might learn. We want to prepare thoroughly for polygraphing him and because he is going to Switzerland for Christmas, it is understood that he will return here in a week or so for further discussions and for a polygraph.

(Casey to President, 12/23/86)

Finally, Charles Allen told the Board that he understood that Nir came to Washington in December, and North briefed him on December 23 "on this initiative"—that is, on the program in light of McFarlane's meetings in London. (C. Allen 53) In late December, Allen gave the NSC staff a copy of an August 1984 CIA "burn notice" on Ghorbanifar to the effect that he was a fabricator whose information should not be trusted. (CIA/IG Report 19) On December 24, North met Gen. Uri Simhoni and Col. Moshe Zur, (North calendar), whom his secretary described to Allen and Bernard Makowka as "Israeli intelligence." (CIA/IG Chronology 12)

Ghorbanifar took a polygraph test in the afternoon and evening, January 11, 1986 and showed deception on almost all of the questions. (Memorandum for the Record, "Ghorbanifar Polygraph Examination")[30] One report on the test stated:

He showed deception on virtually all of the relevant questions. He has lied/fabricated his information on terrorist activities and tried to mislead us concerning his relationship with the Farsi line inside Iran. He also has distorted [name deleted] role in Islamic Jihad. Moreover, Ghorbanifar was tested on his involvement in the deal to release the hostages. The test indicated that he knew ahead of time that the hostages would not be released and deliberately tried to deceive us both independently and with "B."

Ghorbanifar provided new information concerning an alleged terrorist plan to attack U.S. interests in Saudi Arabia. He was also tested on this information and was shown to be lying.

It seemed clear from Ghorbanifar's behavior that he realized that the polygraph test indicated deception. While he commented during the test that he was comfortable with all of the test questions, he said that perhaps the machine might indicate some problems on a series of questions concerning Farsi and the rightists inside Iran. He said he had been told by "White House representatives" not to discuss this topic with CIA because the operation was "too far advanced" and if CIA were involved "it would require Congressional briefings." He went on to add that he supposedly expended $800,000 of his own funds for this purpose and has been assured by these "White House representatives" that he will be reimbursed for these expenditures. (Comment: The polygraph operator stated that Ghorbanifar's explanation/rationalization would not influence the test results on the questions being asked in connection with Farsi and his supporters).

In discussing the hostage deal, Ghorbanifar stated he was very comfortable with the questions asked. During one of the breaks in the testing, he commented that the Israelis received $24 million as soon as the shipment was delivered and they are holding all of the funds that the Iranians are requesting be returned. He added that the Israelis told him that they had "doubled" the cost of the shipment apparently because the Americans were involved. He said the Iranians were very upset about the last shipment and might resort to terrorist activities against U.S. interests. He remarked the Iranians have been refraining from these terrorist activities since the negotiations began.

Ghorbanifar is clearly a fabricator and wheeler-dealer who has undertaken activities prejudicial to U.S. interests.

Neither Ghorbanifar nor Ledeen have [sic] been advised about the results of the test. Michael Ledeen asked that he be informed about the results of the test as soon as possible. He was called on the morning of 12 January and told that the polygraph operator will be reviewing the results on Sunday [January 12] and we should have feedback about the test on 13 January.

*(Id.)*

A paper entitled "Comments on Ghorbanifar's Polygraph" noted, in part, that he

(a) Lied/fabricated his information on terrorist activities;

(b) Tried to mislead us concerning his relationship with the "rightist line inside Iran";

(c) He distorted the leadership role of Seyyed Mohammad Khatemi inside Islamic Jihad;

(d) He showed deception on the question of whether he was under the control of the Iranian Government.

The test also indicated Ghorbanifar knew ahead of time that the hostages would not be released despite our providing missiles to the Iranians. He deliberately tried to deceive us on this issue both independently and with the collusion of "B."

("Comments on Ghorbanifar's Polygraph")

The polygraph examiner reported, on January 13, 1986, to the effect that Ghorbanifar was indeed a fabricator of evidence. He noted, moreover, that polygraph examinations in March and June 1984 had produced the same conclusion. On January 11, 1986, Ghorbanifar was tested in "a local hotel" in Washington. "The english [sic] language was used." "Deception indicated to thirteen of the fifteen relevant questions. Inconclusive to the remaining two." Some "relevant" questions, answers, and tracings by the polygraph were:

A. Has IDEN C . . . personally told you he is willing to cooperate with "US" intelligence? ANSWER: Yes.

B. Are you trying to deceive us about IDEN C's actual degree of influence with IDEN E [Islamic Jihad]? AN-SWER: No.

Testing showed deception to question B. Question A is inconclusive due to inconsistent reactions.

Ghorbanifar was questioned about his knowledge of Iranian terrorist activities. "Relevant" questions and answers were:

C. Are you trying to deceive us in any way about the source of the information regarding the three-man team (the IDEN G [Hamad Hassani] three-man hit team)? ANSWER: No.

D. Regarding European-based IDEN B [Iran/Iranian] terrorist, have you deliberately fabricated any of the information you have provided? ANSWER: No.

E. Did IDEN F . . . tell you the Hamburg Team (The IDEN G three-man hit team) killed IDEN L [Aziz Muradi]? ANSWER: Yes.

F. Other than what you have told us, are you aware of ongoing plans targeting "US" persons or interests for acts of terrorism you are not telling us about? AN-SWER: No.

Testing showed deception to questions C, D, E, and F. The test produced similar results when Ghorbanifar was questioned about " 'new' information about terrorist's current plans targeted against 'USG.' While discussing this topic, 'G' was occasionally evasive and often reluctant to answer questions." He also contradicted himself, although he did outline a meeting, during which IDEN C asked an Iranian for 300 kilograms of plastic explosive to use against United States facilities in Saudi Arabia, and a Lebanese

Palestinian Shiite terrorist asked for more efficient Iranian logistical support in delivering $6,000,000 worth of terrorist armaments. ("Polygraph" Division to C/NE/IRAN, 1/13/86)

At the request of the Director of Central Intelligence, Charles Allen interviewed Ghorbanifar for five hours on January 13, 1986. This conversation generated a nine-page report. Director Casey wanted, Allen reported, "to obtain a general overview of the information he possesses, not to conduct a detailed debriefing." (C. Allen, "Interview with Subject [Ghorbanifar]," 1/29/86) Ghorbanifar sought a "more principled" relationship with the CIA, based on his usefulness as "a turn-key project man," rather than an employee. He explained that, when, in 1980–82 the CIA had communicated its mistrust of him to other intelligence agencies, he had retaliated. Ghorbanifar had persuaded individuals whom he could influence not to cooperate with the CIA. *(Id.* at 1–2)

Ghorbanifar explained his present goal was the modification of the Khomeini regime and the alignment of Iran with the West.

> Subject [Ghorbanifar] stated that he wished to work with the US Government and CIA in a number of areas. Clearly, the US hostages held in Lebanon were a high priority. He would continue to work with the White House on this issue; this effort would be kept separate. A second are would be to assist the West in blunting Iranian terrorism. A third area would be working with the Agency to thwart Libyan and Syrian-sponsored terrorism and to assist in the overthrow of Libyan leader Qadhafi. *(Id.* at 2)

With regard to the hostages, Ghorbanifar made three points. High Iranian officials were interested in a new relationship with the United States. They could release, or kill, the hostages. Whether the United States pursued a relationship with Iran would decide the hostages' fate. If the United States missed the opportunity, the hostages would be killed and new terrorist acts would occur.

Ghorbanifar's Tehran contact, Prime Minister Mir Hosein Musavi-Khamenei, and Minister of Oil Gholam Reza Aqazadeh "'will lose face' soon" unless the United

States went forward with arms supplies through Israel. These men told President Ali Khameini that the United States was willing to provide advanced weapons "in return for Tehran's promise to secure the release of US hostages held in Lebanon. They had assured other senior officials that a long-term relationship with the United States was possible and in negotiation; as a result, Iranian terrorist attacks against the United States had ceased for seven months. "Subject stated that 'the Islamic Jihad Organization (IJO)' would strike soon unless a new understanding was reached, perhaps as early as 24 January." *(Id.)*

Subject stated that he had convinced the Prime Minister and the Minister of Oil to trust the United States with Israel acting as an intermediary. Iran had shown "good faith" by paying in advance of arms deliveries in November. When the goods (Hawk surface-to-air missiles) arrived in late November, they were an "old model," costing four times the price "originally" agreed upon. The Hawk missiles are still at Tehran International Airport, awaiting pickup for return to the West. The Prime Minister and others believe they "were cheated." In fact, nine of the 18 Hawks have the Star of David inscribed on them. Subject stated that he has told the Prime Minister that, unless agreement with the United States is reached by 24 January, he would no longer wish to serve as an intermediary in dealing with the United States.

8. As far as his personal situation was concerned, Subject expressed no serious concern. Musavi-Khamenei, . . . and Aqazadeh all owe Subject substantial sums of money. [His Tehran contact], moreover, has been photographed in compromising situations with Western women, an activity that would finish him with the Khomeini fundamentalist government were it to become known. Even though all three individuals are identified with Line Two [fundamentalist faction] and have blood on their hands, he has no fear of them. What concerns Subject is that, if talks break down with the United States, widespread terrorist activity will ensue.

*(Id.* at 2–3) Ghorbanifar said the Prime Minister was willing to accept American military assistance, including advice and an unofficial presence in Tehran, but had been dismayed by the "cheating thing." *(Id.* at 3) Originally, the five American and two Jewish hostages were to have been released in connection with the shipment of HAWKs. Now, Ghorbanifar said, a "terrorist war" was possible. Shiite terrorism in Pakistan, which would prove worrisome to the United States, was likely. He added that the "Iranian Revolutionary Guard Corps (IRGC) can exert control over the Shiite captors of the Americans. All that is required for the Americans to be freed is for Prime Minister Musavi-Khamenei to issue an order and the IRGC will secure their release." *(Id.)* Conversely, the three Iranian officials could ensure the death of the hostages if there were no agreement with the United States. Ghorbanifar feared the Soviets might exploit Iranian factionalism; the second highest official in the Foreign Ministry was pro-Soviet.

Ghorbanifar gave a long exposition on his links with Qadhafi's regime and ability to carry out a "scam" by faking the murder of Margarieff, one of Qadhafi's targets; his sources of information regarding Iranian terrorism; his information about Syrian officials, who with the Polish government, supplied weapons to Iranian terrorist networks; and his knowledge of IRGC—particularly those plotting a *coup de main* against Bahrain.

Characterizing Ghorbanifar, Allen wrote that he

is a highly energetic, excitable individual who possesses an extraordinarily strong ego that must be carefully fed. Intelligent and clearly an individual who has made a considerable amount of money in procurement of arms and in provision of "other services," he is relatively straightforward about what he hopes to get out of any arrangement with the United States. He deeply resents "his treatment" by the Agency in the 1980–82 timeframe and frequently speaks scornfully of a woman with the name "Lucy" from the US Embassy in London who met with him at that time. A personable individual, he also consistently speaks of his love of Iran and the need to change the composition of the current government there. It is difficult to gauge just what Subject's "organization" consist [sic] of but he appears to have influence over or business arrangments with a substantial number of individuals in the Middle East and Europe and inside Iran itself. We have hard evidence that he is close to the Prime Minister, the Minister of Oil, and other senior officials like an official in the Prime Minister's office. There is no question, however, that he exaggerates and inflates for his own reasons some [?of these?] relationships. He is impatient if one tries to pin him down on the specifics of some of the complex plots that he describes. For this reason, the best strategy is to go back over details in a series of meetings so that all aspects of the plot can be determined. This indirect approach takes time but builds rapport with Subject. The worst approach to Subject would be to attempt to lecture him.

*(Id.* at 8–9. Copies to: DCI, DDCI, DDO, DDI, DC/NE, O/ DDO (Clarridge))

At Ghorbanifar's request, on January 23, Allen met a follower of Ayatollah Shirazi, who was visiting the United States. He confirmed Ghorbanifar's connections "in key areas" of the Middle East. (C. Allen, "Meeting with Hojjat ol-Eslam Seyyed Mohsen Khatami," 1/31/86)

# H. The January 1986 Findings

After the December 10 meeting, Poindexter told the Secretary of State on January 5, 1986, the Israelis took action to "revive" the program. Prime Minister Peres' terrorism advisor, Nir, had seen Poindexter, saying

Israel would identify Hezballah prisoners held by Lahad [commander of the Christian South Lebanon Army] in southern Lebanon who were not "bloody" and offer to release them and to provide 3,000 TOWs in exchange for the hostages.

I [Shultz] said that this idea presented all the same problems as before. It would be a payment that "blows our policy," and Israel would have an interest in leaking such a deal. I remarked at the time, "so it's not dead" and noted that "Peres comes to me on some things and to the NSC on others."

I had been told that "Newsweek" had the story of the Kimche-McFarlane meetings, but did not run it. I noted that Kimche may have leaked it deliberately. My impression at the time was that Vice Admiral Poindexter's reaction to Mr. Nir's idea was negative.

The reason for all of that is that I felt that one of the things Israel wanted was to get itself into a position where its arms sales to Iran could not be criticized by us because we were conducting this Operation Staunch and we were trying to persuade everybody not to sell arms. That is what all that is about.

(Shultz, SRB, 37)[31]

CIA General Counsel Stanley Sporkin continued working on a draft Finding, and on January 3, he carried a copy to North. (CIA/IG Chronology 13) His draft offered a choice between notifying Congressional intelligence committees or postponing such notification until the President determined it would be appropriate. (Sporkin 26) North then prepared the necessary documents for Poindexter to submit to the President with the proposed Finding. North's draft Finding did not refer to hostage rescue until Sporkin insisted that it do so. (*Id.* at 22–23; CIA/IG Chronology 13) The draft Finding did not include the option of notifying Congress.

North submitted the package to Poindexter by memorandum dated January 4. North wrote that the Finding was

based on our discussions with Nir and my subsequent meeting with CIA General Counsel Stanley Sporkin

At Sporkin's request, I talked to Bill Casey on [telephone] re the Finding and the overall approach. He indicated that he thought the finding was good and that this is probably the only approach that will work. He shares our goal of achieving a more moderate government in Iran through this process.

(North to Poindexter, Action Memorandum, 1/4/86.) The package included a memorandum from Poindexter to the President and a Finding, dated January 6.[32]

*ACTION*
MEMORANDUM FOR THE PRESIDENT
FROM: JOHN M. POINDEXTER
SUBJECT: Covert Action Finding regarding Iran
This week, Prime Minister Peres of Israel secretly dispatched his special advisor on terrorism with instructions to propose a plan by which [Israel with limited assistance from the U.S.,][33] can act [in concert] to bring about a more moderate government in Iran. [The Israelis are very concerned that Iran's deteriorating position in the war with Iraq, the potential for further radicalization in Iran, and the possibility of enhanced Soviet influence in the Gulf all pose significant threats to the security of Israel. They believe it is essential that they act to at least preserve a balance of power in the region.][34]

The Israeli plan is premised on the assumption that moderate elements in Iran can come to power if these factions demonstrate their credibilty in defending Iran against Iraq and in deterring Soviet intervention. To achieve the strategic goal of a more moderate Iranian government, the Israelis are prepared to unilaterally commence selling military materiel to Western-oriented Iranian factions. It is their belief that by so doing they can achieve a heretofore unobtainable penetration of the Iranian governing heirarchy [sic]. The Israelis are convinced that the Iranians are so desperate for military materiel, expertise and intelligence that the provision of these resources will result in favorable long-term changes in personnel and attitudes within the Iranian government. Further, once the exchange relationship has commenced, a dependency would be established on those who are providing the requisite resources, thus allowing the providor(s) to coercively influence near-term events. [Such an outcome is consistent with our policy objectives and would present significant advantages for U.S. national interests.]

As described by the Prime Minister's emissary, the only requirement the Israelis have is an assurance that they will be allowed to purchase U.S. replenishments for the stocks that they sell to Iran. [Since the Israeli sales are technically a violation of our Arms Export Control Act embargo for Iran,] a Presidential Covert Action Finding is required in order for us to allow the Israeli [transfers to proceed, for our subsequent replenishment sales to Israel, or for other assistance which may be deemed appropriate (e.g., intelligence).][35]

The Covert Action Finding attached at Tab A provides the lattitude [sic] for the transactions indicated above to proceed. If this Finding is signed, we would not interfere when the Israelis unilaterally commence sales and deliveries of TOW missiles during January, 1986. [The Finding also authorizes U.S. sales of] basic TOWs to Israel when they submit purchase orders for replenishing their own stocks.

The Iranians have indicated an immediate requirement for 4,000 basic TOW weapons for use in the launchers they already hold. We would be expected to replace the Israeli stocks in less than 30 days. 4,000 missiles represent [a significant percentage] of all available TOWs in Israel.

[The Israelis are sensitive to a strong U.S. desire to free our Beirut hostages and have insisted that the Iranians demonstrate both influence and good intent by an early release of the five Americans. Both sides have agreed that the hostages will be immediately released upon commencement of this action.][36] Prime Minister Peres had his emissary pointedly note that they well understand our position on [not] making concessions to terrorists. They also point out, however, that terrorist groups, movements, and organizations are significantly easier to influence through governments than they are by direct approach. In that we have been unable to exercise any suasion over Hezballah during the course of nearly two years of kidnappings, this approach through the government of Iran may well be our *only* way to achieve the release of the Americans held in Beirut. It must again be noted that since this dialogue with the Iranians began in September, Reverend Weir has been released and there have been no Shia terrorist attacks against American or Israeli persons, property, or interests.

The Israelis have asked for our urgent response to this proposal so that they can plan accordingly. They note that [conditions inside both Iran and Lebanon are highly volatile and that] the current crisis in the Middle East provides a rationale for a significant [Israeli] purchase of TOWs and expedited delivery on our part. The Israelis are cognizant that this entire operation will be terminated if the Iranians abandon their government or allow further acts of terrorism. In order to provide an answer to Prime Minister Peres, the Finding at Tab A should be discussed[37] with Secretaries Shultz, Weinberger, Director Casey and Attorney General Meese. [Because of the extreme sensitivity of this project, it is recommended that you exercise your constitutional perogative [sic] to withhold notification of the Finding to the Congressional oversight committees until such time that you deem it to be appropriate.][38]

The following Finding was attached:

I hereby find that the following operation in a foreign country (including all support necessary to such operation) is important to the national security of the United States, and due to its extreme sensitivity and security risks, I determine it is essential to limit prior notice, and direct the Director of Cental Intelligence to refrain from reporting this Finding to the Congress as provided in Section 501 of the National Security Act of 1947, as amended, until I otherwise direct.

*SCOPE* Iran

*DESCRIPTION* [Assist selected friendly foreign liaison services, third countries, which have established relationships with Iranian elements, groups, and individuals] sympathetic to U.S. Government interests and which do not conduct or support terrorist actions directed against U.S. persons, property or interests, for the purpose of: (1) establishing a more moderate government in Iran, and (2) obtaining from them significant intelligence not otherwise obtainable, to determine the current Iranian Government's intentions with respect to its neighbors and with respect to terrorist acts, [and (3) furthering the release of the American hostages held in Beirut and preventing additional terrorist acts by these groups.][39] Provide funds, intelligence, counter-intelligence, training, guidance and communications, and other necessary assistance to these elements, groups, individuals, liaison services and third countries in support of these activities. The USG will act to facilitate efforts by third parties and third countries to establish contact with moderate elements within and outside the Government of Iran by providing these elements with arms, equipment and related materiel in order to enhance the credibility of these elements in their effort to achieve a more pro-U.S. government in Iran by demonstrating their ability to obtain requisite resources to defend their country against Iraq and intervention by the Soviet Union. This support will be discontinued if the U.S. Government learns that these elements have abandoned their goals of moderating their government and appropriated the materiel for purposes other than that [sic] provided by this Finding.

Regan remembered that Poindexter brought the idea of the Finding and the draft to the President.

[E]ither on the way back from the west coast or immediately upon our return from the west coast—I'm not sure which—Poindexter told the President that we had had more contacts from the Israelis urging a new line with the Iranians. But he said he wanted to do this in a proper fashion and wanted to have a Finding so that the thing could be put on a regular track and kept moving, if we were going to exploit it. And he brought in a tentative document, a Finding, for the President to sign.

There were a few things that had to be changed in that as a result of discussions, and then there was a formal meeting in the first part of January on this subject, and NSPG, a formal meeting.

As a result of that, the President decided that we should pursue this line, that we should be prepared to sell arms, and that we should make a Finding that would authorize and justify that and that he would sign it.

\* \* \*

It was discussed with the President, the Vice President and myself on January 6 as, "[h]ere's something."[40] You know how you brief the President 24 hours in advance of this next meeting so when [he] is doing his homework he is familiar with the subject.

He was given that piece of paper by John Poindexter at a regular Monday morning meeting, a 9:30 meeting, saying "[t]his is what we're going to discuss tomorrow," and the President signing it for some reason. I don't know. I think it was in error.

(Regan 17–18; 22–23) After the President signed this draft, Sporkin reviewed it and, by hand, added the words "and third parties" after "third countries" in the second line of the "Description." (Sporkin 24–25) The Finding was retyped before the President signed it on January 17; Sporkin's addition was the only change.

On January 7, 1986, the President and his principal advisors met, apparently after an NSPG meeting that morning to consider the Iranian project. As the Attorney General described it:

After an NSC meeting or an NSC type meeting in the Situation Room, a few of us were asked to gather in the Oval Office.

Now, if you have any information that would vary from or amplify on what I know, do not hesitate to bring up the questions. I am trying to recall from memory.

One of the difficulties that I have, and that I suspect others may have, is that I considered this so highly sensitive and classified that I took almost no notes at any time during the thing because I didn't want to reduce anything to paper. I talked with no one about it, up until a certain point, which I will relate.

So, therefore, the memory even a year later, is fairly hazy.

\* \* \*

Anyway, on the seventh, I joined with the President, the Vice President, Cap Weinberger, George Shultz, Don Regan, Bill Casey, John Poindexter, and I was there, and there may have been an assistant to John Poindexter. It may have been Don Fortier. I am not sure. . . . It was not North, to the best of my recollection . . . Bud wasn't there. . . . At that time, the topic was brought up about an initiative to Iran. It was discussed in some detail, largely by John Poindexter, with some participation by Bill Casey.

It dealt with some overtures to be made to what were described as more moderate elements within the Iranian Government, and it was related to establishing a relationship so that we would have some influence in the future at whatever time it was possible for the Iranian Government to change, either with the death of the Ayatollah, or what.

There was also, as I remember, some discussion that these moderate, these more moderate forces, thought that they might effect a change in the government even sooner than that event happening.

They also talked about this being helpful in terms of ending the Iraq-Iran War, trying to get a more reasonable policy where the Iranian Government would be less inclined to participate or support subversion and terrorism in other countries; and it was also talked about these people using their influence to try to help us get our hostages back.

All of these were factors that went into this strategic initiative in regard to Iran.

(Meese 3–5) The Attorney General noted that prior events, such as the arms shipments, were not mentioned; nor was he then aware that the President had signed a Finding the previous day.

As the discussion ensued, it was the idea that these people wanted a showing of our good faith and that that involved the shipment of some limited quantities of arms. They particularly talked about TOW missiles, I believe, and that they, in turn, would show their good faith by using their influence to get the prisoners, the hostages, back.

Again, this is not a precise recollection; but my general recollection is that this was anticipated: that it would take place over a fairly short period of time—30 to 60 days—and that that was kind of the general framework of which everybody was thinking, because they talked about us making available limited quantities of arms, then they would produce hostages as showing that they were really able to do something for us, and that we would then ship more arms if their good faith had been shown by helping us get the hostages.

It was kind of a sequence that these events would follow, along with each other.

There was also a discussion that, because of the extreme sensitivity, it was recommended that the President not inform Congress until we had gotten the hostages back. I vaguely remember there was discussion that as soon as we got the hostages, even on our planes en route to Wiesbaden, that we would notify Congress then, before it became public generally.

So, the subjects, and the discussion of a finding was made at that time, that a finding would be necessary because of the way in which this was to be done, with CIA being involved in the transfer of the weapons.

This was discussed for about an hour and twenty minutes or so. I remember because I consulted back on my calendar, and I had a group waiting for me in the White House Mess that day, and I was late to that luncheon by more than an hour.

Cap and George were opposed to the idea.

I don't remember what the Vice President or Don Regan might have said. Bill Casey was very much in favor of the idea.

My own views were that it was a very close decision. I have called it since a "51–49 decision." But I felt, in the long run, that the risks that were attendant to this probably were worth the potential benefit, and the potential benefits to me were both the opening into Iran and also the assistance that would be provided in getting the hostages back. . . . It was my independent judgment because nobody had talked to me about it beforehand. But it was also as a result of the discussion back and forth, and particularly Poindexter and Casey were the principal protagonists of going ahead and doing this. . . . There was a relatively thorough—I mean, it was very clear that their [Shultz's and Weinberger's] positions were that they were opposed to it, that George felt this was at odds with our policy in regard to terrorism, that it could hurt us with our allies or with friends around the world.

Cap was concerned primarily about the terrorism policy.

The rejoinder, I think by Poindexter, was that this was a special situation and that this was not at odds with our overall policy; it was an exception to the general situation.

I think what most influenced me was the idea that we would be taking—that the risks would be fairly short-term because if it did not work, we would be able to

222

stop it; if this didn't produce results after, say, the first foray, that the thing would be stopped. There was quite a bit of discussion about that, that this would be in stages so that it could be stopped.

We knew, in retrospect, that it did not work out that way.

But that was one of the things that made it, while a close call, more acceptable, as far as I was concerned.

*(Id.* at 6–10)

The Attorney General believed that the President had an adequate understanding of the arguments for and against the project. Nobody described the operational details, apart from the arms transfers from the Defense Department to the CIA. Ghorbanifar's name was mentioned, but not Khashoggi's or other middlemen's and financiers'. The "thinness" of operational security was not raised.

The feeling was that this would not be revealed, or at least not be revealed while the hostages were still in jeopardy, and the risks to the people involved was also discussed, so it was felt that they would not be revealing this.

*(Id.* at 11) The Attorney General had the impression "that the channel would be, sort of, simply from DOD to the CIA to the Israelis." *(Id.* at 12) The President was confident that the Israelis constituted "a relatively secure channel." *(Id.)* Nevertheless, the Attorney General remembered,

there were always, I won't say questions, but I think that the Iranians were the sort of a sticking point, that we had to try this out carefully and be cautious as we implemented this thing, to be sure that these Iranians would be able to or were sincere and would be willing to show good faith.

In other words, I think there was a question mark left about the Iranians that could only be tested by going through with this thing.

At his meeting with the Board on January 26, 1987, the President said he approved a convoluted plan whereby Israel would free 20 Hezballah prisoners, Israel would sell TOW missiles to Iran, the five U.S. citizens in Beirut would be freed, and the kidnappings would stop. A draft Covert Action Finding had already been signed by the President the day before the meeting on January 6, 1986. Mr. Regan told the Board that the draft Finding may have been signed in error. The President did not recall signing the January 6 draft.

The President told the Board that he had several times asked Secretary Weinberger for assurances that shipments to Iran would not alter the military balance with Iraq. He did not indicate when this occurred but stated that he received such assurances. The President also said he was warned by Secretary Shultz that the arms sales would undercut U.S. efforts to discourage arms sales by its allies to Iran.

The President did not amplify those remarks in his meeting with the Board on February 11. [He did add, however, that no one ever discussed with him the provision of intelligence to Iran.]

The Secretary of State also remembered the meeting as occurring in the Oval Office:

> I again stated my views in full. I recall no discussion about a finding then or at any time thereafter, until it was revealed by Vice Admiral Poindexter in a meeting at the White House on November 10, 1986.

> I might say that when he read out that finding, I said that's the first I heard of that. Cap, who was sitting across the room from me, said, "I have never heard of it either."

> I recall no specific decision being made in my presence, though I was well aware of the President's preferred course, and his strong desire to establish better relations with Iran and to save the hostages.

> So I felt at that meeting that Cap was against it and I was against it and everybody else in the room was in favor.

\* \* \*

Well, I stated all of the reasons why I felt it was a bad idea, and nobody, in retrospect, has thought of a reason that I didn't think of. I mean, I think this is all very predictable, including the argument against those who said well, this is all going to be secret or it is all going to be deniable; that that is nonsense.

So, all of that was said. And in that January 7 meeting, I know that I not only stated these things, but I was very concerned about it, and I expressed myself as forcefully as I could. That is, I didn't just sort of rattle these arguments off. I was intense. The President knew that.

The President was well aware of my views. I think everybody was well aware of my views.

It wasn't just saying oh, Mr. President, this is terrible, don't do it. There were reasons given that were spelled out and which are the reasons that you would expect.

\* \* \*

[N]obody said very much. As I made these arguments, Cap basically agreed with them. He didn't restate them. But I took the initiative as the person in the room who was opposed to what was being proposed. I cannot give you a full accounting, but it was clear to me by the time we went out that the President, the Vice President, the Director of Central Intelligence, the Attorney General, the Chief of Staff, the National Security Advisor all had one opinion and I had a different one and Cap shared it.

\* \* \*

The nature of the players the risks when—I would say "when," not "if"—it came forward publicly—the description always was that Israel was going to be the conduit, and, therefore, it would be deniable, and we'd just say well, we don't know anything about it, and it's something Israel is doing, and so on. All of this was argued with, that it wouldn't work.

Regan's recollection differed. He recalled discussion of Congressional notification at the NSPG meeting.

I remember Casey speaking on it and Ed Meese speaking on it at the NSPG on December 7 [sic: January 7], that this should be on a close hold basis . . . and notification given later to the Congress because there were lives involved where we would be dealing here with hostages and because of the sensitivity of the new contacts we were attempting to establish within Iran being blown if there was premature disclosure, that the notification should come later rather than now.

\* \* \*

Now why did the President do it? There are two things, I think. First of all, he does have this feeling, still has this feeling, that we cannot allow Iran to fall into the Soviet camp. Khomeini is 86. He's been reported and reported in ill health and on the verge of death. We have no contacts there. We are alone. Well, not alone, but we are one of six nations that doesn't have an ambassador or some type of relationship with that country.

We are in the position of not being able to be ballplayers there if any type of situation erupts as a result of the Ayatollah and we should have contacts.

Secondly, there is no doubt in our minds that they have an enormous amount of influence on various religious factions within the Lebanon-Syria area. Some of these factions probably have our hostages and they can be instrumental in getting those out, and he wants to keep that avenue open.

I think [that] is what led him to do it.

(Regan 24, 29)

In response to a question about the degree of discussion of the risks, Regan noted:

The President was told, but by no means was it really teed up for him of what the downside risk would be here as far as American public opinion was concerned. There was no sampling. No one attempted to do this. The NSC certainly didn't in any paper or any discussion say that.

I don't believe the State Department in its presentation arguing against this really brought out the sensitivity of this. None of us was aware of that, I regret to say.

(*Id.* at 30) Nor was the President warned that "all hell would break loose" with Congress. (*Id.* at 31) Regan heard, but disagreed with, the opponents of the program.

I recognized the validity of what [Secretaries Shultz and Weinberger] were saying, you know, that we didn't want to be in a position of trading one for one. Give me a hostage, and to get 100 rifles or whatever the price would be. No, we couldn't be in that.

But I have to be a little bit personal here. In my other capacity as head of Merrill, Lynch, I opened an office in Tehran for Merrill, Lynch and have very close connections in Tehran in the era of the Shah during the '70s. I believed in that country and I thought that that country had quite a future. And I recognized that for us, the United States, to have no connections whatsoever with Iran was a foolish thing to do from an international political point of view as well as an economic point of view.

And, accordingly, I was all for keeping a line open to whoever was the constituted government of Iran in an effort to sometime be a player in that country's future.

(*Id.* at 36–37)

The Secretary of Defense had an imprecise recollection of the meeting, except with regard to one point:

The only time that I got the impression the President was for this thing was in January, which was January 6 or 7, and at that time it became very apparent to me that the cause I was supporting was lost and that the

227

President was for it. And shortly after that, we got a call, I didn't, but Colin Powell did, I believe, from John Poindexter who by that time had succeeded, saying there had been such a decision and the President wanted us to proceed with the transfer of this initial set of arms. The numbers changed. I think initially it was 2,000, and went up to 4,000, but they were to be transferred in amounts sort of as drawn.

But we were to transfer them to the CIA and to nobody else. And I made clear that that was the only way that we would operate, that it had to be transferred to the CIA, not directly by us to anyone else because we couldn't do that, and that it had to be an Economy Act transfer, which as you know, means we've got to be paid value for it.

I said we would carry out the Commander-in-Chief's orders to do this, and obviously we would hold it as closely as possible because that was not only the direction but the obvious thing to do.

(Weinberger 14–15)

The President signed a new Finding, identical to the January 6 document with Sporkin's revision, on January 17. He told the Board on January 26, 1987, that the Finding was presented to him under cover of a memorandum from Poindexter of the same date. The President said he was briefed on the contents of the memorandum but stated that he did not read it. This is reflected in Poindexter's hand-written note on the memorandum. That note also indicates that the Vice President, Regan, and Fortier were present for the briefing.

Regan did not recall the event. He wondered if Poindexter had not simply placed the document in the President's daily briefing book for signature during the morning intelligence briefing. (Regan 20, 41–42)

The Action Memorandum to the President to which the Finding was attached differed in few, but material respects from the memorandum submitted January 6. Unlike the earlier memorandum, it noted that the President had already discussed the matter with his principal advisors. It also contained a test for success: if, after 1,000 TOWs were transferred to Iran, the hostages were not released, the program would terminate.[41] The latter part of the memorandum contained the material changes.

Some time ago Attorney General William French Smith determined that under an appropriate finding you could authorize the CIA to sell arms to countries outside of the provisions of the laws and reporting requirements for foreign military sales.

The objectives of the Israeli plan could be met if the CIA, using an authorized agent as necessary, purchased arms from the Department of Defense under the Economy Act and then transferred them to Iran directly after receiving appropriate payment from Iran.

The Covert Action Finding attached at Tab A provides the latitude for the transactions indicated above to proceed. The Iranians have indicated an immediate requirement for 4,000 basic TOW weapons for use in the launchers they already hold. The Israeli's [sic] are also sensitive to a strong U.S. desire to free our Beirut hostages and have insisted that the Iranians demonstrate both influence and good intent by an early release of the five Americans. Both sides have agreed that the hostages will be immediately released upon commencement of this action. Prime Minister Peres had his emissary pointedly note that they well understand our position on not making concessions to terrorists. They also point out, however, that terrorist groups, movements, and organizations are significantly easier to influence through governments than they are by direct approach. In that we have been unable to exercise any suasion over Hezballah during the course of nearly two years of kidnappings, this approach through the government of Iran may well be our *only* way to achieve the release of the Americans held in Beirut. It must again be noted that since this dialogue with the Iranians began in September, Reverend Weir has been released and there have been no Shia terrorist attacks against American or Israeli persons, property, or interests.

Therefore it is proposed that Israel make the necessary arrangements for the sale of 4,000 TOW weapons to Iran. Sufficient funds to cover the sale would be transferred to an agent of the CIA.[42] The CIA would then purchase the weapons from the Department of Defense and deliver the weapons to Iran through the agent. If all of the hostages are not released after the first shipment of 1,000 weapons, further transfers would cease.

On the other hand, since hostage release is in some respects a byproduct of a larger effort to develop ties to potentially moderate forces in Iran, you may wish to redirect such transfers to other groups within the government at a later time.

The Israelis have asked for our urgent response to this proposal so that they can plan accordingly. They note that conditions inside both Iran and Lebanon are highly volatile. The Israelis are cognizant that this entire operation will be terminated if the Iranians abandon their goal of moderating their government or allow further acts of terrorism. You have discussed the general outlines of the Israeli plan with Secretaries Shultz and Weinberger, Attorney General Meese and Director Casey. The Secretaries do not recommend you proceed with this plan. Attorney General Meese and Director Casey believe the short-term and long-term objectives of the plan warrant the policy risks involved and recommend you approve the attached Finding. Because of the extreme sensitivity of this project, it is recommended that you exercise your statutory prerogative to withhold notification of the Finding to the Congressional oversight committees until such time that you deem it to be appropriate.

At the bottom of this page appeared:

Recommendation

*OK      NO*

"<u>RR</u> per JMP" That you sign the attached Finding.

Prepared by:
Oliver L. North

Attachment

The President made the point to the Board that arms were not given to Iran but sold, and that the purpose was to improve the stature within Iran of particular elements seeking ties to the Iranian military. The President distinguished between selling arms to someone believed to be able to exert influence with respect to the hostages and dealing directly with kidnappers. The President told the Board that only the latter would "make it pay" to take hostages.

The President told the Board that he had not been advised at any time during this period how the plan would be implemented. He said he thought that Israeli government officials would be involved. He assumed that the U.S. side would be on its guard against people such as Mr. McFarlane had met in London in early December. He indicated that Director Casey had not suggested to him at any time that the CIA assume operational responsibility for the initiative, nor was he advised of the downside risks if the NSC staff ran the operation. He recalls understanding at the time that he had a right to defer notice to Congress, and being concerned that any leaks would result in the death of those with whom the United States sought to deal in Iran.

# VI. The United States Sells Iran 1,000 TOW Missiles.

Before the President signed the Finding of January 17, 1986, North began to lash together the CIA and Department of Defense to implement the plan he had outlined to Poindexter in December and incorporated in Poindexter's memorandum to the President in January. Before January 17, he encountered resistance. Poindexter asked him to discuss the matter with the Director of Central Intelligence. North did so on January 14. He reported that

I[n] A[ccordance] W[ith] yr direction, met w/Casey last night after W'bgr speech at Ft. McNair. Casey then tried to contact Cap but he had already departed. Casey has called urging that you convene a mtg w/ he and Cap ASAP so that we can move on. Casey's view is that Cap will continue to create roadblocks until he is told by you that the President wants this to move NOW and that Cap will have to make it work. Casey points out that we have now gone through three different methodologies in an effort to satisfy Cap's concerns and that no matter what we do there is always a new objection. As far as Casey is concerned our earlier method of having Copp deal directly with the DoD as a purchasing agent was fine. He did not see any particular problem w/ making Copp an agent for the CIA in this endeavor but he is concerned that Cap will find some new objection unless he is told to proceed. Colin Powell, who sat next to me during Cap's speech asked the following questions (my answers are indicated):

Q. Does Copp deal w/ Iranians or Israelis?

A. With the Israelis.

Q. Is the intelligence a prerequisite?

A. It is probably something that can be negotiated but in any event it is not a DoD matter. It is covered in the [January 6] finding and is in fact one of the few means we have to make a long term penetration in Iran. Our ultimate objective of changing/moderating the govt. is served by this.

Q. What cost are the Israelis willing to pay for the basic TOWs?

A. They (thru Copp) have funds to pay Fair Market Value (FMV should be about $4900–5400 ea. depending on age) and to cover the cost of transportation. They do not have enough to pay for I TOW (about $9500 ea.) or TOW II (about $15000 ea.). We have frequently sold the Israelis weaps/materiel at FMV vice the replacement cost to the

U.S. Since we have over [quantity deleted] of the basic TOW in our inventory and cannot even use it in training due to its age, we ought to look at this as an opportunity to collect on a weapon which we aren't using [location deleted] (according to Koch) and will eventually have to dispose of because we cannot sell them off otherwise. (I'm told that Hughes Acft, the mfgr. has an agreement w/ DoD that all normal FMS transactions will be handled as a producer sale in order to keep DoD fm undercutting the production line by selling off old stocks.)

The most recent proposal (Copp as agent for the CIA and sales to the Israelis who then deliver weaps to the Iranians) can only work if we can get the Israelis to come up on their price. I have been unable to contact NIR who is in Europe for a meeting w/ an Iranian. He still does not know that we are aware that the Iranians have offered $10K per TOW. He has however left a message that we must have a go/no go decision today and that conditions in Brt. [Beirut] continue to deteriorate. You shd also have seen yesterday's [intelligence report] which pertains.

(North PROF note to Poindexter. 1/15/86, 12:04:22; 13:01:06)

While coordinating with the Defense Department and the Director of Central Intelligence, North also spoke to Nir about the Israeli-Ghorbanifar side of the transaction. Nir, who had just spent thirty-six hours in Lebanon, "believes that Gorba does indeed have at least $10,000 per Tow [sic] available," North reported to Poindexter on January 15, "and that Gorba probably lied to Schwimmer and that Schwimmer probably lied to Nir re how much there was available. Nir is fully prepared to proceed any way we wish but noted that time is rapidly running out." (North PROF note to Poindexter, 1/15/86, 15:41:44)

Nir explained his sense of urgency later that day.

[H]e believes the GOI [Government of Israel] is about to formally withdraw its offer to assist on this matter so that it cannot be blamed when the AMCITS are killed.

I asked him about [t]he rumor that one had already been killed. He replied that it was probably another of the Jews since they (Hezballah) will undoubtedly kill the Jews first to make their point.

I then asked Nir to reconfirm, the requirements as he understood them. He said that the Iranians want 1000 TOWs, 25 Moslems released by Lahad and the AMCITs and any surviving jews [sic] wd be released along w/ the Brit if they (the IRG) [Iranian Revolutionary Guard] can still find him.

The Israelis are very very concerned that they cannot make a delivery of 1000 TOWs w/o a promise to replenish. Nir points out that he is operating in an evironment which is very hostile since the USG never made good on its promise to promptly replenish the original 504 [sic] TOWs that they shipped in September and that if we had but sent these TOWs as promised it might have been possible to take the further risk of another 1000.

IAW instructions have invited Sec W'bgr to mtg w/ Casey in yr ofc at 1700 on Thursday. It is my sense that by that time we will have a msg fm the GOI that they are withdrawing their offer. Is it possible to arrange a telephone conference call tonight to see if we can make this work?

(North PROF note to Poindexter, 1/15/86, 18:34:47)

To clear up the confusion about what the United States had or had not promised Israel, on January 14, Poindexter asked North to speak to McFarlane.

As I [North] understand it, there was a USG commitment to SELL, over time, replacements to the Israelis for what they sent for Weir. We DO, according to RCM [McFarlane] have a commitment to make this SALE. We did NOT have any agreement on prices or ultimate dates, though it was understood by both sides that the transaction wd be concluded promptly.

(North PROF note to Poindexter, 1/15/86, 13:39:54 (reply to note of 1/15/86) Also on instructions from Poindexter,

234

North spoke again to Nir about how implementation was supposed to proceed, and how it, in fact, proceeded. Problems abounded.

As I understand the current problem w/ the purchase of the 504 [sic: 508]:

—The Israelis received funds adequate to purchase only the basic TOW. Whether this is because Schwimmer pocketed the rest or whether there was a kick-back to [Iranian officals in Tehran], neither Nir nor I know. Gorba told me that he had paid $10000 apiece for these weaps and pocketed $500 for each one delivered.

—When the Israeli purchasing office in NYC, following their normal procedures, made inquiries w/ the Army Materiel Command (AMC) on the availability and price of basic TOWs, the AMC immediately began to question why the IDF wanted to revert to the basic model which was no longer in production and the IDF has already begun purchases of the I TOW for their inventory upgrade. AMC noted that there was an "understanding" with the Mfgr not to compete w/ the production line by selling the older weaps fm army stocks and that selling fm Army stocks wd be the only source available for the basic TOW. At this point, the purchasing office terminated the inquiry since they believed that the purchase wd raise so many questions that it wd leak and complicate further action which, by then, was in the planning stages. The Israelis have made no further effort to purchase the basic TOWs but have been told in an unsolicited call from AMC that the basic model wd have to be the same price as the I TOW so that the AMC can recover replacement costs.

—Nir continues to be apprehensive about going back in to ask his people to ship w/o some kind of guarantee of replenishment whether or not it succeeds in getting the hostages out. He is going to get back to me at 0300 EST re results of his meeting w/ the P.M. I passed yr msg verbatim to include "cool yr plans on going into the Bekka." He laughed and noted that the IDF would have even greater impetus to go into the Bekka if the hostages were killed rather than released, thus there are some who have argued against proceeding on this tack any further since it jeopardizes Israel w/ no promise of return.

*(Id.)* In light of these arrangements and obstacles, North proposed simplifying the mechanics by reducing the number of participants.

At this point I believe that we could proceed along the following lines. Nir goes directly to Gorba (cutting out Schwimmer [and the Tehran contacts]) and gets $10M for 1000 basic TOWs. He then sends 1000 basic TOWs fm Israeli stocks to Iran. hopefull [sic] the hostages are then released. He gives Secord whatever the FMV price is for 504 TOWs from the $10M (should be about $2.8M). Secord then buys and ships 504 TOWs to Israel as replacement for the first exchange (Weir). This process wd at least provide the IDF w/ one third of what they had withdrawn from inventory. It is important to note that in my last discussion with Nir (he doesn't sleep either) he is very concerned about credibility all around. He noted that before they shipped the first 504, they had what they believed to be an ironclad promise to allow them to buy replacements but that all along the way there have been obstacles. He has confided that part of the pressure is indeed political in that he is concerned about a leak inside the cabinet from someone who is disaffected over the drawdown of stocks, but if we wanted him to push for it he would. I believe that Nir himself is both so exhausted and in such jeopardy of losing his job over this that he may no longer be functional. I do not believe that Nir is lying to us. I do believe he is sincerely concerned about the outcome and wants to do what he can—for both Israel and the U.S. He has promptly agreed to every proposal we have made to date except the final one of shipping 1000 TOWs w/o promise of replenishment. He will be back to us. Will advise.

*(Id.)*

The Americans pushed for a meeting with an important Iranian official. McFarlane asked Poindexter to have North find out from Nir when the meeting could take place. Kimche had told Ledeen that January 24 would be convenient. (McFarlane PROF note to Poindexter, 1/14/86, 08:08; Poindexter PROF note to North, 1/14/86, 09:27:35) Two days later, North reported that

> Nir has advised that the 24th still appears good IF we are proceeding w/ the first step of the long range plan to change the govt—ending the hostage problem and getting rid of the 18 HAWK missiles still parked in Tehran. He believes that if the first step is scrubbed that the mtg will be too. He will get back to us on Tuesday next week [January 23] re location and go/ no-go decision if we make an affirmative decision on the first steps re the hostages.

(North PROF note to Poindexter, 1/16/86, 13:39:54)

At the same time, the Director of Central Intelligence, Poindexter, and North expressed concern about Ledeen's role.

> Have told this to Ami [?Nir]. You [Poindexter] should be aware, however, that it is my opinion, based on my meeting w/ Gorba on Monday night [January 13], that Gorba tells Ledeen everything. Ami suspects that there is probably a secret business arrangement among Schwimmer, Ledeen and Gorba that is being conducted w/o the knowledge of any of the three respective governments and that this will result in at least some cross-fertilization of information. This may not be altogether bad if we can keep in touch w/ Ledeen enough to get a feel for what is really going on. I have no problem w/ someone making an honest profit on honest business. I do have a problem if it means the compromise of sensitive political or operational details. We might consider making Mike a contract employee of the CIA and requiring him to take a periodic polygraph. Yes? No?

(North PROF note to Poindexter, 1/16/86, 13:50:49) Further,

> Casey shares our concerns. More recent information tends to indicate that there is even further grounds for concern given what may well be/have been a financial arrangement among Schwimmer, Nimrod[i], Gorba and our friend.

(North PROF note to Poindexter, 1/24/86, 10:40:36) Perhaps because of these doubts, Ledeen ceased to be an official American contact with Ghorbanifar.

# A. Launching "Operation Recovery"

The day after the President signed the Finding, the CIA formally joined the program. Clair George, Director of Operations, Sporkin, and Chief of the Near East Division (C/NE), met Poindexter, North, and Secord and read the Finding. (C/NE (1) 4; George 9) C/NE and North then discussed logistics and financing. "At the meeting on that Saturday [January 18]," C/NE recalled, "it was clear that what was needed was 4,508 TOW missiles, which were to be sold to the Iranians as a portion of a larger strategic effort which would get all the American hostages back out, but would also move to changing the nature of the relationship with the U.S. and the Iranians." (C/NE (1) 4) C/NE thought the program had been "an NSC operation" since November; nothing that subsequently happened changed his mind. *(Id.* at 43, 44)

North instructed C/NE to contact General Powell about arranging for the CIA to purchase the missiles from the Defense Department; C/NE found Powell already working on the problem. Powell directed C/NE to consult Major General Russo, Assistant Deputy Chief of Staff for [Army] Logistics, about pricing. When informed that the TOWs would cost some $6,000 each, North told C/NE that old TOWs, useless to the American Army and in less than optimal condition, would suffice. These cost about $3,407 a piece. *(Id.* at 4–6) The Defense Department insisted on being paid value for the missiles; the CIA insisted that its treasury not provide a float; and the Iranians would pay only on delivery. North needed a Swiss bank account to hold the money. C/NE provided an already existing account as the quickest solution to North's problem. Setting up a new account for the sums in question would take time. *(Id.* at 6)

The structure made Ghorbanifar important to success; he raised the necessary "venture capital." *(Id.* at 7) As a result of the polygraph, George decided not to use Ghorbanifar for intelligence or covert actions and, moreover, to terminate CIA relations with Ledeen. (CIA/IG Chronology 14 (1/12 or 13/86)) The Director of Central Intelligence took a more flexible position, and C/NE followed his lead.

> The Director's position when this started up, late January-early February, was Ghorbanifar is a rascal. They had a lot of experience with this guy. He's unreliable. But the channel, there's something in this channel that's working and it's worth a try, and nothing else is working, so let's see where it goes.
>
> And if it doesn't go, we'll turn it off.

(C/NE (1) 23–24)

Deputy Director John McMahon, who had opposed arms transfers to Iran from the beginning, read the January 17 Finding on January 24. "[G]iving TOW missiles was one thing," he remembered telling Poindexter. "[Giving them intelligence gave them a definite offensive edge, and I said that can have cataclysmic results." (J. McMahon 14) He was unimpressed with Poindexter's description of the plan:

> [G]ive some intelligence to the Iranians on the Iraqi front, . . . to establish bona fides that the U.S. really was intent on moving in this direction, and then give them 1,000 TOW missiles and then see what the Iranians did, like release a hostage.
>
> * * *
>
> I objected to that. Poindexter didn't take me on. He didn't challenge that at all, but he said: We have an opportunity here that we should not miss, and we

ought to proceed to explore it; and if it doesn't work, all we've lost is a little intelligence and 1,000 TOW missiles; and if it does work, then maybe we can change a lot of things in the Mideast.

So I came back to the building. Bill Casey was [abroad] at the time. I sent him a cable laying out what was happening, saying we have a directive from the President, a finding to do this, Poindexter said that the Attorney General had checked off on it, and that we were so directed to proceed to support the mission.

And I said, I am so proceeding. I asked for confirmation from Bill to make sure that he was aware of what was happening, and I didn't receive any. Casey had moved on to [country name deleted], so I sent it again to [country name deleted]. And it came back saying: Yes, he has read it and confirmed, and he had seen it.

Then we proceeded to have DoD transfer weapons to us, and we would arrange for the flights over there. All throughout this, I must insist that even at its peak the Agency was only in a supportive role. We took directions, we followed directions.

*(Id.* at 14–16) On January 26, McMahon persuaded North to provide the Iranians only a segment of the Iraqi front. It would show American good faith without giving the Iranians a fighting edge. *(Id.* at 16–17)

According to the CIA Inspector General, North met Ghorbanifar in London before January 24. Among other things, they may have agreed that the United States would provide Ghorbanifar with some intelligence about the Iraqi front. (CIA/IG Chronology 17) Charles Allen transmitted the "limited" intelligence in London on the 26th; Ghorbanifar gave him information about Iranian terrorism in exchange. (C. Allen 13)[43]

When North returned from a late January meeting with Ghorbanifar in London, he prepared "a *notional* timeline for major events in Operation Recovery." (North to Poindexter, draft Action Memorandum, 1/24/86.)[44] "[T]he only persons completely cognizant of this schedule," North wrote, "are: John Poindexter, Don Fortier, Oliver North, John McMahon, Clair George, C/NE, Dewey Clarridge, Richard Secord, Amiram Nir, Prime Minister Shimon Peres." *(Id.)* The timeline was attached:

## Notional Timeline for Operation Recovery

### Friday, January 24

—CIA provide cube and weight data to Copp for a/c loading.

—CIA prepare intel sample for pass to Gorba.

—Copp provide a/c tail # to CIA for pickup. . . .

### Saturday, January 25

—Dispatch intel sample to Gorba via Charlie Allen.

### Sunday, January 26

—C. Allen deliver intel sample to Gorba at Churchill Hotel, London.

—Copp finalize a/c requirements w/air carrier in Oklahoma.

### Monday, January 27

—Gorba place intel sample on 1300 GMT flight to Tehran fm Frankfurt, Germany.

### Wednesday, January 29

—Gorba transfer funds for purchase/transport of 1000 basic TOWs to Israeli account at Credit Suisse Bank, Geneva.

—Israeli account manager automatically transfers deposit fm Israeli account to Copp account in same bank (bank record keeping transaction).

—Copp's account manager automatically transfers $6M to CIA account in same bank (bank record keeping transaction).

### Thursday, January 30

CIA transfers $6M to DoD account by wire service transaction.

—CIA orders movement of 1000 TOW missiles fm DoD storage facility Anniston, Alabama . . .

—CIA bills Copp account $26K for cost of moving 1000 TOW missiles fm Anniston, Alabama . . .

### Sunday, February 2

—Copp travels to Israel for site survey of transfer point (Eliat [sic], Israel).

—Copp proceeds to rendezvous w/Clarridge to establish command post.

### Monday, February 3

—Lahad responds to papal ltr that he will release 50 Hezballah prisoners in 2 groups of 25.

### Tuesday, February 4

—1000 TOWs sanitized and prepared for shipping. . . .

—Copp a/c packers arrive . . . and arrange for Copp a/c to lift TOWs fm Kelly AF Base, San Antonio, TX, on CIA contract.

### Wednesday, February 5

—Copp a/c arrives Kelly AF Base for loading.

—CIA provides remainder of first intel sample to Gorba at Iranian Embassy in Bonn, Germany.

### Thursday, February 6

—Copp a/c commence lifting TOWs fm Kelly AF Base to transfer point at Eliat, Israel.

—Isreali AF "sterilized" 707 a/c arrives at transfer point for loading.

—Copp aircrew arrives Eliat, Israel, to pilot Israeli a/c.

—Remainder of first intel sample flown fm Germany

to Tehran in diplomatic pouch on scheduled Iran Airways flight.

**Friday, February 7**

—Israeli "sterile" a/c piloted by Copp crew commences movement of TOWs fm Eliat to Bandar Abbas, Iran, via Red Sea route.

**Saturday, February 8**

—Delivery of 1000 TOWs completed.

—25 Hezballah released by Lahad.

—Returning Israeli a/c pickup 18 HAWK at Tehran airport for return to Israel.

**Sunday, February 9**

—All U.S. hostages released to U.S./British or Swiss Embassy.

—Second group of 25 Hezballah released by Lahad.

—Israelis return $5.4M to Gorba when HAWKs land in Israel.

**Monday, February 10**

—Gorba transfers funds to Israel account for purchase/transportation of 3000 TOWs (amount transferred is sufficient to cover purchase of 508 additional TOWs owed to Israel for Weir release and all transportation costs).

—Israelis transfer funds to Copp account at Credit Suisse Bank, Geneva.

—Copp transfers funds to CIA account for purchase/transportation of 3508 TOWs ($21.048M).

—Four (4) remaining Lebanese-Jews released by Hezballah.

**Tuesday, February 11 (Anniversary of Iranian-Islamic Revolution)**

—Khomeini steps down.

—CIA transfers $21.048M to DoD account for purchase of 3508 TOWs at $6K each.

—CIA starts moving TOWs . . . fm Anniston, Alabama, in lots of 1000.

## Thursday, February 13

—Copp packers return . . .

## Tuesday, February 18

—Copp a/c pickup 1000 TOWs at Kelly AF Base, Texas; deliver to transfer point (Eliat).

—Israeli "sterilized" 707 a/c w/Copp crew commences delivery of 1000 TOWs to Iran.

## Thursday, February 20

—Copp a/c pickup 1000 TOWs at Kelly AF Base, Texas; deliver to transfer point (Eliat).

—Israeli "sterilized" 707 a/c w/Copp crew commences delivery of 1000 TOWs to Iran.

## Saturday, February 22

—Copp a/c pickup 1000 TOWs at Kelly AF Base, Texas; deliver to transfer point (Eliat).

—Israeli "sterilized" 707 a/c w/Copp crew commences delivery of 1000 TOWs to Iran.

## Monday, February 24

—Copp a/c returns . . . pickup 508 TOWs for delivery to Israel.

—Collett (British hostage) and Italian hostages released and Buckley remains returned.

## Tuesday, February 25

—Second sample of intel provided to Gorba at Iranian Embassy in Bonn, Germany. . . .

By early February, CIA had put in motion the acquisition of the weapons, designated a Swiss bank account, and arranged for two Boeing 707s to be at the disposal of General Secord at Kelly Air Force Base. (CIA/IG Chronology 18)

## B. FORWARD

On February 5, North traveled to London. (North calendar) According to the NSC chronologies, he met Ghorbanifar, Nir, and Ghorbanifar's Tehran contact.[45]

Ghorbanifar told the Board

Let's say this meeting is somewhere around between first of February till fifth of February. It took place in Frankfurt . . . The Iranian delegation stayed also in Hotel Intercontinental, in Frankfurt—a mixture of Iranian authorities, from Prime Minister's [office] and Iranian officers from intelligence department.

This is a historical meeting, after seven years of break, that the two top officials of the two countries, they come together for such an important meeting, such an important mission, to work out against the intelligence against the Russians, against the Iraqis, and also to clean the mess [the November 1985 shipment of HAWKs].

(Ghorbanifar 131–32) On the American side, Ghorbanifar said, were North, Secord, and someone identified to Ghorbanifar as "one of the top senior officers from the CIA. His hair was all white, white hair, good looking—baby face.[46] . . . No[t] Cave. Cave came later on for making the total disaster." *(Id.* at 134) Nir, who was always identified as an American in meetings with Iranian officials, *(Id.* at 135–36), also attended. Ghorbanifar described a "happy" scene, with Americans kissing Iranians. *(Id.* at 136) The military men talked, and

Mr. North told him [Ghorbanifar's Tehran contact] that if you want to know that we were good feeling, good gesture, we were not going to cheat you now. We take out what we brought back in mistake [the 18 HAWKs] and we give you 1,000 TOWs. And then the

Iranian kissed them and they made again dinner party.

*(Id.* at 137) The next day, Khashoggi lent Ghorbanifar $10 million to pay for the missiles; Khashoggi insisted on a 15–20% return to pay finance costs. On February 7, Ghorbanifar said, he [Khashoggi] deposited the money in Lake Resources' Swiss account. North "told us that this time no Israeli deal. Off. This is ourself we directly will dealing." *(Id.* at 138)

> The money was paid to Lake Resources directly, and then they delivered the stuff. There was no talk of release of hostage. There was no hostage. So it is proof to you that there is no deal on hostage. There is no deal for hostage, tit for tat—give me, take this. You understand clearly it was a policy. It was a very big policy, very important strategic policy to go into water. No question about who is going.

*(Id.* at 142)

Whether or not this meeting took place as described by Ghorbanifar—his description does not resemble C/NE's of the Frankfurt meeting, February 24–25 (C/NE (1) 18-20)—North returned from London on February 7 (North calendar), with the operation in full swing. The next day or the day after, he met Charles Allen, C/NE, Noel Koch from the office of Assistant Secretary of Defense Armitage, and Secord to review the schedule. TOW missiles would be delivered, hostages released, and Buckley's body returned by early March 1986. (C. Allen 14) At North's request, C/NE made flight arrangements for Southern Air Transport, a former CIA proprietary, to fly into Kelly Air Force base. (CIA/IG Chronology 19)

The United States Army made a record of its role in the TOW transfer because of Congressional reporting requirements. Under the Intelligence Authorization Act for Fiscal Year 1986, transfers of defense articles or services by an intelligence agency worth $1 million had to be reported to Congressional intelligence committees. Once apprised of this statute, the Army General Counsel advised Russo that where the Army "support[s] another agency, it is responsible to make the necessary notification." (Russo, note, 2/13/

86, on Crawford to Marsh, 2/13/86) "During the course of coordination with OSD (M[ajor] G[eneral] Powell) and O[ffice of the] S[ecretary of the] A[rmy] G[eneral] C[ounsel], questions were asked as to the responsibility for end item usage. This was identified as a responsibility of the receiver." (Russo, "Support for Intelligence Activities," 2/25/86.) The "receiver" was Southern Air Transport, operating under the direction of General Secord and Colonel North.

The Army's involvement began on January 18 when it received a request to deliver 3,504 (later increased to 4,509) TOW missiles to "the receiver" at Redstone Airfield, for an unknown purpose and destination. Transfer depended on receipt of funds by the receiving agency. It was delayed. On February 10 and 11, a total of $3.7 million was deposited (by Ghorbanifar) in the CIA account used to pay for 1,000 TOW missiles. (CIA/IG Chronology 19) Having received certification that the money was available, the Army delivered the first 1,000 missiles on February 13–14.

North's and Secord's reports complete the story of the delivery. North's notional timeline had to change. On February 13, 1986, North wrote Poindexter that

Operation RESCUE is now under way. 1000 items are currently enroute [sic] . . . from Anniston[,] Alabama. Copp is enroute to Ben Gurion Apt [airport] to conduct final briefing for his flight crews who arrived today and commenced fam flights on the two Israeli 707s. All 1000 items will lift off from Kelly AFB at 1400 on Saturday. 500 will be delivered to Bandar Abbas to arrive at dawn on Monday [February 17]. The meeting we had wanted has now been slipped to Weds [February 19] by Gorba. We will explore a second mtg/agenda/location/participants w/ him at this mtg per yr dir. Second 500 will go to Bandar Abbas on Friday vice Thurs. Copp, North plan to meet in Frankfurt on Tues. [February 18] along w/ one of Dewey's people to wire my hotel room for mtg. Carrying the luggage C/NE gave me for this purpose is too much of a hassle going thru customs/airport security in Europe.[47] If all goes according to plan, Lahad will release 25 Hezballah . . ., hopefully on Friday. This wd keep our schedule for releasing the Americans on for Sunday, Feb. 23. Something to pray for at church that day.[48]

(North PROF note to Poindexter, 2/13/86, 21:29:47)

On February 18, 1986, North asked Poindexter to authorize the issuance of alias documentation for the delegation that would travel to Germany to meet Ghorbanifar and his Tehran contact on the 19th. (C/NE (1) 14) His memorandum reproduced Secord's February 18 report of the first delivery of 500 TOWs.

> Aircraft returned safely to Ben Gurion this morning at 0730 EST. Seventeen HAWK missiles[49] aboard. Gorba called one hour ago. [Ghorbanifar's Tehran contact]

will head Iranian side of meeting in Germany along with five others. Iranians will provide all names after we give names and titles to them through Gorba. All will arrive via private plane in Frankfurt, Thursday [February 19] p.m. Meeting to start at 1700 in Iranian Embassy (sic) for two hours. Iranians have asked for second delivery of 500 TOWs on Friday a.m. They say they will release all hostages, if, *repeat*, if [intelligence is good]. They say we will get hostages Friday or Saturday. They envision a future meeting in Iran with us to consider next steps while we are delivering balance of TOWs (3,000). We have already rejected embassy as meeting site. Suggested following names from our side:

Nir (Office of Israeli Prime Minister)

MGEN Adams (Director, Current Intelligence—DIA) (AKA—Secord)

William Goode (Office of President)

Albert Hakim (Support Assistant to Director DIA)

(Secord to North, 2/18/86, [?received at] 8:30 a.m., in North to Poindexter, 2/18/86) North identified Hakim for Poindexter as "VP of one of the European companies set up to handle aid to resistance movement. He is fluent in farsi [sic] and would need one time alias documentation as a DIA official." *(Id.)*[50] Secord, using the alias Major General

248

Adams, also needed documents—"[t]o date, CIA has refused to provide him with any alias documentation."

North wrote, "we appear to be much closer to a solution than earlier believed. [The attendance by an official from the Prime Minister's office] at the Frankfurt meeting tends to support our hope that this whole endeavor can succeed this week, if we *appear* to be forthcoming." *(Id.)*

On February 20, North, Nir, C/NE, and Secord met Ghorbanifar in Frankfurt. (North calendar) They expected the official from the Prime Minister's office, but he did not appear. C/NE remembered that: "we told Ghorbanifar to let us know when his Iranian friend came, that we were going home, and that we wouldn't be back until we had a confirmation that the Iranian had come off from Tehran and was waiting." That happened within a week. (C/NE (1) 13)[51]

(CIA/IG Chronology 19) On February 20, a deposit of $7.85 million was made to an Iranian account at Credit Suisse in connection with the delivery of the TOWs.

On February 24, North went to Frankfurt to meet the official from the Iranian Prime Minister's office. He returned through London. In Frankfurt, he, Secord, Hakim, Nir, Ghorbanifar, and Iranian officials held the meeting the Americans thought was going to occur the 20th. North returned to Washington on February 26 and reported on the meeting the next day to the Director of Central Intelligence, Poindexter, and McFarlane. He wrote McFarlane:

Just returned last night from mtg w/ [official from the Iranian Prime Minister's office] in Frankfurt. If nothing else the meeting serves to emphasize the need for direct contact with these people rather than continue the process by which we deal through intermediaries like Gorbanifahr [sic]. Because CIA wd not provide a translator for the sessions, we used Albert Hakim, an AMCIT who runs the European operation for our Nicaraguan support activity. [C/NE] accompanied so that I wd have someone along who wd provide "objective" account.

Throughout the session, Gorbanifahr intentionally distorted much of the translation and had to be corrected by our man on occasions so numerous that [the Iranian official] finally had Albert translate both ways. Assessment of mtg & agreement we reached as follows: — [the Iranian official] has authority to make his own decisions on matters of great import. —He does not have to check back w/ Tehran on decisions take [sic]. —The govt. of Iran is terrified of a new Soviet threat. —They are seeking a rapprochement but are filled w/ fear & mistrust. —All hostages will be released during rpt during the next meeting. —They want next mtg urgently and have suggested Qeshm Is. [sic] off Bandar Abbas. —They are less interested in Iran/Iraq war than we originally believed. —They want technical advice more than arms or intelligence. —Tech advice shd be on commercial & military maintenance [sic]— not mil tactics—they committed to end anti-U.S. terrorism. —They noted the problems of working thru intermediaries & prefer dir. contact—noted that this was first USG/GOI contact in more than 5 yrs. [sic] Vy important—recognizes risks to both sides—noted need for secrecy. —stressed that there were new Sov. moves/threats that we were unaware of[.] While all of this could be so much smoke, I believe that we may well be on the verge of a major breakthrough—not only on the hostages/terrorism but on the relationship as a whole. We need only to go to this meeting which has no agenda other than to listen to each other to release the hostages and start the process. Have briefed both JMP and Casey—neither very enthusiastic despite [C/NE]/North summary along lines above. Believe you shd be chartered to go early next wf [sic] —or maybe this weekend—but don't know how to make this happen. Have not told JMP that this note is being sent. Help. Pls call on secure yr earliest convenience. Warm, but fatigued regards, North.

(North PROF note to McFarlane, 2/27/86, 8:54:13)

C/NE recalled:

This is the second meeting. This is the first meeting with [the official from the Prime Minister's office], the second February meeting. This is the first time we've had somebody like this out. It should be a very interesting experience. This is a man who . . . is on the low end of the scale in intelligence for [his former profession], and he's an even dumber member of the Iranian Prime Minister's office, but he's full of a little fear and a little trepidation and a lot of distrust of the U.S., for we truly are the great Satan in his eyes.

But he has been promised hundreds of Phoenix missiles, howitzers, TOWs; just about anything else he wants, he's going to get in this channel. He's promised that by Ghorbanifar in order to get him to this meeting. And we are promised that all the hostages will come out after the first two transactions, and that we are going to have a meeting with Rafsanjani and President Khameini within the first two months of this procedure, and one of the things in the scenario was that sometime in April there was a precise date given that Khomeini was going to step down and that he was going to resign all powers.

This is extraordinary nonsense. Essentially Ghorbanifar, as a negotiating technique, lied to both sides to get them to the table, and then sat back and watched us fight it out. It was a real slugging match. It was awful.

At the end of the first meeting, which was at 3:00 a.m. on the 25th, we agreed to nothing except that we would have another meeting the next day.

The next day's meeting was an agreement that we would proceed immediately to ship in 1,000 TOWs as a sign of our good faith and that [the Iranian official] would immediately arrange for one or two hostages to be released as a sign of their good faith. We left the meeting; nothing happened. No hostages.

The communications were still going through Ghorbanifar. We had several hints at this meeting with [the Iranian official] that he wasn't happy with Ghorbanifar. Ghorbanifar was clearly very concerned that this Farsi speaker, Hakim, would in some way arrange to cut him out and have direct contacts with [the Iranian official].

There was enormous distrust all the way around. Nir

251

was insistent that we keep Ghorbanifar in it. They had a relationship that went back with him prior to the revolution. So they know him well, and they recognize his limitations. They recognize that he's a congenital liar, but they know how to deal with it and they know how to use him.

(C/NE (1) 18–20)

On February 26 and 27, 1986, the official from the Prime Minister's office remained in Frankfurt to coordinate the shipment to Bandar Abbas with his colleagues in Tehran.

The morning of February 27, North heard from Secord. The second 500 of the 1,000 TOWs had been delivered to Iran.

> 707 has signaled success and due to land at Ben Gurion in a few minutes.
> Met with Nir and Gorba this a.m. for one hour. Nir continues to agonize over the two soldiers, while Gorba worries about money matters and how he can stay in the center as the indispensable man. Nir then left for Tel Aviv. Subsequently, Gorba, Abe [Albert Hakim], and I met with [the Iranian official] for about one hour. Abe did beautiful job of rug merchanting with [the Iranian official] and also helped Gorba's ego a lot. He was extremely interested in Russian intentions. He propagandized a lot about Iranian fighting spirit and we assured him Americans respected Iranian people. He emphasized need for quick meeting at Kish[52] and said he would possibly, *repeat,* possibly surprise us by getting some hostages released before meeting. [S]uggest you make contingency plan to accommodate early release (i.e., as early as Sunday). So, bottom line is on to Kish ASAP to seize the potential opening now created.

("Copp 2/27/86 1020. 161455Z Feb. 86")

North wrote the following note on this message:

"1120 EST—707 Back at B.G. Apt.

Gorba got 13,200/missile Gets $260/missile Gives $50/missile to Ledeen.

(Handwritten note on *Id.*)

The Board has seen no evidence supporting the implication contained in this Document, and Ledeen "flatly" denied receiving any commissions in connection with the arms transfers to Iran. (Ledeen (1) 63)

North reported his later activities of February 27 to McFarlane:

Since the missive of this morning, met w/ Casey, JMP, [C/NE], Clair George and all have now agreed to press on. Believe we are indeed headed in the right direction. Just finished lengthy session w/ JMP he indicated that he has passed substance to you and has given me dates that you are not avail.

Will endeavor to sched. mtg so that these do not conflict but noted to JMP that it was their call as to date of mtg. Just rec'd msg fm Secord via secure device we are using. [The Iranian official] has again reaffirmed that once we have set a date we shall have a very pleasant surprise. Dick & I believe that they may be preparing to release one of the hostages early. Dick also indicated that yr counterpart at the mtg wd be Rafsanjani. Nice crowd you run with! God willing Shultz will buy onto [sic] this tomorrow when JMP brief[s] him. With the grace of the good Lord and a little more hard work we will very soon have five AMCITS home and be on our way to a much more positive relationship than one which barters TOWs for lives.

I value your friendship and confidence very highly and did not mean to infer that you had revealed these exchanges. By asking that you not indicate same to JMP I was only informing that I had not told him anything of it so as not to compromise myself at a point in time when he needs to be absolutely certain that this can work. He is, as only you can know, under tremendous pressure on this matter and very concerned that it go according to plan. My part in this was easy compared to his. I only had to deal with our enemies. He has to deal with the cabinet. Many thanks for yr. trust. Warm regards, North.

(North PROF note to McFarlane, 2/27/86, 20:11:51)

Meanwhile, McFarlane had written North that afternoon:

Roger Ollie. Well done—if the world only knew how many times you have kept a semblance of integrity and gumption to US policy, they would make you Secretary of State. But they can't know and would complain if they did—such is the state of democracy in the late 20th century. But the mission was terribly promising. As you know I do not hold Gorbanifar [sic] in high regard and so am particularly glad to hear of [the official in the Prime Minister's office] apparent authority.

I have just gotten a note from John asking whether or not I could go some time next week and the President is on board. I agreed. So hunker down and get some rest; let this word come to you in channels, but pack your bags to be ready to go in the next week or so. Incidentally, I have had periodic requests from Mike [?Ledeen?] to assist in getting visas for [sic] Gorbanifar to come to Switzerland . . . I have refused. Surely if they have any real bona fides they can get a visa in Tehran from the Swiss embassy or somewhere else. I do not intend to tell Mike any of this new info. Recommend against your doing so. Bravo Zulu.

(McFarlane PROF note to North, 2/27/86, 16:02:23)

North replied in the evening.

Am reading things out of sequence due to fatigue. Many thanks for yr note. Have responded to most of this in my reply re exchanges—before I read this one. Yr concerns re Mike are shared here. WILCO re the passing of info. He means well but poses a significant problem. Nir says he has info that Mike has a financial relationship w/ Gorba, Nimrodi and perhaps Schwimmer. If true, this is not good. We also know that Gorba tells Mike everything and that is an additional reason to get Gorba out of the long range picture ASAP. We will still need to have him involved in the TOWs transactions since he manages the financial end for the Iraniansin [sic] Europe. We ought to sit quietly and think about how we handle Mike so that he does not start talking out of disgruntlement (if that's a word). Have asked JMP for a session w/ you and Dick Secord as soon as possible after Dick returns tomorrow night fm Eur where he is setting up an arms delivery for the Nic resistance. A man of many talents ol' Secord is. Must be off. Am supposed to make a speech on aiding the Nic resistance to a group of supporters. Best regards. North.

(North PROF notes to McFarlane, 2/27/86, 20:22:22)

On February 28, Poindexter told the Secretary of State that the hostages would be released the following week. According to the Secretary of State:

Poindexter reported nothing about arms. Rather, he said that the Iranians wanted a high-level dialogue, covering issues other than hostages. He said the White House had chosen McFarlane for the mission, and that he would go to Frankfurt, West Germany, to meet with a deputy of Rafsanjani.

I [Shultz] said fine, but asked that Mr. McFarlane be given instructions to govern his negotiations. I was shown these instructions, and I was satisfied with them.

Wholly independent of the hostage issue, Vice Admiral Poindexter said the Iranians had asked for help on intelligence as to what the Soviets were doing on the Iranian border and in Afghanistan. He saw a path to reemerging relations.

Vice Admiral Poindexter said that the hostages would be released at the time Mr. McFarlane was meeting with the Iranians in Frankfurt.

\* \* \*

[T]he presumption was that, after the meeting, they were pursuing this matter, and that, as a result of pursuing it, the Iranians wanted the meeting, and the meeting itself, having it with a high-level person like Mr. McFarlane, the President's former advisor, was a mark of a high-level interest; and the other side of that coin was the release of the hostages. It's sort of like the London proposition returning again, I thought.

It seemed very unlikely to me, but I said well, if you've got that arrangement, that's great.

(Shultz, SRB, 51–52)

## VII. Hostages and Iran Pursued: March–May 1986

By the end of February 1986, the representatives of the United States were disappointed by the results of negotiations with Ghorbanifar and Iranian officials. But disappointment was gilded in hope, and the effort was pursued.

At this time, American policy changed with regard to terrorism. Since the terrorist bombings at the Rome and Vienna airports in December 1985, the United States was prepared to use military force to affirm its rights. In March 1986, units of the Sixth Fleet undertook what was described as a routine assertion of the right of passage through the international waters of the Gulf of Sidra. In the course of that exercise, ships crossed what Qadhafi had designated a "line of death," and Libyan forces attacked them. In April, Libya directed the bombing of a West Berlin discotheque frequented by Americans, and, in response, American aircraft attacked Libyan targets on April 14.

# A. Prologue to a McFarlane-Iranian Meeting, I: March 1986[53]

Preparations for the next meeting with Iranians, in which McFarlane was to participate, immediately began when North returned from Frankfurt. Clair George, with C/NE's support, urged that George Cave join the team as interpreter. C/NE recalled that he had told North on the way home from Frankfurt at the end of February that the government should provide an interpreter. Secord and

Hakim, who is of Iranian origin, had appeared at the first and second Frankfurt meetings, respectively, without prior notice to C/NE. (C/NE (1) 11; C/NE (2) 76) C/NE not only believed that the government could perform the roles assigned to Secord and Hakim, but also thought Hakim had a potential conflict of interest arising from his own business relationships. *(See* C/NE (1) 11–12, 40) C/NE recalled that Hakim was involved in arms transactions "that might or might not be legal. There wasn't any prosecution going against him, but there was a little suspicion . . . And North, to his credit, accepted that advice and we introduced George Cave." *(Id.* at 12)[54]

Cave had served in Tehran and was widely respected for his knowledge of Iran and Farsi. At this time, although retired, he was a consultant to the CIA. (CIA/IG Chronology 20; George 11; C/NE (1) 12; Cave 3) He had been responsible for terminating the CIA's relationship with Ghorbanifar in 1983, and had helped craft Ghorbanifar's polygraph examination in January 1986. (C/NE (2) 76) He joined the team on March 5. When C/NE introduced him to North, (North calendar; Cave 3), he recalled being "a little bit horrified when I found out that [Ghorbanifar] was invoved in this." (Cave 5)[55]

On February 27, the Director of Central Intelligence met with Poindexter, George, and C/NE, (DCI Telephone Calls and Meetings, 1–9/30/86); talking points were prepared on the same day for the Director, possibly for use in that meeting.

Continued discussions on a very serious and important matter and I would like to suggest some guidelines:

(1) The initial meeting should be exploratory only.

(2) We should provide information about the Soviet Union threat to the northern border, about the level and quality of Soviet arms going to Iraq, about the Soviet thrust in Afghanistan . . . That seems like another reason for emphasizing the Soviet aspect. If the fact of the talks leaks, that would be the best way to get public and Arab understanding of the discussions.

(3) The contact should be direct. Israel and Gorbanifar [sic] should not be involved in these discus-

sions. We can't afford any more telephone conversations which the Soviets and others can listen in on.

(4) The first indispensable step is to set up a secure commo channel from the point where the talks are held or some point in that country to Western Europe where further secure conversations can be passed through to Washington. We should have this before discussions begin, and for this purpose we should fly Secord into Teheran as soon as possible.

(5) The group at the meetings should be as small as possible. I recommend that it consist of McFarlane, North, [C/NE], a staffer for McFarlane, and George Cave. George Cave is an ideal interpreter. He speaks not only Farsi, but also Mullah and understands all dialects. He is a known and proven quantity. In contemplation of where these discussions could possibly go, we should avoid having a foreign interpreter, even though the man in Switzerland is accepted and trusted.[56] He should be our man.

(6) These discussions ought to go forward. The President should call Prime Minister Peres, thank him, tell him we are not going to take his man to the meeting because we think it is in the best interest of the two countries not to involve them directly at this time, assure him that we have Israel's interests in mind, and will protect them and report to Peres after the meeting.

(7) We need to continuously plan in case the discussions leak. The fact of discussions between the United States and Iran could change the whole universe. Iraqi resistance could weaken. The Arab world could go mad unless the discussions are carefully and adequately explained. Some element of the explanation could be:

—The Soviets have been talking to both parties for years;

—The Arabs would cheer if Iran could be moderated; and

—Of course, we will do almost anything to get our hostages back.

We should remember that leaking the fact of this meeting could be viewed as working to the advantage of Israel. Only four men in Israel know of the discussions—the Prime Minister, his military secretary (Neer [sic]) who attended the Frankfurt meeting and who is the Prime Minister's terrorism advisor, and Neer's boss in the Prime Minister's office.

(DCI, Talking Points, 2/27/86)[57] At the beginning of March, Robert Gates, Deputy Director for Intelligence, asked that briefing materials on the Soviet threat to Iran be prepared for McFarlane's use. (CIA/IG Chronology 20)

North, C/NE, and Cave travelled to Paris on March 7 to meet Ghorbanifar the next day.[58] On his return from Paris, North reported to McFarlane.

Per request from yr old friend Gorba, met w/ him in Paris on Saturday [March 8].[59] He started w/ a long speech re how we were trying to cut him out, how important he is to the process and how he cd deliver on the hostages if only we cd sweeten the pot w/ some little tid-bits—like more arms, etc. After his speech I allowed as how he was not getting the message, but that I wd reiterate:

—The hostages are a serious impediment to serious govt-to-govt discussions and this must be resolved before we can discuss any further transactions.—We remain ready to go to Kish [Island] or anywhere else to discuss issues of mutual concern as long as the hostages are going to be released during or before this meeting. —The real problem facing Iran—that of Soviet intervention was becoming a reality and the Iranians are in no position to deal w/ this problem. We can help—and are willing to because a free, independent Iran is in our best interests. Unless the hostage issue is resolved quickly and favorably, U.S./Iranian cooperation on opposing the Soviets is out of the question.

Much more said in this respect, but you have the essence. Bob Gates has assembled a nice amt of intel on the Soviet threat. . . . There does indeed seem to be a growing awareness in the USSR that their Iraqi friends are having their asses handed to them and that the situation in Afghanistan is getting worse, not better. . . .

(North PROF note to McFarlane, 3/10/86, 21:10:24)[60]

Cave recalled that, in Paris, Ghorbanifar purported to communicate Iran's present position. He indicated that Tehran was "prepared to do something to get additional hostages released" and was interested in pursuing a political discussion with the United States. (Cave 6) Ghorbanifar presented "a list of 240 line items for HAWK spare parts. This was basically what transpired at that meeting." *(Id.)* Cave remembered much discussion about why no hostages had been released after the delivery of 1,000 TOWs, but no explanation—"just the proposal that the Iranians had indicated to Ghorbanifar that they would be interested in opening negotiations with the United States, both on the political side and the strategic side. The one specific area that was first discussed at this meeting was Afghanistan." *(Id.)*

C/NE recalled frustration after the Paris meeting.

> We had delivered our missiles and the shoe was on their foot, but they were acting like the shoe was still on our foot. Ghorbanifar came to that meeting and said, well, they've decided they didn't want TOWs after all. So the TOWs don't count. What we need now are HAWK spare parts; we don't need any more TOWs. We want HAWK spare parts.
>
> And he presented us a list of HAWK spare parts he needed. So, you now, it's a bag of worms. I was present when North briefed Poindexter after that meeting, and Poindexter at that point was fed up and wanted to just cut if off entirely, forget it. It wasn't going anywhere.

(C/NE (1) 20)

As C/NE noted, the program was not cut off. Based in

part, at least, on reports from Cave, who worked under his direction, C/NE recalled:

> There was a lot of discussion essentially to try to figure out a way to get Ghorbanifar out of it and, North, who you must have sensed by now is a man of a lot of energy and a lot of determination, essentially kept it alive because of the President's personal and emotional interest in getting the hostages out—in my view.

* * *

The political reality of this thing was it would be very nice if you could get a strategic thing done, a real improvement, a real change in Iranian relations, a securing of Iran, again as having a relationship with the U.S. and denied to the Soviets. All that was fine. But the real thing that was driving this was that there was in early '86, late '85, a lot of pressure from the hostage families to meet with the President and there were articles in the magazines about the forgotten hostages, and there were a lot of things being said about the U.S. Government isn't doing anything, not doing anything.

And, of course, what is being done we are desperately trying to keep secret. And there is a lot of fear about the yellow ribbons going back up and that this President would have the same problems that the last President had had with Iranian hostages, Iranian control. We learned as time went on that the Iranians didn't fully control these hostages, but as it was being portrayed until Ghorbanifar got out of it there wasn't any question that we could get all those hostages out through the Iranians.

We had tried to do the same with the Syrians. We had tried the same through the Algerians. . . . There had been several emissaries sent secretly to see Assad. There were a lot of nice words said by Assad, but he never lifted a finger, not once.

On at least two occasions we told the Syrians precisely where those hostages were and the Syrians said we'll

261

do our best to see if we can find these people, and we certainly are going to make sure that nothing is done so that they are harmed as we try to rescue them. But we'll try to get them out right now. But we had intelligence that they weren't doing anything. Nice words, but no action.

So an enormous amount of frustration that there wasn't any other way and that there was an enormous amount of intelligence consistent from the time that Buckley was taken that the captors wanted to have an exchange, that the Kuwaitis would have to release the Dawa prisoners in Kuwait, the ones who were involved in the bombings there in December of '83, and that nothing else would work to get those hostages released.

And that was true until this channel released Weir.

*(Id.* at 21–23)

Prior to the March Paris meeting, Ghorbanifar received word from his Tehran contact that he was having difficulty persuading his government colleagues to respond positively to the delivery of 1,000 TOWs. He insisted that Iran needed 100 surface-to-air missiles but Iran would not accept more HAWKs of the type shipped in November. It was apparent that Ghorbanifar and his Tehran contact had discussed other arms deliveries as well.[61]

McFarlane was concerned by North's reports about the meeting in Frankfurt. He wrote late on March 10:

I guess I'm a little puzzled about the Iranian wiring diagram. From whom are we getting the word concerning a meeting in the Gulf? Is Gorba involved in that dialogue or is that info coming through the Israelis? It strikes me that it is probably OK to keep Gorba in the dark—to the extent that is possible to do if there is another channel. Gorba is basically a self-serving mischief maker. Of course the trouble is that as far as we know, so is the entire lot of those we are dealing with. The Soviet threat is the strategic menace and I would guess that they would like to avoid having the Russians in Iran. But it is going to take some time to get a feel for just who the players are on the contemporary scene in Teheran [sic]. So the sooner we get started the better.

(McFarlane PROF note to North, 3/10/86, 22:14:24)

On March 11, North answered McFarlane:

[Ghorbanifar] is aware of the Kish mtg and is basically carrying our water on the mtg since he is still the only access we have to the Iranian political leadership. It wd be useful, I believe, for you to talk w/ George Cave, the Agency's Iran expert. He shares our concern that we may be dealing only w/ those who have an interest in arms sales and their own personal financial gain. . . . Will advise. If you wd like to meet w/ George, pls let me know and I will arrange.

(North PROF note to McFarlane, 3/11/86, 07:23:34) On March 11, Poindexter told the Secretary of State "that this arrangement [a McFarlane-Iranian meeting in Frankfurt] had fallen through, apparently because Mr. McFarlane objected to the idea." (Shultz, SRB, 52)

Just before North, C/NE, and Cave went to Paris, Howard Teicher, who at that time was working on Libyan matters, again became involved in the matter. C/NE told him in the last week of February "I hope you're getting a lot of rest, you're really going to be tired." (Teicher 16) Teicher subsequently met with Fortier, Rodman, and North. He "was briefed orally on the President's January 17 finding, and advised that [he] would be providing staff support to Mr. McFarlane, travelling with him to Tehran, when the arrangements were completed that would permit a delegation to travel to Iran for meetings with the senior Iranian leadership." (Id. at 17) Teicher recalled being informed in general terms about a shipment of TOWs, "a joint operation with the Government of Israel," and that the Finding specified that Congress would not be informed at this time. He remembered remarking that he understood Congress was normally informed and being told that the Attorney General believed exceptions were permitted, as in this case.

Teicher was instructed to work with Rodman and North on terms of reference for McFarlane's use, and submit them to Fortier. (Id. at 17–18) Teicher later submitted a draft of terms of reference to North. (Teicher 2). An unsigned, undated draft document may be this draft (original spelling and grammar):

We are concerned with three problems of mutual interest:

1. . . . .

2. Soviets. The Soviets are deeply concerned about the possibility of an Iranian military victory in Iraq. The 1972 treaty of friendship between Iraq and the USSR calls for consultation between the two powers when Iraqi territory is threatened by hostile military action. The wording of this treaty is not specific so the Soviets have considerable latitude in deciding on actions to on the actions to take in their own interests. . . . The Soviets see the collapse of Iraq as greatly weakening their influence in the Arab Middle East. To date the Soviets have shied away from direct military assistance, but they have keep [sic] open the military supply line to Iraq. They have also increased their intelligence support to Iraq. This was particularly apparent during the Val fajr 8 offensive. Further Iranian successes in its war with Iraq might lead to Soviet military moves along the Iranian border. These moves would be the threatening type in hopes of drawing off Iranian troops from the Iraqi front. . . .

3. Syria. The Syrians are concerned about the consequences of an Iranian victory in Iraq. They see the inevitability of a clash of interests in Lebanon between the Syrians and the Shiah. An Iranian victory in Iraq will strengthen Shiah resolve in Lebanon. The Syrians also do not want a fundamentalist Islamic state in Iraq. Assad has been trheatened [sic] by fundamentalist movements in Syria in the past and has been forced to deal very harshly with them. The bombardment of Hama being the best example. Syria would like to see Iraq weak, but not overrun by Iran. Assad is already being forced to consider the possibility that relations with Iran are going to become strained

at some point in the future. Syria's most immediate concerned [sic] is its growing problem with
the Hizbullah [sic] movement in Lebanon. . . .

# B. Prologue to a McFarlane-Iranian Meeting, II: April–May 1986

The exchanges of fire with Libya in March and April
1986 complicated, but did not interrupt, attempts to
schedule a meeting between McFarlane and important
officials of the Iranian government. Toward the end of
March, Ghorbanifar travelled to Tehran, North reported
to McFarlane on March 20, "and returned with a proposed
meeting scenario that is being communicated to us thru
the Israeli, Nir, fm Peres' office. Still don't have details yet
since his secure comms down, but should have necessary
info tomorrow." (North PROF note to McFarlane, 3/20/
86, 07:21:03. 1986 PROF notes)[62] On March 25:

[The Iranian official in the PM's office] called the
phone drop that Dick Secord had given him. Al Hakim, who [sic] we passed off as a "White House interpreter" at the Frankfurt mtg. spoke to [the official]
twice yesterday [March 25]. The bottom line of the
calls is that [the Iranian official] wd like to have us
meet w/ the Iranian side next week at Kharg Island.
Supposedly, during the mtg the hostages wd be released and we wd immediately start delivering the 3k
TOWs and agree at the mtg to the delivery of spare
parts which they desperately need. They profess to be
very concerned about the nature of the Soviet threat
and want all we can give them on that score. Not sure
at this point how real this offer is, but he says Rafsanjani wd come as the head of the Iranian side. If this
looks like a go—and we shd know more tomorrow
when the next phone call is scheduled—how are you
for travel during the week of 31Mar-4Apr?

In part to work on scheduling, Ghorbanifar came to the United States at the beginning of April.[63] At the end of March and beginning of April, Ghorbanifar complained to Charles Allen and Nir about two calls from Hakim in which Hakim claimed to speak for the President. According to Ghorbanifar, Hakim said that there was no longer any reason for Ghorbanifar to be involved. (C. Allen, "Conversation with Subject," 4/2/86. CIA Docs.) Partly to reassure him, North invited Ghorbanifar to the United States on an urgent basis. He came on April 3, by Concorde. On April 7, North reported the meeting to McFarlane.

Met last week w/ Gorba to finalize arrangements for a mtg in Iran and release of hostages on or about 19 Apr. This was based on word that he had to deposit not less than $15M in appropriate acct. by close of banking tomorrow. Have talked at length w/ Nir who is handling him on thie [sic] bank xfer and Nir believes that Gorba may be having trouble closing the final arrangements back home. Per request of JMP have prepared a paper for our boss which lays out arrangements. Gorba indicated that yr counterpart in the T[ehran] mtg wd by Rafsanjani. If all this comes to pass it shd be one hell of a show. Meanwhile we have some evidence that Col Q. [Qadhafi] is attempting to buy the hostages in order to stage a propaganda extravanganza. As farfetched as this may seem, CIA believes it is a distinct possibility. Bottom line: believe you shd avail yrself of this paper @ yr earliest convenience. Wd like to see you anyway. Am going home— if I remember the way.

(North PROF note to McFarlane, 4/7/86, 23:18:58)

Cave recalled meeting Ghorbanifar on April 3–4 with Charles Allen, C/NE, and North. Ghorbanifar reported that the Iranians now proposed a meeting. According to Ghorbanifar, "the Iranians were looking at the hostage situation and hoping that they could get all the hostages released in return for consideration on arms, specifically the HAWK missiles and the HAWK missile parts and the

TOWs." (Cave 6–7) The Americans gave him a list of available HAWK spare parts.

Now, on the pricing, the way we handled the pricing is we calculated up all our costs, and this included the cost of the items, whatever shipping costs we had to pay for packing, guards, what have you, and we would give this figure to Colonel North.

*(Id.)*

North's memorandum for Poindexter to forward to the President reviewed the negotiations and specified how the profits on the sale of weapons to Iran could be spent. The Board has obtained no evidence that Poindexter showed this memorandum to the President.

*Background.*—In June 1985, private American and Israeli citizens commenced an operation to effect the release of the American hostages in Beirut in exchange for providing certain factions in Iran with U.S.-origin Israeli military materiel. By September, U.S. and Israeli Government officials became involved in this endeavor in order to ensure that the USG would:

—not object to the Israeli transfer of embargoed materiel to Iran;

—sell replacement items to Israel as replenishment for like items sold to Iran by Israel.

On September 13, the Israeli Government, with the endorsement of the USG, transferred 508 TOW missiles to Iran. Forty-eight hours later, Reverend Benjamin Weir was released in Beirut.

Subsequent efforts by both governments to continue this process have met with frustration due to the need to communicate our intentions through an Iranian expatriate arms dealer in Europe. In January 1986, under the provisions of a new Covert Action Finding, the USG demanded a meeting with responsible Iranian government officials.

On February 20, a U.S. Government official met with an official in the Iranian Prime Minister's office—the first direct U.S.-Iranian contact in over five years. At this meeting, the U.S. side made an effort to refocus Iranian attention on the threat posed by the Soviet Union and the need to establish a longer term relationship between our two countries based on more than arms transactions. It was emphasized that the hostage issue was a "hurdle" which must be crossed before this improved relationship could prosper. During the meeting, it also became apparent that our conditions/demand had not been accurately transmitted to the Iranian government by the intermediary and it was agreed that:

—The USG would establish its good faith and bona fides by immediately providing 1,000 TOW missiles for sale to Iran. This transaction was covertly completed on February 21, using a private U.S. firm and the Israelis as intermediaries.

—A subsequent meeting would be held in Iran with senior U.S. and Iranian officials during which the U.S. hostages would be released.

—Immediately after the hostages were safely in our hands, the U.S. would sell an additional 3,000 TOW missiles to Iran using the same procedures employed during the September 1985 transfer.

In early March, the Iranian expatriate intermediary demanded that Iranian conditions for release of the hostages now included the prior sale of 200 PHOENIX missiles and an unspecified number of HARPOON missiles, in addition to the 3,000 TOWs which would be delivered after the hostages were released. A subsequent meeting was held with the intermediary in Paris on March 8, wherein it was explained that the requirement for prior deliveries violated the understanding reached in Frankfurt on February 20, and were [sic] therefore unacceptable. It was further noted that the Iranian aircraft and ship launchers for these missiles were in such disrepair that the missiles could not be launched even if provided.

From March 9 until March 30, there was no further effort undertaken on our behalf to contact the Iranian

Government or the intermediary. On March 26, [the official in the Prime Minister's office] made an unsolicited call to the phone-drop in Maryland which we had established for this purpose. [He] asked why we had not been in contact and urged that we proceed expeditiously since the situation in Beirut was deteriorating rapidly. He was informed by our Farsi-speaking interpreter that the conditions requiring additional materiel beyond the 3,000 TOWs were unacceptable and that we could in no case provide anything else prior to the release of our hostages. [The Iranian official] observed that we were correct in our assessment of their inability to use PHOENIX and HARPOON missiles and that the most urgent requirement that Iran had was to place their current HAWK missile inventory in working condition. In a subsequent phone call, we agreed to discuss this matter with him and he indicated that he would prepare an inventory of parts required to make their HAWK systems operational. This parts list was received on March 28, and verified by CIA.

*Current Situation.*—On April 3, Ari Gorbanifahr [sic], the Iranian intermediary, arrived in Washington, D.C. with instructions from [his Tehran contact] to consummate final arrangements for the return of the hostages. Gorbanifahr was reportedly enfranchised to negotiate the types, quantities, and delivery procedures for materiel the U.S. would sell to Iran through Israel. The meeting lasted nearly all night on April 3-4, and involved numerous calls to Tehran. A Farsi-speaking CIA officer in attendance was able to verify the substance of his calls to Tehran during the meeting. Subject to Presidential approval, it was agreed to proceed as follows:

—By Monday, April 7, the Iranian Government will transfer $17 million to an Israeli account in Switzerland. The Israelis will, in turn, transfer to a private U.S. corporation account in Switzerland the sum of $15 million.

—On Tuesday, April 8, (or as soon as the transactions are verified), the private U.S. corporation will transfer $3.651 million to a CIA account in Switzerland. CIA will then transfer this sum to a covert Department of the Army account in the U.S.

—On Wednesday, April 9, the CIA will commence procuring $3.651 million worth of HAWK missile parts (240 separate line items) and transferring these parts to . . . This process is estimated to take seven working days.

—On Friday, April 18, a private U.S. aircraft (707B) will pick-up the HAWK missile parts at . . . and fly them to a covert Israeli airfield for prepositioning (this field was used for the earlier delivery of the 1000 TOWs). At this field, the parts will be transferred to an Israeli Defense Forces' (IDF) aircraft with false markings. A SATCOM capability will be positioned at this location.

—On Saturday, April 19, McFarlane, North, Teicher, Cave, [C/NE], and a SATCOM communicator will board an aircraft in Frankfurt, Germany, enroute [sic] to Tehran.

—On Sunday, April 20, the following series of events will occur:

 —U.S. party arrives Tehran (A-hour)—met by Rafsanjani, as head of the Iranian delegation.

 —At A + 7 hours, the U.S. hostages will be released in Beirut.

 —At A + 15 hours, the IDF aircraft with the HAWK missile parts aboard will land at Bandar Abbas, Iran.

*Discussion.*—The following points are relevant to this transaction, the discussions in Iran, and the establishment of a broader relationship between the United States and Iran:

 —The Iranians have been told that our presence in Iran is a "holy commitment" on the part of the USG that we are sincere and can be trusted. There is great distrust of the U.S. among the various Iranian parties involved. Without our presence on the ground in Iran, they will not believe that we will fulfill our end of the bargain after the hostages are released.

—The Iranians know, probably better than we, that both Arafat and Qhadhaffi [sic] are trying hard to have the hostages turned over to them. Gorbanifahr specifically mentioned that Qhadhaffi's efforts to "buy" the hostages could succeed in the near future. Further, the Iranians are well aware that the situation in Beirut is deteriorating rapidly and that the ability of the IRGC [Iranian Revolutionary Guard Corps] to effect the release of the hostages will become increasingly more difficult over time.

—We have convinced the Iranians of a significant near term and long range threat from the Soviet Union. We have real and deceptive intelligence to demonstrate this threat during the visit. They have expressed considerable interest in this matter as part of the longer term relationship.

—We have told the Iranians that we are interested in assistance they may be willing to provide to the Afghan resistance and that we wish to discuss this matter in Tehran.

—The Iranians have been told that their provision of assistance to Nicaragua is unacceptable to us and they have agreed to discuss this matter in Tehran.

—We have further indicated to the Iranians that we wish to discuss steps leading to a cessation of hostilities between Iran and Iraq. . . .

—The Iranians are well aware that their most immediate needs are for technical assistance in maintaining their air force and navy. We should expect that they will raise this issue during the discussions in Tehran. Further conversation with Gorbanifahr on April 4, indicates that they will want to raise the matter of the original 3,000

TOWs as a significant deterrent to a potential Soviet move against Iran. They have also suggested that, if agreement is reached to provide the TOWs, they will make 200 out of each 1,000 available to the Afghan resistance and train the resistance forces in how to use them against the Soviets. We have agreed to discuss this matter.

—The Iranians have been told and agreed that they will receive neither blame nor credit for the seizure/release of the hostages.

—The residual funds from this transaction are allocated as follows:

—$2 million will be used to purchase replacement TOWs for the original 508 sold by Israel to Iran for the release of Benjamin Weir. This is the only way that we have found to meet our commitment to replenish these stocks.

—$12 million will be used to purchase critically needed supplies for the Nicaraguan Democratic Resistance Forces. This materiel is essential to cover shortages in resistance inventories resulting from their current offensives and Sandinista counter-attacks and to "bridge" the period between now and when Congressionally-approved lethal assistance (beyond the $25 million in "defensive" arms) can be delivered.

The ultimate objective in the trip to Tehran is to commence the process of improving U.S.-Iranian relations. Both sides are aware that the Iran-Iraq War is a major factor that must be discussed. We should not, however, view this meeting as a session which will result in immediate Iranian agreement to proceed with a settlement with Iraq. Rather, this meeting, the first high-level U.S.-Iranian contact in five years, should be seen as a chance to move in this direction. These discussions, as well as follow-on talks, should be governed by the Terms of Reference (TOR) (Tab A) with the recognition that this is, hopefully, the first of many meetings and that the hostage issue, once behind us, improves the opportunities for this relationship.

Finally, we should recognize that the Iranians will undoubtedly want to discuss additional arms and commercial transactions as "quids" for accommodating our points on Afghanistan, Nicaragua, and Iraq. Our emphasis on the Soviet military and subversive threat, a useful mechanism in bringing them to agreement on the hostage issue, has also served to increase their desire for means to protect themselves against/deter the Soviets.

RECOMMENDATION

That the President approve the structure depicted above under "Current Situation" and the Terms of Reference at Tab A.

Approve—— Disapprove——

(Unsigned, undated memorandum, "Release of American Hostages in Beirut.")

The following "Terms of Reference" for a "U.S.-Iran Dialogue" were attached:

I. BASIC PILLARS OF U.S. FOREIGN POLICY

—President Reagan came into office at a time when Iran had had a certain impact on the American political process—perhaps not what you intended.

—The President represented and embodied America's recovery from a period of weakness. He has rebuilt American military and economic strength.

—Most important, he has restored American will and self-confidence. The U.S. is not afraid to use its power in defense of its interests. We are not intimidated by Soviet pressures, whether on arms control or Angola or Central America or Afghanistan.

—At the same time, we are prepared to resolve political problems on the basis of reciprocity.

—We see many international trends—economic, technological, and political—working in our favor.

## II. U.S. POLICY TOWARD IRAN: BASIC PRINCIPLES
### A. U.S. Assessment of Iranian Policy

—We view the Iranian revolution as a fact. The U.S. is not trying to turn the clock back.

—Our present attitude to Iran is not a product of prejudice or emotion, but a clear-eyed assessment of Iran's present policies.

—Iran has used "revolutionary Islam" as a weapon to undermine pro-Western governments and American interests throughout the Middle East. As long as this is Iran's policy, we are bound to be strategic adversaries.

—Support for terrorism and hostage-taking is part of this strategic pattern. We see it used not only against us, but against our friends. We cannot accept either. Your influence in achieving the release of *all* hostages/ return of those killed (over time) is essential.

—We see your activity in many parts of the world, including even Central America.

—The U.S. knows how Iran views the Soviet Union. But subversion of Western interests and friends objectively serves Soviet interests on a global scale.

—Thus, our assessment is that a decisive Iranian victory in the war with Iraq would only unleash greater regional instability, a further erosion of the Western position, and enhanced opportunities for Soviet trouble-making.

—The U.S. will therefore do what it can to prevent such a development. We regard the war as dangerous in many respects and would like to see an end to it.

### B. Possible Intersection of U.S.-Iranian Interests

—Despite fundamental conflicts, we perceive several possible intersections of U.S. and Iranian interests. I propose to explore these areas.

—First, the U.S. has had a traditional interest in seeing Iran preserve its territorial integrity and independence. This has not changed. The U.S. opposes Soviet designs on Iran.

—Second, we have no interest in an Iraqi victory over Iran. [Discussion of US-Iraq Relationship] We are seeking an end to this conflict and want to use an improved relationship with Iran to further that end.

—Third, we have parallel views on Afghanistan. Soviet policy there is naked aggression, a threat to all in the region. Our mutual friends—China and Pakistan—are threatened. We have ties with different elements of the Mujahideen. But our objective is the same: the Soviets must get out and let the Afghan people choose their own course.

## C. U.S. Objective Today

—We have no illusions about what is possible in our bilateral relations. Perhaps this meeting will reveal only a limited, momentary, tactical coincidence of interests. Perhaps more. We are prepared either way.

—In essence, we are prepared to have whatever kind of relationship with Iran that Iran is prepared to have with us.

## III. SOVIET MILITARY POSTURE

—[Discussion of Soviet interests in Iran]

—Afghanistan illustrates the price the Soviets are ready to pay to expand areas under their direct control.

—Summarize Soviet capabilities along border and inside Afghanistan which could threaten Tehran.

—U.S. is aware of Soviet activity in Baluchistan, air strikes.

—Iranian support to Sandinista regime in Nicaragua aids and abets Soviet designs—makes U.S.-Iranian relationship more difficult ($100 million in oil last year, plus arms).

—U.S. can help Iran cope with Soviet threat.

## IV. AFGHANISTAN

—[Discussion of situation in Afghanistan]

## V. HARDWARE

—We may be prepared to resume a limited supply relationship.

—However, its evolution and ultimate scope will depend on whether our convergent or our divergent interests come to loom larger in the overall picture.

—What does Iran want?

("Terms of Reference U.S.-Iran Dialogue," 4/4/86)[64]

Ghorbanifar conveyed the Iranian response to Allen on April 8. He said "he had 'good news,'" asserting that an agreement had been reached in accordance with Washington's wishes." (C. Allen, "Conversation with [Ghorbanifar]," 4/8/86) He claimed to be "working the problem through Line One adherents, i.e. those conservative elements within the Iranian Government that are concerned over the Soviets and who do not believe that the clerics should necessarily be in charge of all government activities." (*Id.*)

During April, other activities, including the strike against Libya, occupied the attention of those responsible for the Iran operation. Progress toward the long-promised high-level meeting with representatives of the Iranian government was slow. On April 16, North wrote Poindexter that:

Recognize that all are very busy. Have been unable to get thru to you or Don [Fortier] via phone/appointment. [C/NE] and Gates have urged that Cave and North proceed tomorrow to meet with [the Iranian official] and Gorba in Frankfurt on Friday, and return to Washington on Saturday. All this based on a series of phone calls btwn Gorba/[the Iranian official]; North/ Nir; Nir/Gorba; Allen/Gorba over the last 72 hours.[65] In order to arrive for a Friday mtg Cave/North wd fly out tomorrow night to arrive Friday a.m. No deposit has been made yet because Nir does not want to risk losing the money if the operation is not going to go to closing.

He doesn't need the 240 parts. We have a problem on our side in that over 50 of the parts now do not appear to be in stock or are no longer made for our version of the system. Nir is checking in their older inventories to see if they have them on hand. Please advise soonest, must make reservations.

(North PROF note to Poindexter, 4/16/86, 16:40:45) Poindexter replied:

You may go ahead and go, but I want several points made clear to them. There are not to be any parts delivered until all the hostages are free in accordance with the plan that you layed out for me before. None of this half shipment before all are released crap. It is either all or nothing. Also you may tell them that the President is getting very annoyed at their continual stalling. He will not agree to any more changes in the plan. Either they agree finally on the arrangements that have been discussed or we are going to permanently cut off all contact. If they really want to save their asses from the Soviets, they should get on board. I am beginning to suspect that [the official in the PM's office] doesn't have much authority.

(Poindexter PROF note to North, copy to Thompson, 4/16/86, 21:08:42)

The President said he had no knowledge of the diversion prior to his conversation with Attorney General Meese on November 25, 1986. No evidence has come to light to suggest otherwise. Contemporaneous Justice Department staff notes of North's interview with the Attorney General on November 23, 1986, show North telling the Attorney General that only he, McFarlane, and Poindexter were aware of the diversion.

North reported the last days' activities to McFarlane on April 21.

Both Charlie Allen and Nir have been in touch w/ Gorba in an effort to set up a meeting with [the Iranian official] in Europe. We know that [the Iranian official] is apparently trying to extract additional concessions from us prior to releasing the Americans. George Cave, our resident expert believes that [the Iranian official] had probably received some kind of authority to cause the release of the hostages prior to our Libyan action and that the current delays and efforts to force new concessions are a consequence of internal disputes over what the Iranians shd do about this matter in the wake of the U.S. action in Libya. Gorba has been out of touch all day and Cave/North cancelled the trip to Frankfurt for a second time because we do not want to meet again w/ only Gorba. The Kilburn tragedy has us very concerned because there appears to be some possibility of Syrian complicity in Kilburn's death and the same could happen to our other hostages if the Syrians are able to put their hands on them.

If the mtg takes place this week it would still be a minimum of eight and a maximum of 10 days from deposit of funds before we can assemble the requisite parts. We do not believe they will make this deposit until after the mtg. We also need to make it known that we simply do not have some of the parts requested since we have modernized our HAWK systems. I have sent Nir a coded msg asking him to determine whether or not they have in stock the items which we lack. If it is determined that they do not have them we will have to determine the effect this will have on the understanding we reached last week w/ Gorba. Nir believes that the Israelis will be able to give us an answer in the next 2 days. Cave and North are prepared to lunch again tomorrow if Gorba surfaces and has set up a mtg w/ [his Tehran contact]. Bottom line: earliest timeframe for RCM/Cave/North trip to Iran is 30 April and this will slip a day for every day of delay in the Frankfurt mtg & its complementary financial transaction.

(North PROF note to McFarlane, 4/21/86, 20:31:28) Poindexter transmitted North's note to McFarlane and added the following cover:

> [The Iranian official] wants all of the HAWK parts delivered before the hostages are released. I have told Ollie that we can not do that. The sequence has to be 1) meeting; 2) release of hostages; 3) delivery of HAWK parts. The President is getting quite discouraged by this effort.
>
> This will be our last attempt to make a deal with the Iranians. Next step is a Frankfurt meeting with Gorba, [the Iranian official], North and Cave. Sorry for the inconvenience.

(Poindexter PROF note to McFarlane, 4/21/86, 20:31) McFarlane agreed with Poindexter's outline. "Your firmness against the recurrent attempts to up the ante is correct," McFarlane responded. "Wait them out; they will come round. I will be flexible." (McFarlane PROF note to Poindexter, 4/22/86, 20:35:17)

In North's view, the situation warranted continued pursuit of the meeting and consummation of the transaction. He received support from Major Julius Christensen, a member of the Director of Central Intelligence/Hostage Location Task Force. On April 24, Christensen sent North an analysis of options to secure the release of the hostages. On balance, he concluded that "the back channel initiative" could succeed. But he noted that arms shipments could affect the balance in the Iran-Iraq war and that the longer the operation lasted the greater the risk of exposure. He attached a fuller analysis of the options—doing nothing, diplomatic efforts, Waite, paying ransom, and using force, unilaterally or multilaterally. He looked to the NSC for guidance. (Christensen to North, 4/24/86) In turn, North wrote Poindexter on April 29:

> We are seeing increasing evidence of Libyan efforts to buy the hostages and other signs of increasing disarray inside Lebanon. Further, there is increasing indication of seepage around the edge of our hostage project. Bottom line: [the Iranian official] knows this and wants to proceed quickly with a release. [Available

information indicates that [the Iranian official] does indeed have the requisite authorities to bring this all to a conclusion. We are, at this point concerned only that he may be unable to proceed because of the two radars issue and that the timing of their delegation to Beirut should be such that the delegation is already there by the time we arrive in Tehran—and that they not wait to dispatch it until we arrive. Casey and company believe that we have made too big a deal over the radars issue noting that they were proposed with the original parts list and we should not be treating them as separate items. They note that no one else sees them as such and that I should not have presented them as separate items. They believe that we can order them up from the normal logistics acquisition process that they have established with the Army and that they will simply be delivered as they are made available. In any event—all here agree that Cave, North and Nir ought to go to meet w/ [the Iranian official]. Agency has prepared foreign Documents as necessary. If you approve, we wd depart Thurs p.m. [May 1], commercial to Frankfurt then to Tehran Friday via private jet over Turkey. If you do not believe that we can proceed with the radars I will try to convince them to take what we have in terms of parts and if necessary some of the TOWs as acceptable alternatives. We know . . . that Gorba has tried, unsuccessfully to date, to convince [the Iranian official] that this is the preferred course of action.

(North PROF note to Poindexter, 4/29/86, 19:46:06) According to the CIA Inspector General, the NSC staff and CIA received word that Iran would welcome a high-level American delegation to Tehran. (CIA/IG Chronology 22)

At this time, the Secretary of State again heard that the operation had not died. While at the Tokyo economic summit, Under Secretary Armacost cabled a report from Ambassador Price in London about Khashoggi's efforts to interest Tiny Rowlands, a British entrepreneur, in the transactions with Iran. Rowlands met with Khashoggi, Nir, and Ghorbanifar. Nir outlined the plan, indicating that the shipment of spare parts and weapons to Iran . . . Nir and Khashoggi told Rowlands

[t]he scheme, moreover, was okay with the Americans. It had been cleared with the White House. Poindexter allegedly is the point man. Only four people in the U.S. government are knowledgeable about the plan. The State Department has been cut out.

(Armacost to Shultz (State cable), 5/3/86)

The Secretary of State recalled that:

That same day, I sought out Vice Admiral Poindexter with the President's party, but found Mr. Regan. That is, I got this in the morning. We were in the midst of these meetings. You know how they are. And I read this thing.

So I am in one part of the hostel; the President and his staff—Regan, Poindexter, and so on—are in another part. So I just marched over to their wing of the hotel to find whoever I could find, and I wound up finding Don Regan. Everybody else I could not get to.

I told Mr. Regan and I showed him this—I said that he should go to the President and get him to end this matter once and for all. I opposed dealing with people such as those identified in the message and said it would harm the President if the activity continued.

Mr. Regan, I felt, shared my concern, said he was alarmed and would talk to the President.

I later learned that Vice Admiral Poindexter reportedly told Ambassador Price that there was no more than a smidgen of reality to the story. "Smidgen" is his word. When I got to him, I told Vice Admiral Poindexter my feelings, but he did not share my concerns.

He claimed that we were not dealing with these people; that that was not our deal.

I told him the President was very exposed.

Soon thereafter I recall being told by both Vice Admiral Poindexter and Mr. Casey that the operation had ended and the people involved had been told to "stand down."

\* \* \*

During this period [May 1986], I heard from time to time of reports that the operation may have resumed —that is, through the things that roll around on the grapevine. I heard nothing official to this effect, however.

(Shultz, SRB, 53–55)

Ambassador Price also called Poindexter with the same news. Poindexter wrote North a summary of the tale.

I told Charlie [Price] that there was only a shred of truth in this and the US connection was highly distorted. Tiny told [Bob] Frasure [on Price's staff] that he didn't like the deal and did not want to get involved unless it was an American operation. I told Charlie to advise him not to get involved.

What in the hell is Nir doing? We really can't trust those sob's.

(Poindexter PROF note to North, 5/3/86)

North replied at length, seeming to inform Poindexter of the way the operation was financed.

I agree that we cannot trust anyone in this game. You may recall that nearly a month ago I briefed you to the effect that Tiny Roland [sic] had been approached and we went back through Casey to tell these guys that the whole thing smelled very badly. We know that Khashoggi is the principal fund raiser for Gorba and that only after Gorba delivers a cargo does he get paid by the Iranians. We do not believe that Tiny is still engaged in this effort. Nir has been told to stay off the skyline on the issue. The story you had relayed to you by Price was the one made up by Nir to cover the transaction and Clair George reported it to us when the issue first came up several weeks ago. At the bottom line, this typifies the need to proceed urgently to conclude this phase of the operation before there are further revelations. We all know that this has gone on too long and we do not seem to have any means of expediting the process short of going to Iran. In that regard, George [Cave] and I are leaving tomorrow at 0700 to meet with Gorba in London. We intend to tell him that unless a deposit is made by the end of the week, the whole operation is off. We wd then have Gorba call [his contact in the PM's office] in our presence and have George reinforce the criteria for proceeding: We go to Tehran; within 24 hrs all hostages releases; 8hrs [sic] later we deliver the 240 parts; within 10 days we provide those parts which cannot fit on the a/c. In return we get to raise the issues of Nicaragua, no more terrorism and help for the Afghan resistance. This SEEMS to be what [the Iranian official] has already said he has gotten the "authorities" at his end to accept, but we want to be sure before we proceed. Lord willing, Gorba will then make the requisite deposit on Thursday, we will start to assemble the cargo by Friday, and the following weekend we will go to Tehran. We all hope.

(North PROF note to Poindexter, ?5/5/86, 22:34:44)

North went to London on May 6. The evening before, Poindexter instructed him: "Do not let anybody know you are in London or that you are going there. Do not have any contact with Embassy . . ." (Poindexter PROF note to North, 5/5/86)

Cave remembered that the first May meeting set the stage for the trip to Tehran. Cave spoke to the Iranian Prime Minister's office to fix the arrangements. They haggled over what the Americans would bring with them, the Iranians asking for all the HAWK spare parts. Agreement was reached on one-quarter—one pallet. Ghorbanifar said

we would be meeting with the Prime Minister, the President, Khameini, possibly Hashemi Rafsanjani, and another well-known conservative Ayatollah, named Ayatollah Farsi. He was one of the original candidates for president in the election when Bani Sadr was elected President.

(Cave 8) Ghorbanifar informed the Americans that financing had been arranged, and that he would deposit funds "in an account controlled by Mr. Nir. We eventually got the money in our account on the 16th of May, and that was a deposit from General Secord into the account we had in Switzerland, in Geneva."[66]

Cave told the Board that the CIA had no idea where the money went after Ghorbanifar made the deposit into Nir's account, "nor do we have any idea of how much was deposited." *(Id.* at 9)

When North returned to Washington, he wrote Poindexter that

> I believe we have succeeded. Deposit being made tomorrow (today is a bank holiday in Switzerland [May 8]). Release of hostages set for week of 19 May in sequence you have specified. Specific date to be determined by how quickly we can assemble requisite parts. Thank God—He answers prayers.

(North PROF note to Poindexter, 5/8/86, 8:07:46)

## C. Excursions: May 1986

The way was now clear for McFarlane to visit Tehran. While planning the trip, other issues continued to occupy the NSC staff. The United States received information about Iranian terrorist operations to be conducted against the United States. Poindexter wondered if Ghorbanifar should be reminded "that we thought we had a committment [sic] from them on future terrorist activity against US." (Poindexter PROF note to North, 5/13/86, 19:08) On May 15, North replied in two parts. First, he noted that everybody shared Poindexter's concern. Some members of the team thought the Syrians had recruited important members of Hezballah. Others, like Cave, blamed factionalism with Iran's ruling group.

> Nir is already aware of this and intends to note to Gorba that his $15M is at great risk if one of these events does indeed happen. Gorba is probably not the best interlocutor on this matter and we wd stand a far

284

better chance talking directly to [the official in the Prime Minister's office]. It wd be worthy of some consideration to do just that before we go all the way through with the execution of what is now in motion. Cave and North are still prepared to go if you think it wd help. I do. So does George.

(North PROF note to Poindexter, 5/13/86)

North's second note informed Poindexter that his wish had been carried out, and warned of Ghorbanifar's having "penetrated" the CIA.

Nir and Copp are with Gorba. Both have made points as you urged. In response, Gorba has promised that every effort will be made to stop unauthorized actions being undertaken by Hezballah or Iranian activists in the field. He has also provided the following which was transmitted a few minutes ago via Dick's secure device: "As you remember fm London, Gorba suggested we get together with Howaldi Al Homadi (or Hamadi) of Libya whom Gorba claimed to be the head of internal security and de facto number 2 man in the country. Nir checked this in his records and indeed Homadi is head of internal security and in key govt position plus connection to terrorists abroad. . . . Homadi does not believe that this is an effective channel since FoMin is not well connected. Homadi is willing to come to any point in Europe to meet with North or other appropriate official without preconditions. Homadi willing to deliver three things—no more attacks against U.S.; work out schedule to get terrorists out of Libya; to transfer business contracts from East-Bloc [sic] to West. In return, Homadi wants to settle misunderstandings btwn Libya and U.S. to include some kind of mutual public expressions. Willing to come anywhere in Europe given one week's notice. Gorba says Homadi sees himself as heir apparent to Qadhafi, knows about USG plans to use exiles for new Libyan govt; says it will not work." END OF NIR MESSAGE FROM GORBA.

There may or may not be anything to what Gorba has said of Homadi wanting to meet w/ North or other

USG official. . . . I have not passed any of this to any but you. Nir has asked that we protect him and not reveal his involvement in this to CIA. Nir is, as you know, operating w/o Mossad back-up and has considerable concern about the CIA becoming more knowledgeable about his activities. Based on what Gorba has just told us, Nir has reason to be concerned.

(North PROF note to Poindexter, 5/15/86, 21:36:09) "The CIA are really bunglers," Poindexter replied. You had better pass most of this to Casey directly. I would not pass it to anybody else. Leave me out of it. We need to think about a message to pass back to Homadi thru Gorba next week." (Poindexter PROF note to North, ?5/16/86)[67]

In the course of informing Poindexter that he had passed Ghorbanifar's information to the Director of Central Intelligence and Clarridge, North told Poindexter that the Nicaraguan resistance

now has more than $6M available for immediate disbursement. This reduces the need to go to third countries for help. It does not, however, reduce the urgent need to get CIA back into the management of this program. We can only do this by going forward with the reprogramming proposal and getting the requisite authorities for CIA involvement. Unless we do this, we run increasing risks of trying to manage this program from here with the attendant physical and political liabilities. I am not complaining, and you know that I love the work, but we have to lift some of this onto the CIA so that I can get more than 2-3 hrs of sleep at night. The more money there is (and we will have a considerable amount in a few more days) the more visible the program becomes (airplanes, pilots, weapons, deliveries, etc.) and the more inquisitive will become people like Kerry, Barnes, Harkins, et al. While I care not a whit what they say about me, it could well become a political embarrassment for the President and you. Much of this risk can be avoided simply by covering it with an authorized CIA program undertaken with the $15M. This is what I was about to say in the meeting today[68] and a point that I believe Shultz does not understand in his advocacy of Third [sic] country solicitation. I have no idea what Don Regan does or does not know re my private U.S. operation but the President obviously knows why he has been meeting with several select people to thank them for their "support for Democracy" in CentAM. In short, we need to proceed with the $15M. Shall I work this up?

(North PROF note to Poindexter, 5/16/86) Poindexter authorized North to prepare a paper "for the $15M reprogramming." (Poindexter PROF note to North, 5/17/86) He added: "I understand your concern and agree. I just didn't want you to bring it up at NSPG. I guessed at what you were going to say. Don Regan knows very little of your operation and that is just as well." *(Id.)* When North suggested that, before departing for Tehran, he and Poindexter have a quiet meeting with the President and McFarlane, without papers, and that Poindexter might want to include the Secretaries of State and Defense and the Director of Central Intelligence, Poindexter responded negatively: "I don't want a meeting with RR, Shultz and Weinberger." (North PROF note to Poindexter, 5/19/86; Poindexter PROF note to North, 5/19/86)

# D. Tehran: May 25–28, 1986

Notes made by the NSC Executive Secretary indicate that at the daily national security briefing on May 12, 1986, VADM Poindexter discussed with the President the hostages and Mr. McFarlane's forthcoming trip. The notes indicate that the President directed that the Press not be told about the trip. Notes made by the Executive Secretary on May 15, 1986, indicate that the President authorized Mr. McFarlane's secret mission to Iran and the Terms of Reference for that trip. Those notes indicate that the trip was discussed again with the President on May 21.

After the President approved the trip,[69] Poindexter relied on North to make arrangements. At the same time, he kept informed and made his views known. North's first plan required that the delegation stay in Israel for most of the weekend, May 23-25, and that Poindexter approve a request for aircraft. (North PROF note to Poindexter, 5/19/86, 12:03) Poindexter had

problems with this plan. An a/c request is too closely linked to what is happening. I don't see how we can use a military a/c. Why do you have to stay so long in Israel? I had in mind you would travel separately, RDVU [rendez-vous] in Israel at a covert location, and proceed to Iran.

(McFarlane (1) 30)

(Poindexter PROF note to North, 5/19/86)

Late on May 19, North prepared a detailed plan

We will endeavor to do it any way you want but we are experiencing significant logs [logistics] problems which are considerably eased by the use of a military a/c which can deliver the people, communications equipment (classified SATCOM, beacons, etc.) and still provide a modicum of rest. The present plan includes the A/C as a part of the OPSEC in that RCM has reason to use such an A/C. . . . The same applies to a lesser extent to RCM. The following sched is what is driving us:

Weds; May 21
1000—Copp dep for final sched mtg w/ Gorba
1000—240 Items arrive for final packing/sanitizing by CIA.

Thursday; May 22
1000—240 items + 508 TOWs moved fm to Kelly AFB by CIA
1400—Commercial 707 (#1) arrives Kelly to load most of 240 items
  30—Copp arr. Geneva
1700—Commercial 707 (#1) Dep Kelly for Israel w/ bulk of 240 items aboard
  45—North Dep Wash. for London
2000—Copp Dep Geneva for Israel w/ 707 Special Crew for IAF 707 via Lear Jet.

Friday; May 23

0100—G–3 Dep Andrews w/ Cave, Teicher, CIA communicators (2) plus equipmt

0200—G–3 P/U RCM at Laguardia [sic] (speech that evening in NYC)

0230—Copp arr. Israel w/ 707 Spec Crew

1400—G–3 w/ RCM arrive Gatwick; P/U North

1400—Commercial 707 (#2) Dep Kelly AFB w/ 508 TOWs for IDF enr Israel

1400—Commercial 707 (#1) Arr Israel w/ bulk of 240 items; commence xfr to IAF 707s prior to commencement of Sabbath.

Saturday; May 24

0800—G–3 w/ RCM; communicators & party arrive Israel —start rest period

1700—Commercial 707 (#2) Arrives w/ 508 TOWs & remainder of 240 items; complete xfr of 240 items to IAF 707s after sunset (end of Sabbath)

2200—IAF 707 (#A) w/ Copp special crew & RCM party dep Israel enr T.

2200—bulk of 240 items transloaded fm Commercial 707 (#2) to IAF 707 (#B).

Sunday; May 25

0830—RCM & party on IAF 707 (#A) arrive T. prepared for mtgs.

Monday; May 26

0800(?)—U.S. parties turned over to CRS or ICRC in Brt. [Beirut]

1000—IAF 707 (#A) Arrive T. w/ bulk of 240 items.

In the plan above all times are local. As indicated in earlier discussions we have had on this matter every effort is being made to preserve OPSEC. Because of real world constraints on what can fit in the a/c we will load part of the 240 on 707 #2 and they will be handled separately when they arrive in Israel w/ 508 IDF TOWs. We have tried to compartment the whole effort at . . . Kelly AFB so that no two work shifts at either location has a clear picture of what is being loaded out via the two commercial 707s. The same thing applies to the 707 aircrews (3 of them) which we are providing for this mission. No one crew knows about the other, nor will they see each other. For example, the crew that is going out with Copp to fly the IAF 707 (#A) w/ RCM & party does not know about the two 707s arriving frm Kelly. The only part of this operation that we are not doing ourselves is the CIA comms, beacons and documentation for the party. ALL other arrangements have been made through Copp or affiliates and if we have to, I suppose we can arrange to fly RCM and the communicators out on their own. Quite frankly, however, I do not see the vulnerability of using a military G–3 which will considerably ease our clearance problems given the hour of the day/night in which we are moving. We now have, I believe, a G–3 (or two) available which do (does) not have the usual USA marking on the side. Finally, the length of stay in Israel is not, in my opinion excessive, given the rather reigorous [sic] schedule we are attempting to accommodate. We are being driven by Sabbath requirements in Israel, Ramadan in T. and an awareness that the situation for our four in Beirut looks more desperate by the day. In an effort to address all of these competing and conflicting concerns (to include the availability of commercial 707s, cleared special mission crews, and the peculiar demands of low profile work schedules at . . . Kelly AFB and in the IAF) we have had one hell of a circus. In short, the use of a military G–3 would provide a much needed respite from the havoc of trying to answer all of these issues all over again without further risking OPSEC. It can be done, but it would be much better if we did not have to.

(North PROF note to Poindexter, 5/19/86, 23:00:07)

Poindexter then wondered about using a CIA aircraft: what did the Director of Central Intelligence use when he travelled. (Poindexter PROF note to North, 5/20/86) North replied that CIA aircraft in the United States lacked the necessary range, and available CIA proprietary aircraft were overseas and lacked certificates necessary to fly in the United States. The Director of Central Intelligence used military aircraft, but that option, North wrote, "is in the realm of too hard." He proposed "to make other arrangements." (North PROF note to Poindexter, 5/20/86, 10:38:12) Poindexter noted that

It is not that it is too hard; I just don't think it is a good idea. Leaks at this point could be disastrous. This is different from other secret missions in that anybody that knows anything (or thinks they know something) connected with this mission will be sorely tempted to talk about it afterwards if it is successful. Let me know what you work out.

(Poindexter PROF note to North, 5/20/86, 14:10:03) Later on May 20, North sent Poindexter another schedule and itinerary for the delegation:

This further re transportation arrangements for RCM & party: Cave + Teicher + Communicators will depart IAD aboard Private (Democracy INC.) G–3, stops in NYC to p/u RCM. G–3 Proceeds direct to Rhein Main military airfield, cleared thru customs by CIA . . . North . . . picked up in London by Lear 35 owned by Democracy INC. European subsidiary. Lear 35 drops North at commercial side of Rhein Main, North passes thru customs/immigration as Goode, proceeds to military side to rvs [rendez-vous] w/ RCM party. RCM party on arrival at FM offloads from G–3, transloads to CIA 707 (if available) or to chartered Swiss Challenger a/c for direct flight to Tel Aviv. Still having local point clearance problems for bringing G–3 into RM w/o customs/immigrations clearances. We are going to have to bring . . . Frankfurt into this to work out clearances. Will talk to him tonight via PRT–250 @ approx 0300. Shd have answer shortly thereafter . . . today provided recommended turnover points for hostages. We have sent one of our Democracy INC couriers to deliver flight schedule and turnover info to Gorba in London. Gorba scheduled to go to Tehran on Thursday [May 22]. Copp departure for Geneva/Tel Aviv postponed 24 hrs fm original schedule in order to complete coordination of RCM flight planning. Norta [sic] still on schedule to depart Thurs pm for . . . London. Complete ops plan and annexes being prepared for yr use during op. Will prepare in advance necessary paperwork and cables for dispatch of Hostage debrief team, Nightengale Medevac support and hospitalization alert for Wiesbaden-all of which wd be dispatched only when hostages are released. Will also have required checklist for alerting State to notify families, move same to Europe for reunion. OPLAN includes three sets of press guidance—appropriate to various circumstances which could occur on mission.[70] Finally, need guidance as to whether or not you want to predeploy. . . . It wd be good insurance if things get screwed up during/after turnover of hostages—particularly if turnover does not result in hostages being brought all the way to our embassy. All involved believe it is unlikely that Iranians can get them this far with or without help from Hezballah. Most likely is release at one of the few Western Embassies remaining in W. Beirut or at AUB Hospital. We also suggested the Military Hospital crossing on the green line as a possibility. At the afternoon planning mtg [C/NE] suggested that we look at the Finding again to determine whether we can sell certain items of hardware to IRAQ in concert w/ what we are doing in Iran. He believes that such a step wd add considerably to our leverage in the area if this activity is uncovered by the Sovs. I share his concern. Far too much is being said over the open telephone by Gorba for them to be completely ignorant. Finally, we have several policy issues which need to be addressed.

—RCM should be able to suggest to the Iranians that we are willing to put a permanent Comms unit (2 CIA) into Tehran to facilitate future exchanges of information—w/o a middle man/[sic]

—What do we do if they can only spring one two or three of the hostages after making a good faith effort?

—What do we do if, after 72 hrs, nothing happens?

These are the kinds of things I had envisioned for discussion in the private mtg w/ RR. At the very least, you shd talk to RCM about these things, preferably face to face. While we all expect this thing to go peachy smooth, it may not. RCM, is taking no small risk in this endeavor—just flying around the way we will have to. He doesn't have to take this kind of chance. I know that everyone is very busy, but it wd, in my humble opinion, be thoughtful if you can find a few minutes to discuss the issues above w/ him and say good by. While I'm confident he'll be back next week, I could be wrong and it might be a very long time before anyone sees him again.

(North PROF note to Poindexter, 5/20/86, 15:37:49) In the afternoon of May 22, North submitted to Poindexter an updated schedule for the trip. It did not materially differ from the versions prepared on the 19th and 20th.

The updated schedule was part of a package of materials North prepared. It included an "Operations Plan," which defined the objective as: "To secure the return of four American hostages [Jenco, Anderson, Jacobsen, and Sutherland] who continue to be held by Hezballah elements in Lebanon." (North to Poindexter, "Hostage Recovery Plan," 5/22/86, Tab I, "Operations Plan") The "Concept" was: "Provide incentives for the Government of Iran to intervene with those who hold the American hostages and secure their safe release." *(Id.)* The CIA was responsible for delivering "supplies" to Kelly Air Force Base; providing an interpreter, communicators and their equipment, and travel documents; providing an intelligence briefing package, with photographs; "[f]und maintenance and test/calibration of two Phase I radars at Letterkenney, PA. Investigate availability of two Phase II radars from DOD/FMS channels"; provide a communications schedule, including frequencies; recommend site and conditions for the release of the hostages in Beirut. "Democracy Inc. Charter" was to provide two Boeing 707s to transport "supplies" from Kelly to Tel Aviv. "Democracy, Inc." would provide two vetted crews for the Israeli aircraft; a Swiss Air Learjet to transport Secord from Geneva to Tel Aviv on May 22; a "CANAIR Challenger for delegation airlift from Dulles to Ramstein AFB on Friday, May 23;" and six Blackhawk .357 magnums in presentation boxes. Secord would act as liaison by secure communications between the CIA/NSC and the delegation. The Israelis were to provide funds for 508 TOWs (to replenish Israeli stocks after the August/September 1985 transfers, (CIA/IG Chronology 24)); two black 707 aircraft for transport to Tehran; and a "liaison officer" to the American delegation.

NSC responsibilities constituted the longest list. They included the senior emissary; liaison with the White House; contingency press guidance; and arranging for the debriefing of hostages and the reunion of families, among other details. The Defense Department's role consisted of providing equipment and supplies "through intermediaries," transport for the hostage reception team and transportation in connection with the release of the hostages. The delegation would carry alias passports. There would be no rehearsal. *(Id.)* The schedule noted that McFarlane would board a CIA proprietary 707 at Ramstein for the trip to Tel Aviv.

North's package also included "Terms of Reference" for the delegation. It had been printed at various times since the draft of April 4, but had undergone no material change since then. The "Terms of Reference" were boiled into an outline and talking points for the delegation.

The day North submitted his package, Ledeen saw Peter Rodman, Deputy Assistant to the President for National Security Affairs (Foreign Policy). Rodman wrote Poindexter that Ledeen

urge[d] that we use our Iranian channels as a vehicle for stirring up dissidence within Iran, rather than for (as he puts it) cutting deals involving arms for hostages.

Mike says his contact Gorbanifahr [sic] has access and influence with a dissident Ayatollah . . . as well as with disloyal elements spread throughout the military and the bazaars. There is great potential here, Mike feels, for a U.S. covert program to undermine the regime. He claims that both Bill Casey and Bud agree with this, and that it's a perfect program for Dewey Clarridge's operation.

The obstacle, he says, is that we are following an alternative approach that is too much hostage to the hostage problem.

I said nothing to Mike, but I have to say that I have long had a similar concern that we might be gearing our policy too much to the hostage issue rather than to the strategic menace that the regime represents. The special one-page finding of a few months ago put the hostages in a properly subordinate place among our objectives—but in practice our approach seems to require a hostage release as an early token of good faith. . . .

Perhaps this is something for you to discuss with Casey, with Bud, and with Ledeen.

(Rodman to Poindexter, 5/22/86)

McFarlane recalled that Poindexter asked him to attend a briefing on the trip in the last week of May.

I was asked by the Admiral to come by and get my instructions that he said had been approved by the President—these were about four pages—the political agenda. Here are the political issues that you should develop and they dealt basically with our view of our interests in the Middle East, our view of Iranian conflicts with us and disagreements, basically—terrorism, the continuity of the war, the expansion of fundamentalist influence in other moderate regimes in the area, and, separately, our view of their vulnerabilities to the Soviet Union and our sense of milestones for dealing with specific issues that might over time get us toward a more stable relationship.

And I asked again. I said, is the Secretary of State and Defense, DCI, the President all on board with this. He said, well, they are involved in the preparation of these instructions. He said that, and they are involved in this decision, yes. The President has approved it. And then these instructions. The positions haven't changed. The Secretary of State is against the arms component of it, as is the Secretary of Defense.

(McFarlane (1) 33-34) McFarlane had the sense the instructions represented an NSPG "product." He was not aware that his aircraft would carry military equipment to Iran until he arrived in Tel Aviv. (Id. at 34)

McFarlane's delegation—McFarlane, North, Cave, Teicher, Nir, and a CIA communicator—left Tel Aviv for Tehran on May 25. Secord and one communicator remained in Tel Aviv. According to Cave, the Israeli government pressed for Nir's participation, and McFarlane ultimately decided to include him. (Cave 10) The aircraft carried a pallet of HAWK spare parts, which was loaded in Israel. The delegation also carried a chocolate cake from a kosher bakery in Tel Aviv—"more of a joke than anything else between North and Ghorbanifar." (Teicher 10)

McFarlane sent Poindexter two reports of the meetings; Teicher made detailed memoranda of conversations. McFarlane's first cable reported:

> Delegation arrived Tehran Sunday morning. Absence of anyone to receive us for over an hour and recurrent evidence anxiety ineptitude in even the most straightforward discourse makes it clear that we must take a step back from the history of the past 8 years and put our task in a different light.
>
> It may be best for us to try to picture what it would be like if after nuclear attack, a surviving Tatar became Vice President; a recent grad student became Secretary of State; and a bookie became the interlocutor for all discourse with foreign countries. While the principals are a cut above this level of qualification the incompetence of the Iranian government to do business requires a rethinking on our part of why there have been so many frustrating failures to deliver on their part. The other reason for the several snafus has been the extreme paranoia that dominates the thinking of the political leadership here. More about this later. First let me debrief the meetings that have been held before giving you a sense of where and how fast matters can progress.
>
> Once matters were sorted out at the airport, we were met by Gorba and [the official from the Prime Minister's office] taken to the Hilton Hotel and installed in the top floor along with considerable security (CI) people from their side. After a short rest we convened our first meeting at 1700 local Sunday afternoon. It was a foundation session in which we established that we

acknowledged the Iranian revolution; had no interest or intention in trying to reverse it; indeed believed that a strong independent, non-aligned Iran was in the U.S. interest but that such a situation was unlikely to be possible in our judgement for a number of reasons. First, it seemed clear to us that the Soviet Union was prepared to go quite far to prevent an Iraqi defeat in the war and may well have ambitions vis a vis Iran that we would be pleased to discuss during our talks. For our part, we can envision restoration of a normal relationship with Iran but not under circumstances in which they work against our interests WHETHEPPj$i.u#ERRORISM [?whether by support of terrorism] or support for subversion of our interests in Nicaragua and elsewhere.

Our interlocutors were [officials in the Iranian Prime Minister's office]; Gorba and one other functionary.

Their response to all this was on the whole expressed in a spirit of good will. "We are open to a stable relationship with the U.S. but it will not be easy to overcome a bitter history etc etc" but in a larger sense the central message to us was how uncertain, fearful and timid these third and fourth level officials were. Further, it has become more and more clear that while Gorba has brought us to the beginning of a dialogue with the GOI, he has done it with considerable hyperbole, occasional lies and dissembling. Our interlocutors' defensiveness was expressed through a diatribe about how we hadn't brought enough supplies and thus were acting in bad faith. This was easily rebutted and they were put on the defensive regarding their failure to produce on the hostages but it made clear the need to get beyond their level if we are to do any serious business here. The meeting ended on a harmonious note. They asked that we propose an agenda for today's meetings. We did so last night; basically an abbreviated statement of the TOR paper I reviewed before leaving. [page cut off] brought with us. We recalled them later in the evening and in no uncertain terms let them have it for Iran's breach of faith and insolent behavior that we expected to be corrected forthwith.

This morning, after apparently considerable internal to and fro on their side, [name deleted] was dispatched to apologize and to say that they wanted the meetings to succeed. (Late entry: beginning with our arrival and frequently since Gorba has continued to say "The hostages will be released and things are going in the right direction and don't worry" and other rhetorical irrevelancies.) [name deleted] also said that their leaders had designated an official with higher authority than they to come to meet with us this afternoon (Monday). I made clear that if he was coming to spend needless time discussing the supplies or other forms of niggling that he could do so with the staff.

He arrived at about 9:45 tonight and lasted until just about 1:45 Tuesday morning. As it turned out this man [a senior foreign affairs advisor] was a considerable cut above the bush leaguers we had been dealing with. In the course of the 4 hour meeting it became evident that the three Iranian leaders—Rafsanjani, Musavi (Prime Minister) and Khamenei (President) are each traumatized by the recollection that after Bazargan met with Brzezinski in the Spring of 1980, he was deposed (so strong was popular sentiment against doing business with the Great Satan). Today the force of events and self interest has brought them to the point of realizing that we do have some common interests (vis a vis the Russians, Afghanistan and perhaps even against Iraq.) But they still cannot overcome their more immediate problem of how to talk to us and stay alive. But from the tenor of this last man's . . . statements, conviction and knowledgeable expression of what is possible in the way of a stable cooperative relationship, I believe we have finally reached a competent Iranian official—and that's good.

Nevertheless we cannot, in my judgment be swooned by serious dialogue without acts. Thus I did not meet with this man as a firm signal that although we have come to set in motion a sustained process, we must first set aside a number of obstacles—notably by the release of the hostages. This was forcefully stressed to [name deleted] tonight and we have received throughout the day periodic reaffirmations that steps are in motion, we are working on it, don't worry etc. etc. etc. With that in mind, when he comes back tomorrow to go discuss—the agenda, I intend to have him meet with the staff with perhaps an intervening summons for him to come visit with me to try to set some specific milestones for moving ahead. These would include: 1. An end to the extreme rhetoric on both sides (although we will call it as it is if there is a recurrence of terrorism against us) 2. The establishment of a communications capability between us full time as soon as possible. 3. The positioning on the ground here a technical expert to get us away from these endless exchanges of requests for items they don't need.

With regard to the hostages we have and will continue to make clear that their release is the sine qua non to any further steps between us. And if that has not happened by tomorrow night, they are aware that we will leave and that the balance of this shipment will not be delivered nor will any change to our stance be considered.

As to my judgment on where we stand, it seems clear that we are dealing with people at the top who: 1. Understand that they have an important interest in trying to establish a dialogue that leads to a measure of cooperation with us. 2. That doing so requires that they deliver on certain kinds of behavior e.g., release of the hostages and no further terrorist acts against us. 3. Are very fearful for their own vulnerability to factional attack if they are discovered in this dialogue before they can condition the people to a different perception of the U.S. 4. Are trying to run a country with almost no competent officials below the very top and need help.

So we are on the way to something that can become a truly strategic gain for us at the expense of the Soviets. But it is going to be painfully slow. As we proceed we cannot be gulled by promises of what will happen

tomorrow—at bottom they really are rug merchants.
But little by little we can make progress because it is a
matter of self interest for both of us to do so.

I will give you a more thoughtful fill tomorrow after
our meetings—it is now 3:35 a.m. local. I feel that we
have entered a sensible process and finally gotten a
competent interlocutor on the other side. If you have
any special instructions before we meet tomorrow
please let me know. Hope you had a nice weekend.
Your guys are doing a fantastic job as is Cave and the
communicator who is near death.

MEMORANDUM OF CONVERSATION
SUBJECT: U.S.-Iran Dialogue
PARTICIPANTS:

*U.S.*
Robert C. McFarlane
Oliver L. North
George Cave
Howard R. Teicher

*Israel*
Amiran Nir

*Iran*
[A Deputy Prime Minister]
[Assistants to the Prime Minister]
DATE: May 25, 1986
PLACE: Tehran, Iran, Independence Hotel
TIME: 5:15 p.m.

[The Iranian official] opened the plenary meeting. He
said he was very happy to see the U.S. delegation here.
Hoped this will be a useful trip with good results.
Expressed regret for inconvenience at the airport.
"Ready to begin negotiations and talks." After intro-
ducing his colleagues [the Iranian official] said the
main purpose of this meeting is to prepare an agenda
for other political discussions.

*McFarlane* expressed on behalf of the President his
pleasure to be in Iran to start what the U.S. hopes will
be sustained discourse. *McFarlane* made the following

opening statement: "The President asked that I portray for your leaders U.S. goals, the basis of disagreements, and try to find common ground for cooperation. Perhaps I could propose a format for our exchanges. First a session for an exchange on fundamental issues. In such a session we could present our goals, the nature of the peace we seek in the M.E. and more broadly. We could then turn to how we see our responsibilities vis-a-vis the USSR, and what we see as important to U.S. security interests in other parts of the world. We can also describe how we see the history of U.S.-Iranian relations going back 10 years. In these talks, on bilateral matters, we would hope to make clear that the U.S. accepts the Iranian Revolution and has no wish or presumption of influencing it in any fashion."

*McFarlane* stressed "the U.S. hope that from this day forward, the U.S. and Iran can proceed where interests converge. No doubt there are elements of Iranian policy that the U.S. will disagree with. But it is important we understand the disagreements." After a general discussion of the global and bilateral agenda, *McFarlane* suggested that it might be useful for experts to exchange information, e.g., nature of Soviet intentions and capabilities in this part of the world. "I'd like to stress something at the beginning. Obviously we've had disagreements over the past eight years. But the U.S. recognizes that Iran is a sovereign power and we should deal on the basis of mutual respect, not intimidation. That's why before we begin high-level talks we put behind us hostage-taking which has occurred in the past. We are pleased that informal talks resulted in agreement on release of American hostages. Once that is completed we can begin serious talks. I want to stress our appreciation for your hospitality, especially during Ramazan [sic]. All of us are pleased to be here. This can lead to an historic new beginning."

[The Iranian official] replied that "he wanted to lay a groundwork regarding certain issues before meetings begin. This revolution was totally depending on God, independent Iranian power and unique ideology.

301

These factors allowed this revolution to come into being. This revolution came to power because for years the nation was under dictatorial pressures. These pressures contributed to the revolution's success. I am sure you can feel how the nation and people think after so many years under pressure. Iran can now act freely. What do you expect from them now that they are free? I want to express a very important point. This revolution cost much blood. After so much blood, the people don't want hostility directed against them. The leader and the people expressed their will to look forward, not to the past. The key question to the past eight years may help explain why our relations were not good. We have a famous saying "Past is a mirror for the future." It is not the time to discuss what went wrong over past five years, but I want to emphasize a few points. We don't want to align with East or West, but that doesn't mean we don't want relations. Iran had relations with the U.S.A. at first. But refuge for the Shah and interference in our internal affairs damaged relations. U.S. refuge for the Shah was bad but your military action was a demonstration of hostile intent. All the points combined led to break in confidence in U.S.G. To rebuild bridge of confidence will take time. We are moving toward this goal. Best proof and reason we are moving is informal meetings and your presence here in Iran. You know better than anyone that your presence here is most important development in this process. Believe we will reach this goal by fulfilling the necessary steps that have already been agreed to. I didn't want to review the past but I needed to mention the background."

Turning to the agenda, [the Iranian official] said he needs to make the agenda clear for Iranian leaders. "The first item should be U.S. goals in the area. The basic priority is to build a bridge of confidence. Both Iran and the U.S. must build confidence and trust. Once bridge of confidence is established then other priorities can be addressed and solved. We expect from you that the U.S. will supply physical support to Iran. U.S. support will be with us. This is best way to build confidence. For the U.S.A. to demonstrate that it is with Iran."

*McFarlane* welcomed climate of [the Iranian's] remarks. Bodes well for talks. "We agree that we should take advantage of certain measures that were agreed in the informal talks. Regarding the commitment of the U.S. to turn a page, this is expressed by my presence on behalf of the President. The corresponding commitment on the part of your government to put the past behind us is to use your influence to secure the release of captive Americans. They are not held by Iran but the captors are also subject to Iranian influence. Finally as an earnest showing of our good faith, we are prepared to transfer certain items which may be of assistance. We have brought some of these with us. In virtually all cases we could handle via aircraft. If not, other items will follow as this sequence evolves. Perhaps we could start discussions tomorrow morning on goals. At the conclusion of this discussion, we could have specialized sessions on the Soviet Union and Middle East situation."

[The Iranian official] specified Soviet intentions, Afghan issues, Lebanese affairs, Middle East peace, Iran-Iraq war, Kurdistan. "What is your view about Iraq? It's regime?"

*McFarlane* said, "We are prepared to discuss all of those issues. Let us begin with a long session where we can make summary comments on each topic. Then later, when talking about Soviet capabilities, perhaps experts could meet. But the general threat and how to meet it can be done in a general session. In order to have clarity we can write out the agenda tonight."

[The Iranian official] changed the subject, stating that "for humanitarian reasons we have acted on your hostages. But we expected more than what came on the aircraft."

*McFarlane* answered that we could not bring it all on the plane. But the rest can be brought forward.

[The Iranian official] reiterated the humanitarian dimension, noting that ["]Iran did not take these people captive."

*North* expressed U.S. gratification for Iran's humanitarian assistance. He asked what Tehran wants the U.S. Government to say about Iran's role. The U.S. does not want to embarrass Iran. But if the Iranian government would be served by a U.S.G. statement it can be made. "We hope this will happen in next few hours."

[The Iranian official] said that Iran took this step as a humanitarian act. "We started the process, but cannot forecast when it will happen. We can discuss this affair later. We expect anyhow to receive more items from you so that we will be in a better position with our leaders. I want to make this point very clear. Iran has been at war for six years. Fao was a great accomplishment. We are expecting more equipment."

*McFarlane* stated that the agreement which was concluded will be fulfilled to the letter. "A bridge of confidence is a useful metaphor. I have come as an expression of good will. In addition to my own presence, we put items on the aircraft which can be brought forward. The corresponding act on your side, a humanitarian gesture, involves the release of our people. While separate and not related, these acts do contribute to mutual confidence. You have my word, the bond of my country, that we will fulfill our agreement."

[The Iranian official] replied that "what Iran expected is not here, but as a humanitarian gesture, Iran will send a delegation to Beirut to solve that problem while expecting Iranian logistics needs to be met." He emphasized that no one knows about the McFarlane team's presence in Tehran. The Air Force is suspicious since someone is still on the plane. [The Iranian official] suggested that he stay at the hotel instead.

*McFarlane* said, "we can't do that. Although his presence on the plane may complicate suspicions, he performs communications functions as well as logistics

304

accountability. We can give instructions for him to stay out of sight."

[The Iranian official] said there is no problem with communications. But having him staying on board is a problem because he's at the military airfield.

*McFarlane* stated that "we need communications all the time. Otherwise there is no way to communicate with the President."

[The Iranian official] stressed there is a security problem with Air Force questioning.

Turning back to substance, *McFarlane* said, "this is a good beginning. We do have much to do and very little time." He argued that the U.S. team's presence here should be kept brief for security.

[The Iranian official] opined that "everything depends on good will and restored confidence. But there are some things which cause doubt. We were told that one-half of the equipment would be brought with McFarlane. You did not bring one-half. This behavior raises doubts about what can be accomplished."

*McFarlane* forcefully interjected to end the Iranian official's protests. "Let's be clear. I have come. There should be an act of goodwill by Iran. I brought some things along as a special gesture. So far nothing has happened on your side. However, I am confident it will."

[The Iranian official] apologized, stressing that he and his colleagues are not decision-makers. "We just give you a message and take your message. But we told our leaders that you would bring one-half of the items." S9307.

*North* noted that the aircraft has weight and fuel limitations.

[The Iranian official] commented that some of the spare parts are used.

Angrily, *McFarlane* replied that "I have come from

305

U.S.A. You are not dealing with Iraq. I did not have to bring anything. We can leave now!".

[The Iranian official] said that "We promised things to higher authorities regarding one-half of the items we purchased. Could you have told us it would only be one-fourth due to technical flight requirements? Now we will have internal problems."

[The Iranian official] stated that this problem can be solved in parallel with the other problem. A special delegation has already left to deal with the humanitarian problem. "We have all done what we should do. We respect our guests' need."

The meeting concluded at 7:00 p.m.

PARTICIPANTS:

*U.S.*
Robert C. McFarlane
Oliver L. North
George Cave
Howard Teicher

*Israel*
Amiram Nir

*Iran*
[A] Deputy Prime Minister
Assistant to the Prime Minister

DATE: May 26, 1986
PLACE: Tehran, Iran, Independence Hotel
TIME: 3:30 p.m.

*North* stated that "we are confused and concerned. We have tried for months to come to a point where we could talk government-to-government. Some in our government opposed. McFarlane favored. I was convinced that necessary arrangements had been made. We received President Reagan's permission to proceed. We have now been here for over a day and no one will talk with us. Where are we going? Nothing is happening."

[The Iranian official] replied that he wondered "why

we came to this situation. We were both happy last night. Why are you now confused? We are working to make things happen. We have similar problems with our people, but don't see any insurmountable problems. I understand McFarlane is unhappy about something. I want to see McFarlane."

*North* spoke privately with McFarlane who agreed to see [the two Iranian officials] at 3:30. The meeting resumed at 3:30 with McFarlane. [The Iranian official] stated he is at McFarlane's service to solve his problems. "I want to remove obstacles. Sorry, I want to solve problems, misunderstandings, so they won't be repeated."

*McFarlane* said he was pleased to hear that [the Iranian official] was committed to solving problems. "My purpose in coming was to establish a basis of trust and after that to address important problems. Before coming, my President and I believed preliminary problems affecting mutual trust were resolved by the staff. On your part, bringing about the release of hostages. On our part, providing some defensive supplies. But upon arriving, I learned that the steps had not been taken by your government. That is disappointing. The more important purpose is to share with your Ministers how to restore a basis of trust between us. There are crucial matters related to the Soviet Union, Afghanistan and Iraq that we should discuss. But we cannot begin to address these matters until preliminary problems are solved. Perhaps your government is not ready to deal with these larger issues. Maybe we should wait for another day. But I must depart tomorrow night. I would like to meet with your Ministers. But I cannot if preliminary problems have not been solved. I have no more to say."

[The Iranian official] said, "We seem to be moving in a positive direction. I hope we will overcome these problems. Yesterday we mentioned the Air Force problem. We are only concerned over leakage. There is no problem sending someone to the plane whenever they need to. We thought it understandable that you would go back and forth to communicate. On top of everything else, you are our guest and we respect our guest on top of all else. The delay at the airport was due to your early arrival. Our main problem is that we cannot inform staffs. Regarding your gifts, we held them for security reasons. We will bring them back now, same as passports. The delay is due to the difficult effort needed to make everything work out. At 4:00 p.m., a gentleman with higher authority will be here."

*McFarlane* repeated that "there are important things to discuss about the future. But this entire visit will surely provide us with indications of your commitment and good faith. So far the experience has not been a happy one. I am here to deal with larger problems. As soon as problems you are working on are solved, I am prepared to meet with your Ministers. No other meetings are necessary."

[The Iranian official] said he had no authority to decide on these matters. The important authority will arrive at 4:00. *McFarlane* said he would not meet the person. He came to meet with Ministers. The staff can meet this other person.

[The Iranian official] argued that the Iranians were having problems trying to arrange a Ministerial meeting. "We have to build up to that stage."

*McFarlane* said he did not want to interfere with [the Iranian official's] problems. "Work with my staff."

[The Iranian official] said his government had now appointed a high authority to follow up. This will help to open the stage.

*McFarlane* expressed his great disappointment. "We understand it takes time to make a decision to renew a dialogue with the U.S. But I must return to Washington tomorrow night. The preliminary problem in Lebanon must be overcome. I hope your Minister will come to my country next year. He will be received by my President. As I am a Minister, I expect to meet with decision-makers. Otherwise, you can work with my staff."

[The Iranian official] said at the start of relations, there are always misunderstandings.

*McFarlane* agreed, wishing the Iranians "good luck."

The meeting was ended at 4:00 p.m.

PARTICIPANTS:

*U.S.*
Oliver L. North
George Cave
Howard Teicher

*Israel*
Amiram Nir

*Iran*
Senior Foreign Affairs Advisor
Assistants to the Prime Minister

DATE: May 26, 1986
PLACE: Tehran, Iran, Independence Hotel
TIME: 9:30 p.m.

[The Foreign Affairs Advisor] said he was very pleased to welcome the delegation in Tehran.

*North* stated that "we have a great opportunity to establish a relationship between our countries. There is a long history of unfortunate relations which cannot be forgotten in a minute. Men of good will have a chance to build a bridge of confidence. We may be able to work toward a common goal. Hope you've seen the proposed agenda. It provides a basis for discussion between our leaders. There is a technical agenda as well. All contribute to this great opportunity. I explained our respective commitments and the process to the President. Perhaps we came prematurely, with our hopes too high. Our hope was to remove certain hurdles to a better relationship. We understand it is hard for both our countries. But we have acted in good faith. The key is in your hands. It is not easy to turn that key. Misunderstandings have occurred. We have put them aside."

[The Foreign Affairs Advisor] said "you did a great job

coming here given the state of relations between us. I would be surprised if little problems did not come up. There is a Persian saying: Patience will bring you victory—they are old friends. Without patience, we won't reach anything. Politicians must understand this."

*North* thanked [the Foreign Affairs Advisor], noting that this shows the value of being able to talk. "There are factions in our governments that don't want something like this to succeed. This is why McFarlane grew angry when things didn't take place as I suggested they would. He took a risk urging our President to do this. There is great opposition to this project. We have to be able to show progress, not for personal reasons, but for the future. This is not a deal of weapons for release of the hostages. It has to do with what we see regarding Soviet intentions in the region. We accept the Iranian revolution and respect your sovereignty. Some people want to ensure that our countries find a common foundation for the future."

*North* continued that there are areas of agreement and disagreement. "What we had hoped was to agree on the direction for a dialogue between Iran and the U.S. Political decisions will be required. We may not agree this week or year. But this process must begin. It can begin in total secrecy, with certain non-political actions."

[The Foreign Affairs Advisor] asked whether the U.S. can keep a secret?

*North* said "We will try. But one of the greatest liabilities is a lack of secure communications."

*Nir* said there are ideas on this problem. It is a subject for technical discussions.

*North* offered to show the Iranians a device. "We can secretly put someone here. We know the Soviets are trying to find out what we are up to. We know the Soviets know a little bit about this and are trying to find out more. They will make a major effort to expose us. Our major hope is to pacify this opposition through

310

technical [sic] measures. If your government can cause the release of the Americans held in Beirut, 10 hours after they are released, aircraft will arrive with HAWK missile parts. Within 10 days of deposit, two radars will be delivered. After that delivery, we would like to have our logistics and technical experts sit down with your experts to make a good determination of what is needed. We need a technical survey. It must be done very secretly. However, if we go home without setting aside obstacles, there will be new obstacles."

[The Foreign Affairs Advisor] asked which obstacles?

*North* replied, "The release of the U.S. citizens. You said it was difficult for us to come here. We also know it was difficult for you to invite us."

*Nir* said that the back and forth on arms has tested the patience of the President. Hostage release is important as demonstration of Iranian influence and good will.

[The Foreign Affairs Advisor] asked to hear about the U.S. perception of the Soviet threat.

*Teicher* summarized the Soviet military posture and threat around Iran. There are 26 divisions. The military districts in the Trans Caucasus have been reorganized and improved. Exercise activity has intensified with respect to military action against Iran. The Soviets are increasing the frequency of their cross-border strikes into Pakistan and occasionally Iran, while initiating a terror campaign in Pakistan. He stressed the importance of beginning a dialogue on the Soviet Union for both Iran and the U.S.

[The Foreign Affairs Advisor] said, "there are training camps for Mujhadeen in Iran. Weapons and logistics support are provided. We are ready to send troops into Afghanistan. The Russians already complain about Iranian bullets killing Russians."

*North* asked if it would help to provide the Mujhadeen with TOWs?

[The Foreign Affairs Advisor] said the T–72 is not the best weapon against the Mujhadeen. Gas, napalm, and other criminal actions are their biggest problem. One million innocent victims. "Primary difficulty is not TOWs, though, we can cooperate with you in this area. The chemical warfare equipment is too developed. We need help curing wounded. Many die due to lack of first aid. Do you have anything more to say about Russians?"

*Cave* said we have eight hours worth of briefing materials.

[The Foreign Affairs Advisor] said he was ready for a detailed intelligence briefing, and agreed to the agenda without change. "We are ready to listen in all areas. Though we know we won't agree in every area, we will agree on some subjects. We have to bring up some subjects from the past, around the revolution. We don't need to discuss what came before. We believe that the United States Government from 1356 (one year before the revolution) made mistakes against all peoples. Our own belief is that our revolution is greater than the French or Russian Revolutions. There have been more changes. Today we feel many in the third world are thinking as revolutionaries like us."

"You see many pictures of Khomeini in the Afghan trenches,["] [the Foreign Affairs Advisor] continued. "He is their leader. We see the Imam's picture in South Africa, Lebanon, and West Africa. There are protests in Marrakesh. We didn't send this picture in the mail. We have no relations with Morocco that would allow us to give them the Imam's picture. The influence of this revolution has passed to many Moslems. Islamic countries express themselves honestly. But there is bad propaganda against us in America and Europe. We have been victimized by more terrorism than anyone else. The President, Prime Minister, Minister of Justice, 10 percent of Parliament, clerics, and innocent, have all been killed by terror. What the Afghans are doing is not terrorism. But we don't call action in South Lebanon against Israel terror."

"We are against kidnapping," [the Foreign Affairs Advisor] said. "What happened here was exceptional. Because of one exceptional act we should not be considered terrorists. When we turn to the subject of our relations, there are many serious things to say. We saw past U.S. leadership trying to destroy all the bridges of confidence. We did not start confronting you. This was not the clergy, army, jor [sic] party. It was the people. In such a revolution, there is no law and order. Not one drop of American blood was spilled one year after the revolution. American military advisors took all their belongings, as well as things they should not have taken. The memoirs of Ambassador Sullivan show it was a mass revolution. But the U.S. supported Bakhtiar, who confronted us harshly. We do not accept that. We did not see you sitting alone doing nothing. If there is only one other country in the world against the Soviets, it is Iran. We have a famous saying: Enemy of your enemy is your friend. You don't see it this way. Because we are neither east nor west, you are both pulling us. Neither the U.S. nor the Soviet Union likes independent states."

[The Foreign Affairs Advisor] said, "I am sorry to be so harsh. But I need to be frank and candid to overcome differences. We have the same problem that you have. Some here oppose relations with the U.S. I am happy to hear you believe in an independent sovereign Iran. We are hopeful that all American moves will be to support this dialogue. But we feel the whole world is trying to weaken us. We feel and see the Russian danger much more than you. You see the threat with high technology. We feel it, touch it, see it. It is not easy to sleep next to an elephant that you have wounded. To weaken Iran does not mean the Soviets want Iran. It means they want to reach the warm waters of the Gulf. Our Gulf neighbors know this. We share thousands of kilometers of land and water border. If we are weakened, you can forecast what will happen."

After a pause, [the Foreign Affairs Advisor] continued, "When we accepted your team with McFarlane, it symbolized a new political development here. But there has been a misunderstanding. When we accepted his visit, it did not mean a direct dialogue would occur on the spot. It is too early at this stage."

The discussion adjourned for a watermelon break. Detailed discussion resumed over difficulty of spare parts delivery. [The Iranian official] said he would try to arrange for an Iranian 747.

[The Foreign Affairs Advisor] resumed the discussion of bilateral relations. "Our relations are dark. They are very bad. Maybe you don't like to hear it, but I must be outspoken. The Iranians are bitter. Many Iranians call America the Great Satan. The first revolutionary government fell because of one meeting with Brzezinski. As a government, we don't want to be crushed tomorrow. We want to stay in power and solve these problems between us. We should not insist on special issues or a Ministerial meeting. There was no agreement that when McFarlane led the team it would lead to Ministerial meetings. Let us turn the key in a way that will work. We don't see the release of hostages as the key. You all must know that establishing this dialogue is the greatest challenge. China, Russia, Lebanon are easy. If you wanted formal meetings, McFarlane would have been received differently."

*North* stated that he had told McFarlane that he would meet Speaker Rafsanjani, Prime Minister Mousavi, and President Khameini. "I was told this would happen," North said. McFarlane and Kissinger made three trips to China to set up meetings for the President.

[The Foreign Affairs Advisor] asked why was McFarlane promised there would be Ministerial meetings?

*North* repeated that Ghorbanifar, in [George Cave's] presence, had stated that the U.S. team would meet with the senior leadership.

[The Iranian official] interjected that it had been previously agreed that North would come to Tehran to make arrangements and set the agenda. But North did not come. "We did not mention McFarlane. The last

314

phone call did not mention Ministerial meetings. We did not agree to such meetings for McFarlane. We keep our word."

[The Foreign Affairs Advisor] said the Iranian side wants to solve the whole problem. "Iran does not just want to discuss spare parts. I want to state clearly, we do not encourage terror. Even the Imam officially condemned skyjacking. We accept that we have influence in Lebanon. Many Islamic groups in Lebanon respect the revolution. We sent a man to Lebanon. We are very hopeful that we can help you and solve this problem. By solving this problem we strengthen you in the White House. We are waiting for an answer. As we promised, we will make every effort. We are working right now. We hope to get you news about the situation tomorrow. We will finish the job without waiting for the other parts. Regarding the agenda, we are willing to discuss all the items you proposed, especially where we have mutual interest. Afghanistan, the Soviets, Iran-Iraq War, Lebanon. We are ready to discuss. We have some objections to your positions on some of these issues. I have been appointed to represent Iran in this dialogue. I hope this will be a good start."

*North* asked whether [name deleted] thought it was possible to convince those who hold the Americans to release them?

"I answered you," [the Foreign Affairs Advisor] replied. "They're difficult to deal with. But anything we start we are hopeful about."

*North* said if that succeeds, the other aircraft and other things would be delivered. "Can a *secret* meeting be arranged with McFarlane and your leaders?"

[The Foreign Affairs Advisor] said he would have to wait or come back. "You can be sure that this will be conveyed. But 10 days is so early. We believe that after the hostages are free and the deliveries completed, there will need to be more positive steps."

*North* argued that he did not believe we should further the relationship with give and take. [The Iranian

315

official] got bad advice. Some of the parts Iran asked for it does not need. "Why do you need twenty radars? You should fix your radars rather than buy new ones."

*Nir* said, "we need to deliver a system that would allow both sides to exchange technical data, advice, and information. A long-term system is required. Such a development can only be agreed at the top."

[The Iranian official] said Nir was right. But North said the U.S. already knows what is needed.

[The Foreign Affairs Advisor] said Iran worries about the Russians. "They have missiles that can reach Tehran, as well as high altitude jets. You can't compare quality and quantity of our weapons. But the will of the Iranian people is greater than the Soviet people. I myself have a sister with two sons who were martyred in the war. One body was not even found. Two others are handicapped. All four were volunteers. I have a young brother who was not accepted as a volunteer. He took his older brother's ID when he returned from Ahwaz. Martyrdom is great. We congratulate the family of martyrs with congratulations and sorrow. During Ramazan we ask God to let us be a martyr if we are to die. Ramazan is the night of fate and power. Russians sell their rifles and prisoners for cash. Such a Russian can't fight an Iranian. But if we try to get such technology to strike them they will not fight. Islam tells us to be strong to prepare to fight. Millions of Soviet Moslems listen to our influence. Many believe the Imam is their leader, not Gorbachev. They are real Moslems. Secret groups in the Soviet Union print the Koran and distribute it. Their heart is on this side of the border. If we put aside nuclear power, we don't think Russians will take advantage of Iran. Of course everything is possible with these people."

[The Foreign Affairs Advisor] continued, "We appreciate and want to discuss everything with you. There is $2.5 billion deal. No one knows what it is. Rafsanjani said officially Iran is ready to buy weapons from America. This was a very positive statement. We really find more confidence and trust in our discussions. We hope in this way we can have a general dialogue before we come to the technical level. We want TOWs, especially with technicians. Easier to operate than MILAN. We would appreciate your advice on F-14/phoenix and harpoon missiles. You know how our people face you in public. When the spare parts come on a large-scale, the public will naturally know where they come from. The Air Force, land forces, Pasdarans will see. But they don't need to know about the dialogue, etc. Naturally, after some of this movement, our leaders could meet and accept this change officially. We rule on the basis of the people. We respect our people's will. This is our policy. The people hear the Parliament. Three sessions a week. We have to prepare the people for such a change. Step by step. We need to prepare the nation. Meetings between U.S. and Iranian leaders will take place publicly in this context. If you are serious about solving problems, I am sure official trips and high-level meetings will take place. The Iman has said we are ready to establish relations with all the world except Israel. But you have to remove the obstacles. This is why we are ready to discuss the agenda as you gave it with some changes. Speed up what has been agreed. You are a real superpower. I hope you don't mind being a superpower. You have much more capability. A few 747s can carry a lot in one day. We would be very pleased to discuss our specific needs."

*Teicher* asked why the meetings cannot take place now. "Rafsanjani has acted and spoken in a way that indicates Iran could benefit from a dialogue. [The Foreign Affairs Advisor] just stated that Imam said Iran is ready to establish relations with all the world except Israel. What is the problem?"

[The Foreign Affairs Advisor] explained that the leadership is affected by people and influences people. It is an interactive condition. "It's not whatever the Imam says. His word is accepted because he talks from the heart of the people. This is why the leadership of Iran is not something dogmatic. It is not a dictatorship, religious or otherwise. The leadership depends on wisdom of public opinion. After death of Brezhnev, Iran sent a delegation. The leadership was attacked by the nation for this act. No one went out to Chernenko's funeral. If you are serious, everything can be solved."

*North* said, "The U.S. wants to help Iran so others won't attack it. We need to work to broaden this understanding. I will urge McFarlane to meet with [The Foreign Affairs Advisor]. He doesn't always take my advice. Such is the fate of all advisors." North also asked the Iranian delegation to consider whether Iran would want the U.S. Government to express appreciation to Iran if four Americans go free.

[The Iranian official] said, "Understanding can lead to action."

[The Foreign Affairs Advisor] proposed reconvening at 10:00 a.m. on May 27 to review the agenda. "We should keep the Iranian experts out for now to keep the numbers small. Let us keep it political. We can decide later if experts are to be included. That agenda may be different. We will decide on a framework to implement what we agree to and how to establish secure communications. That will require high-level agreement."

The meeting ended at 1:50 a.m.

PARTICIPANTS:

*U.S.*
Oliver L. North
George Cave
Howard R. Teicher

*Iran*
[Senior Foreign Affairs Advisor]
[Assistants to the Prime Minister]

DATE: May 27, 1986
PLACE: Tehran, Iran, Independence Hotel
TIME: 10:00 a.m.

*North* expressed the U.S. team's gratitude that discussions can be continued. He noted that he had recommended that McFarlane meet with [the Foreign Affairs Advisor].

[The Foreign Affairs Advisor] said there was some news about the hostages. "We heard early. But I felt you were sleeping. There is a development which requires a decision. Our messenger in Beirut is in touch with those holding the hostages by special means. They made heavy conditions. They asked for Israel to withdraw from the Golan Heights and South Lebanon. Lahad must return to East Beirut, the prisoners in Kuwait must be freed, and all expenses paid for hostage-taking. They do not want money from the U.S. Iran must pay this money. We told them these conditions must be reduced. We can't make this work. We are negotiating. We are ready to pay for humanitarian reasons. We are negotiating other conditions. We are hopeful these negotiations will succeed."

[The Iranian official] complained that "only a portion of the 240 spare parts had been delivered. The rest should come. This is an important misunderstanding." (McFarlane called [the Foreign Affairs Advisor] down to his suite at this point in the discussion.)

*North* said, "The U.S. would provide the additional items on [the Iranian official's] list to the extend [sic] we can as soon as possible if they're still made. As soon as possible relates to funding. Even with countries where we have formal military ties, our law requires prior payment."

[The Assistant to the PM] opined that "many things are not written in law. In the same way we can finance your hostages you can find a way to finance our purchases."

*Teicher* explained how the U.S. Government sells military equipment, especially the interaction between the Congress and the President. "Our current sales to Iran are not following normal procedures and cannot be routinized."

*Nir* asked whether it might be agreed that "since the U.S. Government cannot deliver without advance payment and Iran cannot pay in advance, we will examine mid-term financial arrangement possibilities, such as Ghorbanifar and oil deals?"

On this note, the discussion broke up into separate lengthy corridor talks. After the Iranians departed, around noon, McFarlane stated that [Foreign Affairs Advisor] understood what steps Iran must take to restore U.S. confidence. But he referred to some sort of documents or letters held by Ghorbanifar. No member of the U.S. team was aware of these letters. McFarlane had emphasized that he must shortly leave, and that an opportunity for improved relations was being wasted. McFarlane said he would draft a MEMCON of his one-on-one discussion.

Lunch was served at 12:30 p.m.

Please deliver the following message from Robert McFarlane to Admiral Poindexter as soon as possible.

I have just completed a three hours one-on-one meeting with . . . the official designated by Rafsanjani/Musavi and Khamenei as their spokesman and whom I mentioned in my first cable which you received this morning.

It was a useful meeting on the whole. I say that in the sense that I was able to present a thorough foundation brief of our purposes and priorities internationally with specific explanation of our goals and intentions in the Middle East generally and with specific regard to Iran. I made clear that regarding Iran we sought a relationship based upon mutual respect for each other's sovereignty, territorial integrity and independence; that we believed in non intervention in the affairs of all states (and expected them to do the same thing). I then developed a brief of our sense of the Soviet objectives in the Middle East which are to expand its influence so as to ultimately be in the position to disrupt the resource flows of the area and exploit its geography for self interest. It's instruments for achieving these goals are the radical Arab states. . . . The Soviets would go to considerable length to prevent Iraq from losing to Iran, for if they did lose, Soviet credibility would be catastrophically damaged in the area. We would expect the Soviets to give Iraq all the support they needed and if this were not enough, then they would pressure Iran directly with military force.

I went on to explain that our policy remained to seek an end to the war and not to favor victory by either side; in their case since we were concerned for what their larger purposes were in the Middle East. On the surface they appeared to us to be determined to expand their influence through the spread of Islamic fundamentalism, relaying (sic or sp) on the use of terrorism to achieve their purposes. Consequently, I stated that they should understand that we were not prepared to give them a level of arms that would enable them to win the war.

That said, however, we were prepared to enter a dialogue to determine where there might be common interests and that Afghanistan appeared to be a leading case in point. We would also want to discuss Nicaragua (and their support for the Sandinistas) as well as Lebanon.

Finally, I proposed a specific work program to try to inject a little momenium [sic] into the process. As a first item, I proposed that both sides lower the rhetoric toward the other (although we would continue to call it as we saw it if terrorist acts were committed against Americans by Iranians). As a second measure, I proposed that we commit now to a sustained political dialogue in an effort to bridge differences here [sic] possible (even though some disagreements would remain eternal). This meeting should be secret but could take place within two weeks either here in Tehran or in a third country or in the U.S. Finally, I stated that since the Russians were no doubt monitoring the telephone calls that had been the basis of bringing us to this point, it would be wise to take direct secure means of communications and that could be done very easily. I also stated that while we could not envision providing a significant level of arms, that we might consider having a technician visit and remain on site to help them get more from what they have (as you know he listened attentively and then responded in low key fashion. Stressing that there are a number of areas where we have fundamental disagreements but also a number of areas where there are common interests. He went through the areas of disagreement but in a rather pro forma fashion. He then got to the clincher —their efforts to free the hostages in Lebanon. He reported that Hizbollah had made several preconditions to the release: 1. Israeli withdrawal from the Golan; 2. Israeli withdrawal from Southern Lebanon; 3. Lahad movement into East Beirut and 4. some (undefined) to pay the bills the hostages have accumulated. How's that for Chutzpah!!! He hurriedly added (before I unloaded on him) that "these demands are not acceptable and we are negotiating with them and believe that the only real problem is when you deliver the times we have requested."

I responded that I was glad to hear that his government wanted to solve problems and set a political dialogue in motion but that I had to say that the other matters he had stated led me to believe that such a dialogue would never get started at all. I then explained for him the history of how we have reached this point (bearing in mind that he has been getting only the Gorba/[Tehran contact] versions). I then carefully recounted how in the course of the past year, we had negotiated agreements only to have them altered at the last moment or delays imposed which had led to an extremely high level of frustration on the part of the President and that he had only reluctantly agreed to this meeting under a very clear and precise understanding of the arrangements. I then went over in detail what those arrangements were: 1. The U.S. would send a high level delegation to Tehran. They would bring with them a portion of the items they had requested and paid for (which we had done). 2. Upon our arrival, they had agreed to secure the release of the hostages promptly. 3. Upon release of the hostages to our custody, we would call forward the balance of items that had been paid for and those that had not been paid for would be dispatched as soon as payment had been received.

At this point he became somewhat agitated wanting to know just who had agreed to these terms. (I fingered Gorba and [his contact in the Prime Minister's office]). He stated that these were not the terms as he understood them. The basic difference was that they expected all deliveries to occur before any release took place. I stated firmly that while misunderstandings happen, I was confident that it had not been our side for we had two witnesses to the agreement. More importantly, however, regardless of misunderstandings, there was simply no latitude for altering the agreement at this time. Due to the tortured history I had recounted, the President had reached his limit of tolerance and that this visit was the last attempt we would make. My instructions were to return tonight to Washington. I stressed that we were prepared to call the other aircraft forward as soon as we received word that the hostages were released and even to do so within a couple of days after we had left if they were not released tonight but there was no possibility of changing the terms.

He was obviously concerned over the very real possibility that his people (Gorba and [his Tehran contact] had misled him and asked for a break to confer with his colleagues. I agreed noting that I had to leave tonight. (Actually, I don't have to leave tonight but recognizing that we have been here for three working days and they have not produced I wanted to try to build a little fire under them.) Right now they are under the understanding that we will all be leaving. They asked whether I could leave anyone behind and I said no.

Separately the rest of our delegations had been meeting to go over a letter that they had drafted which purported to show what we had agreed to in Frankfurt. This had been discussed last night as well, with Gorba basically, convincing an increasingly uncomfortable [Iranian official] that our interpretation was surely plausible to him. Ollie, Cave and Nir are all confident of their ground but understand the probability that Gorba or [the Iranian official] or both over-sold their accomplishment.

At this point it is hard to know where this will lead. We have heard nothing from Beirut—have you? I tend to think we should hold firm on our intention to leave and in fact do so unless we have word of release in the next six or seven hours. I can imagine circumstances in which if they said tonight that they guarantee the release at a precise hour tomorrow we would standby, but not agree to any change in the terms or call the aircraft forward.

Please convince [sic] this to the President and we will proceed as directed. My judgment is that they are in a state of great upset, Schizophrenic over their wish to get more from the deal but sobered to the fact that their interlocutors may have misled them. We are staying entirely at arms length while this plays out. We should hear something from them before long! However, when you get word it may be best if you call me on the prt 250—Bob Earl can arrange it for you.

Warm regards to all.

PARTICIPANTS:

*U.S.*
Robert C. McFarlane
Oliver L. North
George Cave
Howard R. Teicher

*Israel*
Amiram Nir

*Iran*
[Senior Foreign Affairs Advisor]
[Assistants to the Prime Minister]

DATE: May 27, 1986
PLACE: Tehran, Iran, Independence Hotel
TIME: 5:00 p.m.

[The Foreign Affairs Advisor] began the discussion with a report from Beirut. "The last contact with our man in Lebanon reported that he was able to eliminate three demands: the withdrawal of Israel from the Golan, South Lebanon and the transfer of Lahad to East Beirut. The people who hold the hostages believe they can solve the world's hunger problem! We will solve the money problem. The only remaining problem is Kuwait. We agreed to try to get a promise from you that they would be released in the future. The only problem is that the men here are not in agreement. These documents are in Ghorbanifar's handwriting. This is what I told you about this morning. If there has been a mistake in our agreement, it is not our fault. Maybe Ghorbanifar made a mistake. The problem is very simple. The only thing to discuss is what comes first and what comes later. The intentions of the two groups, based on what's written here, leads me to believe that agreement should be possible. I think we can come to a final agreement since you are an important person in your country. We, like you, want to solve this problem and get on with it."

*McFarlane* said it is apparent the Iranians are making a determined effort to bring this problem to a conclusion. "I am grateful. This spirit, if it had been present in our first encounter, would have made clear we could reach some agreement. Unfortunately, we have reached this point after a year and three efforts where we thought we have an agreement. This has affected the President's view of our ability to reach an agreement. He kept trying due to his belief that there were larger problems we should turn to. This affected his faith in our ability to work together. So he was willing to try once more and he believed we had come to an agreement. But his instructions in sending me here were that if this fourth try did not achieve results it was pointless to pursue an ineffective dialogue. I can understand that there may have been misunderstandings and I don't point to any bad faith. But my President's instructions are firm: without results we are to discontinue the talks. These are very firm instructions. All the items that have been paid for are loaded and posed for release the minute the hostages are in our custody. Their prompt delivery within 10 hours is our solemn commitment. With regard to the problem raised by the captors, the Da'Wa prisoners, it is much on our mind as it has been raised before. Our position is derived from our policy which respects all nations' judicial policies. We cannot ignore their process. I am sad to report all this. I respect what you said. I will report to my President but I cannot be optimistic."

[The Foreign Affairs Advisor] proposed a slight change, "Since the plane is loaded why not let it come. You would leave happy. The President would be happy. We have no guilt based on our understanding of the agreement. We are surprised now that it has been changed. Let the agreement be carried out. The hostages will be freed very quickly. Your President's word will be honored. If the plane arrives before tomorrow morning, the hostages will be free by noon. We do not wish to see our agreement fail at this final stage."

*McFarlane* underscored "how much I appreciated your statement of your country's opposition to hostage-taking. Such behavior is inconsistent with your country. Bearing in mind the possible misunderstanding, can we separate the issue? As a humanitarian gesture? We delivered hundreds of weapons. You can release the hostages, advise us, and will deliver the weapons."

[The Foreign Affairs Advisor] said, "OK." "But he (presumably Rafsanjani) would like for the staff to reach an agreement on what's been previously worked out. He wants your agreement for the staff to work out an agreement. This will be a difficult task. Might be difficult to get it done tonight. Can extend you stay [sic]? Or perhaps just the staff. Perhaps if we can reach agreement on this the staff can stay and complete the work?"

*McFarlane* expressed appreciation for [the Foreign Affairs Advisor's] willingness to try to work out an agreement. "I will seek the President's decision. I cannot know what he will say. But I should say in his most recent communication he pointed out I have been here three days. It should have been enough. But I will report again."

[The Foreign Affairs Advisor] suggested trying to solve the problem as fast as possible. "We will try to do it in a manner that will please your President. Problems like this can only be solved at the last minute. With all the problems we have, we want to solve them in a good atmosphere. They call us liberals, but revolutionaries do not accept this. The staffs must reach a mutually acceptable solution, then the problem will be solved. Something is apparent in our letters. I am not blaming the staffs. We want to reach a new understanding."

*McFarlane* agreed to try, while noting that "staff agreements must be approved by our leaders."

The meeting ended around 6:00 p.m.

PARTICIPANTS:

*U.S.*
Oliver L. North
George Cave
Howard R. Teicher

*Israel*
Amiram Nir

*Iran*
[Senior Foreign Affairs Advisor]
[Assistants to the Prime Minister]

DATE: May 27
PLACE: Tehran, Iran, Independence Hotel
TIME: 9:30 p.m.

*North* thanked [the Foreign Affairs Advisor] for returning the passports. He also stated that the plane needs gas.

[The Foreign Affairs Advisor] directed [the Iranian official] to take care of it.

*North* then presented the draft proposal for the evolution of relations, noting that "McFarlane is not pleased, but he gives Iran until 0400 to consider this proposal." ([Foreign Affairs Advisor] and his aids studied it. Their faces displayed anxiety. They each ask about the timing of deliveries. They repeatedly ask each other about the spare parts.).

[The Foreign Affairs Advisor] asks "How are we supposed to free the hostages by 0400?"

[The Assistant to the Prime Minister] acknowledged that they are in contact with those who hold the hostages. "We are negotiating. There is still a lot of work to do. We cannot make a final decision on when they will be released!"

*North* said he did not understand the timing problem. "With McFarlane earlier today you told us they would be free by noon."

[The Foreign Affairs Advisor] agreed he had said that earlier today. But it is now late. Our dispute is over the lack of complete agreement. What can you say about the [sic] held in Kuwait?"

*North* proposed a statement like: "The U.S. will make every effort through and with international organizations, private individuals, religious organizations, and other third parties in a humanitarian effort to achieve the release and just and fair treatment for Shiites held in confinement, as soon as possible."

The Iranians ask to think about the proposal.

McFarlane and [the Foreign Affairs Advisor] meet privately.

About 11:30 p.m., after more wrangling between McFarlane and [The Foreign Affairs Advisor], McFarlane concludes that they're just stringing us along. He gives the order to pack and depart. We discovered 15 minutes earlier that all day the plane was not refueled, leaving us semi-stranded. The pilot is now en route to refuel.

The meeting ends at 11:40 p.m.

PARTICIPANTS:

*U.S.*
Robert C. McFarlane
Howard Teicher
Oliver North

*Iran*
Senior Foreign Affairs Advisor

DATE: May 28, 1986
PLACE: Tehran, Iran, Independence Hotel
TIME: 2:00 a.m.

[The Foreign Affairs Advisor] asks for a delay until 6:00 a.m. They will get answer on the hostages by then.

*McFarlane* replies that if "you give us a time we will launch the aircraft so that it will land here two hours after the hostages are in U.S. custody."

[The Foreign Affairs Advisor] said he would be back in touch before 6:00 a.m.

The meeting ended at 2:10 a.m.


PARTICIPANTS:

*U.S.*
Robert C. McFarlane
Oliver L. North
George Cave
Howard R. Teicher

*Israel*
Amiram Nir

*Iran*
[Senior Foreign Affairs Advisor]
[Assistant to the Prime Minister]

DATE: May 28, 1986
PLACE: Tehran, Iran, Independence Hotel/ Mehrabad Airport

TIME: 7:50 a.m.

The Iranian official appears at 7:50 a.m. Regarding the hostages, he says, "they think two can get out now but it will require 'joint action' on the other two." *McFarlane* says, "It is too late. We are leaving."

[The Foreign Affairs Advisor] arrives at 8:00 a.m. He repeats the proposal made by [the Iranian official]. *McFarlane* tells him it won't work. "You are not keeping the agreement. We are leaving."

They try to slow us down but McFarlane has made up his mind. By 8:00 a.m. we are on our way to the airport.

As we board the aircraft [the Iranian official] pleads, "Why are you leaving?" *McFarlane* told him to tell his "superiors that this was the fourth time they had failed to honor an agreement. The lack of trust will endure for a long time. An important opportunity was lost." We left Tehran at 8:55 a.m.

These memoranda were distributed to the State and Defense Departments, CIA, and JCS in December 1986. (Teicher to McDaniel, 12/11/86.)

George Cave, using his alias "O'neil", also made a record of the meetings. He noted that

Tuesday was a day of marathon negotiations with the Iranians stalling for time and trying to get the most out of the American delegation. The American delegation stuck by the terms of the orginal agreement and insisted that after the terms of the Frankfurt agreement were met, we would meet and discuss in detail their needs and the outline of our two countries' future relations. The American delegation proposed a specific timing for a subsequent meeting. During the late afternoon it was agreed that the American team would draw up an agreement which would be discussed later in the evening. To save time O'neil began working on a translation which was later completed by he and Gorba.

During Tuesday's negotiations, all the demands of the

hostages holders evaporated except for the demand for the release of the Shi'ite prisoners in Kuwait. Goode [North] handled this part of the negotiations by firmly stating that the United States would not interfere in the internal affairs of Kuwait, particularly in an instance where Kuwaiti due legal process had been carried out. We would however seek to better the condition of the Shia prisoners through the good offices of international organizations such as the Red Cross and the Red Crescent. Goode warned that as far as the well being of the Shi'ite prisoners in Kuwait was concerned, there had better not be any more terrorist activity directed at the Royal family in Kuwait.

The draft agreement was the subject of intense negotiations with the Iranians making some counter proposals which were designed to gain them more time. Talks broke off around midnight with the Iranian delegation saying it wanted to caucus. For the next two hours, heated discussions were held within the Iranian delegation. [The Iranian officials] both said that the other would be responsible if nothing comes of the negotiations. Finally, shortly before two on Wednesday morning, [the Assistant to the PM] asked to see McFarland [sic]. He wanted assurances that we would deliver the remaining spare parts two hours after the hostages were released, and would stay after the arrival of the spare parts to discuss additional Iranian needs. He also asked for more time to get control of the hostages. McFarland gave [the Assistant to the PM] until 0630 wednesday [sic] morning to arrange for the release of the hostages. The American delegation retired to grab a couple of hours sleep knowing that we had at least out-frazzled them.

Cave's account terminated with the last conversations before the delegation returned to Israel. Washington reported before they left that it had seen no evidence that "the hostages were about to be released or that anything unusual was taking place." *(Id.)*

The agreement drafted during the evening of May 27 provided:

On this twenty seventh day of May 1986 and the sixth day of Khordad in the year 1365, the Government of the United States of America and the Government of the Islamic Republic of Iran, in a spirit of mutual understanding, and recognizing the importance of building respect, trust and confidence hereby agree to the following sequence of steps designed to lead to a new era of bi-lateral relations:

(1) The United States Government will cause a 707 aircraft to launch from a neutral site at 0100 in the morning to arrive in Tehran, Iran at 1000 on the morning of May 28, the seventh day of Khordad. This aircraft will contain the remainder of the HAWK missile parts purchased and paid for by the Government of Iran, a portion of which was delivered on May 24.

(2) The Iranian Government, having recognized the plight of the hostages in the Lebanon, and in the spirit of humanitarian assistance, agrees to cause the release and safe return of the living American hostages and the return of the body of the deceased American and that this release will be completed not later than 0400 Tehran time.

(3) It is further agreed by both sides that if by 0400 Tehran time, the hostages are not safely in the hands of U.S. authorities, the aircraft with the HAWK missile parts will be turned around and will not land in Iran and the U.S. delegation will depart Tehran immediately. If, howerver [sic], the hostages are released at 0400, as indicated above, the U.S. delegation will remain in Tehran until 1200 Noon on May 28, 1986.

(4) The Government of the United States commits to deliver to Bandar Abbas, Iran, two phase one IHIPIR radar sets, fully compatible with the HAWK missile system now in the possession of the Iranian government. This delivery to take place after the arrival of the hostages in U.S. custody and within ten days after the receipt of payment through existing financial channels for these radar

systems. It is further agreed that the government of the United States will make every effort to locate and identify those items from the original list of 240 parts which were not immediately available, and to provide those available as soon as possible after payment is received and the hostages are in U.S. custody.

(5) Both Governments agree to a continuation of a political dialogue to be conducted in secrecy until such time as both sides agree to make such a dialogue public. It is agreed by both sides that this dialogue shall include discussions on the Soviet threat to Iran, the situation in Afghanistan, Nicaragua, and other political topics as may be mutually agreed. Both sides agree in advance that these discussions will include consideration of further defense needs of Iran.

(6) Both Governments recognize that the lack of a clear channel of communications has contributed to misunderstanding and confusion in the past and agree that this problem is best resolved by having the United States provide a secure channel of communications between our two governments by placing a secure satellite communications team, and appropriate equipment secretly in

Tehran. The Government of Iran agrees that the U.S. communicators will be accorded normal diplomatic privileges and immunity on an informal basis and without attribution.

Cave's report ended with comments and a recommendation, including:

2. It is quite possible that the Iranian side was negotiating under the impression that we were only interested in a deal for the hostages. This would explain why they tried so hard to get us to do more in exchange for the hostages, i.e., the 20 hawk [sic] batteries and 18 additional hipar radars. It was therefore a good idea to leave a translation of the draft agreement with them as it will give them something to chew on.

McFarlane issued a stern warning that we are getting fed up with overatures [sic] from them that don't pan out. We are interested in a long term political and strategic relationship, and if Iran does not pick up on this opportunity it may be years before there is another one.

3. Ramadan was certainly a factor in how the negotiations went. aslo [sic] the problem caused by not being able to see anyone in a position of power. The people we were negotiating with were a couple of rungs down the ladder. The fact that [the Iranian official's] breath could curl rhino hide was no help either. On the positive side was the change in the attitude of the Iranian delegation. By tuesday [sic] they were begging us to stay.

4. We also may have the problem of the dishonest interlocutor. The Iranian side made it clear that one of the problems in our negotiations was the fact that prior to our meeting, Gorba gave each side a different picture of the structure of the deal. O'neil made the point to [the Assistant to the Prime Minister] that the letters they received [sic] were from Gorba, not the U.S. government. We will have to lean heavily on Gorba in the future.

5. Since both Gorba and [the Iranian official] stand to make a lot of money out of this deal, they presumably will work hard to bring it off. Gorba has very special reasons for seeing that the deal goes through. The serious problem we must address is whether the Iranians can gain control of the hostages. The French don't think they can. This could be our real problem. The Iranian side may be most willing, but unable to gain control.

RECOMMENDATION

Through hindsight it would have been better for Goode and O'neil to have gone in first to handle the initial negotiations. We should not have subjected a senior U.S. official to the indignities he was forced to endure. We have made the point to the Iranians that the draft agreement must be finally negotiated by senior responsible officials from both sides. If we have a subsequent response from the Iranian side it is strongly recommended that Goode and O'neil meet with the Iranian side somewhere in Europe to continue the negotiations.

(May 1986 Hot Docs.).

# E. Post Mortem

Most American accounts of the meetings conform more or less faithfully to the contemporaneous written record. Ghorbanifar's account is different.

According to Ghorbanifar, the meetings started badly because they were inadequately prepared. Ghorbanifar proposed that North and he go to Tehran first to prepare the way. The Americans refused. (Ghorbanifar 161) Ghorbanifar's Iranian interlocutors were incredulous at the notion that McFarlane would arrive without preparation, but agreed to welcome him "if he comes with the whole of what he has promised to come here, the spare parts, okay." *(Id.* at 162. *See also* 168)

The American delegation arrived two hours earlier than Ghorbanifar thought they would; as a result, they waited an hour and a half at the airport until the Iranian officials arrived. *(Id.* at 163–64) From the beginning, the Iranians were disappointed that the Americans had brought less than all the spare parts alleged to have been promised. Ghorbanifar recalled that the Americans raised the hostage question as something to be resolved before progress could be made on other subjects, and that this condition was mentioned for the first time since February. *(Id.* at 165–66) Ghorbanifar stressed that McFarlane's arrival and treatment were remarkable in light of the recent history of Iranian-American relations and the fate of Iranian officials such as Barzagan who met with American officials. They discussed cooperation against the Soviet Union, which also was remarkable. This fact contradicts, Ghorbanifar said, the image of the meetings conveyed in the press as negotiations about an arms-for-hostages trade, facilitated by self-interested arms traders. *(Id.* at 166–68)

Ghorbanifar remembered that Ayatollah Khomeini approved the meetings, and that he, Ghorbanifar, arranged for the head of the Majlis foreign relations committee to meet McFarlane. According to Ghorbanifar, "the Parliament is everything in Iran, the Majlis, and he is the number one for foreign affairs." *(Id.* at 169) This man urged McFarlane not to press the Iranians, but to give them time.

> that we cook the way we want the Ayatollah Khomeini to pave the ground for this, to make it ready, prepare for him. Don't push him. From the first place, Mr. McFarlane was insisting on we have nothing to discuss and nothing is going on to get to this agenda if the whole four American hostages are not released. . . . He waited one day. I pushed the Iranian side every day. Do something. He is here. You will have to save his face.

> After three days the man came to him and said, Mr. McFarlane, I have good news for you. We accepted the whole agenda, approved that we go and we coordinate. And the good news to that is this: we prepared the old man. Everything is ready right now. It was seven in the evening, and I have six witnesses—Mr. Nir, Mr. North, Cave, and the other gentleman and myself.

*(Id.* at 170-71) The Iranian said the Lebanese were proving difficult, but that it was possible to arrange the immediate release of two hostages.

Ghorbanifar remembered that McFarlane stormed out of the room in response to this message. Nir and North eventually persuaded him to return. Despite the pleadings of the Iranians and what Ghorbanifar described as the "panic" of Nir and North at McFarlane's behavior, McFarlane behaved as if he were giving an ultimatum, Russian-style. *(Id.* at 171–73) The Iranians continued to plead; the Majlis foreign affairs expert said Khomeini had agreed to release the hostages first, but McFarlane

> said no, if by six o'clock all the hostages are not out, I leave. He says, okay, take two now and give us another day. No. And he left at six o'clock. And, believe me, I saw the tears in the eyes of North, Nir, and everybody.

> Why he did so? I know why. I tell you why. Number

one, he had $15 million in his pocket. We were a hostage to him. Number two, the Iranians, they are not real politicians. The people came to him. They were so soft and they were so open to him; they explained to him deeply how they are in disaster. They need the help of the United States financially—I mean the support-wise, logistic-wise, military-wise. And he is a smart guy.

He found out that in such a catastrophe and that situation they are. They are really in need of it. And, besides that, he says what the hell is this. I know now all the big shots. I have their telephone number. We have relation. We go out. We have the money. We have them. We know their need. They will follow. Who needs this man, middle man? Who is he?

So he checked out and he left. And they left the poor guys alone in Tehran. I stayed one day, two days in Tehran. I told them this issue is so big that nobody can leave it on the air. Let me go and talk to them and finalize what I can do. But there is no way I can do unless you do something. First we have to do something.

*(Id.* at 173–74)

McFarlane's recollection corresponded to his contemporaneous record. In addition, he noted that the Iranians confiscated the pallet of spare parts, but that no additional delivery was made because no hostage was released. In Israel on the trip home, McFarlane was disappointed.

North said well, don't be too downhearted, that the one bright spot is that the government is availing itself of part of the money for application to Central America, as I recall, although I took it to be Nicaragua.[71]

After returning to the United States, Cave remembered evaluating the situation. "It was quite clear that Ghorbanifar was lying to both sides in order to blow this deal up as big as he could." (Cave 24) Cave learned from the Tehran trip that the Iranians had less control over the holders of the hostages than the Intelligence Community believed. He also concluded that the Kuwaitis held the key to the hostage problem. American hostages would not be released until Kuwait released the Dawa prisoners. *(Id.* at 41-42).

## VIII. The End of the Beginning: June-July 1986

When McFarlane's delegation returned to the United States, nearly a year had passed since the NSC staff formally floated the idea of contacting Iranian political factions through the medium of arms. In that time, Israel and the United States sold Iran 1,508 TOW missiles, 18 HAWK missiles, of which 17 were returned, and some HAWK spare parts. In addition, the United States had provided Iran with briefings on the U.S. perception of the Soviet threat and the Iran-Iraq War. The NSC staff's involvement had been ancillary at the beginning; as time passed, the staff increasingly influenced, and then directed the operation.

All those involved hoped that these transfers would lead to the release of Americans held hostage in Lebanon and form the basis for a new relationship with Iran. In this period, one American hostage had been released, and at least one had died in captivity. Whether a new relationship was being formed remained (and remains) to be seen.

## A. Aid to the Nicaraguan Resistance

In the late spring, 1986, the Administration directed its energy to persuade Congress to fund the Nicaraguan resistance. Absent Congressional appropriations, the Administration looked to third countries to help the resistance pay its bills. The Assistant Secretary of State for Inter-American Affairs told the Board:

[B]y spring [1986], we were running out of money. The $27 million was running out. It ran out about in June or July, and at that point, it was also clear to us that though both Houses [of Congress] had voted the hundred million, we weren't going to get it that fast.

We knew we'd get it before or believed we'd get it

before the adjournment. But, in any event, we were out of money.

It was at that point that we made a solicitation to another government for a kind of bridge to extend the $27 million until we had the $100 million.

\* \* \*

We had discussed in the department [of State] on several occasions whether we should utilize the authority which we believe we had to go to a third government. I don't remember the dates of those discussions, but the Secretary's staff has those dates. I mean, there are notes of those discussions. It was in the spring—March, April, May, starting—as authority to obligate the $27 million ran out March 31. After that, we were dealing with the pipeline, which we knew would last about two months, ten weeks, something like that.

I got actual authority to go ahead and make a particular solicitation in July, as I recall it. There is cable traffic on this. It was from the Secretary, and we sent a cable—this was done through the embassy in that country—saying do you think they'll give, and there was a sort of back and forth with the Ambassador. The secretary decided that we should go ahead and make the request, which I then did.

The actual solicitation was made by me, not by the Ambassador, in London, meeting with an official of that government.

They ultimately said yes.

Let me back up a step.

Before I went off and made the solicitation, it was clear that they might say yes. They, after all, agreed to meet us on a matter of highest importance. I don't know whether they knew what it was going to be, but it was certainly plausible.

So, we needed a place to put the money. When [sic: What] I did was to go to [the] head of the Central American Task Force at CIA and say—and I must say that I am relying on his memory of this as I don't remember this conversation. But I asked him about it a couple of weeks ago, and so, this is his account of it.

It was so how do I do this? I mean, can UNO, the Nicaraguans, the Contras, can they set up an account? How do we do this?

He said yes, he would pass a message to them to set up an account, which would receive any money, the number of which I would give to the foreign official, and then that would be the place that they would receive the money.

Chairman Tower: Set up an account where?

Mr. Abrams: It didn't matter to me, and I think—I don't actually know the answer to that any more, but there are records that the CIA has—I believe the answer is Panama. Actually, they dispatched, a message was passed to an official of UNO, "Go open an account," because there may be some money being put in it.

So they did that.

I asked the same question more or less the same day, probably even the same hour, of Ollie North—what do I do here? I think there may be some money coming in for the Contras, can we set up an account?

Again, I don't have much memory of that conversation either, and I haven't asked Ollie for obvious reasons. So I don't know what his memory, if any, is of that.

At any event, at some point later, like a week later, probably, both of these guys gave the index cards with an account number and the name of the bank on it.

I then went to Charlie Hill, who is the Executive Assistant to Secretary Schultz. . . . Well, for the account number which was given to me by Ollie North, [the bank] was Credit Suisse, in Geneva. . . . To continue, I went to Charlie Hill, who is Executive Assistant to

340

the Secretary and said now what do I do? I asked both these guys and they both came up with accounts.

So Charlie and I kicked it around. This was the first week in August, as I recall. We decided to use the account number that been provided by Ollie, on the grounds that it looked, oddly enough in retrospect, kind of cleaner because we were unsure, first of all, whether this account had any relationship to any other Agency account. We wanted a separate account. And, I would have to say there was probably some institutional rivalry there; that is, this is something State was doing, why should we get the CIA involved in the distribution of funds, because I don't know who was a signatory for that. I still don't—for that account.

\* \* \*

I then gave the account number that Ollie had given me to this foreign official.

(Abrams 3–7)

According to the head of CIA's Central American Task Force, the Nicaraguan resistance started to incur debt after they used up the $27 million; by the middle of July 1986, that debt amounted to over $2.5 million. (H/CATF 38) This CIA official told the Board:

In early August of 1986, when we were seeing this debt problem, which had been a focal point of discussion, saying my God, the resistance is going to run out of money and they are going to start starving to death; we ought to get this law passed. We knew we weren't. We were running into summer recess, even though both chambers had passed the bill. And we had a number of discussions about how are they going to survive for the next three months.

The obvious answer was solicit some money from someplace. So State Department, who had the writ and the charter to do that, went out and looked at the possibilities and came up with Brunei, obviously. One day I got a phone call on Thursday from Elliott [Abrams] saying we have a possibility to solicit some

341

money from the Sultan of Brunei. Only the Secretary and I are aware of it. I am going to be making a trip. How should we deposit this money? How should we handle it?

And I said, well, the best way, the mechanisms that I would prefer to use, which are an Agency-controlled bank account and so on and so forth, are not—the other mechanisms are too hard to start up. The best way to do it is to get the resistance forces, one person in particular in whom we have complete trust and confidence, to open a bank account, and you put the money in a bank account and make him accountable to you for how it's used.

And he said that sounds like a good idea. I'll open a bank account. So I got hold of this particular individual and asked him to open a bank account in the Bahamas. I wanted to stay away from Cayman Islands and Panama. And he did open up a bank account and had it co-signed with his financial officer. And I gave Elliott the account number. And that's all.

I subsequently asked the individual if any money had been deposited and asked Elliott if he thought the mission had been successful, and the answers to both were, Elliott, I don't know, and to the individual, he said no, no money has been deposited. We subsequently checked and no money was deposited in that account.

And that's the last I thought or heard of it until . . . I received a phone call [from the Deputy Director for Operations] saying, my God, did you give Elliott a bank account in Geneva. And do you have a private bank account in Geneva? And I said no, who are you talking about? Well, the FBI says that you gave Elliott a bank account in Geneva, to which Elliott deposited $10 million from the Sultan of Brunei, which is missing.

And I said, wait a minute, something's badly wrong here. That was the first time I knew that Elliott—then we got it sorted out after about a few hours of almost frantic phone calls, and it was the first I knew that

Elliott apparently had gotten another, allegedly had gotten another bank account from Ollie North in Geneva.

General Scowcroft: He didn't tell you he was not going to use your account?

[Head of Central America Task Force]: No, he never told me that. That probably left me as speechless as anything in this whole endeavor, that that $10 million which we sorely needed and still do need—I mean, it would be the margin of comfort even in today's operation—went into a bank account in Geneva and disappeared. It just left me dumbstruck and still does. I still find it hard to believe.

(H/CATF44–47)

On June 10, 1986, early in the process thus described to the Board, North wsrote Poindexter:

Hopefully you have by now been informed that UNO/ FDN safely released the eight West Germans this evening just before dark at the religious commune at Presillas. Franklin is headed North in attempt to get across the Rama Rd before the Sandinistas can close in on him. At this point the only liability we still have is one of DEMOCRACY INC.'s airplanes is mired in the mud (it is the rainy season down there) on the secret field in Costa Rica. They hope to have it out by dawn. On a separate but related matter: The reason why I asked to speak to you urgently earlier today is that Ray [?Burghardt] called Elliott Abrams regarding the third country issue. Elliott has talked to Shultz and had prepared a paper re going to [other third countries] for contributions. Elliott called me and asked "where to send the money." I told Elliott to do nothing, to send no papers and to [sic] talk to no one further about this until he talks to you. He is seeing you privately tomorrow. At this point I need your help. As you know, I have the accounts and the means by which this thing needs to be accomplished. I have no idea what Shultz knows or doesn't know, but he could prove to be very unhappy if he learns of these others countries aid that has been given in the past from someone other than you. Did RCM [McFarlane] ever tell Shultz?

I am very concerned that we are bifurcating an effort that has, up to now, worked relatively well. An extraordinary amount of good has been done and money truly is not the thing which is most needed at this point. What we most need is to get the CIA re-engaged in this effort so that it can be better managed than it now is by one slightly confused Marine LtCol. Money will again become an issue in July, but probably not until mid-month. There are several million rounds of most types of ammo on hand and more ($3M) worth on the way by ship . . . Critically needed items are being flown in from Europe to the expanded warehouse facility at Ilopango. Boots, uniforms, ponchos, etc. are being [sic] purchased locally and Calero will received $500K for food purchases by the end of the week. Somehow we will molify the wounded egos of the triple A with not being able to see RR. We should look to going back to a head of an allied government on the blowpipes if we are going to do anything at all about outside support in the next few days, and I wd love to carry the letter from RR . . . if we are going to move on something. Meanwhile, I wd recommend that you and RCM have a talk about how much Sec Shultz does or does not know abt [third country assistance approaches] so that we don't make any mistakes. I don't know [one of those governments] knows since Fred never told me. At this point I'm not sure who on our side knows what. Help.

(North PROF note to Poindexter, 6/10/86, 23:21:54) Poindexter replied:

Out of the last NSPG on Central America Shultz agreed that he would think about third country sources. I wanted to get an answer from him so we could get out of the business. As I understand the law there is nothing that prevents State from getting involved in this now. To my knowledge Shultz knows nothing about the prior financing. I think it should stay that way. My concern was to find out what they were thinking so there would not be a screw up. I asked Elliot at lunch.[72] He said he had recommended Brunei where Shultz is going to visit. They have lots of money and very little to spend it on. It seems like a good prospect. Shultz agrees. I asked Elliot how the money could be transferred. He said he thought Shultz could just hand them an account number. I said that was a bad idea not at all letting on that we had access to accounts. I told Elliot that the best way was for Brunei to direct their embassy here to receive a person that we would designate and the funds could be transferred through him. Don't you think that is best? I still want to reduce your visibility. Let me know what you think and I will talk to George. I agree about CIA but we have got to get the legislation past.

(Poindexter PROF note to North, 6/11/86.) In another message, Poindexter added: "We should not mention Brunei to anybody. elliot said only schultz and hill are aware." [sic] (Poindexter PROF note to [?Burghardt]):

"With respect to private solicitations," Abrams told the Board,

we never did any of that. As a matter of fact, the state of our knowledge of that was limited. We had intelligence reporting, which improved over time as the restrictions on what the Agency could do with the Contras were reduced. We had better information on what was being received, better information on what was being received, better in 1986 than in 1985.

We in the department never made any other solicitation for anything from anybody. One time, this summer, I would say, General Singlaub called me from Asia . . . and said I can get some aid for the Contras, through me, if you will just sort of let this foreign government know, just tell their ambassador—I don't remember who I was supposed to tell—this is official.

I said I can't do that. It's just not right; I can't do that.

He said well, then, I'm going to blow it. But I just couldn't do that.

So that was the only other time when I was asked, in a sense indirectly, to solicit, and said no.

We had virtually no, we had no information on who was paying for it. CIA people have testified that they were able to trace money back to secret bank accounts but couldn't get behind the bank secrecy laws; and they have testified that they knew the arms were coming from [a foreign country]; that is to say, the last stop before Central America . . . , but they could not go beyond that and find out who was paying.

Well, I have to say that we did not think it was our job to find out who was paying, since it seemed to us, as long as it didn't violate the Neutrality Act or the Arms Export Control Act that it was legal and proper.

Once or twice we, in particular, actually CIA and not State, came up with some facts that indicated a violation of the Neutrality Act, a shipment of arms from the U.S., and we reported that to the Department of Justice.

But we did not engage in nor did we really know anything about this private network. We knew that it existed. We knew it in part because somebody was giving the Contras guns.

We knew it also because you couldn't be in Central America and not know it.

We have significant military assistance through El Salvador via Ilopango Airport, which is the Salvadoran Airport.

Also, we ran a good proportion of the $27 million in humanitarian aid through Ilopango Airport.

(Abrams 11–13)

Congress authorized $100 million in assistance to the Nicaraguan resistance at the end of June 1986.

In June, the pressures on North worried McFarlane. He wrote Poindexter that

[i]t seems increasingly clear that the Democratic left is coming after him [North] with a vengeance in the

election year and that eventually they will get him—too many people are talking to reporters from the donor community and within the administration. I don't [know] what you do about it but in Ollie's interest I would get him transfered or sent to Bethesda for disability review board (appartwently [sic] the Marine Corps has already tried to survey him once[)]. That wuld [sic] represent a major loss to the staff and contra effort but I think we can probably find a way to continue to do those things. In the end it may be better anyway.

(McFarlane PROF note to Poindexter, 6/10/86) Poindexter indicated he would think about McFarlane's concern. (Poindexter PROF note to McFarlane, 6/11/86)

In the middle of July, Poindexter asked to see North. After the meeting, North wrote:

The opportunity to discuss the Central America issue with you was welcome and at the same time, disturbing. In view of last night's CBS piece and this morning's appalling Washington TIMES item, I can understand why you may well have reservations about both my involvement in Nicaragua policy and even my continued tenure here. Since returning a few minutes ago I have been told that even my luncheon engagement with my sister yesterday is in question. Under these circumstances, and given your intention that I extricate myself entirely from the Nicaragua issue, it probably wd be best if I were to move on as quietly, but expeditiously as possible. I want you to know that it is, for me deeply disappointing to have lost your confidence, for I respect you, what you have tried to do and have enjoyed working with you on a number of issues important to our nation. On the plus side of the ledger we have had a close relationship on several initiatives that could not have been accomplished without absolute trust between two professionals. At the same time you should not be expected to retain on your staff someone who you suspect could be talking to the media or whom you believe to be too emotionally involved in an issue to be objective in the development of policy options and recommendations.

347

I know in my heart that this is not the case, but as I said in our discussion yesterday, we live in a world of perceptions, not realities. I have taken the liberty of forwarding to you a memo transmitted two weeks ago which I wd like to be sure you have had a chance to see—mostly because it predates the current controversy. I want to be sure that you do indeed know that I have and will continue to tell you the truth as I see it—for I deeply believe that this is the only honorable thing to do. That this, and the relationships established in the region over the past five years are no longer enough to enable me to serve in the various policy fora on Nicaragua is, for me, unfortunate. Nonetheless, I consider myself to have been blessed to have had the chance to so serve for as long as I did. Finally, to end on a substantive note, you should be aware that Gen Galvin will be here for DRB sessions on Mon & Tues next week and wd vy much like to have the chance to meet privately with you. He has suggested any time after 1630 on Tues, but is amenable to yr schedule as long as he will not have to absent himself from DRB sessions. Given the controversy that rages over the CINC-SOUTHCOM role in the project, I strongly recommend that you see him if at all possible.

(North PROF note to Poindexter, 7/15/86, 12:21:30) Poindexter replied:

Now you are getting emotional again. It would help if you would call Roger Fontaine and Jerry O'Leary and tell them to call off the dogs. Tell them on deep background, off the record, not to be published that I just wanted to lower your visibility so you wouldn't be such a good target for the Libs. As it has worked out both you and Vince will represent NSC on Elliot's group. Don't go intodetail [sic]. I do not want you to leave and to be honest cannot afford to let you go. By the way they are making a big mistake by calling Rod a soft liner. He disagrees with Stan Turner and Bernie as much as I do.

NEW SUBJECT: I can see Jack Galvin this afternoon. Let me know how the calls go.

(Poindexter PROF notes to North, 7/15/86, 14:06;
14:07:02; 14:09:02) The matter was straightened out as far
as concerned North's relationship with Poindexter later in
the month. *(See* North PROF note to Poindexter, 7/23/86,
15:05:39; Poindexter PROF note to North, [7/23/86])

Afterward, North wrote Poindexter about the need to
turn over certain material in Central America to the CIA.

We are rapidly approaching the point where the
PROJECT DEMOCRACY assets in CentAm need to
be turned over to CIA for use in the new program.
The toal (sic or sp) value of the assets (six aircraft,
warehouses, supplies, maintenance facilities, ships,
boats, leased houses, vehicles, ordnance, munitions,
communications equipment, and a 6520' runway on
property owned by a PRODEM proprietary) is over
$4.5M.

All of the assets—and the personnel—are owned/paid
by overseas companies with no U.S. connection. All of
the equipment is in first rate condition and is already
in place. It wd be ludicrous for this to simply disappear
just because CIA does not want to be "tainted" with
picking up the assets and then have them spend $8M–
10M of the $100M to replace it weeks or months later.
Yet, that seems to be the direction they are heading,
apparently based on NSC guidance.

If you have already given Casey instructions to this
effect, I wd vy much like to talk to you about it in
hopes that we can reclama [sic] the issue. All seriously
believe that immediately after the Senate vote the
DRF will be subjected to a major Sandinista effort to
break them before the U.S. aid can become effective.
PRODEM currently has the only assets available to
support the DRF and the CIA's most ambitious estimate is 30 days after a bill is signed before their own
assets will be available. This will be a disaster for the
DRF if they have to wait that long. Give our lack of
movement on other funding options, and Elliot [sic]/
Allen's plea for PRODEM to get food to the resistance
ASAP, PRODEM will have to borrow at least $2M to
pay for the food. That's O.K., and Dick is willing to do

349

so tomorrow-but only if there is reasonable assurance that the lenders can be repaid. The only way that the $2M in food money can be repaid is if CIA purchases the $4.5M+ worth of PRODEM equipment for about $2.25M when the law passes. You should be aware that CIA has already approached PRODEM's chief pilot to ask him where they (CIA) can purchase more of the C–135K A/C. The chief pilot told them where they can get them commercially from the USAF as excess-the same way PRODEM bought them under proprietary arrangements. It is just unbelievable. If you wish I can send you a copy of the PROJECT DEMOCRACY status report which includes a breakdown of assets. It is useful, nonattributable reading.

(North PROF note to Poindexter, reply to note of 7/15/86, 14:07)

# B. Hostages and Iran, June-July 1986: "Stalemate"

On May 29, McFarlane, North, and Teicher reported on the Tehran trip to the President, accompanied by Poindexter, Regan, and the Vice President. They informed the President that the Iranians had asked for the delivery of all HAWK spare parts before hostages would be freed. The United States delegation had rejected this proposal, but agreed with the Iranians to establish a secure communications network. Contact would continue. McFarlane argued that no new meeting should take place until all hostages were freed. (McDaniel log) McFarlane recalled this report to the President.

I told him that I had talked to people and that while I thought that there were people legitimately oriented toward change that they had not yet gotten to a position of confident ability to act. I had not met with Rafsanjani. He must have felt vulnerable, as Mr. Brzezinski's meeting with Barzagan had led to certain consequences, and he probably was fearful about it. But that ought to tell us something and that I thought it was unwise to continue anything further.

350

If they wanted to have political meetings that is a judgment we could make, but that there ought not be any weapons transfers.

The President didn't comment really, but that was not untypical. He would often hear reports, say that he would think about it, and that was—and he didn't react to me and I left, and that's the last I heard about it.

Chairman Tower: And that ended your involvement in the matter!

McFarlane: Yes, sir.

(McFarlane (1) 45) On June 2, the CIA instructed the Army "to put the radar transfer action on 'hold,' a status which continued until 30 July 1986." (Army/IG Report 9)

While McFarlane's delegation was negotiating in Tehran, the President heard discussion about using force to free the hostages. (McDaniel log, 5/28/86) Once North returned, Poindexter sought his views on the subject. He wrote North

I am beginning to think that we need to seriously think about a rescue effort for the hostages. Is there any way we can get a spy into the Hayy Assallum area? See Charlie's [Allen] weekly report [on hostage locations]. Over a period of time we could probably move covertly some . . . people into Yarze.

(Poindexter PROF note to [?North], 5/31/86)

North was not prepared to replace the program with force. He

[f]ully agree[d] that if the current effort fails to achieve release then such a mission should be considered. You will recall that we have not had much success with this kind of endeavor in the past, however. After CIA took so long to organize and then botched the Kilburn effort, Copp undertook to see what could be done thru one of the earlier DEA [Drug Enforcement Agency] developed Druze contacts. Dick has been working with Nir on this and now has three

351

people in Beirut and a 40 man Druze force working "for" us. Dick rates the possibility of success on this operation as 30%, but that's better than nothing.

In regard to U.S. military rescue ops, JCS has steadfastly refused to go beyond the initial thinking stage unless we can develop some hard intelligence on their whereabouts. We already have . . . one ISA officer in Beirut but no effort has been made to insert personnel since we withdrew the military mission to the LAF. If we really are serious, we should start by getting CIA to put a full time analyst on the HLTF [Hostage Location Task Force] and then organizing a planning cell-preferably not in the pentagon [sic], but at CIA, to put the operation together. Dick, who has been in Beirut, and who organized the second Iran mission, is convinced that such an operation could indeed be conducted. My concern in this regard is that JCS wd insist on using most of the tier 2 and 3 forces in such an undertaking. If you want me to task this thru the OSG we will do so, but [I] urge that we start by you having Casey staff the HLTF as there has been a certain amount of planning undertaken on this matter already. It might be useful to sit down w/ Dewey and Moellering on this after next week's OSG meeting (Thursday 1500-1600 [June 12]) if you have the time. We can probably brief you in about 20 min max.

(North PROF note to Poindexter, 6/3/86, 11:42:43)

At his morning national security briefing on June 6, the President is said to have approved military planning to rescue the hostages as well as reviving [previously planned efforts]. (McDaniel log) Poindexter asked the Director of Central Intelligence to intensify efforts to locate the hostages. (Poindexter to DCI, 6/19/86. CIA/IG Chronology 19) By July, the United States had asked Israel to help. *(See* North PROF note to Poindexter, 07/11/86, 07:27:44)

Meanwhile, the United States knew that at least Ghorbanifar refused to treat the Tehran meeting as the end. On June 6, he pressed [his contact in the Prime Minister's office] for another meeting with the United States. He promised that the United States would deliver the remaining HAWK spare parts and, if Iran paid in advance, the radars. [The Iranian official] seems to have treated Ghorbanifar's advocacy as nothing new, to have been unimpressed with his idea, and inclined to drop the initiative.

Claiming that Ghorbanifar told him that [the Iranian official] wanted to talk, George Cave, using his alias "O'neil," called [the Iranian] on June 13.

[The official in the PM's office] said that this was not true, but "our friend" [Ghorbanifar] had been pressing him to go through with the deal.

O'neil then asked what we should do about the situation. B replied that he did not know why we didn't complete the deal when in dubai [sic] [?Tehran]. O'neil interrupted to state that he had a suggestion. We should first meet in Europe to make sure there were no misunderstandings as happened before. Then our gorup [sic] would go to Dubai [coverterm for Tehran] at an agreed upon date. Upon arrival in Dubai the four boxes [hostages] would be turned over, then the rest of the spares would arrive and later dependeing [sic] on timeing [sic] the two Quties [coverterm for HAWK radars] would arrive. We would stay until everything was delivered. B said that the meeting in Germany was not necessary and that deal was unacceptable to them. He proposed that we arrive with the remaining 240 spares, then two hostages would be truned over [sic]. When the two radars arrive, the two other hostages would be turned over.

We haggled abit [sic] O'neil insisting on our deal and he insisting on his. O'neil suggested that meeting in Germany was necessary and B finally agreed that if really necessary he would come. He parrried [sic] the request that the H [?] also attend. He added that it would be very difficult to get away at this time.

When discussing the possible trip to Dubai, B suggested that it not necessary for the chief to accompany group that comes.

Since discussion was getting nowhere, O'neil suggested that he was in [a] position to decide on B insistance [sic], and there for it best [sic] that O'neil confer

353

with his superiors and B with his and O'neil will get back to him in one or two days. At the end B stated that it should not be that we give such importance to who does what first, once this deal is completed there are many important issues that we must discuss. He again insisted on the need of the US to demonstrate good faith.

O'neil asked if the hostages were now under their control because at one point B said that he did not know if their delegation was still in Lebanon. B hesitated to answer k—this [sic] one but said that they could get them. O'neil said "then they are in your hands" and B said they were (note O'neil doubts this is true).

The next day, the Iranian official told Ghorbanifar that Iranian officials were prepared to meet American representatives in Europe if the remaining HAWK spares and radars were delivered first. If all equipment were delivered, all hostages would be freed; if half the equipment, half the hostages.

Ghorbanifar and his Tehran contact discussed the matter for the rest of June. On June 20, Ghorbanifar provided the Iranian official with a detailed analysis of the price and the availability of the remaining HAWK spare parts. According to Ghorbanifar, 177 units would cost $3,781,600 in addition to the $24,173,200 Iran already had paid. He reported that, as a gift, the United States would add ten diesel generators essential to operating the HAWK system, and had offered to provide test and calibration equipment and technicians to operate it. At his morning national security briefing the same day, the President discussed both [our] ability to rescue hostages and next steps with Iran. The President is said to have decided that there would be no meetings with Iranian officials until the hostages were released. (McDaniel log) The next day, Ghorbanifar and the Iranian official argued pricing, using an oil transaction as cover.

"[P]er instructions" from the official in the Prime Minister's office, who had unsuccessfully tried to reach him, Cave called the Iranian June 22.

2. Although there was a lot of talk one thing emerged and that is that the B's people want to somehow go through with the deal. The difficulties that dealing with us was causing them [sic]. The B emphasized that there are many people that oppose dealing with us. When O'neil asked if this was causing his group political difficulties, he confirmed that this was the case. His problem is that they must appear to have made a good deal. He pointed out that the previous release of the one person in return for the 1,000 had not left them in good oder [sic] as the 1,000 were not that important, and they had to return the other materials.

3. O'neil stated that we were very much interested in the deal and a long term relationship between the two companies, but the chief of our company was insisting on the release of our embargoed 4,000,000 dollars [coverterm for hostages] before we delivered the remainder of 240 [HAWKs] spares and then the two large boxes [radars]. What was interesting at this point is that the B did not say there could be no deal on this basis. He said that some fromula [sic] must be worked out whereby we can deliver what we promised at much the same time as they deliver the 4,000,000. For the first time he said that they needed political currency to deliver on their end. He stated that they have a serious problem with the 4 million in explaining why it is that they need it. This has been a serious problem in their negotiations with those that control the 4 million. When O'neil asked the direct question can they gain control of the 4 million, the B hesitated but said that this was within their capabilities. He said that if we had stayed in Dubai [Tehran] a few days longer they could have delivered 2 million immediately. He emphasized in answer to an O'neil question that they could not specifically say exactly when the 4 million would be transferred, but this was still in their power, despite the fact that the situation where the 4 million are held was continually deteriorating. The B urged that we try to do this deal as soon as possible, so that our two companies could have a meaningful future relationship. O'neil said that he would call back at approximately the same time on 23 June.

4. The B continually spoke of the serious problems that trying to consumate [sic] this deal was causing him and his colleagues. He urged O'neil to contact the merchant [Ghorbanifar] to get all the details. He would try to contact the merchant immediately to provide as much background as possible. The B on several occasions said that there was [sic] considerable forces arrayed against this deal and he considered himself in some danger. Most interesting note is that during this conversation the B insisted that they want to go through with deal. Although he bordered on the inarticulate at times, long pauses and some relapses into his old song and dance, he did not reject our position outright. O'neil's reccomendation [sic] is that we sit down and talk it out with him in in [sic] person, we may get more out of this than the transaction we are interested in.

Two days later, North reported to Poindexter that the Iranian official was trying to reach Cave again.

As of this minute they they have not yet connected. We are trying to have him call back. Nir advises that [the Iranian official] called Gorba about an hour ago in a state of great agitation to say that he was trying to get Sam [O'neil] to arrange for the release of one U.S. hostage. Nir believes it to be sincere and that we may really be close. I am not so sure but [C/NE] Sam and Charlie [Allen] all think it may be real. We'll see. Sam will call me later tonight and I'll come back into here or CIA to receive the report. Wd be nice to have some kind of secure voice to save these middle of the night trips. Will advise in a.m. of any developments.

(North PROF note to Poindexter, 6/24/86, 21:28:15)

At about the same time, a successful rescue began to look possible. North wrote in late June:

You should also be aware that CIA believes that they have made a major breakthrough on the location of at least two of the hostages. The info is being carefully analized [sic] before passing to JSOC, but there hasn't been this much enthusiasm on the issue in a long time. Our other effort seems to be at a standstill w/Ashgari

[sic] [Ghorbanifar] and [his Tehran contact] screaming at each other about prices and Geo. Cave telling [the Iranian official] that we are fed up w/the whole thing and are tired of being insulted by people who "pretend to be able to do things they cannot."

(North PROF note to [?Poindexter], reply to note of 6/25/86)

Ghorbanifar told the Board that Cave's telephone calls "every night" created a problem in Tehran. He recalled Cave.

saying the President said this, McFarlane said this, Poindexter said this, and making a lot of confuse [sic] for Iranians. Because he doesn't know there are three groups that must come together to make a decision.

General Scowcroft: Who was Cave talking to when he called?
Mr. Ghorbanifar: To the man who is the head of this operation, the special aide to the Prime Minister, the number one in his office.

(Ghorbanifar 175)

The official in the Prime Minister's office and Ghorbanifar held a number of discussions at this time. The Iranian official complained that the United States charged six times the 1985 price for the weapons at issue. Ghorbanifar tried to explain the pricing, while complaining that his financial problems had forced him into hiding. He needed $5 million to avoid ruin. On June 30, Ghorbanifar told his Tehran contact that the Americans again explained the high prices, and had suggested that, once the matter was resolved and relations were improved, the United States would assist Iran to obtain loans from international banks and American agencies. Ghorbanifar then proposed, without indicating who may have originated the idea, that Iran obtain the release of one hostage to coincide with the July 4 celebrations and the centennial of the Statue of Liberty. He added that, within twenty-four hours of such release, the United States would ship the rest of the HAWK spare parts. The radars would follow, and Iran would effect the release of the last two hostages. The Iranian official

357

doubted a hostage could be released by July 4; for one thing, there had to be agreement on the price of the materiel. Ghorbanifar agreed they had to solve the price problem before the timing of the hostage releases could be fixed.

Cave also spoke to the official in the Prime Minister's office about the price of HAWK spare parts on June 30. Cave reported that:

1. This was fairly lengthy call during which B [the official in the Iranian Prime Minister's office] continued to harp on the Price [sic] of the 240 items. Sam [O'neil] told him that we had sent a copy of the prices to the mercahnt [sic] [Ghorbanifar]. These constituted the prices that the middlemen paid for the goods. B wanted to -know [sic] if Sam had a copy so he could relate some of them to B. Sam said that he did not have a copy of the prices. During the course of the conversation, B would inisist [sic] on discussing kpricing [sic]. He refused to be stonewalled and said that he was under enormous pressure to get some adjustment in the pricing. When Sam asked about the Micro [sic] fiche list. He confessed that he had not sent it but would on the morrow. Th;is [sic] is some kind of indicator that such a list might not exist [sic]. However, he does have something and suspect it might be an old invoice. He said that his superiors are shocked that the USG would selll [sic] them parts at black market prices. Sam -pointed [sic] out that he was buying from the merchant. B was insistant that some th;ing [sic] must be done on pricing as they were not prepared to pay six times -pricing [sic].

2. Sam told him that something must break soon as the Chief of our comp[any] is fed up with the whole deal. He was must [sic] disturbed at the way our delegation was handled in Dubai [Tehran] and is on the verge of corking off the while [sic] deal. This did not seem to make a great impression on B. Sam also said that he and Goode [North] are in deep trouble for having recomended [sic] the deal in the first place. B said that we were in no more trouble than he was on

358

his end. Sam said that we were then all in the same trench together.

3. At one point in the pricing argument, Sam pointed out that we do not cheat on prices, were they displeased with the [?HAWKs]? when [sic] B kept insisting on some kind of break in the price, Sam told him that as far as we were concerned they could buy the parts elsewhere. This deal was set and it would have to go -through [sic] and mercahant [sic].

4. Toward the end of the conversation, B made a plea to Sam to do something about the end of the price if at all possible. He also extracted a promise from Sam to call him back tomorrow.

According to the CIA/IG report, Cave obtained the following letter, purportedly written by Ghorbanifar to his Iranian contact, on 8 July 1986.[73]

My dear and esteemed brother [B]:

After greetings, I feel it is necessary to state the following points with respect to the American issue, which for a year has taken up everyone's time and has become very unpleasant:

If you remember, we had some very lengthy telephone conversations Monday and Tuesday [30 June and 1 July]. I stressed the fact that the essence of a [good] policy is to identify the moment, exploit the occasion, and recognize the proper and appropriate time in order to take advantage of them and to get concessions. I said that Friday was the 4th of July and the celebration of the 210th anniversary of the American Independence as well as the 100th anniversary celebration of the Statue of Liberty in New York. For this reason, there was going to be a very elaborate and majestic celebration titled 'Liberty Day' in New York at the foot of the Statue of Liberty. The Americans were calling it the Celebration of the Century; and the US President and the President of France will be hosting the celebration; for it is the day of liberty and celebration of freedom. [I said] that if we could mediate for the release of the American hostage clergyman

359

on Thursday, 3 July, and he could attend these celebrations—as he is clergy—we could exploit it and benefit from it a great deal; we could get the Americans to accept many of our demands. Naturally, as usual, nobody paid any attention to my suggestions. The Americans were expecting us to take at least these steps for them. Anyway, the Americans are saying that last year after the Iranians mediated the release of an American clergy, M. Mier [sic] who was kept hostage in Beirut, they [the Americans]—as a goodwill gesture and as a first step—made available to Iranians 504 [sic] TOW missiles. Also, during the year since then, they [the Americans] have taken the following positive and constructive steps as a sign of goodwill and utmost respect toward the Islamic Republic. However, in return, the Iranians have not made the slightest attempt nor shown the smallest sign—even discreetly—to improve relations:

1. After the clergyman's release, whenever and wherever American officials talked about countries supporting and nurturing terrorism, they did not include Iran; also, the Chief Justice of the Supreme Court [translator believes he means Attorney General of the United States] in an official interview, mentioned Libya, Syria, South Yemen, and Cuba as the countries supporting, protecting, and strengthening terrorism.

2. With regard to the Iran-Iraq war, the US Department of State, in an official note, strongly condemned the use of chemical weapons.

3. The American Ambassador at the United Nations was the first person to vote for official condemnation of Iraq for the use of chemical weapons.

4. [Issuance] of an official announcement terming the Mojahedin-e Khalq Organization terrorist and Marxist; the [issuance] of a circular to the Congress and to all American firms and institutions, and banning of any and all types of assistance to the opponents of the regime of the Islamic Republic of Iran.

5. Opposition to the decrease in oil prices; so much so that Mr. George Bush, the Vice President, on two

occasions during speeches and interviews announced that the reduction in oil prices would ultimately be harmful for the United States and that oil prices should increase.

6. Dispatch of two US planes with more than 1,000 TOW missiles on two separate occasions, at cost price.

7. Dispatch of a high-ranking 5-man team from the White House and the Defense Department for a meeting with B and his accompanying team, and the provision of certain preliminary military data on Iraq with an agreement that more complete and comprehensive data should be made available in subsequent meetings and after the final agreement.

8. Arrival of a very high-ranking delegation from the White House headed by Robert McFarlane, Mr. Reagan's special assistant and advisor, together with five high-ranking civilian and military officials for a 4-day stay in Tehran; they brought more than one-fifth of the requested spare parts for missile systems; further, some complete military, technical, and intelligence information and data with regard to Soviet threats against Iran, and the military and political——[sic][74] of that government [USSR] with full details on [plan for] invasion of Iran; Soviet activities in Kurdestan, Baluchestan, and Iraq; [Soviet] cooperation with opponents of the Islamic regime; and above all, a clear and explicit announcement by the US Government that it considers the regime of the Islamic Republic stable and it respects that regime. Also, that the USG does not in any way oppose that regime; and promises that it has no intentions or plans to bring it under its [sphere of] influence, create changes, or interfere in its internal affairs. Later, Minutes [sic] of the meeting and agreement were submitted, reflecting the goodwill and total cooperation of the United States with the Islamic Republic; specifically with respect to the war and other problems threatening this regime. [You may read these Minutes again.]

The Americans are saying: "We were treated in an insulting and unfriendly fashion; they made us return empty-handed while we were ambassadors of friendship and assistance."

The gentlemen themselves know the details of the events better than anyone else.

As you know, the US officials in Tehran reiterated over and over that in exchange for what they proposed, they only expected that our [Iranian] authorities should mediate and use their religious and spiritual influence for the release of the four American hostages who have been kept in Beirut for more than two years; that by this humanitarian deed, they could bring happiness to the families and children waiting to see their fathers; and that they could further be free in every respect to provide us [Iranians] with secret and necessary support.

They made it very clear that they are fully prepared and willing to provide [Iran] with all types of political, economic, and weapons cooperation and accord, on the condition that such assistance should not be considered part of [a bargain for the release of] hostages; but rather it should be considered a goodwill and better relations and friendship gesture by the United States.

Prior to the arrival of the US team and myself in Tehran on 25 May 1986, there was full agreement that upon arrival of the high-ranking US delegation in Tehran, bringing some of the requested items, the Iranian authorities would begin immediately mediating for the release of all American hostages in Beirut all, together and collectively. And that after this, the remaining items requested by Iran would arrive in Tehran. The US team would stay in Tehran until the rest of equipment [items]—among them the large HP radars—also arrived in Tehran. Further, there was supposed to be official agreement and commitment for providing the rest of Iran's weapon needs, as well as secret agreements in some political and economic areas. The Americans were to leave Iran only after all of these stages had been completed.

However, although the 10-man US team and their

giant special aircraft was in Tehran for four days, unfortunately nothing was accomplished. You well remember that on the last day of the stay, His Excellency [redacted][75] in the presence of you and another gentleman, insisted several times that everyone should agree for the time being about the mediation for the release of two hostages. But Mr. McFarlane did not accept this and stated that they were there [in Tehran] and were prepared to discuss and solve some basic and strategically important issues and to stand by you [Iranians]; all of these must be solved together, so that no problem remained and the way could thus be paved for everything once and for all.

I must [at this point] remind you that in 1985 there were 45,703 deaths on US highways, and that during the same year, 1,301 Americans died as a result of choking on their food [gluttons]. Thus, we must not put the Americans under such pressure that they end up including these four [hostages] as part of the above statistics, and we end up losing this historic opportunity which has combined one whole year of hardship and difficulties with some heavy expenses for me.

You know that this matter has been tangled for 45 days. I can assure you that the Americans neither can nor will be able to take another step along this path unless we should at least carry out as a preliminary and beginning step that which was [redacted][76] was insisting upon. I also believe that whatever we want to do and whatever decision you make, must be carried out within the next 2–3 days.

Now, there are only three solutions; I have totally convinced them [Americans] and they are in total agreement with all of the three solutions. I believe and strongly recommend that the first solution be chosen:

1. You should immediately pay in cash the amount for the items that have already arrived, including the remaining 177 items. The money for the 240 items, as well as the money for the two HP's, should be paid

through the London branch of Bank Melli Iran on 30 July, that is, in 21 days.

2. That same evening, you should mediate and release two of the hostages.

3. Within a maximum of 24 hours after this, the Americans would deliver all of the 240 items, that is approximately 4,000 spare parts and two giant HP's at Bandar Abbas.

4. Immediately after receiving all of the above items and their full inspection, you should take immediate steps for the release of the remaining two hostages. Also, for humanitarian and religious reasons, you should mediate for identification of the burial place of the hostage who died last year [W. Buckley] so that his body can be transferred to the United States to be buried next to his mother as was his wish.

5. Seventy-two hours after the delivery and receipt of all the 240 items of [HAWKs] and the two HP's and the release of all hostages, a high-ranking US team will be present in Geneva, Frankfurt, or Tehran—as you wish —and will take careful steps with respect to providing the proposed Minutes of the meeting and will make a commitment. Further, the team will study the matter of the remaining HP's and helicopter spare parts and all other needs and requirements of the Iranian army. In this regard, agreement as to the date for their delivery could be specified. Meanwhile, they [Americans] are ready to send immediately technical experts and equipment for testing and repairing them.

Second solution, which would require more time and would entail more headaches:

1. You should pay in cash the amount for the items that have already arrived, including the remaining 177 items. The money for the 240 items should be paid through issuance of a check via London branch of Bank Melli Iran on 20 July, that is in 11 days.

2. That same evening, you should mediate and release one of the hostages.

3. Within 12 hours after this, they will deliver all of the 240 items in Tehran.

4. Immediately after receiving fully and accurately all of the 240 items in Tehran, you must mediate and release the same day two more hostages and must pay the money for the two HP's.

5. Within a maximum of 24 hours after the release of these two hostages and the payment of the amount for the HP's, the radar equipment will be delivered at Bandar Abbas.

6. After the complete and correct delivery of the two HP's, you will mediate and take steps for the release of the last [fourth] hostage as well as the body of William Buckley.

7. Seventy-two hours after receiving all of the 240 items of [HAWKs] and the two HP's and the release of American hostages, a high-ranking US team will be present in Geneva, Frankfurt, or Tehran—as you wish —and will take careful steps with respect to providing the proposed minutes of the meeting and will make a commitment. Further, it will study the matter of the remaining HP's and helicopter spare parts and all other needs and requirements of the Iranian army. And in this regard, agreement can be made as to the specific date for their delivery. Meanwhile, they [Americans] are ready to immediately send technical experts and equipment for testing and repairing them.

8. I personally and on my honor—whatever way you deem it proper—would guarantee and make commitment that immediately after carrying out the last phase—that is, after the delivery of the 240 items and the two HP's and after the release of all American hostages, within a maximum of one month—I shall deliver in Tehran 3,000 TOW missiles at a cost of $38.5 million which is the cost to the Americans themselves, plus 200 Sidewinder missiles mounted on F-4 and F-5 planes, again at cost. Naturally, [only] if you make the money available to me—not like this [last] time when you did not leave anything for me.

Third solution:

Since I have tried to be a mediator for good, I do not wish to be a cause of misdeeds. I have tried to bring [the two sides] together and create friendship, and not to cause further division, hostility, and alienation. Thus, if you do not find either of the above-mentioned solutions advisable, return immediately the exact items that they brought so that the whole case can be closed and we can pretend nothing happened, as if 'no camel arrived and no camel left' [old Persian saying]. Everyone can thus go his own way. Hopefully, in the future, [when] conditions and circumstances are once again suitable, steps can be taken. I mean we should not 'put a bone inside a wound' [another old Persian saying, meaning not to make things worse]. There is no reason for it. If I have encountered great difficulties and many material, spiritual, and prestige problems soley due to friendship, good intentions, honesty, belief, and trust, it was simply for the love of [my] country and my friendship with you and it does not matter. I hope good and generous God will compensate me for it, as my intentions were all good.

I beg you to take a speedy and decisive step and make a quick decision on this issue, for the good and the welfare of the Islamic Republic.

Thanking you and with highest respect,

Manuchehr Qorbanifar
signed 9 July 1986

"In June and July," Charles Allen told the Board,

there seemed to be sort of a stalemate. In early July, Colonel North called me out of a meeting—I was lecturing to a group at the Office of Personnel Management—and stated that he had been assured by Amiram Nir, special assistant to the Prime Minister, Peres at that time, of Israel that another American would be released very shortly. He at that stage briefed some of the senior people in the government.

We sent a hostage briefing team to Wiesbaden and no

release occurred, and we brought the team back.[77] Colonel North was deeply disappointed and he said that he had been admonished by Admiral Poindexter on this, and he cut off all contacct with Amiram Nir at that stage and asked that I talk to Amiram Nir for a period of two or three weeks.[78]

(C. Allen 21)

The Secretary of State told the Board that, on July 2,

Mr. Armacost wrote me a memo, informing me "that there is renewed 'conjecture' that the NSC-sponsored search for a U.S.-Iran deal for hostages will produce an early result. The story is that one hostage may be released tomorrow in Lebanon."

Arms were not mentioned. I do not recall having seen this memo, but this reported "conjecture" would have added nothing to my knowledge of the matter. You heard this from time to time.

(Shultz, SRB, 56)

In the middle of July, two senior foreign government officials visited Tehran. One of them reported a feeler by Rafsanjani to the effect that the Americans knew what had to be done to improve relations. North wrote Poindexter on July 10 that:

[y]ou will recall that several months ago the [name deleted] initiated direct discussions with the Iranians on the matter of our hostages. This is the third such overture they have made on our behalf. In addition to the information in the cable, . . . [of the [country deleted] Embassy in Washington] made the following comments:

—The perception of a Soviet threat to Iran is a concern that has reached the highest levels of the Revolutionary Government.

—There are obviously members of the Iranian Government who foresee the possibility that "given the right conditions" Iran could "cause the release" of the American hostages.

—Although none of the Iranian officials responded positively to [Director General of the [country deleted] Foreign Ministry's] suggestion that direct secret discussions be initiated between the U.S. and Iran, it was not rejected.

Rafsanjani noted that "the U.S. Government knows what it should do."

—The [country deleted] have clearly explained to the Iranians that they are reporting directly back to the American Government on these contacts.

From this and earlier meetings, it is apparent that the [country deleted] have been able to establish and maintain a direct link at the highest levels of the Iranian Government. Given the stalemate on other initiatives and our inability too ensure that we are in direct contact with responsible Iranian officials we may be able to use this most recent [country deleted] visit to Tehran as an opportunity to establish such a contact. [Name deleted], who has acted as our conduit for these matters, has suggested that they have the ability to pass a secure communication directly to Rafsanjani through their ambassador in Tehran.

It is important to note that, during the meeting, [name deleted] pointedly asked whether we had conveyed our willingness to eventually normalize U.S.–Iranian relations when our "officials were in Tehran." A direct response was avoided and [name deleted] was advised that our willingness to talk with the Iranians is "common knowledge." It is disturbing that the visit may also be common knowledge.[79]

North proposed sending the following message:

We have reported the results of the June 27–29 discussions to the American Government and they have asked us to relay the following message in highest confidence. The highest levels of the American Government are prepared to open direct and private discussions with responsible officials who are empowered to speak on behalf of the Iranian Government. They have asked us to tell you that under the right conditions, the American Government is prepared to take steps leading to a normalization of relations between your Government and theirs. If you are agreeable, a senior American official is prepared to meet with responsible representatives of your government at the time and place of your choosing. They are prepared, as you have suggested, to make an appropriate gesture of goodwill.

(North to Poindexter, 7/10/86, "Non-Log") In his memorandum to Poindexter, dated July 17, North indicated that Poindexter approved sending this message.

On July 17, North reported a second opportunity for direct contact with the Iranian government to Poindexter. The Secretary of State had been given a memorandum by a foreign official on "US-Iran Relations," reporting a recent conversation in Tehran.

At the conclusion of my discussions in Tehran, Dr. Larijani, Irani Deputy Foreign Minister stated that he wanted to raise a matter that was highly sensitive. He requested that it should be treated with appropriate confidentiality and that I should convey it in [country deleted] at a 'suitable' [country deleted] to decide the level at which to raise the issue with the Americans.

2. Larijani said that since the beginning of the Irani revolution, the United States of America had adopted an implacably hostile policy towards Iran. Apart from attempts at physical intimidation, the Americans had tried to undermine the Irani revolution through various means and especially by giving moral and material support to Iran's enemies. Larijani said that the Americans should appreciate that the Irani government and people could not compromise on the Irani revolution which had been brought about through supreme sacrifices by the Irani people. They would defend the revolution to the last drop of blood.

3. The American government should appreciate, however, that Iran and America shared similar strategic interests in the region. The danger of pro-Soviet, Marxist interests asserting themselves in the region was growing rapidly. After Afghanistan, the Marxists

had taken over in South Yemen. Pro-Soviet, Marxist elements were strongly entrenched in other countries in the region and especially in Egypt, North Yemen, Kuwait and Iraq. Even in the Gulf countries there was disillusionment with the established order which could be overthrown by forces that would adopt an anti-US and pro-Soviet policy. Iran viewed these developments with concern. Iran felt that, despite its physical resources, the United States would not be able to influence developments especially, at a time of internal convulsions. Iran, on the other hand, had a greater capacity to influence and pre-empt such developments.

4. Larijani's remarks indicated that, despite Iran's rhetorical invective against USA, Iran wanted an easing of relations on substantive matters with USA and that Iran wanted [country deleted] to play the role of intermediary in attempting a better understanding with the American government.

(Tab II to North to Poindexter, 7/17/86)

In his covering memorandum, which was labeled "Non-Log," North wrote:

When we first commenced direct discussions with the Iranians, we established an immediate objective of recovering our hostages and longer-term goals of ending the Iran-Iraq war and normalizing the U.S.-Iranian relationship. . . . To date, we have been unable to establish a direct contact with Iranian officials who are willing/able to take such steps.

It is entirely likely that the visit of [the foreign minister of a friendly nation] presents an opportunity to have him contact appropriate Iranian officials with a message from the USG. The memorandum provided to Secretary Shultz by Larijani . . . indicates that various officials in Iran do indeed wish to establish such contact.

When we first discussed this matter, it was indicated that the point of contact for [a foreign official] to deliver our message would likely be Musavi-Khamenei, the Iranian Prime Minister. Given Musavi's radical past, it is unlikely that he would be as positively disposed as Rafsanjani, who is more widely known as a "pragmatist." In a meeting this afternoon with George Cave, he volunteered that it was "too bad we did not have enough trust [in this country] to carry a message to Rafsanjani, since they are apparently close." Cave is unaware of this initiative.

In order to insure consistency with the earlier message delivered by [an official of a second friendly country] and messages we hope to have delivered by other trusted interlocutors, a verbatim message rather than talking points has been prepared. . . . At this point, two actions need to be taken:

—Secretary Shultz should review the proposed message at Tab III and, if he concurs, it should be passed to [the foreign minister of the first friendly nation] for personal delivery to the Iranians.

—We should seek to have the message delivered by [him] to Rafsanjani rather than Musavi.

(North to Poindexter, 7/17/86)

# C. Jenco

Whether or not Poindexter acted on North's proposals to try to use these two nations' access to the Iranian government, on July 21, the United States obtained a clear indication that a hostage might be freed soon. North reported that:

We have just been told by Nir that "the Iranians claim to have taken action this morning to release one hostage." . . . I have asked CIA to alert [appropriate personnel in] Beirut and no others to the possibility in order to preclude a repeat of Jul[y] 4. We have not put any other USG assets on alert. RELATED SUBJECT: Absent further developments on this approach, George Cave will proceed to Frankfurt to meet w/ Tabatabai,[80] the cousin of the man I met w/ here. T is alledgedly well connected to Rafsanjani and several other of the so called "pragmatists." Purpose of the meeting is to determine T's real access and willingness to act as an interlocutor. If bona fides prove out he could also be used to pass the same message we sent back via [a third country]. In that regard, who was [that country's emissary] to give our message to on the Iranian side?

(North PROF note to Poindexter, 7/21/86, 18:04:38) Poindexter informed North the same day that [the emissary] was to pass the message to "the Iranian FM [Foreign Minister]. Don't tell anybody including Cave about this." (Poindexter PROF note to North, 7/21/86, 20:10:14) North in turn replied:

Roger, WILCO. Am concerned, however that if tonight's [information] does indeed bear the fruit promised, that we may be confusing an already difficult situation. Maybe that's not as bad as it might otherwise be since those guys will all get the message eventually if anything develops.

(North PROF note to Poindexter, 7/21/86, 20:20:23)

On July 25, Poindexter wrote North:

Bob Oakley must have told Shultz about a discussion that took place in OSG. Shultz called me about a Cave meeting in the next few days. I vaguely remember that you told me something about this. George just wanted to be sure that we did not have any disconnect between what [the emissary] will be telling them and what Cave tells them.

(Poindexter PROF note to North, 7/25/86, 11:33:17) In his reply, North reminded Poindexter where the various communications stood.

Cave is meeting w/ [a relation of a powerful Iranian official] and Tabatabai to determine level of access and current political sentiments toward the present regieme [sic]. He was prepared to pass a message identical to the one we sent thru [a friendly foreign official] but I held it back when you advised that the FoMin, not Rafsanjani was to be the recipient. We have likewise sent no message back thru [the other friendly government]. At the present, the only active courier is [the emissary of the first country] and the only recipient is the FM. Cave will report his findings when he returns from Frankfurt and we can then determine whether we wish to use any of these new contacts as interlocutors. Also related: Nir and [the official in the Iranian PM's office] are both out of their respective pockets. Charlie agrees that it is entirely possible that they are meeting in Europe.

(North PROF note to Poindexter, 7/25/86, 18:43:42)

On July 26, Father Lawrence Jenco was released. McFarlane wrote Poindexter: "Bravo Zulu on Jenco's release. Do you correlate this to the anxious calls that have come since the trip to Iran and our insistence that they move first? Or is it really a Syrian effort?" (McFarlane PROF note to Poindexter, 7/26/86[81] Poindexter explained how it had come about in his reply:

Thank you. It is directly related to your trip out there. The Syrians only entered at the last minute. Gorba finally convinced [his Tehran contact] after numerous telephone calls that they should come forward with a humanitarian gesture. Gorba either on his own or as Nir's agent is out a lot of money that he put up front for the parts. [the Tehran contact] has been unwilling to pay him since all of the material has not been delivered. Gorga [sic] has cooked up a story that if Iran could make a humanitarian gesture then the US would deliver the rest of the parts and then Iran would release the rest of the hostages. Of course we have not agreed to any such plan. Nir and Gorba are in London. [The Iranian official] is enroute [sic]. I am trying to decide whether to send Ollie and George Cave. The problem is that if parts aren't delivered, Gorba will convince [his Tehran contact] that we welched on the deal. Although through several conversations Cave has repeated to [the Tehran contact] what our position has been—all of the hostages out before anything else moves[,] I have aboutdecided [sic] to send Ollie to make certain our position is clear. It seems to me that we may have some leverage over [the official in the

PM's office] now since he is out on a limb in Tehran and may fear for his own safety.

(Poindexter PROF note to McFarlane, 7/26/86, 14:58:07)

McFarlane agreed with Poindexter's approach.

I agree with your strategy; to send Ollie and to reaffirm our position. Of course the unknowables are: 1. Do they—as they have said—no longer have control over the others (Itend [sic] to believe they do still have control over all; Jenco ought to be able to throw some light on that). 2. Will [the Iranian official] have the courage and influence in Tehran to be able to recommend the release of allwithout [sic] something coming from us. I tend to doubt it. He is a simple [person] way over his head and afraid of his own shadow; not the kind to take risks or to trust foreigners he cannot begin to understand. But it is likely that the higher ups—[a senior foreign policy advisor] (the most senior guy we met) will understand and respect that we are sticking to our original position. Over time, constancy is respected. 3. Finally however, there is the risk that even the higher ups will see no great downside in killing one of the remaining hostages. I'm afraid that's just a risk we will have to run for to do otherwise will lead to a thousand reoccurences [sic] of this scenario in the months ahead as they see that we really can be strung out.

(McFarlane PROF note to Poindexter, 7/26/86, 21:53:58)

On July 26, the day of Jenco's release, Poindexter "[b]riefed [the] President on secure phone," (Poindexter, handwritten note on North to Poindexter 7/26/86), from a paper by North on "what we know of the Jenco release," for Poindexter to give the President. (North to Poindexter 7/26/86)

The release of Father Lawrence Jenco is a second positive step in our protracted and difficult dialogue with the Iranians. Father Jenco's release undoubtedly comes about as a result of Bud McFarlane's trip at the end of May and the continuing direct and indirect contacts we have had with Iranian officials. Our Israeli contacts and the Iranian intermediary in Europe advise that the Iranian Government now expects some reciprocal move on our part—though exactly what, we are uncertain.

[Available information] indicate[s] that the decision to release Father Jenco was make in Tehran on or about July 21. On Wednesday, July 23, our Israeli point of contact advised us that "if, as we hope, a hostage is released, it will be Jenco." It was also on this date that the Israeli point of contact (Amiram Nir) told the Iranian intermediary in Europe that the USG was breaking off all contact on this matter. We have also learned that July 24 was a key date in the most recent release:

—The Iranian Government paid their European intermediary $4M on Thursday, July 24, as partial payment for HAWK missile parts which were removed from our mission aircraft at the end of May. (It is important to note that in order to pay the Israelis for the HAWK missile parts, the Iranian intermediary in Europe borrowed more than $15M and has been under threat of death from his creditors. The Israelis regard this payment as further proof that the Iranians wish to continue the contact with the U.S. on the hostage issue.)

—Father Jenco has told Ambassador Eagleton . . . in Damascus that it was on Thursday, July 24, that he was separated from the other American hostages in Beirut and delivered to a location in the Bekka Valley. It was from this location in western Lebanon that he was subsequently released to Lebanese authorities, who in turn delivered him to a Syrian military checkpoint.

Our next step will be to have two USG representatives meet with the Israeli and Iranians in Europe, if possible, tomorrow in an effort to determine Iranian expectations. This is not a negotiating session, but rather an attempt to maintain contact and, if possible, assess how we should now proceed. To our knowledge, no new Israeli deliveries have occurred and all remaining

HAWK missile repair parts are still in a covert depot in Israel.

(Tab I to North to Poindexter, 7/26/86)

With this memorandum, North attached a memorandum from the Director of Central Intelligence on the "American Hostages."[82]

After discussing the release of Father Lawrence Jenco with Charlie Allen and Dewey Clarridge, I believe it is important that you have our assessment of this development and prospects for release of additional hostages.

First, it is indisputable that the Iranian connection actually worked this time, after a series of failures. You will recall that the [Iranian official]-Ghorbanifar connection also resulted in the release of Reverend Weir in September 1985. Syria played no role either in the release of Weir or Jenco. After the impasse in Tehran over in late May, [the Iranian official] continued to initiate direct contact with one of my officers, George Cave, even though the Iranians had been told that we were no longer interested in pursuing the matter. The fact that [this official] persisted in contacting us indicates his desire to arrange a "deal" with Washington either through Ghorbanifar or, if necessary, with Cave. He also clearly wanted to keep a channel open. Amiram Nir, Special Assistant to the Prime Minister of Israel on Counter-Terrorism, has also played a critical role in a determined effort to force Iran to begin the release of American hostages. He has been supported by Prime Minister Peres and Defense Minister Rabin in this endeavor. In order to make the terms of the arrangements more palatable, Israel, on its own, offered additional arms "to sweeten the deal." . . .

[We received information on 21 July that the Iranian official] had taken action with other Iranian authorities to release one hostage. To reinforce this commitment, he transferred $4M to a West European bank to pay his European intermediary for the HAWK spare parts removed from our mission aircraft in May. On Wednesday, July 23, when no hostage had been released. Ghorbanifar was instructed to inform [the Iranian official] that "the deal was off." On Thursday, July 24, the Israelis [obtained information] indicating Jenco would be released.

In return for the release, [the Iranian official] probably expects to receive most of the HAWK spare parts not yet delivered, along with additional military equipment that Israel unilaterally has added to the arrangement. Once this equipment is delivered, [the Iranian official] stated that Iran would take action to obtain the release of one more hostage and would pay the remainder of the money owed to the Iranian intermediary for the HAWK spare parts. According to [our information, the Iranian official] apparently expects to then receive the two HAWK radars and the remainder of the HAWK spare parts, although it is unclear as to the timing of these additional deliveries. [The Iranian official], moreover, indicated a willingness to meet with U.S. officials again on these matters, either in Tehran or "somewhere else" — presumably Western Europe.

This is how we see the current situation:

   —The Ghorbanifar-[Iranian official] connection has worked for the second time — and another American has been released.

   —Ghorbanifar is an uncontrollable factor, but appears to respond generally to Nir's direction.

   —Nir has every reason to work for further releases of our hostages. Peres and Rabin have put their reputation on the Ghorbanifar-[Iranian official] connection and support Nir fully in his endeavors. There would be a considerable loss of face for Nir and his superiors if the link were broken. This connection appears to be the only hope they have for recovering their own missing soldiers.

   —[The Iranian official] has now acted and likely expects the United States to respond quickly in turn by delivering most of the remaining HAWK spare parts. He probably believes the United States is also supplying the additional military equipment that has been promised.

—If the deliveries do not occur, [the Iranian official] will lose badly with his superiors in Tehran and matters could turn ugly, especially since the Lebanese Hezballah captors probably are not pleased with the Jenco release.

—If there is not USG contact as a result of Jenco's release, it is entirely possible that Iran and/or Hezballah could resort to the murder of one or more of the remaining hostages.

In summary, based on the intelligence at my disposal, I believe that we should continue to maintain the Ghorbanifar-[Iranian official] contact and consider what we may be prepared to do to meet [the Iranian official's] minimum requirements that would lead to release of the rest of the hostages. Although I am not pleased by segmented releases of the American hostages, I am convinced that this may be the only way to proceed, given the delicate factional balance in Iran. I also see resolution of the hostage issue as potentially leading to contacts with moderate factions in Iran that we may be able to deal with in the longer term.

(Casey to Poindexter, 7/26/86)[83]

On July 26, North wrote to Poindexter that

Cave is departing Geneva tonight to meet North/Secord in Frankfurt tomorrow (Sunday) morning. Nir and Ghorbanifar depart London tomorrow and have called [Ghorbanifar's Tehran contact] to meet them in Frankfurt, GE, Sunday morning. The purpose of the meeting is to assess Iranian expectations and ability to release the remaining Iranian hostages.

(North to Poindexter, 7/26/86) North prepared talking points for the meeting, which Poindexter approved on July 26. (North to Poindexter, 7/26/86)

—You have seen the President's statement regarding the release of Father Jenco. This is very much in line with what your people had suggested.

—Our government remains prepared to open direct and private discussions with your government leading to a normalization of relations.

—We recognize the important role played by your government in the release of Father Jenco and regard this to be a very positive step.

—It is important that there not be any misunderstandings or false expectations regarding the release of Father Jenco.

—On every occasion, including our meetings in Tehran, we made it clear that we were not going to barter over the lives of human beings.

—While we are not empowered to negotiate with you regarding any further deliveries of materiel, it is important that you recognize that the understanding we proposed in Tehran is still operative. We have been instructed to report back to our government any changes to this proposal.

—We continue to believe that a direct channel of communication, which will prevent misunderstandings is important. As we indicated in Tehran, we are prepared to dispatch a secure satellite communications team to Tehran to facilitate this communication.

("North/Cave Talking Points," Tab II to North to Poindexter, 7/26/86)

North and Cave met with Nir and Ghorbanifar the afternoon of July 27. North reported:

Lengthy meeting this afternoon with Gorba and Nir followed by discussion with [the official in the Prime Minister's office] via phone. Following are salient points. [The Iranian official] believes he has demonstrated his ability to perform and has expectations we are now prepared to deal. Despite our earlier and current protestations that we want all hostages before we deliver anything, this is clearly not the way they want to proceed. They see clearly that the ball is now in our court. In discussion with [the Iranian official] he repeatedly asked quote—"When are you going to deliver". While [the official] made no specific threat, he noted that he was under intense pressure and could not totally control events. We will call him back 28 July at 1100 Frankfurt time and urge that he come to Europe for a meeting and to do nothing rash in the meantime. We are trying to make this idea attractive —using [his interest in the U.S. establishing] a "special account" for him as an incentive. Jenco has expressed a desire to thank the three world leaders responsible for his release. The Pope, The Archbishop of Canterbury and RR. The first two intend to oblige. Can we deliver on the last? Unodir [unless otherwise directed] we will call [the Iranian official] in A.M. and urge him to meet us in Europe ASAP. Since it will take him several days to get authorization to come, we plan to return to D.C. via Pan Am 061 on 28 July and report to JMP in evening. Please advise via this channel if other instructions obtain. Warm regards. North/Cave.

Bottom line, is that if we want to prevent the death of one of the three remaining hostages, we are going to have to do something.

[Handwritten at bottom: "Put this in a sealed envelope and have Ollie pick it up." JP]

(Document misdated 6/27/86) Another version of this message contained the following:

P.S. Please call Dewey and tell him George will send hard copy to he [sic] and [C/NE, CIA DO] in A.M. via NIACT.

(Id.) Yet another version, bearing the word "done" with a tick mark next to the P.S., has the following handwritten note: "Read all to JMP, except P.S. 7/27 1830." (Id.)

According to North's calendar, North met Jenco in Germany on July 29. On the same day, he set forth his views on the next steps regarding hostages in a memorandum to Poindexter.

The debrief of Father Jenco has proceeded well and he continues to cooperate fully with our team. Though Jenco's geographic knowledge is understandably limited by the brief time he was in Beirut before he was seized and the conditions of his captivity, he has made every effort to answer our questions.

[Terry] Waite is accompanying Father Jenco to meetings with the Pope and the Archbishop of Canterbury on Wednesday and Thursday. Father Jenco is scheduled to meet with the President on Friday, August 1, at 2:00 p.m.

Based on information derived from the Jenco debrief, our discussions with Ghorbanifar, Nir, and [the Iranian official]; and the videotaped and private messages delivered by Jenco, we have drawn the following conclusions:

—Jenco was released as a direct result of action taken by [the official in the Iranian PM's office] on or about July 21.

—Though Iranian influence over the hostage holders is still considerable, the captors themselves are increasingly disenchanted with the Iranian relationship:

—The delay between [the Iranian official's] "instruction" to the captors on July 21 and the actual release on July 24 was likely occasioned by the hostage holders need to find a new prison site, arrange for the videotape by Jacobsen, place their story in *An Nahar*.

—The Iranians have been unable to deter the Syrians from moving in strength against Hezballah strongholds in Lebanon.

—The continued reluctance of the Hezballah itself to follow precise Iranian instructions on *how* to release the hostages is seen as an indi-

381

cation of efforts by Hezballah to demonstrate at least partial independence.

—[The Iranian official] believed that he had consummated an arrangement with the Americans through Ghorbanifar on the terms for release of the hostages.

—[The Iranian official's] expectations regarding the immediate delivery of the 240 HAWK missile parts were apparently transmitted to higher authority in Iran. Discussions with [him] in Europe (Sunday, July 27) and calls *from* him today indicate that [he] is in considerable personal jeopardy as a consequence of not having received what he believed we promised.

—It is entirely possible that if nothing is received [the Iranian official] will be killed by his opponents in Tehran, Ghorbanifar will be killed by his creditors (they are the beneficiaries of a $22M life insurance policy), and one American hostage will probably be killed in order to demonstrate displeasure.

—Although the Dawa 17 in Kuwait continue to be mentioned as the ultimate demand on the part of the hostage holders, Jenco himself does not believe this and we have not seen reference to this issue since our meeting in Tehran (Tab B).

It is obvious that the conditions for the release of the hostages arranged between Ghorbanifar and [the Iranian official] are unacceptable. Nonetheless, we believe that Ghorbanifar acted on what he considered to be the following arrangement:

*Step 1:* One hostage released and $4M to Ghorbanifar for items removed from the aircraft in Tehran during the May visit (Ghorbanifar received the $4M on July 28).

*Step 2:* Remainder of 240 parts plus full quota of electron tubes (Item 24 on Iranian parts list) and 500 TOWs delivered to Iran.

*Step 3:* Second hostage released and Ghorbanifar paid for remainder of 240 parts.

*Step 4:* 500 TOWs and 1 HIPAR radar delivered.

*Step 5:* Third hostage released and Ghorbanifar paid for one radar.

*Step 6:* Meeting in Tehran to discuss future followed by release of the last hostage and delivery of second HIPAR radar.

We believe that the mixture of HAWK parts and TOWs is designed to satisfy both the military and the revolutionary guards in Iran. At this point, [the Iranian official] will probably be able to retain his credibility if just the 240 parts are delivered from Israel. We believe that he can be convinced to follow-up this delivery with a meeting in Europe to discuss next steps.

At such a meeting, we should endeavor to produce a concrete schedule that is agreeable to both parties and which allows all remaining hostages to be released simultaneously. The Jenco release . . . indicate[s] that this is clearly within the power of the Iranians, if they are so inclined. While they will continue to haggle over prices, timing, and sequence, the delivery of the 240 should help to assure the Iranians that we will keep *our* word. It is important that a face-to-face meeting occur so that we can establish the terms rather than having Ghorbanifar negotiate for us. Finally, even after the parts are delivered, we still retain some leverage over [the Iranian official]:

—He has been told that we have video tapes and photographs of him meeting with us in Tehran and he is concerned that we could make these public.

—He also wants assurance of asylum in the U.S. should "things go wrong." He has been told that we are prepared to offer such and need to meet with him to arrange exfiltration procedures. We intend to use this ploy as a further reason for establishing a direct communications link in Tehran.

## RECOMMENDATION

That you brief the President regarding our conclusions on the Jenco release as indicated above and obtain his approval for having the 240 HAWK missile parts shipped from Israel to Iran as soon as possible, followed by a meeting with the Iranians in Europe.

(North to Poindexter, 7/29/86) Poindexter initialed "Approve" and wrote: "7/30/86. President approved. JP." A member of the Hostage Location Task Force reported, on July 30, that

Charlie Allen advises that the President today approved further shipments of arms to Iran in response to the release of Rev. Jenco. Apparently, internal White House disagreements over who was responsible, the Syrians or the Iranians and, ultimately, the [Ghorbanifar-Iranian official] connection.

The Vice President was in Israel on July 29. While there, he met with Nir. The Vice President told the Board that, before the meeting, he had been uneasy, and tried to call Poindexter.

Failing to contact Poindexter, Mr. Bush spoke to North who indicated that the Israeli Prime Minister thought the meeting with Mr. Nir was important for the Vice President to meet with Nir. According to the Vice President, North had originally requested that the Vice President meet with Nir on the basis that the Israeli Prime Minister thought the meeting was important. North's position was apparently confirmed when after the meeting with Nir, the Israeli Prime Minister asked Mr. Bush how the meeting had gone. The Vice President indicated that there had been no discussion of the Nir meeting between himself and the Israeli Prime Minister.

(W. Clark McFadden II, "Discussion with the Vice President," 12/29/86) The Vice President expressed concern to the Board about what he perceived as the extent to which the interests of the United States were in the grip of the Israelis. Now, according to the Vice President, the Israelis themselves may be in some sense seeking cover. Vice President Bush related that his discussion with Mr. Nir was generally about counterterrorism. There was no discussion of specifics relating to arms going to the Iranians, e.g., the price of TOW missiles was never raised.

*(Id.)*

The Vice President's Chief of Staff, Craig Fuller, attended the meeting and memorialized it:

THE VICE PRESIDENT'S MEETING WITH MR. NIR—7/29/86 0735-0805

PARTICIPANTS: The Vice President, Mr. Nir, Craig Fuller

DATE/TIME: 7/29/86 0735-0805

LOCATION: Vice President's suite/King David Hotel, Jerusalem

1. SUMMARY. Mr. Nir indicated that he had briefed Prime Minister Peres and had been asked to brief the VP by his White House contacts. He described the details of the efforts from last year through the current period to gain the release of the U.S. hostages. He reviewed what had been learned which was essentially that the radical group was the group that could deliver. He reviewed the issues to be considered—namely that there needed to be ad [sic] decision as to whether the items requested would be delivered in separate shipments or whether we would continue to press for the release of the hostages prior to delivering the items in an amount agreed to previously.

2. The VP's 25 minute meeting was arranged after Mr. Nir called Craig Fuller and requested the meeting and after it was discussed with the VP by Fuller and North. Only Fuller was aware of the meeting and no other member of the VP's staff or traveling party has been advised about the meeting. No cables were generated nor was there other reporting except a brief

385

phone call between Fuller and North to advise that "no requests were made."

3. Nir began by indicating that Peres had asked him to brief the VP. In addition, Nir's White House contacts with whom he had recent discussions asked him to brief the VP.

4. Nir began by providing an historical perspective from his vantage point. He stated that the effort began last summer. This early phase he said "didn't work well." There were more discussions in November and in January "we thought we had a better approach with the Iranian side," said Nir. He said, "Poindexter accepted the decision."

5. He characterized the decision as "having two layers—tactical and strategic." The tactical layer was described as an effort "to get the hostages out." The strategic layer was designed "to build better contact with Iran and to insure we are better prepared when a change (in leadership) occurs." "Working through our Iranian contact, we used the hostage problem and efforts there as a test," suggested Nir. He seemed to suggest the test was to determine how best to establish relationships that worked with various Iranian factions.

6. Nir described Israel's role in the effort by saying, "we activated the channel; we gave a front to the operation; provided a physical base; provided aircraft." All this to "make sure the U.S. will not be involved in logistical aspects." Nir indicated that in the early phase they "began moving things over there."[84]

7. Before a second phase a meeting was desired. Nir indicated a February meeting took place with "the Prime Minister on the other side." Nir did not make it clear who else attended the meeting. He said the meeting was "dramatic and interesting." He said "an agreement was made on 4,000 units—1,000 first and then 3,000." "The agreement was made on the basis that we would get the group," Nir said. "The whole package for a fixed price," he said.

8. Although there was agreement the other side changed their minds and "then they asked for the other items," according to Nir. "We were pleased because these were defensive items and we got to work with the military," said Nir. He continued, "there were 240 items on the list we were provided and we agreed to it."

9. A meeting was organized for mid-May in Tehran to finalize the operation. The VP asked Nir if he attended the meeting and Nir indicated he did attend. Nir said, "two mistakes were made during this phase." "Two people were to be sent to prepare for the meeting but the U.S. had concerns about McFarlane," according to Nir. He described the meetings as "more difficult—total frustration because we didn't prepare." And he said, "their top level was not prepared adequately." During the meeting in Tehran the other side kept reminding the group that "in 1982 there was a meeting which leaked and the Prime Minister was thrown out of office." Nir said that at the end of the May meeting, "they began to see the light." "McFarlane was making it clear that we wanted all hostages released," Nir reported and, "at the last moment the other side suggested two would be released if those at the meeting stayed six more hours." According to Nir, "the Deputy Prime Minister delivered the request (to delay departure) and when the group said 'no,' they all departed without anything."

10. According to Nir, "the reason for delay is to squeeze as much as possible as long as they have assets. They don't believe that we want overall strategic co-operation to be better in the future. If they believed us they would have not bothered so much with the price right now." Further, according to Nir, "there are serious struggles now within the Iran power groups. Three leaders share the view that we should go ahead but each wants to prove his own toughness."

11. Turning to what Nir said was the final or most recent phase, he reported, "we felt things would just die if we didn't push forward to see what could be

delivered. They asked for four sequences, but we said no to talks until they showed something."

12. According to Nir, he told them about 10 days ago he would cancel the deal. Then nine days ago their Prime Minister called saying that they were taking steps to release one—the Priest. The second one to be released would be Jacobson. The Prime Minister also said that one would be released and then "we should give some equipment." Nir indicated to the VP that the bottom line on the items to be delivered was understood to be the same or even less but it was not the way the deal was originally made. The items involved spares for Hawks and TOWs. No denial or approval was given according to Nir. Nir said he made it clear that no deal would be discussed unless evidence is seen of a release.

13. On Tuesday or Wednesday a message was intercepted between Tehran and the guards according to Nir. On Friday, three hostages were taken out and on Saturday Janco [sic] was taken out, put into a trunk and driven to a village in the Bakka [sic] Valley. Nir then described what Janco reported with regard to the conditions under which he was held and what he knew of the other hostages including Buckley. (I assume we have detailed briefing already.) The VP asked Nir if he had briefed Peres on all of this and he indicated that he had.

14. Nir described some of the lessons learned: "we are dealing with the most radical elements. The Deputy Prime Minister is an emissary. They can deliver . . . that's for sure. They were called yesterday and thanked and today more phone calls. This is good because we've learned they can deliver and the moderates can't. We should think about diversity and establish other contacts with other factions. We have started to establish contact with some success and now more success is expected since if these groups feel if the extremes are in contact with us then it is less risky for the other groups—nothing operational is being done . . . this is contact only."

15. Nir described some of the problems and choices: "Should we accept sequencing? What are alternatives to sequencing? They fear if they give all hostages they won't get anything from us. If we do want to move along these lines we'd have to move quickly. It would be a matter still of several weeks not several days, in part because they have to move the hostages every time one is released."

16. Nir concluded with the following points: "The bottom line is that we won't give them more than previously agreed to. It is important that we have assets there 2 to 3 years out when change occurs. We have no real choice than to proceed."

17. The VP made no commitments nor did he give any direction to Nir. The VP expressed his appreciation for the briefing and thanked Nir for having pursued this effort despite doubts and reservations throughout the process.

BY: CRAIG L. FULLER [initialed:] "CF 8/6/86"

## IX. New Wine in Old Bottles? July-November 1986

Jenco's release coincided with expressions of interest by Iranian officials in improved relations with the United States. At the same time, three Americans remained hostage in Lebanon. American officials, already dissatisfied with Ghorbanifar as an intermediary, were ready to try other channels of communication with Iran. American goals remained unchanged.

# A. Sequentialism

Pursuant to the President's decision of July 30, 1986, on August 3, the United States delivered twelve pallets of HAWK spare parts to Iran. ("Adams" [Secord] to [?North], 8/2/86) Israel provided logistical assistance. (CIA/IG Chronology 28; Maximum Version 8; Historical Chronology 13)[85] On August 2, Secord reported:

1. Planning to operate 707 TAIL No. EI-ptm fm Ben Gurion to Bandar Abbas. Cargo Wt. 48000 lbs. 12 Pallets. ETD 2400L–2100Z and ETA is 0730L–0400Z. Rt

of flt is down red sea, East btwn S. YEMEN and Socotra to vic Char Bahar, Direct to Bandar Abbas. Expect
EI-PTM to contact Bandar Abbas approach control,
circa 0700L–0330Z on VHF 124.2 Pt. 2. Pls ensure
authorities in Bandar Abbas know we are coming and
are ready to off load and refuel the 707. Fuel is expected to be free as in the past. Past experience shows
that the authorities at Bandar Abbas are not in the
picture and much confusion results. pls get Sam
[O'neil] to emphasize this to the Australian
[coverterm for official in Iranian Prime Minister's of-
fice]. We wd like to get out of Bandar Abbas and return
here in Daylight hours. Pt. 3. 707 will transmit ops
normal position reports in blind to IAF command post
on HF/SSB Freqs Night: 8739 or 5605 or 10475 or
3115; Day: 8858 or 11290 or 12600. Reports will be
given abeam jidda, socotra and approaching B. Abbas.
Pt. 4. It is now 7 hrs til planned takeoff. If coord w/
Tehran cannot be accomplished, we plan 24 hr delay.

("Adams" [Secord] to [?North], 8/2/86)

Shortly before taking a vacation. North went to London on
August 7. (North calendar)[86]

Toward the end of August, after returning from vacation, North reported to Poindexter the latest Iranian and
Nicaraguan information.

We have had an intensive series of discussions w/ Nir,
Gorba and [Ghorbanifar's Tehran contact] over the
past 48 hrs. It is not clear whether Nir/Gorba are
aware that we are talking directly to . . . . Basic proposal as outlined to you over phone remains unchanged; i.e., sequential release for sequential deliveries. We must, however resolve the problem of how
to provide the parts which we promised but do not
have in stock. [C/NE] has assigned an officer to work
w/ Army logistics in an effort to find (or manufacture,
if necessary) the missing/wrong items. Both Gorba
and [his Tehran contact] have been told not to ship the
63 defective/wrong parts back and that we will
backhaul them on the next delivery. Copp has been
told to keep a crew in readiness for a further mission

390

and has been apprised of the general parameters of the arrangement. He notes that from a logistics perspective, the sequential arrangement is preferable in that it requires only one crew and one A/C throughout thus reducing visibility and enhancing OPSEC. We should have a better fix on availability of parts early in the week and meanwhile have told Gorba and [the official in the Prime Minister's office] that both sides should bring a technical expert familiar w/ the appropriate system to the meeting. [The Iranian official] told Geo. [Cave] this morning that it wd be best to bring an expert w/ us to Tehran for the meeting and he could see for himself what the problems are. Having discussed this proposal this a.m. w/ both Clarridge and Cave we all believe this to be the best course of action, especially if we can leave our "technical expert" and a communicator behind in Tehran. CIA is now looking for a good Ops officer who is familiar w/ the system. Dick already has one identified but CIA wd prefer to use its own officer if they can find one. We should get back to [the Iranian official] w/ an answer by Monday [August 25]. All of us rate the risk to be relatively low, particularly given the experience we had in May. If you approve, we wd use [false] documents (as we did in May) and go in via the Iran Air flight to/from Frankfurt. Estimated time on mission wd be two days. We wd plan to go over a weekend to reduce visible absence fm D.C.

NEW SUBJECTS: . . .

On the hostages—I just don't know. One of the things that has concerned me for some time was the report that you got from Copp [Secord] about how the parts really help their problem for lack of test equipment, not ordering all of the right parts and the lack of knowledge of the system. If we get into a sequential arrangement, we really have to be prepared to deliver a lot more material and arrange a rather continuing technical arrangement. Of course that could all be done, but after the hostages are released. I just don't see how we can have such a continuing relationship until that happens. . . . Before we agree to a sequential arrangement I think we ought to straighten out

391

our committment on the 240—that alone will help establish our good faith that we aren't trying to cheat them. Then we should wait a bit and see what [a friendly country approach] delivers. . . .

(Poindexter PROF note to North, reply to note of 8/23/86, 15:52) On August 5, Secord met with the Relative of a powerful Iranian official (the "Relative").

Secord reported to North:

1. Following is summary report of three long meetings —total circa eight hours—with Iranian gp visiting Brussels. Meetings took place August 25 in three segments. Iranian side was [the Relative], and [a] former Iranian Navy officer—20 years—and alleged London businessman now—definitely an important agent for Rafsanjani gp and possibly Savama. Our side included me—true name—Abe [Hakim] in true name, and [another Iranian expatriate], our agent. Meetings constituted comprehensive tour de force regarding Iran/Iraq War, Iranian views of U.S. and other western policies, Soviet activities, activities of nearly all important Iran government figures, hostage matters, activities in the Hague, and Iranian forces equipment and materiel shortages.

2. Special interest items included claim that an "Al Haig gp" and "a Senator Kennedy gp" have recently tried to meet with [the Relative]—he has declined— he wants to deal with the Presidents [sic] representatives. [The Relative] is very sharp, well educated youngman [sic]—speaks no English. [He] is well-known favorite of [Majlis speaker] Rafsanjani . . . They badly need air defense items, armor spares, TOWs, gun barrels, helo spares, and tactical intelligence. I told them all things negotiable if we can clear the hostage matter quickly. [The Relative] knew great deal about McFarlane msn to Thn. He also knows all about [the official in the Prime Minister's office], Gorba, Israeli connection, and this gps financial greed. Gorba was nastly [sic] classified as a crook. [The Relative's] wealth of current information but also volunteers to discuss hostage matter and USG connection

with Rafsanjani in next 10 days. He will then return to Brussels for meeting with us. [The Relative] said categorically he would not screw up [official in Prime Minister's office, Cave] efforts but would carefully examine them for feasibility. [The relative] will recommend two courses to Rafsanjani:

a. Assist in current . . . effort [by official in Prime Minister's office] to release hostages or start new effort.

b. Provide us with current intelligence on their location, etc., . . . [The relative] says there are many specific things USG can do in the Hague and on Voice of America programming to help start USG/GOI talks—he will give us documents on these subjects at next meeting.

3. Numerous military supply problems were discussed and I will detail these for you later this week in Washington. FYI: They need oil barter deals.
4. My judgement is that we have opened up new and probably much better channel into Iran. This connection has been effectively recruited and he wants to start dealing. Recommend you plan on bringing George to next meeting in two weeks or less.

(Secord ("Copp") to North, 8/26/86)[87]

On August 27, the Relative informed Secord that the Iranians were trying to buy TOWs in Madrid at a cost of $13,000 each. Secord thought it was "a big steal." The United States was not involved, and the Relative reportedly worried that the transaction could upset the effort to establish a new relationship with the United States. (Secord to [?North], 8/27/86; North to Poindexter, 9/2/86)[88]

On September 2, North formally proposed trying to use the new connection with the Relative. He wrote Poindexter: *NEXT STEPS WITH IRAN*

*Ongoing Activities*

There are currently five separate activities underway which are related to resolution of the American hostage situation and a potentially broadened relationship with the Government of Iran:

—*[Third Country] Initiative:* [The Foreign Minister] has been given a message for delivery to the Iranian Foreign Ministry indicating a willingness on the part of the USG to improve relations with Iran and to undertake direct, private discussions with responsible Iranian officials. No response has yet been received.

—*[Another Third Country Connection]:* [It's] Ambassador in Tehran during a meeting with Rafsanjani discussed the hostage situation and further U.S.-Iranian contacts. Rafsanjani, for the first time, suggested certain materiel (F-14 spare parts and embargoed helicopters) as items that could cause Iran to act on behalf of the American hostages. Per instructions, [that government was] advised that such "barter arrangements" were unacceptable to the U.S. and contrary to our policy. [They] remain willing to advise Rafsanjani that we are prepared to hold private discussions with the Iranians.

—***

—*[The Relative]:* In coordination with the CIA, Copp and two of his associates met for two days last week with [the Relative] indicated a full awareness of the May trip to Tehran and the ongoing activity involving [the official in the Prime Minister's office] and Ghorbanifar. [The Relative] clearly indicated that he had c specific mandate from [Rafsanjani] to meet with USG official seeking a means for "getting beyond the hostage issue" and [the Relative] starting a dialogue with the USG. [The Relative] has returned to Tehran and has since informed us of a pending TOW sale through Madrid and further indicated that he is prepared to proceed with further discussions. He has further noted that the government in Tehran is very concerned over Soviet activities in the Gulf and is aware that a "final victory" over Iraq will not be possible. There is considerable evidence that [the Relative] is indeed a bonafide [sic] intermediary seeking to establish direct contact with the USG for Rafsanjani's faction within the Government of Iran.

—*[Official in Prime Minister's Office]/Ghorbanifar:* Since the release of Father Jenco, that portion of the 240 parts which was available has been delivered. The Iranians have advised through Nir that at least 63[89] of the items delivered are improper or inoperable. Further, 299 of the items promised have not been received. They have offered to return the damaged/incorrect parts, but have been told to return them on a "future delivery flight." The Iranians continue to insist on a sequential delivery process and in a meeting in London with Nir a specific seven step delivery/release pattern was proposed:

—Deliver 500 TOWs and the 39 electron tubes for the HAWK system previously requested.

—[Hostage] released.

—Deliver 500 TOWs and one of the HAWK radars previously requested.

—[Hostage] released.

—Meeting in Tehran to discuss broadened relationship, Soviet intelligence, etc.

—Deliver remaining radar and 1000 TOWs while we are in Tehran.

—[Hostage] released and Buckley's body delivered.

CIA concurs that the [Iranian official]/Ghorbanifar connection is the only proven means by which we have been able to effect the release of any of the hostages. Though the sequential plan is not what we prefer, the commodities and quantities are within the framework of our original understanding. CIA believes that we should proceed

expeditiously with the Ghorbanifar connection
and pursue the other five alternatives as subsidiary efforts.

(Tab I, "Next Steps with Iran," to North to Poindexter,
9/2/86) The copy obtained by the Board of North's Action
Memorandum, to which this document is attached, shows
a check mark next to the word "Approve."

North was impatient for Poindexter's approval of the
plan. He wrote McFarlane that evening:

> We still have no response fm JMP re proceeding w/
> the sequential release proposal outlined to you some
> time back. Have now undertaken to have Casey raise
> same w/ JMP tomorrow at thr weekly mtg. The things
> one must do to get action. Am hopeful Bill can push
> hard enought [sic] to move on the matter. Nir will be
> here next week and will raised [sic] enough hell to
> move it if it hasn't all fallen apart by then. The basic
> problem, as you know, is that we dither so long on
> these things that by the time we're ready to go to bat,
> the rules have changed again. I agree w/ yr assess-
> ment that the next mtg in Tango [Tehran] is unlikely
> to be for some time. My hope is that we will not be
> trying to adjust yr sched for next June for this mtg.

(North PROF note to McFarlane, 9/3/86, 20:12:50)

At the same time, the families of the hostages called
North to complain about the " 'deal' " being made for
Daniloff, a *U.S News & World Report* journalist arrested in
Moscow, apparently in retaliation for the arrest in New
York of a suspected KGB agent. North reported on Sep-
tember 8:

> Some, like Jacobsen's son Paul accused us of being
> callous to the LebNap victims—and unwilling to pres-
> sure the Kuwaitis because the issue has "slipped from
> the public eye and that we are willing to make deals
> for Daniloff because it was more important to the
> President because of the visibility." All indicated that
> they are planning to hold a press conference later this
> week to "turn the heat on" the Administration. My
> rejoinder that no deal for Daniloff was in the mill was,

because of earlier press coverage to the contrary, not taken seriously. Bob Oakley has made a similar effort w/ the same unfortunate results. This afternoon, Louis Boccardi, President of the AP came to see me. He is supportive of our policy on terroprism [sic] and on the hostage issue—and notes that we are not credible in saying that a deal was not in the making. He pointedly noted that this could well have an effect on Terry Anderson's fate in that the Hezballah could not but take heart from the talk of our willingness to deal with the Soviets over Daniloff. While it was an amiable discussion, I was impressed by his concern that no matter what we do now re Daniloff, we are going to be perceived as having made a deal that will hurt chances for Anderson's release and jeopardize his other reporters elsewhere. He made cogent observation that I think is relevant: "I sure hope that you are dealing with someone regarding Terry and the others in Lebanon—and that you can keep it quiet—that's the only way that any of this will work."

(North PROF note to Poindexter, 9/08/86, 19:08:10)

On the same day, North updated his paper on "Next Steps with Iran" for Poindexter to use with the President. In North's view:

[The Relative] continues to indicate that he has a specific mandate from [Rafsanjani] to meet with USG officials seeking a means for "getting beyond the hostage issue" and starting a dialogue with the USG.

—*[Iranian official]/Ghorbanifar:* Pursuant to guidance, efforts were made over the weekend to convince [the Iranian official] to release of [sic] all three Americans simultaneously. He steadfastly rejected this proposal citing the intransigence of the captors and Iranian inability to ensure results.

—Since last week, CIA and Army Logistics have located a significant number of HAWK parts which had previously been listed as "unavailable." We now believe that the total "package" will be sufficient to entice the Iranians to proceed with the sequential release pattern proposed in the London meetings.

—Since Sunday [September 7], [the Iranian official] has sought, in dozens of calls, to contact Abe [Hakim], Goode [North], Sam [Cave] and Copp [Secord]. This afternoon, when Sam returned call to him he told Sam that his "boss approved of the meeting that was to take place" and referred specifically to the meetings two weeks ago with [the relative] in Brussels. CIA evaluates this information as confirmation that Rafsanjani may be moving to take control of the entire process of the U.S. relationship and the hostages.

Other Issues

This weekend, . . . an eleven minute address by the Shah's son [was broadcast] over Iranian T.V., by pirating the national network broadcast frequency. This broadcast reportedly sparked protests in Tehran and elsewhere by supporters of the Shah's family. [The Iranian official], in one of his calls to Sam, asked pointedly how it was that we could profess to "accept the Iranian revolution as fact" and still sponsor such an event.

Separate intelligence reporting indicates that a major Iranian offensive is likely to occur on/or about Monday, September 22—the anniversary of Iraq's attack against Iran in 1980. Given the urgency of calls from Iran and Rafsanjani's apparent willingness to endorse U.S./Iranian discussions, Iran may be making all possible attempts to acquire requisite arms to support this "final offensive."

Director Casey conducted a review of the Iranian project today and has directed his people to initiate necessary preparations for acquiring the parts promised in earlier discussions with the Iranians. CIA continues to believe that the [Iranian official]/Ghorbanifar connection is the only proven means by which we have been able to effect the release of any of the hostages. Though the sequential plan is not what we prefer, the commodities and quantities are within the framework of our original understanding. CIA believes that we should proceed expeditiously with arrangements to implement the sequential plan proposed by [the Iranian official]—with hopes that we could improve on it in discussions with Rafsanjani's representatives when they arrive in Europe. In this regard, our window of opportunity may be better than it will ever be again, if we are able to consummate the release of the hostages before the Iranian offensive begins.

(Tab I ("Supplement Next Steps with Iran") to North to Poindexter, 9/8/86) North also attached a report from Charles Allen about a threat to kill the hostages. Allen wrote that "we" believe that the captors were frustrated that they were no closer to freeing the Dawa prisoners than when they captured Buckley.

More and more, we suspect that some Hezballah leaders would be willing to settle for the release of the Americans and French in exchange for Shia prisoners held by Antoine Lahad's Southern Lebanese Army.

(Allen to Poindexter, 9/8/86, Tab II to North to Poindexter, 9/8/86)

The President considered the new Iranian interlocutor, the prospects for a hostage release, and the possibility of a rescue operation at his morning briefing on September 9. (McDaniel log) Later that day, North and Poindexter discussed the hostage problem. Allen reported to the Director of Central Intelligence on September 10 that he had seen North shortly after this meeting. Allen wrote:

2. Poindexter has given Ollie new guidance on the American hostages, namely:

. . .

—Ollie is to continue to develop links to the Iranian Government through Albert Hakim and Dick Secord of Stanford Technology Associates. (Hakim, as you are aware, has links to [the Relative]. [The Relative] apparently is attempting to arrange for Ollie and George Cave to meet with

Rafsanjani, presumably with the next shipment of arms to Tehran.)

—Ghorbanifar will be cut out as the intermediary in future shipments of cargos to Iran, if at all possible. To cut Ghorbanifar out, Ollie will have to raise a minimumm [sic] of $4 million.

—If there is no other channel for financing future arms shipments, then Ghorbanifar will be used as a last resort.

3. Ollie is greatly relieved by Poindexter's decisions because he feared that John and the President would shut down completely this back channel to Iran because of the kidnapping yesterday of Frank Reed.[90]. . .

[Handwritten note]—Reed released immediately

(C. Allen to DCI, 9/10/86)

On September 10, Nir met with Poindexter and North in Washington. To prepare Poindexter for the meeting, North wrote:

Nir is coming to the U.S. at the urgent request of Prime Minister Peres. Incoming PM Shamir and outgoing PM Peres have agreed that Nir will remain in his current capacity after the change of government in October. You will be meeting with Nir the day before you meet with Defense Minister Rabin. It is likely that Nir has been given the task of approaching the USG on the matter of the hostages and counter-terrorism—leaving to Rabin broader security issues.

Nir arrives in the wake of renewed terrorist attempts against Israel, the Istanbul Synagogue attack, and the seizure of another American in Beirut. The Israeli government has been anxious to consummate the hostage release plan worked out with Iran. Undoubtedly, Peres would like to achieve the release of the Israeli soldier believed to be held by Hezballah before leaving office in October. The Israelis recognize that this morning's seizure of another American in Beirut jeopardized all previous plans in this regard.

It is important to note that Nir has become partially aware of our contact with [the Relative]. He is not aware that we have been advised that the Iranian delegation will be headed by Rafsanjani's brother Mahmoud Rafsanjani, the former Ambassador to Damascus. The Israelis were initially concerned that the USG was moving to establish a separate channel which would not include the release of the Israeli soldier seized in February. Under instructions, Nir advised that his government's position remained as follows:

—The Government of Israel has supported this joint effort for over a year and has not at any time acted unilaterally.

—The Government of Israel expects that the effort to obtain the release of hostages held in Lebanon will continue to be a joint endeavor and include U.S. demands for the release of the Israeli hostage.

Nir has been told that we will continue to support these two objectives and that the U.S. and Israel will work together to that end.

Your talking points at Tab I provide a rationale for how contact was established with Rafsanjani and how we expect to proceed. Please note that your talking points indicate that Nir will participate in these discussions. Nir will also be meeting with Director Casey, the OSG-TIWG principals, and Father Jenco, and has asked to meet with the Vice President—who he met with in Israel. The Vice President has not yet agreed to this meeting.

*RECOMMENDATION*

That you use the points at Tab I during your meeting.

## Talking Points

Meeting with Amiram Nir

—Glad we could have this opportunity to talk

again. Understand you have a number of important meetings during your four days here.

—We are certainly pleased that you will be continuing in your current capacity during the political transition in October.

—I believe our joint efforts to safely recover the hostages in Lebanon and to broaden our relationships with Iran are important to both our nations.

—The President recognizes that were it not for your efforts that Weir and Jenco would not yet be free.

—We are committed to continuing our joint efforts to achieve the release of all of our citizens— yours and ours.

—In that spirit of cooperation, I want to make you aware of an opportunity that we became aware of last week.

—In the process of investigating a possible illegal diversion of TOW missiles to Iran, Copp made contact with an agent in [country deleted] working the sale.

—The European agent indicated that [the Relative] was involved with this purchase. Copp met with [the Relative] in Brussels on August 25, 1986 and advised him that it will not be possible to obtain TOW missiles without the help of the USG.

—[The Relative] . . . , was clearly interested in this possibility and also raised the following points:

 —He was checking on obtaining TOWs for Moshen [sic] Rafsanjani who is Speaker Rafsanjani's brother, who suspected the $16 million deal would not be possible.

 —[The Relative] had been probed by representatives of Senator Kennedy and former Secretary of State Haig concerning the possible release of the hostages.

—[The Relative] also knew full details of our meetings in Tehran last May to include the fact that "Miller was an Israeli."

—Queried Copp re Iran-Iraq war and Soviet designs in the region.

—Noted that Rafsanjani is now head of "Supreme War Council" and wants to change perception of current military situation and establish basis for truce talks with Iraq.

—Provided details on immediate needs re TOWs, HAWKs, technical spares, and other technical assistance.

—Provided three scenarios for "getting beyond the hostage issue:"

• Provide us with intelligence on current locations and let us (U.S. and Israel) handle the problem.

• Let [the official in the Prime Minister's office] project continue.

• Rafsanjani personally intervenes to free hostages.

—Would it be possible to set up a meeting between a personal representative of Rafsanjani and a high-level USG contact?

—Yesterday, the Presient [sic] approved proceeding with a meeting with the Rafsanjani representative.

Poindexter approved North's talking points. (North to Poindexter, 9/9/86)

North had additional news about the abduction of Reed.

[The Relative] called Abe [Hakim] last night to advise that Reed was not, repeat not, held by Islamic Jihad, that no Iranian "influenced" groups were responsible, and that Iran wd do whatever they could to find him and either return him or tell us where he is being held.

We have not yet gotten a call from [the official in the Prime Minister's office]. back to Sam [O'neil—Cave] on this matter, but hope the news will be the same on that front. If it is, we may well be getting somewhere w/ the highest levels of the present regieme [sic].

(North PROF note to Poindexter, 9/11/86, 07:17:56)

On September 13, Poindexter informed North that he had discussed "our plans on the hostages" with the Director of Central Intelligence "and he is on board. Also went over the Secord matters. Bill agrees Secord is a patriot. He will check into our suspicions. I told him he could get more detail from you." (Poindexter PROF note to North, 9/13/86, 12:01:00)

The Prime Minister of Israel visited Washington in the middle of September; the Iran operation constituted one of the topics addressed. Nir saw Poindexter and North. As instructed by Poindexter, North prepared briefing papers.

You are scheduled to meet with Ami Nir again this afternoon at 1:30 p.m. for 10 minutes. Purpose of this meeting is to debrief Nir on his meeting with Peres over the weekend. You will then be able to brief the President on Peres' views regarding the several on-going and contemplated initiatives with the Israelis. . . .

Issues, which Prime Minister Peres may raise privately with the President, are outlined at Tab III. Nir notes that it is unlikely that Peres will discuss any of these with anyone else in the room.

RECOMMENDATIONS

. . .

2. That you brief the President on the initiatives outlined at Tab III.

Approve "JP Done"

*POSSIBLE PERES DISCUSSION ITEMS WITH THE PRESIDENT*

Amiram Nir, the Special Assistant to Prime Minister Peres on Counter-Terrorism, has indicated that during the 15 minute private discussion with the President, Peres is likely to raise several sensitive issues:

\* \* \*

emphasizing his new role as Foreign Minister. He feels frustrated by the lack of progress and may suggest several areas wherein the U.S. could boost the image of Israeli flexibility.

—*Hostages:* Several weeks ago, Peres expressed concern that the U.S. may be contemplating termination of current efforts with Iran. The Israelis view the hostage issue as a "hurdle" which must be crossed enroute [sic] to a broadened strategic relationship with the Iranian government. It is likely that Peres will seek assurances that the U.S. will indeed continue with the current "joint initiative" and ensure that we will include the two missing Israelis in the process. In that neither Weir nor Jenco would be free today without Israeli help (particularly in logistics), it would be helpful if the President would simply thank Peres for their discrete [sic] assistance.

[Marginal note in Poindexter's handwriting: Thanks for assistance on Weir and Jenco. Will continue to work Iran with you. Include 2 missing Israelis in it.]

—*Israeli Arms:* On Friday night, Defense Minister Rabin offered a significant quantity of captured Soviet bloc arms for use by the Nicaraguan democratic resistance. These arms will be picked up by a foreign flag vessel this week and delivered to the Nicaraguan resistance. If Peres raises this issue, it would be helpful if the President thanked him since the Israelis hold considerable stores of bloc ordnance, compatible with what the Nicaraguan resistance now uses.

[Marginal note in Poindexter's handwriting: Rabin, Very tightly held.].

(North to Poindexter, 9/15/86)

Once past the visit of the Israeli Prime Minister, the United States entertained [the issue of the Relative]. The morning of September 17, North wrote Poindexter

> We are planning to bring him [the Relative] into the U.S. at the end of the week, via parole papers thru Istanbul. Iranians can go to Turkey w/o visas and parole papers avoid the necessity of stamping a visa in his passport—a complication which frequently causes major problems for those living in Iran. We (Cave, Clarridge, C/NE, North) decided to honor their request to keep this first meeting private (w/o Nir/Israelis) and to have it here so that they can confirm that they are indeed talking to the USG. We knew this when you and Nir met on Monday, but I had not yet had the chance to brief you. We will have a follow-up mtg with [the Relative] in Europe and we will work Nir back into this op then. In the interim, Clair [George] has put a hold on bringing [the Relative] in because he does not know whether you have "approved the operation." Wd you pls call Casey and tell him to get on with moving the guy in so that we don't embarass the hell out of ourselves w/ Rafsanjani.

(North PROF note to Poindexter, 9/17/86, 07:56:26) Poindexter replied that he had already enlisted the approval of the Director of Central Intelligence on September 13. "If Clair [George] has a problem," Poindexter noted on North's memorandum on surveillance for [the relative], "he should talk to Casey." (Poindexter note on North to Poindexter, 9/17/86)

North orchestrated preparations for the visit, which included electronic surveillance . . . (North to Poindexter, 9/17/86, enclosing Casey to Meese, 9/17/86, with Poindexter's concurrence, and memorandum by Odom) He reported to Poindexter:

> Casey called and told me what he wanted to do. I don't think [Clair] George will be a problem. He was actually enthusiastic about Cave's talking to Khomeini's relative * * *.

406

(Poindexter PROF note North, 9/17/86, 14:35:04) He also explicitly responded to Poindexter's note on the memorandum:

> Per your note on the surveillance package I called Casey and told him we need to get on with the parole paperwork in that you had already agreed—and had furthermore just endorsed the surveillance request. He acknowledged yr approval for the plan but said he as [sic] concerned about Shultz. He said he planned to tell Shultz in general terms that we were talking to another high level Iranian and that we would fill him in after the interview. I protested that experience showed that Shultz would then talk to * * * or * * * who would in turn talk to * * *—and that * * * could well be the source of the Jack Anderson stuff we have seen periodically. Casey Agreed [sic] to proceed with the INS parole paperwork for the Relative and the visa for his escort but noted that he would still talk privately to Shultz about this. We are now underwaywith [sic] getting [the Relative] aboard a chartered jet out of Istanbul. CIA could not produce an aircraft on such "short notice" so Dick has chartered the a/c thru one of Project Democracy's overseas companies. Why Dick can do something in 5 min. that the CIA cannot do in two days is beyond me—but he does. How the hell he is ever going to pay for it is also a matter of concern, but Dick is a good soldier and never even groused about it. You may want to talk to Sec Shultz about [the Relative] before Casey does. I will prepare a memo for you as soon as we talk to him.

(North PROF note to Poindexter, 9/17/86, 12:59:11)

North relied on Secord to bring [the Relative] to the United States. (North PROF note to Poindexter, 9/17/86, 16:19:33) Secord reported to North, also on September 17, that:

> [The Relative] will want intell info and a scheme for future provision of same. In the past, Casey has wanted to establish comms in Tehran and this might be the vehicle. We should give some very good OB data in narrative form so that he can take it back and

make an impact. The stuff we used for [the official in the Prime Minister's office] will have changed. It is no big task for an analyst to prepare such a briefing. I know there is skepticism about this new connection, but we will fail if we do not use our senses and produce something of use. Next he will want some kind of secure voice device for use in telecoms back here to us in the next few weeks or months—there are a number of these items available commercially and I would hope that CIA could supply same in a briefcase for him to take back. Finally, [the Relative] will want to talk about war material and its relation to a long-term connection from U.S to Iran. My opinion is that he and his group are attaching more importance to a long-term relationship than to any short-term quick fix, such as a few thousand TOWs. He will, however, have a list of needed items and will no doubt suggest some kind of shipment to clear the hostage matter and to firmly establish direct USG to GOI transactions and to eliminate the Gorbas and [official in Prime Minister's office]. Thus, if I'm right, CIA must deliver the goods re good OB and come up with suitcase secure phone device.

(Copp to Goode [North], 9/17/86, 1720)

# B. The Second Channel in Washington

On September 19 and 20, North, Secord, and Cave (as O'neil) met with the Relative and the Iranian expatriate who had introduced him. The two days of negotiations were surreptitiously taped. North reported to Poindexter on September 20 that:

> Talks going extremely well. They and we want to move quickly beyond the "obstacle" of the hostages. Sincerely believe that RR can be instrumental in bringing about an end to Iran/Iraq war—a la Roosevelt w/ Russo/Japanese War in 1904. Anybody for RR getting the same prize? . . .

(North PROF note to Poindexter, 9/20/86, 12:04:15) Poindexter replied two days later: "Good on the talks. Will look forward to debrief. Ok on trip to London." (Poindexter PROF note North, 9/22/86, 8:37:02)

North gave Poindexter a preliminary report on September 22:

Talks with [the Relative] commenced on Friday night and proceeded almost nonstop until Sunday at 1100 when he departed for Istanbul aboard charter. George and Dick agree that things went extremely well. He is assured that the GOI is dealing directly with the USG and that the mutual interests of both parties transcend the "obstacle" of the hostages—but that this problem must be solved first. Much credit in this goes to Dick, who established the initial contact in Brussels. [The Relative] wants to set up a "joint committee" in Turkey or Portugal for resolving the issues which separate us—an idea which would then lead to putting a discrete [sic] communications team in Tehran. At one point he asked if Secord could return with him to advise on how to set this up. He asked specifically for a sign from the USG that we are indeed moving in the right direction and we agreed to a carefully constructed phrase in a VOA broadcast which would mention the nations which denied access to the hijacked PA 73 a/c—and include Iran in the list. He will be back to us later in the week after he has met with the leadership in Tehran. In discussing what we could do for them he raised the issues of 2M homeless in Iran, the collapse of the economy and the destruction of their oil industry. He complained bitterly about the French effort this spring which he said was designed only to get their hostages out and to help Chirac get elected. We noted that RR could not be reelected, that his motivation was to bring about an honorable end to the killing in the Iran/Iraq war, and to reestablish a positive relationship with the Iranian government that would lead to Christians, Jews and Moslems living in peace with one another. On a number of occasions he was told that RR believed deeply in the teachings of our Holy Book, a copy of which was on the table,

409

and reference was made to a number of pertinent passages (e.g. Gen. 15:7-21; Gal. 3:7; etc.). At one point he noted to George that RR being a man of God had removed the only argument they had—that Allah was supposed to be on their side. He has promised prompt action on the hostages, is looking for assurances that we will not walk away once they use their influence to get them free and noted that the USG should stop other attempts to make contact w/ the GOI to prevent confusion within the factions at home. He expressed several concerns about the [Ghorbanifar] channel and admitted that they believed someone close to [Ghorbanifar's Tehran contact] was working for the KGB. He expressed great concern that the Soviets could exploit confirmation of the contact by making the contact public and doing great mischief in Iran and the U.S. and by rapidly escalating their assistance to Iraq or even intervening in Iran. We did all we could to feed this anxiety. Nir has been calling regularly to exhort us to move on the next shipment. Because [the Relative] has asked us to wait to see what the result of his discussion in Tehran is, we have decided to stall by telling Nir and Gorba that we must have a meeting w/ [the official in the Prime Minister's office] before we can proceed. We have told Nir that you and RR are very concerned about the two new hostages and that we cannot proceed w/ further deliveries until such a meeting takes place. [The Relative] has asked that for the time being we leave the Israelis out of this because of the problems at home. Contrary to what Nir said here, [the Relative] did know that Nir was an Israeli. We will put together a summary of the talks by my return Wednesday. You can brief RR that we seem to be headed in a vy positive direction on this matter and have hopes that the hostage resolution will lead to a significant role in ending the Iran/Iraq war.

(North PROF note to Poindexter, 9/22/86, 9:22:57) In the course of the meetings, [the Relative] asked that the United States "stop other attempts to make contact [such as those through [third countries] now that we were in direct discussions." (North PROF note to Poindexter, 9/20/86, 12:06:57.) "Geo Cave will brief Casey this after-

noon on the results of the discussions w/ [the Relative],"
North wrote Poindexter. "Casey has asked what we are
doing abt bringing Sec State up to speed on results. I told
him this was your call. Casey is urging a mtg on Weds.
among you, Casey, Cave and me to discuss situation prior
to discussion w/Shultz. Can we schedule same?" (North
PROF note to Poindexter, 9/22/86, 12:00:49)

Apparently, the Director of Central Intelligence discussed the relative's visit with the Secretary of State, North
wrote Poindexter the afternoon of September 22:

> FoMin Velayati is one of the few non-clerics at the top
> of the GOI. He is a technocrat, reportedly a conserva-
> tive and relatively close to Rafsanjhani [sic]. He re-
> portedly is a member of the "War Council" which
> determines the distribution of resources and funds
> within the Iranian government. According to [the Rel-
> ative], Velayati participated in the meetings regarding
> our earlier diplomatic approaches to the GOI and
> evaluated these initiatives as sincere. [The Relative]
> reports, however, that Velayati was not in the final
> sessions they had which authorized [the Relative] trip
> to the U.S. In these sessions Rafsanjhani, Moshen [sic]
> Rafiq-Dust and Mohammed Hosein Jalalai along with
> Musavi-Khamenei made the decision for him to come
> to the U.S. and to be assured that he was indeed talk-
> ing to the top of the USG. Re the Casey/Shultz discus-
> sions: Casey informs that he told Shultz, alone, that the
> CIA was assisting in bringing [the Relative] into and
> out of the U.S. for talks and that he (Casey) wd get
> back to Shultz at some point in the future on what had
> transpired. According to Bill, Shultz simply said
> "OK."

(North PROF note to Poindexter, 9/22/86, 14:35:55)

North also prepared a full memorandum of conversation
to Poindexter on September 25 which had additional material including the statement: "I want to tell you that
unless one of the three men sitting here in the room right
now (North, Secord, Sam O'Neill) contact you, there is no
official message." North noted that "[t]he only other copy

of this memorandum of conversation has been given (by hand) to the DDO of CIA." (North to Poindexter, 9/25/86)

The Secretary of State told the Board that he heard nothing about Iran from July 2, 1986, when Under Secretary Armacost sent him a memorandum he does not recall reading and October 31, 1986, when, after making a speech in Los Angeles, someone asked him about a hostage release. "I was totally barn-sided. I had no idea what was taking place." (Shultz, SRB, 56–57)

On September 24, North provided Poindexter with materials for a meeting among Poindexter, the Director of Central Intelligence, Cave, and C/NE to discuss the September 19–20 conversations.

During the discussions, [the Relative] asked for a "discrete [sic] public sign" that he could use to support his debriefing back in Tehran. We decided that a VOA editorial, broadcast in Farsi, which mentions the Iranian Government's denial of flight clearance to the hijacked Pan Am flight, would suffice. At Tab II is a VOA editorial regarding the hijacking of Pan Am Flight #73.

We appear to be in contact with the highest levels of the Iranian Government. There is no doubt that [the relative] is far more competent and better "connected" than our other interlocutor, [the official in the Prime Minister's office]. It is possible that the Iranian Government may well be amenable to a U.S. role in ending the Iran-Iraq war. This, in and of itself, would be a major foreign policy success for the President. We, therefore, need to determine how we will proceed from here on with the Iranians. Specifically:

—Should we proceed with the "joint committee" proposed by [the Relative] during our discussions.

—Who, if anybody, at the State Department should be brought into this activity.

RECOMMENDATION

That you review the attachments prior to your meeting.

Approve "IP" Disapprove

(North to Poindexter, 9/24/86) North attached Cave's summary of the meetings.

([Cave], "Rundown of Visitor's comments on 19/20 Sept 86," Tab I to North to Poindexter, 9/24/86)

North also attached a draft of a Voice of America editorial entitled "International Cooperation Against Terrorism," in which, as promised to the Relative, Iran among others, was thanked for its assistance in the successful resolution of the PanAm Flight 73 hijacking. (Tab II to North to Poindexter, 9/24/86)[91]

Cave recalled that, at the meetings on September 19 and 20, "an enormous amount of progress was made." (Cave 17) Cave told the Board that "we were talking to someone at the political level, even though the gentleman was very young." *(Id.)*

[W]hen we were in Tehran, at the political and strategic level, we really didn't get anywhere. But at this meeting [September 19–20], he proposed to us that we form a joint commission of four U.S. members and four Iranian members, that we meet in secret and come up with a program for improving U.S.-Iranian relations.

He also discussed in great detail their concerns about Afghanistan, the Soviet Union, and the Persian Gulf. He told us that they had taken our advice and in early September had sent their Oil Ministry [sic], under cover of doing OPEC business, on a trip around the Persian Gulf to talk to the Saudis, the Kuwaitis and the United Arab Emirates, and had gotten what they had considered a rather positive response, particularly from the Saudis.

At that meeting, we also gave them a briefing on what we considered to be the Soviet threat toward Iran.

We also agreed at that meeting that at the next meeting they had, which was going to be in early October, we would give them a briefing on our view of the war, their war with Iraq. We also gave them at the Septem-

413

ber meeting a briefing on our view of how the insurrection in Afghanistan was going against the central government and the Soviets, and they promised at the next meeting that they would give us their views.

*(Id.* at 18–19)

To C/NE, this meeting had been remarkable for another reason. He told the Board that [the Relative]

immediately presented bona fides in the sense of saying, look, we can't get all your hostages out. It was the first time we had heard that in this channel. Always before the promise was don't worry about a thing; we can get them all. He said, we can get two out, maybe three, but we can't get them all.

(C/HE (1) 38) According to Charles Allen, the "new channel" informed the Americans in September that Khomeini's son "briefed the father in great detail . . . [and] the Iranians had decided that it was worth talking to the Americans not just for arms but, I think, for broader reasons." (C. Allen (1) 19–20)

# C. Frankfurt

In the immediate aftermath of [the Relative's] visit, events seemed to move quickly. North wrote Poindexter on September 26 that

[t]his morning, immediately after the VOA broadcast of our PA-73 message, [the Relative] deposited $7M in the numbered Swiss Account we gave him last week. The money will be transferred by noon (EDT) to another account in another bank. In order to save time, I have told Dick to pay CIA's account for the remaining HAWK parts and the 500 TOWs so that they can be assempbled [sic], packed and moved to [location deleted]. UNODIR, CIA will commence acquisition as soon as they receive the money—though nothing will be shipped to final destination until we have had the follow-on discussion w/ [the Relative] and reached an understanding on the "obstacle." We believe he will want to meet on the week of October 6–10—* * *.

Nothing will move from . . . until you so approve. Will sit down tomorrow w/ the CIA logistics guy who is doing the ordering to see if for once they can get it right.

(North PROF note to Poindexter, 9/26/86, 09:47:48)

A week later, North submitted the views of his team (Cave, Clarridge, C/NE, Secord, and North) on "Next Steps for Iran." They argued for the program discussed with [the Relative], who added pressure for acceptance.

North reported on October 2:

[The Relative] contacted Dick this morning and asked that George, Dick and I meet him on Monday in Frankfurt. He claims to have just returned to Tehran from Beirut and that he will have good news regarding the "obstacle" (hostages). I am preparing a paper for you which will include the travel approval for Goode and a bible for [the Relative]—since he is bringing a Koran for the President. We will also use the opportunity of this meeting to set Nir straight on how we are going to proceed. He is beside himself at the delay in action since he was here—and we can, I believe take care of that whole problem in the next few days. Will include our collective recommendations (from George, Dick and me) in the package. Hope to have it to you this afternoon. Warm regards, North p.s. PLEASE authorize us to be polygraphed re this Woodward mess. You, the President, WE need to find the person who is doing this. p.p.s. On the Costa Rican airstrip: it is a C-135K, not a C-130. We had to sell the C-130 last month just to keep Project Democracy afloat (actually an L-100, the commercial variant of the C-130). The airplane in the photo—and referenced in the memo is a smaller precedent to the C-130 w/ 2 reciprocating piston engines and two ram jets outboard (like the old P2V Neptunes).

(North PROF note to Poindexter, 10/02/86, 15:11:48.) A week later, North submitted "Next Steps for Iran" to Poindexter.

[The Relative] called Dick this morning to advise that he had just returned from Beirut and would very much like to meet with us in Frankfurt, Germany, on Monday, October 6. He indicates that he has "good news" regarding the hostages and that he wishes to get past the "obstacle" as quickly as possible. An appropriate travel approval is attached at Tab I.

George Cave is taking a well-deserved "mini-vacation" in Rome. We are telling all callers that he is in the hospital for tests on his back. In accord with [the Relative] request, the U.S. side would be represented by: Sam O'Neil, Copp, and Goode.

This meeting also affords us the opportunity to deal with the issue of Israeli cooperation. Nir has been calling daily (often several times) urging that we get on with the process in our "joint venture." He constantly cites his September 10 meeting with you as the basis for proceeding urgently. Because we have not told him about our intention to pursue the "[the Relative channel]" first, he continues to encourage Ghorbanifar to raise the requisite funds for another delivery. Ghorbanifar, in turn, has a frequent dialogue with [his Tehran contact] in this regard. All of this tends to create confusion among the various participants and an unnecessary OPSEC vulnerability. We need to act now to reduce the number of channels into the Iranians (at least on a temporary basis) and clarify various roles and missions. As is evident on the diagram at Tab II, the various channels of communications are, at the very least, a source of great vulnerability to KGB and other SIGINT penetration.

We (Cave, Clarridge, C/NE, and Copp) believe that we should move promptly on both fronts as follows:

—[The Relative]: O'Neil, Copp, and Goode meet with [the Relative] in Frankfurt on Monday, October 6. [The Relative] has indicated that he has an internal consensus on how to proceed with regard to the hostages "obstacle." He has said that he will bring with him to this meeting "one of the officials we met with in Tehran" and has asked that we bring with us a definitive sample of the intelligence we had discussed when he was here. Based on this, we believe that [a Revolutionary Guard Intelligence official], may well accompany [the Relative]. You will recall that [the Relative's] request for intelligence was very specific (the details were forwarded to you via PROFs). While the sensitivity of providing this information is well-recognized, it must also be noted that intelligence was given a higher priority by [the Relative] than any other assistance we could provide. In the Casey-C/NE-Cave-North meeting we had with you after [the Relative] departed, we all agreed that it was unlikely that providing such information would change the course of the war. Further, we all recognized that the information need not be accurate and that it was highly perishable given the dynamic nature of the conflict. In short, we believe that a mix of factual and bogus information can be provided at this meeting which will satisfy their concerns about "good faith" and that we can use the "perishible" argument as an incentive for the Iranians to accept a CIA communications team in Tehran. As before, we would not leave any documents with the Iranians, but will provide an exposition during which they could take detailed notes. Director Casey needs to be told to prepare the intelligence for hand-carry to the meeting.

[The Relative] has said he is bringing a Koran for the President. As a reciprocal gesture, we have purchased a Bible which we would present to [the Relative] for him to take back to Tehran with him. Given our earlier discussions (see transcript), it would be very helpful if the President would inscribe a brief note citing a particular biblical passage (Tab III) in the front of the Bible. This particular excerpt is important in that it is a new testament reference to Abraham, who is viewed by Moslems, Jews, and Christians as the progenitor of all the world's nations. It would be most effective if the President hand wrote the inscription and initialed/signed it without addressing the note to any particular person.

—*Nir:* When Amiram was here, we made a conscious decision not to apprise him of our near-term efforts with [the Relative]. We did inform him earlier of the contact and he continues to inquire regarding the status of this initiative. Meanwhile, lacking guidance to the contrary, Nir has sought to stimulate further activity between Ghorbanifar and [the official in the Prime Minister's office]. This has resulted in [this official] calling directly to George's home and office several times daily and considerable confusion regarding why we have not accepted the [Iranian official]/Ghorbanifar "offer" to purchase the remaining HAWK spare parts and 500 TOWs.

From an operational perspective, the current communications arrangements are a command and control/OPSEC nightmare (Tab II). Nir essentially controls our access to both [the Iranian official] and Ghorbanifar and, thus, we often find ourselves reacting to his well intentioned efforts. We believe that we now have an opportunity to change the relationship in such a way that Nir is placed in a supporting role rather than acting as a primary source of control. We also recognize that Israel's participation in this activity is both politically and operationally important. In altering Nir's status, we need to do so in such a way that he and those officials in his government who are cognizant continue to perceive that this is still a "joint venture."

In order to accomplish the objectives outlined above, we propose that on Saturday, October 4, Copp would fly to Tel Aviv and meet with Nir. At the meeting, Copp would use the talking points at Tab IV. In an effort to ameliorate Nir's *angst* over his "new status," we urge that the letter at Tab V to Prime Minister Peres be signed by the President. If you agree, we need your approval of the talking points at Tab IV and a Presidential signature (real or autopen) on Tab V by 3:00 p.m. Friday, October 3.

The steps above are designed to give us a chance to make the new relationship through [the Relative] function without destroying the Ghorbanifar/[Iranian official] channel. We would, in effect, put Ghorbanifar [the Iranian official in the Prime Minister's office] on "hold" until we see what [the Relative] produces. Please note that when Copp briefs Nir in Tel Aviv on Saturday, he will *not* reveal that he is enroute to Frankfurt to meet [the Relative]. Given [the Relative's] strong antipathy toward the Israelis and our uncertainty as to whether or not he knows that Nir (aka Miller) is Israeli, we would tell Nir on Sunday night that we were going to a hastily arranged meeting with [the Relative] which he (Nir) will be unable to make due to a lack of connecting flights to Frankfurt.

[The Relative] has already told us, that shortly after the October 6 meeting, there will be a follow-on meeting of the "joint committee" in which [the official in the Prime Minister's office] will be a participant. Unless we are convinced that the Iranians would recognize Nir as an Israeli, we would intend to invite Nir to this follow-on meeting.

A memo from you to the President has not been prepared for obvious reasons. It is hoped that between now and 3:00 p.m. Friday you will have an opportunity to privately discuss this with the President and obtain his approvals/signatures on the steps indicated above.

(North to Poindexter, 10/2/86) Poindexter approved North's travel request (in the name of William P. Goode); agreed to have the President inscribe a Bible with the designated passage from Galatians;[92] approved talking points for Secord; and agreed to persuade the President to sign the letter to Peres. Poindexter neither accepted nor rejected the request to have the Director of Central Intelligence prepare an appropriate intelligence package by October 4 for the meeting on October 6. *(Id.)*

The second attachment to this memorandum was a dia-

gram of the communications between "Tango" [Tehran]—
Merchant (Ghorbanifar), [the official in the Prime Minister's office], [the relative], [the Iranian expatriate] and
[Secord's Iranian agent].—and the United States team—
Goode (North), Sam (Cave), Charlie (Allen), Copp (Secord),
and C/NE. Apart from Cave and [the official in the Iranian
Prime Minister's office], who sporadically communicated
one-on-one, and Allen and Ghorbanifar, who also communicated directly, the others talked through middlemen.
Ghorbanifar generally used Nir; while those in the second
channel used Hakim (Abe). *(Id.* at Tab II) North added the
recommendation:

> Pare the U.S. communicators down to no more than
> *two* individuals (who either compare notes directly
> each day, or report to a common supervisor); e.g., Sam
> and Copp, who *both* report daily to North. Cut Char-
> lie, C/NE and anybody else *out*. Have them stop com-
> munications cold turkey (to support cover story of
> [old] channel being blown, rolled up, and *finished).*

*(Id.)*

Secord's instructions for his meeting with Nir on October 4 noted:

> The objective of this discussion is to improve our con-
> trol of events in this joint effort to establish a strategic
> relationship with Iran. The talking points below are
> intended to establish the parameters of your discus-
> sion and are designed to elicit further cooperation:
>
>> —ADM Poindexter has directed that I see you
>> regarding our current Ghorbanifar/[Iranian offi-
>> cial] channel and discuss with you ways in which
>> we can move together to accomplish our mutual
>> objective—a strategic relationship with Iran.
>>
>> —We have fairly strong evidence that [the Iranian
>> official] was directly involved with the seizure of
>> the second new hostage in Beirut (Cicippio).
>>
>> —We believe that the first new hostage (Reed)
>> was taken by elements other than Hezballah—
>> although they *may* have him in their hands now.

—We think that [the official in the Iranian Prime Minister's office] may have believed that he could bring additional pressure to bear on us to commence further deliveries by seizing another hostage (or hostages).

—Quite the contrary is true. The President is adamant that we will *not* move forward on this channel until we resolve the new hostage issue.

—We are also concerned that the two new hostages (or at least Cicippio) represents a clear violation of the "understanding" we have had with the Iranians on anti-U.S. terrorism since June of last year.

—We do not want to engage in a process that results in new hostages just to bring "pressure to bear." Nor will we continue this process if, when the current hostages are released, more are taken, simply to elicit further deliveries of arms.

—Aside from this very strong policy objection to continuing, we have, as you know, had repetitive financial and communications dufficulties [sic] with Ghorbanifar. While we could debate as to whether or not Ghorbanifar had received all that was due him by the Iranians, the most important factor is potential OPSEC risk.

—In an effort to "keep things moving," Ghorbanifar has made commitments in our name which are patently beyond our ability to meet. This has resulted in increased expectations on the part of the Iranians.

—We know * * * that neither [the official in the Prime Minister's office] nor other Iranian officials in Tehran trust Ghorbanifar.

—Finally, both of us know that [the Iranian official], himself, is not intellectually astute enough to realize the importance of our contact nor the sincerity of our desire to establish an official government-to-government relationship.

421

—In short, this channel is *not* serving our mutual objective: the reopening of a strategic relationship with Iran.

—The President has directed that we will *not* proceed with any further receipt of funds from Ghorbanifar nor deliveries to [his Tehran contact] until we resolve these issues.

—Several months ago, I apprised you of a contact with [the relation of a powerful Iranian official]. The USG decided to pursue this contact to determine its validity.

—We are confident that [the Relative], the man I met with in Brussels, has been franchised to act as a liaison between the U.S. and Iranian governments.

—When Prime Minister Peres was in Washington last month, the President assured him that we are going to continue this effort as a joint project. [Poindexter penned a questionmark in the margin next to this point].

—I have been instructed to seek out a second meeting with [the Relative] as soon as it can be set up and that I will act as the U.S. intermediary until we establish direct contact with government officials from our side.

—Once we have established direct USG contact with [the Relative], we intend to introduce you into this process under the same conditions as obtained when you went to Tehran with us.

—Based on my initial meeting with [the Relative] and the intelligence we have been able to collect, we believe that this contact may well prove to be the one that both your government and mine have been seeking.

(Remember Nir has been told that you "came upon" [the Relative] as a consequence of looking into the possible diversion of TOWs through Spain/Portugal during an investigation undertaken in late July/early August.)

—While we explore the sincerity of the nephew and confirm his ability to speak for the Iranian government, we want to keep the Ghorbanifar/ [Iranian official] channel on "hold."

—To that end, we have told Sam—who is in the hospital—he is to contact [the Iranian official] and tell him that:

—there must be a meeting with [the Iranian official] before we proceed any further;

—the issue of the two new hostages has become a strong, negative factor in proceeding at all;

—this matter (the two new hostages) must be resolved before we will take any further steps for any further deliveries;

—the problem is not the merchant and his financing, but rather the two new hostages;

—coantrary to what he [the Iranian official] may expect, there will be *no* further deliveries until we have met and resolved this matter;

—we have asked [the Iranian official] to meet with us in Frankfurt on October 9—we do not yet have an answer.

—I intend to meet with [the Relative], somewhere in Europe or Turkey, hopefully this week. I will then report back to Washington on my findings and a follow-on meeting will be set-up—in which we will attempt to have you included.

—I want to caution you, however, that in my meeting in Brussels [the Relative] indicated that he and others in Tehran are aware that you are an Israeli—and knew it when you went to Tehran.

423

—Neither of us want this contact, if it is indeed what I think it to be, to founder because of this.

—I have been instructed to find a way to have you in the meeting in which Goode and Sam will serve as the USG representatives.

—If the meeting with [the Relative] this week goes well, I would expect that all of us could meet with him next week.

—In the interim, if [the Iranian official] does indeed agree to meet with us under the conditions we have established, we should proceed with that meeting.

Poindexter met with the Director of Central Intelligence and his Deputy the evening of October 2. (DCI Telephone Calls and Meetings; Gates, Memorandum for the Record, 10/3/86) In addition to discussing the proposal to provide Iran with military information . . .

Both North and Poindexter reported on the new channel to McFarlane. On October 3, North invited McFarlane to review the transcripts of the September 19–20 meeting. (North PROF note to McFarlane, 10/03/86, 22:08:16) Poindexter expressed enthusiasm about the meetings:

We have made contact with [the Relative of a powerful Iranian official (the "Relative")]. Two meetings so far. One here in US. Ollie, Cave and Secord meet with him this weekend in Frankfort [sic]. Your trip to Tehran paid off. You did get through to the top. They are playing our line back to us. They are worried about Soviets, Afghanistan and their economoy [sic]. They realize the hostages are obstacle to any productive relationship with us. They want to remove the obstacle, [The Relative] has been in Beirut, says he has good news for Frankfort. We shall see. Still insisting on group release. If this comes off may ask you to do second round after hostages are back. Keep your fingers crossed.

(Poindexter PROF note to McFarlane, 10/03/86, 20:35:35) McFarlane responded:

Roger; anytime John.

By the way, I watched the news tonight and saw Peggy Say beating up on the Administration for not getting the Beirut hostages out. I haven't heard anything on that score for a while. But I get [sic] the sense that we are pretty much at the mercy of the Iranians.

If you think it would be of any value, I might be able to take a couple of months off and work on the problem. No guarantees and no need for any sponsorship (except for airfares and hotels) but I might be able to turn something up. Think about it.

(McFarlane PROF note to Poindexter, (10/04/86)

On October 5, North flew to Frankfurt. On the 10th, he reported to Poindexter:[93]

Copp has just returned from Frankfurt. According to both he [sic] and Sam, my donkey act with the Relative and [a Revolutionary Guard Intelligence Official] had quite an effect. [The Revolutionary Guard Intelligence Official] told Dick that if he returned home without the hope of further help that he "would be sent back to the front." [The Revolutionary Guard Intelligence Official] gave Dick a proposal closer to the line in my original seven points and asked Dick if there was any way that he could get us to meet before the 3 Nov. meeting I had suggested. Dick told him that he would pass the points on but could not guarantee anything. Points as follows:

1. They pay $3.6M next week.

2. We deliver 500 TOWs (no HAWK parts) 9 daysafter [sic] payment.

3. . . .

4. Two hostages (if possible, but no less than one) released w/in 4 days of TOW delivery. If only one hostage released, whole process stops and we meet again.

5. Repeat funding and Delivery [sic] cycle as in steps 1 & 2 above.

6. We send Tech support for HAWKs, update on intel and secure comm to Tehran and provide location/availability or artillery items noted on the original list provided by [the Relative] in Washington mtg.

7. Iran does utmost to secure release of remaining hostages(s).

[The Revolutionary Guard Intelligence Official] told both Sam and Copp that the group holding Reed and Cicippio is not, repeat not, responsive to Iran. Further, that only [Hostage 1] and [Hostage 2] are "immediately available." [The Revolutionary Guard Intelligence Official] begged Dick to let them find out exactly where [Hostage 3] is and "you can rescue him and not ruin us (Iran) with the Hezballah."

Both Sam and Copp believe we should let them stew in Tehran for a few more days and then accept the proposal indicated above. [The Revolutionary Guard Intelligence Official] and [the Relative] both said that Pattis was not now available, but that they were sure they could work it out once things were moving. Only changes from my proposal is sequential nature of their plan and lack of mention of Buckley body & transcript of interrogation. We do not believe that they can be sure of getting all three—all available info indicates [Hostage 3] is held elsewhere. Dick and Sam believe that we will, however, get two back for nothing more than the two sets of 500 TOWs. They point out that the rest of what the Iranians want (a plan for approaching the Kuwaitis, the location/availability of the artillery, and the intel) all can be managed w/o any great complications. [C/NE], Cave and Casey all seem to be convinced that this is best/fastest way to get two more out—probably w/in next 14 days [C/NE] also notes that the situation in Leb is getting much worse and that we may be getting close to the end of the line for any further movement. Finally, all here now believe that these guys do not have Reed/Cicippio, who are probably in hands of Libyan controlled group which earlier bought/killed Kilburn. [C/NE] and Sam believe that these guys may be the only way we can ever get our hands on Reed/Cicippio since their access and info in the Lebanon are so much better than ours.

BOTTOM LINE: Recommend that we wait for their call on Tuesday, if their position is same as above or better, we shd push them to include Buckley remains and transcript and then get on with it. Pls advise.

(North PROF note to Poindexter, 10/10/86, 21:55:31)

Cave told the Board that the most important part of the Frankfurt meeting was the Iranian's statement that he could obtain the release of one hostage. In addition, Cave said, the participants discussed Iran's weapons requirements, the Afghan war, and the Iraq war. Cave recalled that he

gave them a briefing on our view of their war with Iraq. This briefing was structured so that we told them basically the truth, but the stress we placed on the briefing was such that it would give them considerable pause about launching this final offensive that they had been talking about for the last six months.

(Cave 19–20) Cave recalled that the Iranians wanted to end the war in a way they could present as a victory. *(Id.* at 20) The negotiators agreed to meet again toward the end of the month. During that meeting, Cave said, "we caused the 500 TOWs to be shipped. . . . That's when we got Jacobson [sic] out." *(Id.* at 21)

As it happened the Israelis shipped the TOWs because Secord tried to deposit the Iranians' payment for the weapons into a CIA account that had already been closed.

# D. Arms Into Iran, One Hostage Out of Lebanon[94]

North returned from Frankfurt the evening of October 8. (North calendar) By that time, the first signs of the operation's demise had occurred. But the secret drama had another scene to play before it became a public scandal.

Charles Allen told the Board:

. . . I was very troubled in September that the operation was to spin out of control, and I became convinced, without any evidence, but I've been trained all my life as an intelligence officer to make assessments, that perhaps because Secord and Hakim were directly involved and were also directly involved in supplying the contras, and I could not understand this incredible price markup that we were seeing—the complaints were coming from Iran, from Ghorbanifar, from the Special Assistant to the Prime Minister of Israel, although later he didn't raise that issue again, and I think perhaps—it's just speculation—he was advised by the NSC that maybe some of the money was being diverted to the contras.

On 1 October I went to Bob Gates, the Deputy Director, and I said, I am deeply concerned that:

And I added at the end of my conversation, I said, and this first channel that has been shut down by the NSC is a running sore. The creditors are demanding payment and I said this is going to be exposed if something isn't done. I said perhaps the money has been diverted to the contras, and I said I can't prove it. Gates was deeply disturbed by that and asked me to brief the Director.

For one reason or the other, I did not talk to the Director of Central Intelligence until 7 October. I raised that issue at that time about the operational security of the problem. I also raised the issue of diversion to the contras, and Mr. Casey at that stage said Mr. Furmark has just talked to me, and he didn't talk about the contras, but he talked about the problems of the Canadian investors, and that they are threatening to take law suits to try to take some action.

I said to Mr. Casey, I think I should put all my troubles down in a memorandum, and he said that would be good, and on Columbus Day, October 13, I laid out a comprehensive memorandum which laid out what I thought were the original

428

objectives of the NSC initiative—to open up a geostrategic relationship in the long term with Iran, to get the hostage situation out of the way as a stumbling block to any further relations with Iran, and to discourage Iran from conducting terrorism.

And throughout this initiative Colonel North constantly reiterated to the Iranians no more terrorism against Americans. And in fact terrorism against western targets and against Americans have been substantially reduced since 1984.

I presented this memorandum to Mr. Gates on the 14th because I wasn't certain what he wanted. I gave three recommendations—that we immediately set up a planning cell in the NSC headed by an individual like Henry Kissinger, Hal Saunders, Dick Helms—I forgot who else—to really take a hard program review of this whole initiative. What are we trying to achieve? What are our short-term objectives? What are our long-term objectives? What are our options? A critical review of everything. And I said this is the first recommendation.

The second recommendation was to get ready to exposure of this initiative. We don't even have press guidance. We ought to start preparing some. And to get together a group that's familiar with the Ghorbanifar channel and decide how best we can shut it down in an orderly system-like fashion.

The Director was taken by this memorandum, and he took the original, called Poindexter and said I must see you right away. And he and Gates jointly met with Poindexter on the 15th. They presented the memorandum. They talked in considerable detail about it. Poindexter read it carefully in their presence, asked who wrote it. I have known John Poindexter for several years and I admire him greatly. And they said Charlie Allen wrote it, and Admiral Poindexter promised to look into it. And Bill Casey told me that he advised Admiral Poindexter to get a White House counsel involved right away because it contained in the memorandum that there would be allegations of impropriety and shabby conduct by U.S. officials, regardless of how this comes out, if this was publicly exposed.

And at this meeting the Director and Bob Gates called me in after they had returned from seeing Admiral Poindexter and Director Casey asked me to see Roy Furmark again. I saw Roy Furmark on the 16th. I got additional information. I wrote another memorandum on October 17 which I laid out how deeply troubled I was because I could see this thing blowing up and we were going to have an incredible mess on our hands.

I told Mr. Furmark I needed to sit a long time with him and debrief him fully, and I was to see him early—I guess it was about the week of the 20th of October—but it was the 22nd before we could get together in New York. I took George Cave with me, and at that stage Mr. Furmark made an allegation that he had been told by Ghorbanifar that the bulk of the $15 million that had been raised by the Canadian investors and the Arab investor, which Khashoggi had guaranteed, would be repaid within 30 days at 20 percent interest that the bulk of that money had gone to the contras in Central America.

I recorded all this in a memorandum. Mr. Cave and I jointly prepared the memorandum. It went to Mr. Casey. Mr. Casey again was deeply disturbed. He talked to Admiral Poindexter on secure [telephone]. For some reason, the memorandum from Casey to Poindexter was never sent. It fell into the wrong out box. Casey, when this whole thing erupted on the 25th of November, he was deeply upset to find out he had not signed it. He thought it had gone to Admiral Poindexter. But it laid it out starkly that there would be allegations, that Ghorbanifar had made allegations of diversion of funds to the contras.

430

Chairman Tower: And that was October 17 that that memorandum was dated?

Mr. Allen. It was never dated because he [Casey] didn't sign it, but it was October 24—the 23rd of October. I came back and Mr. Cave and I briefed Casey at 9:00 on the 23rd. We told him the whole thing. Mr. Casey was deeply upset and said immediately prepare that memo. For some reason, the memo was never sent, but he talked to Admiral Poindexter again.

Chairman Tower: What occurs to me is that anything that critical, that important, he would have discussed with Admiral Poindexter.

Mr. Allen: He did, and he discussed this whole problem on the 7th. He discussed it in depth with Admiral Poindexter on the 15th, when he said you better get your White House counsel involved immediately.

Chairman Tower: And he was never aware that Poindexter had not gotten the memo?

Mr. Allen: Not until the 25th of November, when Mr. Casey asked me to pull all the memos together, and he said I sent that memo down and I also talked to him on the 24th of October is actually the date it finally got into his in box. But he found out he had not sent it. He was deeply disturbed and upset. As a matter of fact, on the 7th of October he had called Admiral Poindexter. He had met with Admiral Poindexter, along with Mr. Gates, on the 15th. He had also talked to Admiral Poindexter on the 24th about this.

He had given a lot of warning to Admiral Poindexter that this operation was spinning out of control.

I later met with Mr. Furmark on the 7th of November, but at that stage the operation was starting to be exposed in a major way, so the fact that the Canadian investors were threatening a law suit didn't seem to be as significant to me at that stage.

* * *

[The article appeared in the Lebanese paper on the] 3rd of November, and Rafsanjani on the 4th made his statement that McFarlane came uninvited and we locked them up for five days, which was not true, but Mr. Rafsanjani was covering his derriere just a little on that.

I guess my only comments on this was that the new channel that was opened in mid-August, I had some doubts about it initially, but it's turned out to be a very solid channel, that the initiative today is in the hands of the Department of State.

(C. Allen (1) 29–35) Furmark told the Board that, on October 7, he met the Director of Central Intelligence in Washington, and explained that "the Canadians were putting lots of pressure on Adnan [Khashoggi], and that they were going to sue him and he would have to then bring in [sic] the U.S. into the transaction." (Furmark 10)

At the same time the financiers of the arms transfers were pressing, allegedly, to recover their investment, the NSC staff and the CIA prepared to make another shipment of arms to Iran. On October 16, Earl reported a call from chief of the Iran desk at the Agency:

The fool's [sic] want to get Nir to grease the skids in advance on their request for flight clearance to Tel Aviv before they submit the paperwork. I've got the info when you're ready to let Nir know. . . . I recommend you DON't [sic] tell him the flight plan data when you first tell him the thing is approved, however; it's so detailed he'll know we held out on him. Suggest you tell him I'm working w/ the fool's now to develop that info and we'll pass it to him as soon as we have it. Then we can call him again later tonight or tomorrow. New subject: The fool's are leaning forward as far as they can—e.g. the toes [sic] are apparently being palletized in Alabama already—but they can't get everything going until they have the money

($2.037m) in hand. They've asked for a heads up when Copp/Abe deposit it in their Berne account. I've codedup [sic] this request for a heads up/confirmation and sent it to Bob M. [J. Robert McBrien] and [encryption device].

(Earl PROF note to North,[95] 10/16/86, 17:42:53) Coy reported to Earl on the 20th that the chief of the Iran desk had relayed information about 12 pallets, each carrying 44 TOWs.

"Material [TOWs and medicine] is put together and will be shipped from AL when money is avail. Planning delivery to Adam [Nir] in T.A. [Tel Aviv] on Oct 29. (Coy PROF note to Earl, 10/20/86, 11:59:29) On October 21, 1986, Edward Tracy, a booksalesman, was kidnapped in Beirut.

While preparations for another shipment of TOWs continued, North and his team went to Frankfurt for another meeting with the Relative. North left Washington on October 26. (North Calendar) On October 29, Earl relayed a report from North to Poindexter:

Gist of following message already given to you by phone on the plane, but thought you may need some of the details:

For JMP from North. Iranian rep [the Relative] assures us we will get 2 of the 3 US hostages held by Hezballah in next few days—probably Fri or Sat but NLT Sunday. To ensure good coordination w/ all concerned, propose North, [and] Secord . . . proceed ASAP to Beirut to coordinate release of two hostages. If approved, we wd proceed from Frankfurt to Larnaca via charter jet then to Beirut via US military helo to brief our ambassador. . . . Neither Secord nor North wd be visible but wd brief Amb Kelly on details. Secord wd attend because he will have to brief Amb on third hostage as well as remaining three (ie total of 4 Americans) when we get info from Rafsanjani on locations, shd we decide to proceed on a rescue msn when Iranians give us locational info. Press guidance for a Presidential announcement of the release before it becomes known will be developed along lines of quote. The USG is grateful to all those who have assisted in this effort—and that two more AMCITS have been released unquote. Our effort is to have RR make the announcement before CNN knows it has happened, but after the AMCITS are in USG hands, so that RR is seen to have influenced the action and Syrians are not. . . .

(Earl PROF note to Poindexter, 10/29/86, 22:23:43)

North's account to Poindexter omitted the extensive discussion about the third American hostage and what could be done to secure his freedom. North told the Relative that he had already found a technician to work with the Iranians on their HAWK systems, but Secord added that it would be "highly unlikely that we would be allowed to send technicians into Iran, to Isfahan, until we get that guy out." The Relative replied that Rafsanjani "has been taken with the subject of the Phoenix [air to air missile]," and that if the Iranians "could just get a couple of these things working, and if it would hit an . . . Iraqi plane . . . it would be a terrible blow to [Iraqi] morale. . . ." The Relative promised that, if the U.S. would send a technician to help with the Phoenix missiles Iran already had, he would "personally get the third guy out, and . . . could tell [the U.S.] where the rest of the guys [three most recent U.S. hostages] are." North promised the technician, planning to send him in at the same time as the additional HAWK parts. Responding to the Iranian's question on the next delivery of 500 TOW missiles, North answered: "If you get the hostages out, we'll send you a million of them. All you have to do is pay for them. And if you guys get your act together, we'd open up an FMS account and you'd get a better price on them."

Jacobsen was released November 2. North kept hoping others would be released if the story could be kept quiet for a few days. (Coy PROF note to Poindexter, 11/02/86, 4:25:06) It was not to be.

The day after a Beirut magazine published an account of the May trip to Tehran, Teicher wrote Poindexter:

The reports of Bud's trip in pro-Syrian Lebanese newspapers coming on the heels of high-level Iranian visits to Damascus, are the clearest possible signals we could receive that the succession struggle is underway and U.S.-Iranian relations are likely to play an important role in the struggle. Obviously there are many possible interpretations of the story; maybe it was put out by Mugniyas to embarrass Iran for putting so much pressure on him. We may never know the exact reason, but we must not let this opportunity to assess the consequences in Iran of these revelations from slipping through our fingers. I think it would be useful to produce an assessment of the range of possible interpretation, and possible U.S. options. To be fair, I also think it would be appropriate to involve Dennis Ross. He is unaware of the compartment of our activities. Once we finish the analysis, I strongly urge you to discuss our options with Shultz and Casey. At a minimum, we need to determine how best, other than parts, etc., to signal the Iranians in a productive manner.

(Teicher PROF note to Poindexter, 11/04/86, 09:35, through Pearson (lower case in original))

On October 29, North had written Poindexter: "This is the damndest operation I have ever seen. Pls let me go on to other things. Wd very much like to give RR two hostages that he can take credit for and stop worrying about these other things." (North to Poindexter, through Earl, 10/29/86).[96]

# Charts and Narratives

The following charts and accompanying narrative explanations represent an estimate of the arms transactions with Iran based on evidence developed by the Board from interviews and documentary materials.

# TRANSACTION ONE: AUGUST 1985

Step 1—Ghorbanifar provides Khashoggi with $1 million post-dated check on August 17.

Step 2—Khashoggi deposits $1 million in Nimrodi-controlled Israeli account at Swiss bank.

Step 3—Nimrodi notifies Israeli officials of funds having been received.

Step 4—Iran transfers $1,217,410 to Iranian account at Swiss bank[97] on August 27 to pay for shipment.

Step 5—Israel delivers 100 TOW missiles to Iran on August 30.

Step 6—Ghorbanifar notifies Khashoggi that check is covered.

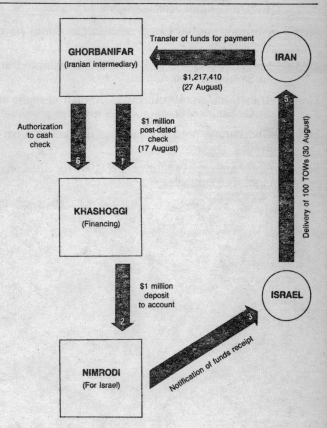

**TRANSACTION ONE: AUGUST 1985 SALE OF 100 ISRAELI TOW ANTI-TANK MISSILES**

GHORBANIFAR
(Iranian intermediary)

IRAN

Transfer of funds for payment

4

$1,217,410
(27 August)

Authorization to cash check

6

$1 million post-dated check
(17 August)

1

5

Delivery of 100 TOWs (30 August)

KHASHOGGI
(Financing)

$1 million deposit to account

2

ISRAEL

3

Notification of funds receipt

NIMRODI
(For Israel)

# TRANSACTION TWO: SEPTEMBER 1985

Step 1—Ghorbanifar provides Khashoggi with $4 million post-dated check.

Step 2—Khashoggi deposits $4 million to Nimrodi-controlled account on September 14.

Step 3—Nimrodi notifies Israeli officials that funds have been received.

Step 4—Israel delivers 408 TOW anti-tank missiles to Iran on September 14.

Step 5—Iran transfers $5 million to Iranian account at Swiss bank on September 18 to cover purchase.

Step 6—Ghorbanifar notifies Khashoggi that check is covered.

Step 7—Ghorbanifar pays Nimrodi $250,000 for additional eight TOW missiles.

# TRANSACTION TWO: SEPTEMBER 1985 SALE OF 408 ISRAELI TOW MISSILES

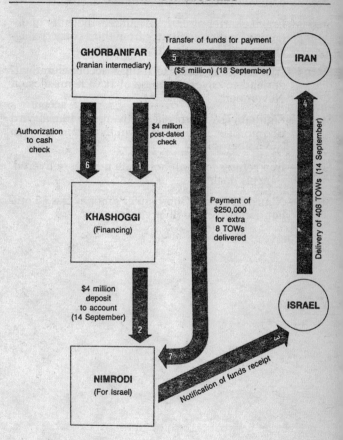

# TRANSACTION THREE: NOVEMBER 1985

**Step 1**—Ghorbanifar deposits $24 milllion to Nimrodi-controlled account.

**Step 2**—Nimrodi notifies Israel of funds receipt.

**Step 3**—Israeli charter aircraft encounters difficulty in obtaining landing clearance from third country staging point. U.S. assistance sought.

**Step 4**—Iran transfers funds to Iranian accounts in Switzerland to cover purchase of HAWK missiles on November 22 and 25.[98]

**Step 5**—Eighteen HAWK missiles delivered to Iran aboard CIA proprietary aircraft flown by Secord crew on November 25.

**Step 6**—Iran refuses to pay for obsolete missiles delivered. Cancels deal.

**Step 7**—Nimrodi returns Ghorbanifar's money less $5 million for HAWKs delivered.

# TRANSACTION THREE: NOVEMBER 1985 ABORTED SALE OF 120 ISRAELI HAWK ANTI-AIRCRAFT MISSILES WITH U.S. DELIVERY ASSISTANCE

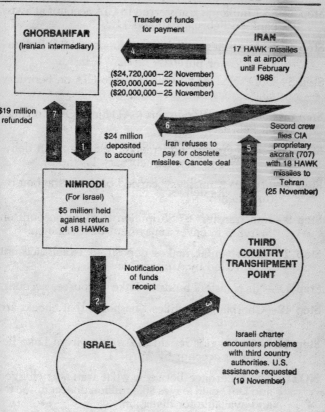

**GHORBANIFAR**
(Iranian intermediary)

Transfer of funds
for payment

**IRAN**
17 HAWK missiles
sit at airport
until February
1986

($24,720,000—22 November)
($20,000,000—22 November)
($20,000,000—25 November)

$19 million
refunded

$24 million
deposited
to account

Iran refuses to
pay for obsolete
missiles. Cancels deal

Secord crew
flies CIA
proprietary
aircraft (707)
with 18 HAWK
missiles to
Tehran
(25 November)

**NIMRODI**
(For Israel)
$5 million held
against return
of 18 HAWKs

Notification
of funds
receipt

**THIRD
COUNTRY
TRANSHIPMENT
POINT**

**ISRAEL**

Israeli charter
encounters problems
with third country
authorities. U.S.
assistance requested
(19 November)

443

# TRANSACTION FOUR: FEBRUARY 1986

**Step 1**—Ghorbanifar provides Khashoggi with four post dated checks for $3 million each.

**Step 2**—Khashoggi deposits $10 million in Lake Resources account on February 10.

**Step 3**—$3.7 million is transferred to CIA account at Swiss bank on February 10 and 11.

**Step 4**—CIA certifies availability of funds to DoD for purchase of 1,000 TOWs.

**Step 5**—DoD signs over 1,000 TOWs to CIA on February 13.

**Step 6**—Southern Air Transport (SAT) flies TOWs to Israel on February 14.

**Step 7**—Secord crew flying Israeli false flag aircraft delivers TOWs to Iran on February 17 and 27.

**Step 8**—17 HAWK missiles[99] carried back to Israel on return flight.

**Step 9**—Iran transfers $7.85 million to Swiss account on March 3 to cover repayment of Khashoggi.[100]

**Step 10**—Ghorbanifar makes deposit to Israeli account controlled by Amiram Nir.

**Step 11**—Nir transfers funds to Lake Resources account.

**Step 12**—Ghorbanifar notifies Khashoggi that checks are covered.

**Step 13**—Khashoggi is repaid $12 million from Lake Resources account by April 11.

**NOTE:** The difference between what Iran was charged and DoD paid leaves $6.3 million unaccounted for and available for diversion.

# TRANSACTION FOUR: FEBRUARY 1985 SALE OF 1,000 U.S. TOW MISSILES

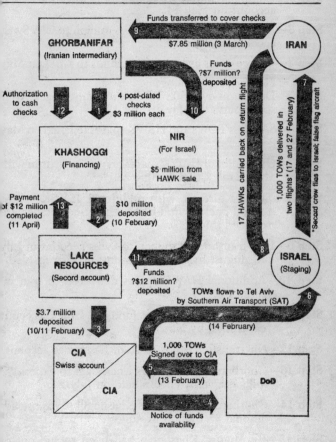

# TRANSACTION FIVE: MAY 1986 (SUPPLEMENTED IN AUGUST 1986)

**Step 1**—Ghorbanifar provides Khashoggi with 3 post dated checks for $1, 6, and 11 million.

**Step 2**—Khashoggi deposits $15 million to Lake Resources account on May 14.

**Step 3**—Lake Resources tranfers $6.5 million to CIA Swiss account on May 15.

**Step 4**—CIA certifies availability of funds to DoD on May 16.

**Step 5**—DoD signs over 508 TOWs and quantity of HAWK spare parts on May 16 and 19.

**Step 6**—SAT flies TOWs and HAWK spares to Israel on May 23 and 24.

**Step 7**—One pallet of HAWK spares arrives in Tehran with McFarlane party on May 25.

**Step 8**—Second aircraft with additional HAWK spares turned back in mid-flight when no hostages are released (May 25).

**Step 9**—Iran transfers $8 million to Swiss account in July and August in payment against goods received.

**Step 10**—Additional HAWK spares delivered to Iran on August 3.

**Step 11**—Ghorbanifar transfers funds to Israeli account controlled by Nir.

**Step 12**—Nir transfers funds to Lake Resources account.

**Step 13**—Ghorbanifar authorizes Khashoggi to expose $3 million against checks held on July 24.

**Step 14**—Ghorbanifar authorizes Khashoggi to expose additional $5 million in August.

**Step 15**—By August, Khashoggi had been repaid out of Lake Resources account $8 million of the $15 million loaned.

# TRANSACTION FIVE: MAY 1986 (SUPPLEMENTED IN AUGUST) PARTIALLY COMPLETED SALE OF VARIOUS U.S. HAWK MISSILE SYSTEM SPARE PARTS

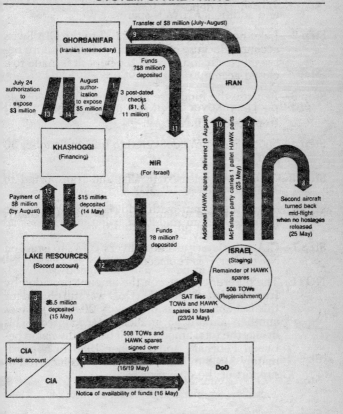

**NOTE:** The difference between the amount charged Iran (as advanced by Khashoggi) and that paid to DoD leaves an additional $8.5 million unaccounted for and available for diversion.

# TRANSACTION SIX: OCTOBER 1986

Step 1—Iranian representatives (the Second Channel) deposit $7 million into Lake Resources account on September 26[101] to cover purchase of 500 TOWs and additional HAWK spares.

Step 2—Lake Resources transfers $2.037 to the CIA Swiss account. Because of a communications failure between North and Secord, the deposit is made to a closed account.

Step 3—Because the funds are not immediately available for DoD, North asks Israel to deliver 500 TOWs from its own inventory.

Step 4—500 Israeli TOWs delivered to Iran on October 30 and 31.

Step 5—500 TOWs released to CIA and transported to Kelly AFB on November 3.

Step 6—TOWs shipped to Ramstein AFB, West Germany, via MAC flight on November 6.

Step 7—CIA proprietary airline delivers TOWs to Israel on November 7 as replacements.

NOTE: The difference between the amount provided by Iran and that paid to CIA (DoD was still unpaid for this last shipment as of January 20, 1987) leaves another almost $5 million unaccounted. This brings the total amount available for diversion between February and October 1986 to approximately $19.8 million less actual costs incurred in support of the operation.

# TRANSACTION SIX: OCTOBER 1986 SALE OF 500 U.S. TOW MISSILES AND VARIOUS HAWK MISSILE SYSTEM SPARE PARTS

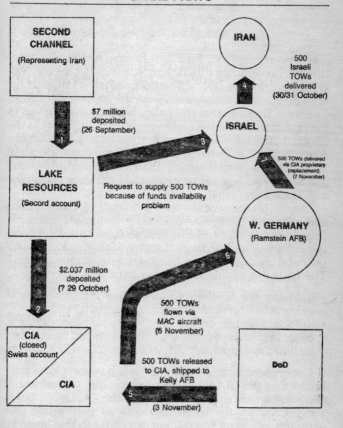

**SECOND CHANNEL** (Representing Iran)

— $7 million deposited (26 September) ① →

**LAKE RESOURCES** (Secord account)

Request to supply 500 TOWs because of funds availability problem

— $2.037 million deposited (? 29 October) ② →

**CIA** (closed) Swiss account / CIA

**IRAN**

500 Israeli TOWs delivered (30/31 October) ④

**ISRAEL** ③

500 TOWs delivered via CIA proprietary (replacement) (7 November) ⑦

**W. GERMANY** (Ramstein AFB) ⑥

500 TOWs flown via MAC aircraft (6 November)

500 TOWs released to CIA, shipped to Kelly AFB (3 November) ⑤

**DoD**

# The NSC Staff and the Contras

In December, 1981, President Reagan signed a National Intelligence Finding establishing U.S. support for the Nicaraguan resistance forces. The policy of covert support for the Contras was controversial from the start—especially in Congress. Concern that this policy would provoke a war in the region led Congress on December 21, 1982 to pass the "Boland Amendment," barring the Central Intelligence Agency and the Department of Defense from spending funds toward "overthrowing the Government of Nicaragua or provoking a military exchange between Nicaragua and Honduras."

Despite disagreement—both within the Administration and with the Congress—the policy continued apace. In September, 1983, President Reagan signed a second Nicaragua finding authorizing "the provision of material support and guidance to the Nicaraguan resistance groups." The objective of this finding was twofold:

- inducing the Sandinista Government in Nicaragua to enter into negotiations with its neighbors; and
- putting pressure on the Sandinistas and their allies to cease provision of arms, training, command and control facilities and sanctuary to leftist guerrillas in El Salvador.

Congressional opposition grew when reports were published that the CIA had a role in directing the mining of the Nicaraguan harbors in summer 1983. On December 8, 1983, Congress tightened the scope of permissible CIA activities, placing a $24 million cap on funds that could be spent by DoD and CIA or any other agency "involved in intelligence activities" toward "supporting, directly or indirectly, military or paramilitary operations in Nicaragua by any nation, group, organization, movement or individual." In October, 1984, Congress cut off all U.S. funding for the Contras, unless specifically authorized by Congress. Section 8066(a) of the Fiscal Year 1985 DoD Appropriations Act provided:

> During fiscal year 1985, no funds available to the Central Intelligence Agency, the Department of Defense, or any other agency or entity of the United States involved in intelligence activities may be obligated or expended for the purpose or which would have the effect of supporting, directly or indirectly, military or paramilitary operations in Nicaragua by any nation, group, organization, movement, or individual.[1]

This legislation presented the Administration with a dilemma: how, if at all, to continue implementing a largely covert program of support for the Contras without U.S. funds and without the involvement of the CIA. As soon as the Congressional restrictions were put into effect, CIA headquarters sent instructions to its field stations to cease all contacts with resistance groups except for intelligence collection activities:

> Field stations are to cease and desist with actions which can be construed to be providing any type of support, either direct or indirect, to the various entities with whom we dealt under the program. All future contact with those entities are, until further notice, to be solely, repeat solely, for the purpose of collecting positive and counterintelligence information of interest to the United States.

From the outset, questions were raised as to whether the provision applied to the NSC staff. Some in Congress argued that the Boland Amendment applied to the NSC staff, since it is "involved in intelligence activity." Executive Order 12333 on covert action and Congressional oversight designates the NSC "as the highest Executive Branch entity that provides review of, guidance for and direction to the conduct of all national foreign intelligence, counterintelligence, and special activities, and attendant policies and programs."

451

But the NSC staff appears to have received different advice. A classified legal memorandum, retrieved from LtCol North's safe, apparently was prepared by the President's Intelligence Oversight Board ("IOB") between March 1 and December 19, 1985. The letterhead and transmittal information had been removed, but the document contained references to "the Board" and "the Board's Counsel" and resembled in form, style and subject matter other memoranda prepared for the NSC staff by the IOB.[2] The memorandum was developed in response to a letter from then Congressman Michael Barnes. It concluded: (1) "the NSC is not covered by the prohibition," (adding by footnote that "LtCol. North might be, as he evidently is on a non-reimbursed detail from the Marine Corps");[3] and (2) "None of LtCol North's activities during the past year constitutes a violation of the Boland Amendment."

After October, 1984, the NSC staff—particularly Oliver North—moved to fill the void left by the Congressional restrictions. Between 1984 and 1986, LtCol North, with the acquiescence of the National Security Advisor, performed activities the CIA was unable to undertake itself, including the facilitation of outside fundraising efforts and oversight of a private network to supply lethal equipment to the Contras.

The Director of the CIA Central American Task Force (CATF), described the inter-agency process on Central America at the time he moved into his job in late September, 1984:

"There was only one point in the appartus [sic] who was functioning and who seemed to be able and was interested and was working the process, and that was Ollie North. And it was Ollie North who then moved into that void and was the focal point for the Administration on Central American policy during that timeframe [until fall 1985.]"

452

# The NSC Staff Steps Into the Void

LtCol North's involvement in Contra support is evident as early as September, 1984, before the October, 1984 ban was in effect. He directed his attention to two areas: operations and fundraising.

## 1. North's Operational Role: September 1984–October 1985

In a memorandum on September 2, 1984 LtCol North informed Mr. McFarlane of a recent air attack launched into Nicaraguan territory by the Federated Democratic Resistance ("FDN"), a major Contra faction. LtCol North said that at a meeting the previous day he and a CIA official involved in Central American affairs had urged Contra leader Adolpho Calero to postpone the attack. Despite Mr. Calero's agreement, the plan was carried out and, in the course of the attack, the Contras lost "the only operating FDN helicopter on the Northern Front."

LtCol North regarded this loss as "a serious blow." He told Mr. McFarlane, "It may therefore be necessary to ask a private donor to donate a helicopter to the FDN for use in any upcoming operation against an arms delivery." Outside help was necessary since "FDN resources are not adequate to purchase a helicopter at this time." He recommended that Mr. McFarlane grant him approval to approach a private donor for "the provision of a replacement *civilian* helicopter."

At the bottom of the memorandum Mr. McFarlane initialed, "Disapprove," and wrote, "Let's wait a week or two." After further thought, Mr. McFarlane apparently changed his mind. He crossed out the above sentence and wrote, "I don't think this is legal."

Two months later, in another memorandum to Mr. McFarlane, LtCol North sought approval to continue providing intelligence support to Mr. Calero. Mr. Calero had requested information from LtCol North to assist him in efforts to "take out" Soviet provided Hind-D helicopters recently shipped to El Bluff, Nicaragua. LtCol North told Mr. McFarlane that he earlier had forwarded Mr. Calero responsive intelligence obtained from Robert Vickers, CIA National Intelligence Officer for Latin American affairs and GEN Paul Gorman. Mr. Calero decided to fly to Washington that day to review with LtCol North a plan to strike the Hinds and a longterm strategy for establishing a Calero-Cruz coalition. The Director of the CIA CATF contacted LtCol North when he learned of Mr. Calero's unexpected trip to Washington, but, citing the new statutory prohibitions, declined an invitation to meet with LtCol North and Mr. Calero.

Director Casey learned of LtCol North's discussions with the CIA official and expressed his concern to Mr. McFarlane that LtCol North had discussed "Calero, Guatemala, MIGs, dollars, etc." LtCol North's November 7 memorandum assured Mr. McFarlane that he had withheld much information in his conversations:

> At no time did I discuss with [name deleted] financial arrangements for the FDN. At no time did I indicate that Calero was attempting to attack the MIGs. I specifically told [the Director of the CIA CATF] that Calero was attempting to collect information on the MIGs in Corinto and would pass this information to a CIA agent in Tegucigalpa if it was available.

In 1985, LtCol North's interest in operational activities with respect to the Contras increased. In a memorandum for Mr. McFarlane on February 6, 1985 LtCol North discussed a Nicaraguan merchant ship, the MONIMBO, suspected of carrying arms via North Korea for delivery to Nicaragua. LtCol North recommended that Mr. McFarlane *authorize Calero to be provided with the information on MONIMBO and approached on the matter of seizing or sinking the ship.* (emphasis added). LtCol North said that Calero would be willing to finance such an operation, but would require operational support. LtCol North suggested a friendly nation's special operations unit might be asked to assist in the operation. Once the ship was seized LtCol North said:

> arrangements would have to be made for removal of the cargo for further transfer to the FDN, since it is unlikely that any of the other Central American states

would allow the MONIMBO to enter their harbors once she had been pirated.

At the bottom of the memorandum VADM Poindexter indicated his agreement: "We need to take action to make sure ship does not arrive in Nicaragua." A note from VADM Poindexter to Mr. McFarlane dated February 7 is attached to the memorandum, suggesting that the issue be raised at a meeting later that day of the Crisis Pre-Planning Group ("CPPG"), an interagency group established under auspices of the NSC system. VADM Poindexter wrote:

Except for the prohibition of the intelligence community doing anything to assist the Freedom Fighters I would readily recommend I bring this up at CPPG at 2:00 today. *Of course we could discuss it from the standpoint of keeping the arms away from Nicaragua without any involvement of Calero and Freedom Fighters.* What do you think? JP (emphasis added).

We have no record on whether this was discussed at the CPPG meeting but understand that the project was abandoned after the friendly government rejected involvement.

On February 6, LtCol North informed Mr. McFarlane of recent efforts by Maj Gen John Singlaub, USAF Ret; to raise funds for the Contras in Asia. LtCol North said that as a result, two foreign governments offered to provide assistance. LtCol North sought Mr. McFarlane's approval to coordinate Singlaub's contacts with these governments:

Singlaub will be here to see me tomorrow. With your permission, I will ask him to approach [X] at the [country deleted] Interests Section and [Y] at the [country deleted] Embassy urging that they proceed with their offer. Singlaub would then put Calero in direct contact with each of these officers. No White House/NSC solicitation would be made. [hand written notes:] Nor should Singlaub indicate any U.S. Government endorsement whatsoever.

We do not know if Mr. McFarlane ever approved this plan, but the Contras eventually received funds from both foreign governments.

LtCol North had further contacts with Mr. Singlaub in March. On March 5 he sent a letter to [an ambassador of a Central American country posted in Washington] requesting "a multiple entry visa" for Mr. Singlaub. LtCol North wrote the Ambassador: "I can assure you that General Singlaub's visits to [your country] will well serve the interests of your country and mine." On March 14, Mr. Singlaub reported to North on his recent trip. He said that he had met with several FDN leaders and that he had agreed to recruit and send "a few American trainers" to provide "specific skills not available within this (sic) current resources." Mr. Singlaub specified that "these will be civilian (former military or CIA personnel) who will do training only and not participate in combat operations."

More direct NSC staff involvement in efforts to gain third country support for the Contras was evident in a memorandum LtCol North sent to Mr. McFarlane dated March 5, 1985. North described plans to ship arms to the Contras via [country deleted], to be delivered in several shipments starting on or about March 10, 1985. The transaction required certification that the arms would not be transferred out of [country deleted]. LtCol North attached copies of such end-user certificates, provided by [country deleted] for nearly "$8 million worth of munitions for the FDN." He told Mr. McFarlane that these end-user certificates are *"a direct consequence of the informal liaison we have established with GEN [name deleted] and your meeting with he [sic] and President [name deleted]."* (emphasis added).

LtCol North's memorandum described the need to provide increased U.S. assistance to [country deleted] to compensate them "for the extraordinary assistance they are providing to the Nicaraguan freedom fighters." LtCol North said:

Once we have approval for at least some of what they have asked for, we can ensure that the right people in [country deleted] understand that we are able to provide results from their cooperation on the resistance issue.

An accompanying memorandum to Secretary Shultz, Secretary Weinberger, CIA Director Casey and Chairman of the Joint Chiefs of Staff Vessey requested their views on increased U.S. assistance to a Central American country, but made no reference to the Contra arms shipments or the end user certificates.

## 2. Private Funding: January–April, 1985

As the March, 1985, Congressional vote on Contra aid approached, elements of the NSC staff focused their efforts on strategies for repackaging the Contra program to increase support on Capitol Hill.

In a memorandum to Mr. McFarlane on March 16, 1985, LtCol North outlined a fallback plan for supporting the Contras should the Congress not endorse resumption of U.S. Government support. LtCol North recommended that the President make a public request to the American people for private funds "to support liberty and democracy in the Americas." Mr. McFarlane wrote in the margin, "Not yet." Nevertheless, he indicated his agreement to some of the accompanying elements of the proposal:

- "The Nicaraguan Freedom Fund, Inc., a 501(c)3 tax exempt corporation, must be established. . . . (This process is already under way)." Mr. McFarlane wrote next to this point, "Yes."
- *"The name of one of several existing non-profit foundations we have established in the course of the last year* will be changed to Nicaraguan Freedom Fund, Inc. Several reliable American citizens must be contacted to serve as its corporate leadership on its board of directors along with Cruz, Calero, and Robelo." (emphasis added). Mr. McFarlane wrote, "OK."

Next to the proposal that "current donors" be apprised of the plan and convinced to provide "an additional $25–30M to the resistance for the purchase of arms and munitions," Mr. McFarlane wrote, "Doubt." LtCol North recommended that Mr. McFarlane consult Secretary Shultz on the proposals, but we have no information as to whether this was done.

457

During this period LtCol North was well-informed about the financial and military situation of the Contras. In a memorandum to Mr. McFarlane on April 11, 1985, LtCol North detailed FDN funding received since the expiration of U.S. assistance:

> From July 1984 through February 1985, the FDN received $1M per month for a total of $8M. From February 22 to April 9, 1985, an additional $16.5M has been received for a grand total of $24.5M. Of this, $17,145,594 has been expended for arms, munitions, combat operations, and support activities.

LtCol North recommended that effort be undertaken to "seek additional funds from the current donors ($15–20M) which will allow the force to grow to 30–35,000." An attachment to this document itemized Contra arms purchases during this period. A sample entry read:

| | |
|---|---:|
| Airlift #2—March 1985: | |
| 750,000 rounds 7.62 x 39 ............... | $210,000 |
| 1,000 RPG-7 grenades .................. | 265,000 |
| 8,910 hand grenades..................... | 84,645 |
| 60—60mm mortars ..................... | 96,000 |
| 1,472 kqs C-4........................... | 47,104 |
| * * * ...................................... | |

On May 1, 1985, a nearly identical memorandum was prepared for JCS Chairman Vessey from LtCol North.

In his March 16 memorandum to Mr. McFarlane, LtCol North also reported that he had checked the legality of his proposals with private legal counsel: "Informal contacts several months ago with a lawyer sympathetic to our cause indicated that such a procedure would be within the limits of the law." He recommended that White House Counsel Fred Fielding "be asked to do conduct [sic] a very *private* evaluation of the President's role." Mr. McFarlane wrote, "not yet" in the margin.

The Board asked Mr. McFarlane whether he was aware of funds received by the FDN during this period. He provided the following written response:

> In May or June of 1984, without any solicitation on my part, a foreign official offered to make a contribution

from what he described as "personal funds" in the amount of one million dollars per month for support of the FDN. He asked my help in determining how to proceed. I asked LTC North to find out where the contribution should be sent. He subsequently obtained the necessary information from the FDN leadership, and I provided it to the donor. I was told it was an FDN bank account in Miami. In early 1985 the same individual advised me that he intended to continue support in that year at approximately double the former rate. I was separately informed by the Secretary of Defense and General Vessey that the total amount of the contribution during 1985 was 25 million dollars.

On an apparently unrelated letter from his secretary dated April 18, 1985, LtCol North sketched the attached diagram linking him with Robert Owen, an American citizen with close ties to the Contras; Andrew Messing, Executive Director of the non-profit organization the National Defense Council; and Linda Guell, Director of "Western Goals." The diagram showed an arrow from LtCol North to Mr. Messing, Mr. Messing to Ms. Guell, Ms. Guell to Owen. Under Owen's name North writes "weapons"; under Messing's, "funds." North's calendar shows that he met regularly with Mr. Messing and Mr. Owen during 1984 and 1985. Sometimes these meetings took place with other figures often linked to the "benefactors" network—*e.g.* John Singlaub, John Hull and Adolpho Calero.

The Board examined the information available to it showing LtCol North's connection to Political Action Committees. The information, which indicated that he had contacts of an indeterminant nature, will be available to Congressional committees.

# Congressional Reactions

On August 15, 1985, Congress authorized the expenditure of $27 million in humanitarian assistance, to be administered by any agency but CIA and DOD. By its terms, the authorization would expire on March 31, 1986.

Congressional scrutiny of LtCol North's activities increased. To varying degrees throughout 1985, Congress had pressed the NSC staff for information about LtCol North's involvement in Contra fundraising and resupply activities. The following exchanges took place.

In a reply to an August 20, 1985 letter from Lee Hamilton, Chairman of the House Permanent Select Committee on Intelligence, Mr. McFarlane wrote:

> I can state with deep personal conviction that at no time did I or any member of the National Security Council staff violate the letter or spirit of the law.

He reiterated his comments in a letter to Congressman Michael Barnes on September 12, 1985:

> I want to assure you that my actions, and those of my staff, have been in compliance with both the spirit and the letter of the law. . . . There have not been, nor will there be, any expenditures of NSC funds which would have the effect of supporting directly or indirectly military or paramilitary operations in Nicaragua by any nation, group, organization, movement or individual. . . .

In a subsequent letter, Congressman Hamilton inquired into the nature of the NSC staff's involvement with the fundraisers. On October 7, 1985, Mr. McFarlane replied to Congressman Hamilton:

> There is no official or unofficial relationship with any member of the NSC staff regarding fund raising for the Nicaraguan democratic opposition.

In response to the question of whether Oliver North "at any time "advise[d] individuals on how they might donate money to the rebels?"

Mr. McFarlane answered, "No."

On October 21, 1985 Mr. McFarlane received an inquiry from Congressman Richard Durbin. Congressman Durbin asked: "Are there any efforts currently underway in the Administration to facilitate the sending of private donations to the contras?"

McFarlane replied: "No."

## Authorization for "Communications" and "Advice"

In December, 1985, Congress passed two measures. The first, contained in section 8050 of the Fiscal Year 1986 Defense Appropriation Act, reenacted the Boland prohibition.[4] The second, set out in section 105(a) of the Fiscal Year 1986 Intelligence Authorization Act, authorized classified amounts for communications, communications equipment training and "advice" for the Contras.

The "communications" and "advice" provisions introduced substantial uncertainty as to whether any US officials—CIA, DOD or the NSC staff—could advise the Contras on the delivery or distribution of lethal supplies. First, the provisions were so ambiguous that even the drafters debated their meaning.[5] Second, applicable statutory provisions were contained in an annex classified top secret, and developed pursuant to a legislative history likewise classified. Whether such secrecy was warranted, it did not enhance common understanding of the statute.

Within the Executive Branch, interpretations differed. The CIA, in a "Question for the Record re 28 January Covert Action Update Briefing," concluded that it was not authorized to provide "specialized logistics training" needed by the Contras. The IOB, by memorandum of April 8, 1986, provided VADM Poindexter a classified legal analysis that concluded that under the "communications" and "advice" provision, *any U.S. agency* may lawfully provide basic military training to the Contras, "so long as such training does not amount to the participation in the planning or execution of military or paramilitary operations in Nicaragua."[6]

# Direct Involvement in Resupply: Fall 1985–Summer 1986

By fall 1985, LtCol North was actively engaged in private efforts to resupply the Contras with lethal equipment.

On November 22, 1985, LtCol North wrote VADM Poindexter that complications in an arms shipment (via a third country) to Iran required Mr. Secord to divert a plane that he planned to use for a Nicaraguan arms shipment. LtCol North told VADM Poindexter that the plane:

was at [city deleted] to put up a load of ammo for UNO . . . Too bad, this was to be *our first direct flight (of ammo) to the resistance field at [x] inside Nicaragua*. The ammo was already palletized w/parachutes attached. Maybe we can do it on Weds or Thurs.

LtCol North said he would meet Mr. Calero that evening to advise him "that the ammo will be several days late in arriving."

One month later, in an internal NSC message to VADM Poindexter discussing the Iran operation, LtCol North wrote:

OpSec concerns are threefold: communications, deliveries enroute to Iran and replenishment of Israeli stocks. To solve the first problem an Ops Code is now in use by all parties. *This code is similar to the one used to oversee deliveries to the Nicaraguan Resistance and has never been compromised.* (emphasis added). [North PROF notes to Poindexter, Dec. 4, 1985].

In a memorandum dated February 18, 1986 to VADM Poindexter, LtCol North referred to Albert Hakim, a private U.S. citizen who was involved in the Iran operation. He stated that Hakim was "VP of one of the European companies set up to handle aid to resistance movements." Several days later, in a message to Mr. McFarlane LtCol North again mentioned Hakim with respect to both Iran and Central America. He wrote: "Because CIA would not provide a translator for the sessions, we used Albert Hakim, an AMCIT who runs the European operation for our Nicaraguan resistance support activity." [North PROF notes to McFarlane, Feb. 27, 1986]

From January to March, 1986, LtCol North received fifteen encryption devices from the National Security Agency for use in transmitting classified messages in support of his counterterrorist activities. These devices enabled LtCol North to establish a private communications network. He used them to communicate, outside of the purview of other government agencies, with members of the private Contra support effort. At least one device was sent to Mr. Secord and another, through a private individual, to a CIA field officer posted in Central America.

We counted some thirty-six messages to LtCol North from members of this Contra resupply network—not including North's replies or additional documents not in our possession. Some of the messages to LtCol North from Mr. Secord, and others: (a) asked him to direct where and when to make Contra munitions drops; (b) informed him of arms requirements; and (c) apprised him of payments, balances, and deficits. At least nine lethal "drops" were coordinated through this channel from March to June 1986; two of these were delivered through [country deleted] ports.

Excerpts from the messages received by LtCol North on this channel follow:

(1) On March 24, 1986, Mr. Secord sent LtCol North a secure message in which he discussed plans for an upcoming "drop" to Contra troops along the Costa Rican border (the so-called southern front):

[X] should have held discussions with [Y] by now re. L–100 drop to Blackies troops. If you have lined up [Z] to go to [location deleted] on the L–100, suggest you call [Y] secure and ensure he does all possible get load released from [location deleted]—also emphasize we ought to drop something besides 7.62; e.g., grenades, medical supplies, etc.

LtCol North's handwritten notes on this document enumerate quantities of various ammunition types.

(2) On April 9, 1986, LtCol North received another secure message from Secord about preparations for a special shipment. North's notations on this message read: "Apr 9–1900. Confirmed arrival [city, country deleted] of L–100 w/load of [specified quantities of] ammo. . . . Confirming drop, Friday 11 April 0030."

(3) On April 12, 1986, LtCol North received a secure message from the CIA field officer confirming a successful drop to the UNO South Force and outlining plans for the next two to three weeks:

[A]ir drop at sea for UNO/KISAN indigenous force area . . . lethal drop to UNO South . . . transfer of 80 UNO/FARN recruits . . . carrying all remaining

463

cached lethal materiel to join UNO South Force. *My objective is creation of 2,500 man force which can strike northwest and link-up with quiche to form solid southern force.* Likewise, envisage formidable opposition on Atlantic Coast resupplied at or by sea. Realize this may be overly ambitious planning but with your help, believe we can pull it off. (emphasis added).

(4) Three days later, the field officer sent another secure message to confirm a delivery to an airbase in a Central American country; he tells LtCol North the delivery is loaded with ammunition "for your friends." He asks LtCol North: "When and where do you want this stuff? We are prepared to deliver as soon as you call for it."

The field officer testified before the Board:

[T]his private benefactor operation . . . was, according to my understanding, controlled by Colonel North." He also informed the Board that all the shipments he was involved in were arms deliveries: "This was all lethal. Benefactors only sent lethal stuff.[7]

The CIA field officer explained the legal regime under which he was operating:

I could not plan or engage in any military operation inside Nicaragua . . . But I could provide information that would allow the safe delivery of material to the people inside; I could pass information concerning potential deliveries to supply them, but not for any specific military operation. In other words, I could be the conduit for information; passing of information was legal or permissible under the agreement reached between the House and the Senate with the Agency under the Boland Amendment . . .

Asked if LtCol North ever discussed the legality of actions with him, the field officer answered,

I asked him, are you sure this is all right—you know, that sort of thing. Are you sure this is okay? He said, yes, yes, all you're doing is passing information.

The field officer was a member of a group that met for three minutes with President Reagan in the Oval Office in

1986. [photo session] The group comprised the Minister of Public Security from a Central American country and his wife, Chief of Staff Regan, VADM Poindexter and LtCol North.

In spring 1986, LtCol North also was involved in other efforts to help facilitate Contra military purchases through third countries. On March 26, 1986, three months after Mr. McFarlane left Government service, LtCol North informed Mr. McFarlane of his efforts (again, with Secord's assistance) to obtain Blowpipe launchers and missiles for the Contras:

> [W]e are trying to find a way to get 10 BLOWPIPE launchers and 20 missiles from [a South American Country] thru the Short Bros. Rep. . . . Short Bros., the mfgr. of the BLOWPIPE, is willing to arrange the deal, conduct the training and even send U.K. 'tech. reps' fwd if we can close the arrangement. Dick Secord has already paid 10% down on the delivery and we have a [country deleted] EUC [end user certificates] which is acceptable to [that South American country].

On April 4, Mr. McFarlane replied to LtCol North, "I've been thinking about the blowpipe problem and the Contras. Could you ask the CIA to identify which countries the Brits have sold them to. I ought to have a contact in at least one of them."

In the same message, Mr. McFarlane also asked: "How are you coming on the loose ends for the material transfer? Anything I can do? If for any reason, you need some mortars or other artillery—which I doubt—please let me know."

When shown the aforementioned message, Mr. McFarlane submitted the following written response:

> Since the area of mortars and artillery is one in which I have expertise, gained through 20 years of experience as an artillery officer, I was prepared to assist LTC North by furnishing information and advice. I did not offer to assist LTC North in negotiating, purchasing, or obtaining mortars or other artillery for the Contras, nor did I ever take any such action.

On May 2, LtCol North informed VADM Poindexter that he believed the Contras were readying to launch a major offensive to capture a "principal coastal population center" in Nicaragua and proclaim independence. North warned that if this occurred "the rest of the world will wait to see what we do—recognize the new territory—and UNO as the govt—or evacuate them as in a Bay of Pigs." He suggested that the U.S. should be prepared to come to the Contras' aid.

Assistant Secretary of State for Inter-American Affairs Elliot Abrams testified that he could recall "a time when Ollie was pushing for the Contras to grab a piece of Nicaraguan territory and proclaim independence." Mr. Abrams said that he might have indicated to LtCol North his support for the plan, but never took the idea seriously: "It was totally implausible and not do-able."

In a May 8 message, LtCol North also informed VADM Poindexter of an Israeli offer to assist in Central America:

> DefMin Rabin sent his MilAide to see me with the following offer: The Israelis wd be willing to put 20–50 Spanish speaking military trainers/advisors into the DRF if we want this to happen. They wd do this in concert with an Israeli plan to sell the KFIR fighter to Honduras as a replacement for the 28 yr old [Super Mystere] which the Hondurans want to replace. . . . Rabin want to meet w/me privately in N.Y. to discuss details. My impression is that they are prepared to move quickly on this if we so desire. Abrams likes the idea.

Mr. Abrams told the Board that he did not recall ever discussing any offer of Israeli assistance to the Contras with LtCol North. Former U.S. Ambassador to Costa Rica Louis Tambs and a senior CIA official stationed in Central America said that to their knowledge Israel never shipped any arms to the Contras.

In a June, 1986 note to VADM Poindexter regarding the third country issue, LtCol North discussed previous solicitations from [two countries deleted]. He told VADM Poindexter:

> I have no idea what Shultz knows or doesn't know, but he could prove to be very unhappy if he learns of the

[two countries deleted] aid that has been given in the past from someone other than you. Did RCM (McFarlane) ever tell Shultz?

Later that day VADM Poindexter replied: "To my knowledge Secretary Shultz knows nothing about the prior financing. I think it should stay that way."

## Concern for Disclosure

By May, 1986 VADM Poindexter became concerned that LtCol North's operational activities were becoming too apparent. He informed LtCol North that he had been notified by an NSC staffer that LtCol North had offered a Danish-registered ship under his control to the CIA—apparently for use in an unrelated operation. On May 15, 1986, in an internal NSC message to LtCol North, entitled "Be Cautious," VADM Poindexter warned:

> I am afraid you are letting your operational role become too public. From now on, I don't want you to talk to anybody else, *including Casey, except me about any of your operational roles. In fact, you need to quietly generate a cover story that I have insisted that you stop.* (emphasis added).

In response to a May 16 note, LtCol North sent VADM Poindexter a message on the status of the Contra project:

> You should be aware that the resistance support organization now has more than $6M available for immediated [sic] disbursement. This reduces the need to go to third countries for help. It does not, however, reduce the urgent need to get CIA back into the management of this program. . . .

In the same message, LtCol North expressed concern about potential exposure of his activities and the consequences for the President. He wrote:

> The more money there is (and we will have a considerable amount in a few more days) the more visible the program becomes (airplanes, pilots, weapons, deliveries, etc.) and the more inquisitive will become peo-

ple like Kerry, Barnes, Harkins, et al. While I care not a whit what they say about me, it could well become a political embarrassment for the President and you. Much of this risk can be avoided simply by covering it with an authorized CIA program.

On June 10, Mr. McFarlane expressed much the same concern:

It seems increasingly clear that the Democratic left is coming after him [LtCol North] with a vengeance in the election year and that eventually they will get him —too many people are talking to reporters from the donor community and within the administration.

On June 24, 1986, H.Res. 485 was introduced, directing the President to provide to the House of Representatives "certain information concerning activities of Lieutenant Colonel North or any other member of the staff of the National Security Council in support of the resistance."

LtCol North was interviewed by the members of the House Permanent Select Committee on Intelligence on August 6, 1986. An internal NSC staff account reported that LtCol North made the following points:

Contact with FDN and UNO aimed to foster viable, democratic, political strategy for Nicaraguan opposition, gave no military advice, knew of no specific military operations.

Singlaub—gave no advice, has had no contact in 20 months; Owen—never worked from OLN office, OLN had casual contact, never provided Owen guidance.

Shortly thereafter VADM Poindexter forwarded the above to LtCol North with the message: "Well Done."

# Summer 1986: Project Democracy[8]

In summer 1986, LtCol North informed Rodney McDaniel, NSC Executive Secretary, of his role in a "new contra management structure." LtCol North told Mr. McDaniel that Vincent Cannestraro, NSC Director of Intelligence Programs, was "not witting of Project Democracy," a term LtCol North used to describe a network of secret bank accounts and individuals deeply involved in Contra resupply activities—including the building of a secret airstrip for use by the Contras in northern Costa Rica.

Mr. McFarlane informed the Board that his only recollection of terms similar to "Project Democracy" occurred during a May trip to Tehran:

> Upon arrival in Tel Aviv, we were met by Major General Richard Secord (USAF Ret). I was told by LTC North that the aircraft being used on the trip had been chartered (I believed by the CIA) from a European concern managed by General Secord. I had known that General Secord had had a prior association with the CIA while on active duty, and this did not surprise me. LTC North also mentioned in passing that General Secord was also associated with the democracy project. . . . At the time, LtCol North's reference to "the democracy project" did not register with me and I did not pursue it with him thereafter.

LtCol North referred to "Project Democracy" or "PD" in a July 24, 1986, internal message from VADM Poindexter. In his note, LtCol North proposed that the CIA buy out "PD" assets when the Congressional ban on CIA activities was officially lifted in October. LtCol North listed "PD" assets totalling $4.5 million dollars. He wrote:

> We are rapidly approaching the point where the PROJECT DEMOCRACY assets in CentAm need to be turned over to CIA. . . . The total value of the assets (six aircraft, warehouses, supplies, maintenence [sic] facilities, ships, boats, leased houses, vehicles, ordnance, munitions, communications equipment, and a 6520' runway on property owned by a PRODEM proprietary) is over $4.5M. . . . All of the assets—and the personnel—are owned/paid by overseas companies with no U.S. connection. . . . It would be ludicrous for this to simply disappear just because CIA does not want to be "tainted" with picking up the assets and then have them spend $8–$10M to replace it—weeks or months later . . . PRODEM currently has the only assets available to support the DRF and the CIA's

most ambitious estimate is 30 days after a bill is signed before their own assets will be available.

VADM Poindexter replied to LtCol North's suggestion: "I did tell Gates that I thought the private effort should be phased out. Please talk to Casey about this. I agree with you."

In a note to VADM Poindexter several months later, LtCol North once again proposed the creation of a private, non-profit organization to manage the Contra support effort. According to LtCol North, this organization would be involved in tasks the CIA could not perform, including raising money, paying for public relations, organizing UNO activities in the U.S., and providing medical treatment for wounded contras. LtCol North tells VADM Poindexter that these activities were *"now all being done by Project Democracy,"* which he said was supposed to be out of the Central America business on or about October 1, when U.S. funds were due to be appropriated.

The construction of a secret airstrip in northern Costa Rica in summer 1985 was apparently one of the operations undertaken by "Project Democracy." In a September 30, 1986, memorandum to VADM Poindexter, LtCol North described Project Democracy's role:

> The airfield at Santa Elena has been a vital element in supporting the resistance. Built by a Project Democracy proprietary, (Udall Corporation S.A.—a Panamanian Company), the field was initially used for direct resupply efforts [to the Contras] (July 1985–February 1986)...the field has served as the primary abort base for aircraft damaged by Sandinista anti-aircraft fire.[9]

According to LtCol North, press reports on the existence of this airfield in September, 1986 "caused Project Democracy to permanently close Udall Corporation, and dispose of its capital assets." (A CIA field officer based in Costa Rica told the Board that Udall Corp. was closely associated with Mr. Secord.)

Two attached diagrams found in LtCol North's safe link Udall Corporation with Lake Resources, the account that emerged often in the context of the Iranian operation. Lake Resources may have been used to transfer funds— probably private—for Mr. Secord's use in Central American operations. In a note on his appointment card for April 3, 1986, LtCol North scribbled himself a reminder: "call Copp [Secord alias], 650k to LAKE." In a secure message to LtCol North on April 16, Mr. Secord reported: "650k received today as reported by the banker."

The CIA field officer told the Board that construction of the Santa Elena airfield was a pet project of U.S. Ambassador Louis Tambs. According to the CIA officer:

When Ambassador Tambs arrived in Costa Rica [July 1985], he called together the Deputy Chief of Mission, the Defense Attache and myself, and said that he had really only one mission in Costa Rica, and that was to form a Nicaraguan resistance southern front.

[The Santa Elena airstrip] was a matter which I had been monitoring, kind of as an aside, but it was essentially the Ambassador's initiative.

When interviewed by the Board's staff on this issue, the Ambassador said that prior to reporting to Costa Rica, he received instructions from the members of the Restricted Interagency Group ("RIG") to aid the Nicaraguan Resistance Forces in setting up a "Southern Front." The members of the RIG were Mr. Abrams, LtCol North and the Director of the CIA CATF. Ambassador Tambs recounted the instructions he received in July 1985:

Before I went (to Costa Rica) Ollie said when you get down there you should open the southern front. In the subsequent meetings and conversations (of the RIG) that was confirmed by Abrams and (name deleted—CIA official). That was sort of our mission.

When asked what this mission meant to him, Ambassador Tambs responded that "the idea was that we would encourage them to fight." He added that he never had any contacts with Contra military leaders and that he only spoke with the "political types."

Ambassador Tambs said that he learned of the airstrip project from a CIA field officer. The officer informed him that private benefactors were behind the efforts to build the airstrip and Mr. Secord coordinated the flights.

Ambassador Tambs recalled that LtCol North asked him shortly after he arrived in Costa Rica whether the Costa

Rican government would "go along" with the airstrip. He said that the Costa Rican government was interested in the airstrip primarily as a resupply station in the event of a Nicaraguan invasion of Costa Rica. As far as he knew, the airstrip was used mainly for refueling before Contra resupply planes returned to "wherever they were coming from."

According to a CIA field officer, Mr. Abrams and LtCol North were also well informed of this project. On a visit to Costa Rica shortly after he was confirmed to his new position Mr. Abrams raised the subject with the CIA officer:

> During the course of this conversation . . . Assistant Secretary Abrams asked me about Point West [another name for the airstrip] . . . I became very upset with Assistant Secretary Abrams for bringing out (sic) the question . . . I thought it should be closely held . . . I said what is this with the airstrip? Where is this known? He said well, this is known in Washington by —Colonel North told me about it and I assume that the [Director of the CIA CATF] knows about it.

Mr. Abrams testified that the Santa Elena airstrip was never used: "My understanding was nobody ever used the airstrip . . . that it had never quite gotten into operation."

When asked about LtCol North's activities and the existence of the Santa Elena airfield Mr. Abrams had no recollection of when he first learned of the airstrip or from whom. Mr. Abrams said that he believed the airstrip had been built by private "benefactors," but that he had no information on who these people were. He added:

> We knew that there were outside benefactors. We knew that the Contras were getting lots of, at least ammunition, getting military equipment—if not arms, then at least military equipment. And I think it is fair to say that everybody involved in the RIG knew that Ollie was somehow connected with this but did not know why . . . I think most of us were careful not to ask lots of questions, other than once in a while, to say is this all okay, is this stuff legal—once in a while. I had some reassurance of that when he said it had been run by the White House Counsel.

472

In August, 1986, Costa Rican authorities took measures to stop further use of the airstrip. U.S. authorities sought to avoid public disclosure of past activities there. Prior to the public disclosure of the Santa Elena airstrip, LtCol North informed VADM Poindexter that he had been tipped off by "our Project Democracy representative in Costa Rica" that the Costa Rican Government was planning to call a press conference to announce "that an illegal support operation for the Contras had been taking place from an airfield in Costa Rica for over a year."

On September 9, LtCol North informed VADM Poindexter that he had completed a conference call with U.S. Ambassador to Costa Rica Louis Tambs, Mr. Abrams and the Director of the CIA CATF who all agreed that LtCol North would call Costa Rican President Arias to insist the press conference be stopped. LtCol North said that they agreed he would take a tough line with President Arias, threatening to withhold U.S. assistance.

LtCol North wrote that Ambassador Tambs and Mr. Abrams reinforced his message:

> Tambs then called Arias from his leave location in W. Va. and confirmed what I had said and suggested that Arias talk to Elliot for further confirmation.—Arias then got the same word from Elliot. . . . At 0300 Arias called back to advise that there would be no press conference.

Reporting after the fact, LtCol North asked VADM Poindexter to understand the grounds for taking steps that LtCol North admitted may have been extraordinary:

> I recognize that I was well beyond my charter in dealing w/a head of state this way and in making threats/ offers that may be impossible to deliver, but under the circumstances—and w/Elliott's concurrence—it seemed like the only thing we could do.

Later that day, VADM Poindexter replied: "You did the right thing, but let's try to keep it quiet."

Mr. Abrams confirmed that LtCol North initiated a conference call on the anticipated disclosure, involving at least Ambassador Tambs, Mr. Abrams and LtCol North. He said they agreed that Ambassador Tambs would call

President Arias, but that they did not agree to threaten to withhold aid money. He said he would not have approved a similar call by LtCol North, since Arias was a head of State. Moreover, he doubted that LtCol North actually called President Arias, since the then newly-elected Arias had little occasion to meet or learn of LtCol North. Ambassador Tambs told the Board that he also doubted North ever placed such a call. The Arias government subsequently announced publicly the discovery and closure of the airstrip.

Another aspect of LtCol North's activities in 1986 involved control of a Danish-registered ship which appears to have been used to carry out a series of weapons deliveries to the Contras through two Central American countries. In April, Mr. Secord informed LtCol North of the status of efforts to purchase the ship:

> Abe [Hakim] still in Copenhagen with our lawyer finalizing purchase of ship. Deal has been made after three days of negotiations. The Danish captain is up and eager for the mission—he now works for us. We are asking . . . for firm fixed price contract of $1.2M for six months. . . . Our rough guess is that our monthly operating costs will be 50K.

In September, 1986, Israeli Defense Minister Rabin, LtCol North, Amiram Nir, and a General Hagai Regev met in Washington and discussed plans for the Israelis to provide Soviet Bloc weapons and ammunition to the United States. LtCol North's communication said the Israelis made the offer. Defense Minister Rabin recently told the State Department that LtCol North made the solicitation and that Israel would give the weapons to the U.S., but not directly to the Contras. According to an internal message from LtCol North to VADM Poindexter, Defense Minister Rabin suggested that LtCol North send a ship in his control to Israel to pick up the weapons. LtCol North asked VADM Poindexter for advice:

> Don't quite no [sic] what to do. Did not want to turn down offer. . . can go ahead and move the whole shipment to [countries deleted]—but still won't have any money to pay off rapidly growing debts. Hate to

turn away offers like this—it will really help in the long run. Any advice?

VADM Poindexter responded later that day, "I think you should go ahead and make it happen. It can be a private deal between Dick and Rabin that we bless."

On September 15, LtCol North reported that:

> Orders were passed to the ship this morning to proceed to Haifa to pick up the arms. Loading will be accomplished during one night and the ship will be back at sea before dawn. Loading will be accomplished by Israeli military personnel.

VADM Poindexter's response an hour later emphasized the need for absolute secrecy:

> Absolutely nobody else should know about this. Defense Minister Rabin should not say anything to anybody else except you or me. In fact I hope Nir doesn't even know about it.

Defense Minister Rabin reported to the State Department that the ship left Israel, but was recalled when it appeared the Iran arms story would become public.

# Who Knew What?

The Director of the CIA CATF recalls that by 1985, the CIA knew the Contras were receiving significant arms deliveries, some running in value in excess of $6 million, and were spending at a rate in excess of $1 million a month. CIA officials sought to locate the source of the funding. The Director of the CIA CATF told us:

> [W]hat we found out was really only one or two people. It was tremendously compartmented inside the resistance organization and no one knew the ultimate source of the money, and very, very few people even know how much there was coming in and out.

Mr. Abrams recalls:

> [W]e did not engage in nor did we really know anything about this private network. We knew that it

existed. We knew it in part because somebody was giving the Contras guns. . . . they were instructed to kind of stay away, as the Agency people were, on the grounds that if you got too close, you would end up being accused of facilitating and so forth.

Richard Armitage, Assistant Secretary of Defense, recalls, "[S]everal of us in those groups said, Ollie. . . . you're not involved in all this, are you? And he said . . . I have broken no laws."

LtCol North and VADM Poindexter do not seem to have sought the President's approval. In his response to a May 16, 1986, message from Poindexter on the status of the Contra project, LtCol North went on to discuss White House knowledge of his activities. LtCol North speculated that the President must know, indirectly, of his Contra activities.

I have no idea what Don Regan does or does not know re my private U.S. operation but the President obviously knows why he has been meeting with several select people to thank them for their 'support for Democracy' in CentAm.

Later that day VADM Poindexter replied to LtCol North: "Don Regan knows very little of your operation and that is just as well."

April 18, 1985

Phil and Randy:

Just wanted to drop a note for
"good luck" before the vote.
We are, as always, grateful for
the work you do to communicate
the President's policy in Central
America. We are all working
tirelessly to educate the American
people on why it is so important
to help the Nicaraguan freedom
fighters.

There are many people who believe
in the cause of freedom and
democracy, but far fewer who are
willing to act to support it.
Your dedication and ambition
are much appreciated.

I hope the enclosed can be of
some use to you. Let me know
if we can help in any way.

Thanks--God bless you!

Fawn *HALL*

Col. North 395-3345

→ Bob Owen ⟶ (MONEY)
  weapons    → Linda Guell
→ Randy messing    Western Goals
  funds    she works → Trips to Germany
  with CAWA    & So Kore
  & Col. PAM →    Last year

N 20 13
12 15 15

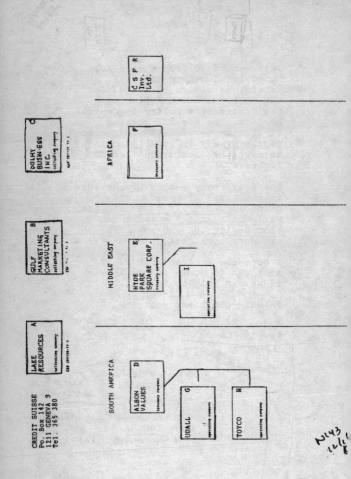

CREDIT SUISSE
Po. Box 142
1211 GENEVA 3
Tel. 365 380

**A** LAKE RESOURCES
collecting company
CB# 284539-77-1

**B** GULF MARKETING CONSULTANTS
collecting company
CB# 211 76 6

**C** DOLHY BUSINESS INC.
collecting company
REF 78/326 97 4

C S P R
Inv.
Ltd.

SOUTH AMERICA

**D** ALBON VALUES
Holding company

**G** UDALL
operating company

**H** TOYCO
operating company

MIDDLE EAST

**E** HYDE PARK SQUARE CORP.
Holding company

**I**
operating company

AFRICA

**F**
Holding company

N143
12/6

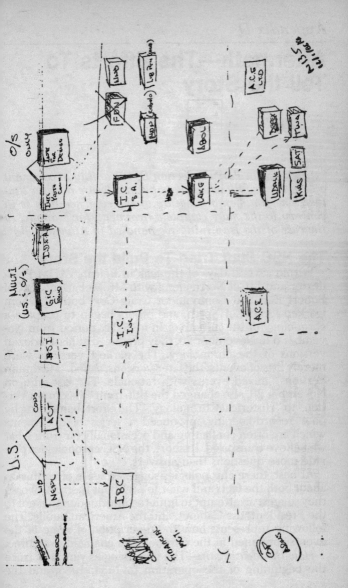

479

## Appendix D

# Aftermath—The Efforts To Tell the Story

*(As noted in Part IV, Section D, our ability to comment on the events following the public disclosure remains limited. The fragmentary nature of the evidence here is in contrast to the more complete treatment, for example, in the case of the Iran initiative handled in Appendix B.)*

## The NSC Staff Tried To Build the Story

Within several days of the leak in Beirut, VADM Poindexter and LtCol North along with Mr. McFarlane, LtCol Robert Earl and Commander Craig Coy, both of whom worked for LtCol North, and others began to prepare a chronology of the initiative. In a 15-day period from November 5 to November 20, they produced at least a dozen versions of the chronology. The earliest versions were merely lists of events; the later versions, called "Maximum Versions" mixed events with rationale. The last edit, on November 20, also changed the title from "Maximum Version" to "Historical Chronology." The effort, hamstrung by poor record-keeping, produced a series of documents which are often conflicting and occasionally far from what we believe transpired. In short, the NSC chronologies provide more questions than answers.

At best, these chronologies suggest a sense of confusion about both the facts and what to say about them. At worst, they suggest an attempt to limit the information that got to the President, the Cabinet, and the American public. The following represents how the description of some of the events contained in the chronologies changed over time.

*How the idea began.*—The chronologies variously trace the beginning of the operation to 1984, 1985, and the

480

spring of 1985. They state that an American citizen sometimes referred to by name, Michael Ledeen, was either approached by or learned from the Israelis that an Iranian expatriate sometimes referred to by name, Mr. Ghorbanifar, could either be useful or wanted to establish a contact with the U.S. government for Iran. In the November 17 maximum version, we learn that the Israelis "analyzed this intermediary's background exhaustively in order to validate his legitimacy" and that the U.S. "established an indirect contact with the Iranian intermediary, through the private U.S. citizen and a senior Israeli official." The version continued that this contact was established through the NSC staff with the "full knowledge of appropriate Cabinet officers." This section does not exist in the November 20 historical chronology.

*August/September, 1985.*—The chronologies are more confused on this section. The November 13 maximum version stated, "in September of 1985, the Israelis advised that they were close to achieving a breakthrough on the hostage situation and would proceed unless we objected. * * * The U.S. judged that the Israelis would persist in these secret deliveries, despite our objections, because they believed it to be in their strategic interest. * * * Shortly after Reverend Weir's release, the U.S. acquiesced in an Israeli delivery of military supplies (508 TOWs) to Tehran. U.S. acquiescence in this Israeli operation was based on a decision at the highest level to exploit the existing Israeli channels with Tehran in an effort to establish an American strategic dialogue with the Iranian government."

By November 17, the story was as follows: "On August 22, 1985, the U.S., through the U.S. citizen intermediary, acquiesced in an Israeli delivery of military supplies (508 TOWs) to Tehran. We were subsequently informed that the delivery had taken place at the end of August, though we were not aware of the shipment at the time it was made." Again, the U.S. decision was made at "the highest level."

On November 18, the chronology read, "On August 22, 1985, a senior Israeli official (David Kimche) visited Washington and met with the National Security Advisor. The Israeli asked us to acquiesce in a single Israeli delivery of defensive military materiel to Tehran. * * * Mr. McFarlane stated that the U.S. could in no way be construed as an

481

'arms for hostages' deal [sic] and that there could be no guarantee that whatever items of U.S. origin Israel sent, could be replaced. We were subsequently informed that the Israelis had delivered 508 TOWs at the end of August."

After a PROF note from Mr. McFarlane to VADM Poindexter on November 18, this section changed drastically. At Mr. McFarlane's suggestion, the arms and hostages were handled as distinct and unrelated examples of bona fides for a broader relationship. The chronology now read that Mr. McFarlane "elevated this proposition to the President within days at a meeting that included the Secretaries of State and Defense and the Director of Central Intelligence." The President, according to this account, could not authorize any transfers of material. Within days, the Israeli offered the option to have Israel ship "modest quantities of material" and would the United States resupply. Mr. McFarlane reportedly would elevate the issue again and, once again, the President said that he could not do so. "We subsequently learned that in late August the Israelis had transferred 508 TOW missiles to Iran." (See the November 18, 1986 PROF note from Mr. McFarlane to Mr. Poindexter).

The November 20 historical chronology added that "(t)he Israelis told us that they undertook the action, despite our objections, because they believed it to be in their strategic interests. * * * After discussing this matter with the President, it was decided not to expose this Israeli delivery because we wanted to retain the option of exploiting the existing Israeli channel with Tehran in our own effort to establish a strategic dialogue with the Iranian government.

*November, 1985 HAWK shipment.*—The early versions of the November shipment offered little commentary; by November 20 the following story emerged: "In mid-November, the Israelis, through a senior officer in the Foreign Minister's office (Kimche), indicated that the Government of Israel was convinced that they were nearing a breakthrough with Iran on a high-level dialogue. The Israeli contacted a U.S. official (North) and asked for the name of a European-based airline which could discreetly transit to Iran for the purpose of delivering passengers and cargo. He specifically noted that neither a U.S. carrier nor an Israeli affiliated carrier could be used. We were assured, at the time, that the Israelis were going to 'try oil drilling parts as an incentive,' since we had expressed so much displeasure over the earlier TOW shipment." Apparently Kimche was given the name of a proprietary and Israel "subsequently chartered through normal commercial contract for a flight from Tel Aviv to Tabriz, Iran on November 25, 1985."

"In January, we learned that the Israelis, responding to urgent entreaties from the Iranians, had used the proprietary aircraft to transport 18 HAWK missiles to Iran in an effort to improve the static air defenses around Tehran. Our belated awareness that the Israelis had delivered HAWK missiles raised serious U.S. concerns that these deliveries were jeopardizing our objectives of meeting with high-level Iranian officials. As a consequence of U.S. initiative and by mutual agreement of all three parties, these missiles were returned to Israel in February 1986."

This version also states that, in a conversation in January, 1986 with Mr. Nir, VADM Poindexter "noted our stringent objections to the HAWK missile shipments in November and noted that the U.S. would have to act to have them returned."

*The January Finding.*—The date is variously listed as the 6th, 9th, and 17th.

*February, 1986 shipment.*—Outside a brief mention on an 11/7 chronology, the early versions contained nothing of the shipment of 1000 TOWs in February. The November 17 maximum version described a "mechanism for transfer of the weapons" with the Iranian intermediary depositing funds through an Israeli account into a "sterile U.S.-controlled account." Using these funds, "the CIA would covertly obtain materiel authorized for transfer from U.S. military stocks and transport this to Israel for onward movement to Iran."

Through this mechanism, "funds were deposited in the CIA account in Geneva on February 11, 1986 and on February 14 1,000 TOWs were transported to Israel for prepositioning. The TOWs were off-loaded and placed in a covert Israeli facility.

"On February 19–21, U.S. and Iranian officials * * * met again in Germany to discuss problems in arranging a meeting among high-level officials. At this meeting, the U.S. side agreed to provide 1,000 TOWs to Iran as a clear signal of U.S. sincerity. This delivery was commenced on the morning of February 20 and completed in two transits to Tehran on February 21."

*May through October, 1986.*—The presentation of the facts of the May trip to Tehran and the use of a second channel is comparatively accurate, though far from complete.

There is little pattern to the inaccuracies of these documents, though it is clear that the authors tried to portray the initiative as an orderly operation and in the best light.

## Mr. McFarlane and the NSC Chronologies

The Board reviewed the different histories offered by Mr. McFarlane in three PROF notes on the 7th, 18th, and 21st of November and in his several testimonies on the Hill and before the Board. His various positions on the question of Presidential authorization in August and September, 1985 have made this question very difficult to resolve. This issue was discussed extensively in Mr. McFarlane's final interview with the Board. What follows are excerpts from that discussion and portions of the relevant PROF notes from Mr. McFarlane.

\* \* \*

Below are excerpts from Mr. McFarlane's testimony before the Board February 21, 1987:

Mr. McFarlane: Well, Mr. Chairman, I appreciate the opportunity to add further.

I will first deal with the November '86 narrative, if you will. On the day that the story was leaked or published in the Beirut magazine Admiral Poindexter called and stated that because of the continuing hope of being able to release or secure the release of other hostages that the White House was going to take a position of essentially not commenting on the story, that he hoped that I would honor that, too, and I assured him that I would.

He stated as well that he was going to begin, at the President's direction, putting together a narrative of events of how the entire policy initiative had been conducted, conceived, approved and so forth. And he stated then in the call that he recalled the meeting in July or August of 1985 in which the President had discussed with his Cabinet officers the pros and cons, the President then reaching a decision later on.

But he said I cannot document that and can you help out. And I said that I would, and I added in the same call that, John, you have very little time on this and I recommend that the President not have a long period of forelorned hopes that I think are unlikely to be fulfilled about further hostages, just based upon past performance. (pp. 2–3)

\* \* \*

It seemed to me, first of all, just thinking about why would I write the memo, well, I was inspired to write the memo because I was being told that a version was coming from the White House to the effect that I had taken this on basically and it wasn't until after the fact that the President had approved this.

General Scowcroft: How did you know that? You didn't have a draft at that point?

Mr. McFarlane: No. I had nothing from the White House on this, but I was receiving word from people indirectly, journalists, that were saying this is what we are being briefed by the White House and I just want you to learn about it.

Well, I had to say that I could fully accept that as a policy advisor to the President and out of loyalty to him I wanted to take full responsibility for all of my own actions, to assure that the President was placed in the best position possible. But one must not avoid the truth. Consequently, I was upset to hear that possibly —this was through hearsay—that possibly the White House might be taking a position which was fundamentally untrue.

Chairman Tower: When you say "the White House," Bud, can you be more specific?

General Scowcroft: Who is in charge of putting all this stuff together?

Mr. McFarlane: Well, the briefings that were being given to magazines referred to here were originally by Mr. Regan, and five days or four days prior, when Admiral Poindexter had called me, he said that he had been tasked, through Mr. Regan, to prepare an account, but already an account was being put out, or so I was told. (pp. 4–5)

\* \* \*

At any rate, my point is in saying that there would have been no reason to write a memo on my part, the point of writing a memo at all is to alter what I was hearing was the White House version, and that was that the President had not approved the Iranian arms sale or provided authority for it by us or anyone else until after it took place. And that's false.

So I sat down and I wrote down the memo. But again having returned from out of town and still not looking at records or calendars, because I was relying upon recollections, I put together a series of events from primarily July spread out until a decision by the President in early September, which in truth occurred in a shorter span of time, a span of time from about early July until the first ten days of August.

Now as one reads the memo, if you refer to it, that series of decisions, first of all to say yes to a political dialogue, secondly, when confronted by an insistence on selling TOWs by us to say no, and then, thirdly, when the Israelis decide that they will take it on their own to sell arms if we agree, and that they can buy replacements from us instead of spreading out in time from the early July until early September, those events take place in about a month's period of time. (pp. 5–6).

\* \* \*

Below is the portion of the memo to which Mr. McFarlane just referred; he sent it as a PROF note to VADM Poindexter dated November 7, 1986, time log 20:30:32:

It might be useful to review just what the truth is.

You will recall that when the Israelis first approached us in June '85, I presented the idea of engaging in a dialogue with the Iranians—no mention at all of any arms exchange at all—and he approved it.

We then heard nothing until August when the Israelis introduced the requirement for TOWs. I told Kimche no.

They went ahead on their own but then asked that we replace the TOWs and after checking with the President, we agreed. Weir was released as a consequence of their action.

My next involvement was to go to London where I presented our willingness to open a political dialogue but that we could not participate in an arms transfer for hostages. Gorbanifar ranted and raved but we did not change our position.

I returned to the States and debriefed the President (with Cap present, and Regan) that we had taken the position of being open to a political dialogue once our hostages were released but not before and ruled out an arms transfer. I also said that Gorbanifar was not to be trusted and recommended that we no longer carry on business with him. You were present John. I then left the government.

Some dialogue must have continued with Gorbanifar between New Year's and April, notwithstanding my recommendation. In April you contacted me to go to Iran to open the political dialogue. I did so. Once there, faced with bad faith on their part (not having released our people and without meetings with the decision makers) I aborted the mission. Ollie can verify all this.

Upon my return, I debriefed the trip and once more

recommended against carrying on the arms connection but waiting them out on the political dialogue.

Returning to Mr. McFarlane's testimony:

On November 7 I could not have documented it for you, and it wasn't until about three weeks later—actually until I got my record of schedule out of storage. Another point I would make, however, about this cross-note that I'm talking about is that there's no question here in that cross-note about prior approval prior to Mr. Weir's release.

I said it then. I've said it since, and it is true today: The decision process had three milestones on it—early July, political without any arms of any kind; mid-July, the Israelis saying political dialogue, but if the United States will sell arms and we responded no; and then early August, in which the Israelis said, well, if we do, and my meeting with Mr. Kimche resulted in our discussion on the pros and cons and so forth, and my going to the President and once more his discussion of it with his advisors, and the decision, yes, that we will replace the sale replacements for any Israeli arms that they may ship. (pp. 6–7)

* * *

I have felt since last November—and that is where we started—that it has been, I think, misleading, at least, and wrong, at worst, for me to overly gild the President's motives for his decision in this, to portray them as mostly directed toward political outcomes.

The President acknowledged those and recognized that those were clearly important. However, by the tenor of his questioning, which was oriented toward the hostages and timing of the hostages, from his recurrent virtually daily questioning just about welfare and do we have anything new and so forth, it is very clear that his concerns here were for the return of the hostages. (p. 11)

* * *

Mr. McFarlane: I think it is accurate and useful to

point out that the motives behind Admiral Poindexter's actions right after the release of the story on November 3 were inspired by concern for hoped-for still getting out more hostages and that was, I think, rather too ambitiously pursued even by the President, who went to the point of denying that anything at all had occurred. And I take it that attitude persisted even into the third week of November, although becoming ever more frail.

It seems to me that by the time the President had made his speech on this, which had not had the intended effect of explaining satisfactorily what had happened that his wish to say something more and at the same time minimize his own role grew to the point that on November 18, by the time that group convened, a principal objective, probably the primary objective, was to describe a sequence of events that would distance the President from the initial approval of the Iran arms sale, distance him from it to blur his association with it.

The November 18 chronology, which I indeed helped prepare, was not a full and completely accurate account of those events, but rather this effort to blur and leave ambiguous the President's role. The language was intended, I would say, to convey the impression that the United States had not expressly authorized the sale of arms either directly from the United States or by the Israelis on behalf of the United States, but, second, to preserve the ability to say that if Israel were to make such sales that they could expect to purchase replacement items from the United States. (pp. 42–43)

\* \* \*

Mr. McFarlane prepared a portion of the chronology on November 18. He sent his edit to VADM Poindexter at 23:06:20 on the 18th. Below is a complete text of that PROF note:

I have just finished reading the chronology. Much of it is coming to me for the first time—primarily the material on what went on between Jan–May '86—and I am not really able to comment on how to deal with that.

It seems to me that I ought to limit my input to what I recall from my involvement before Jan '86 and then from the May meeting. In that context, I would recommend deleting all material starting on the 11/17 (2000) version at page three, penultimate para (i.e. In 1985, a private * * *) down through the third para on the following page (ending with * * * strategic dialogue with the Iranian government.) and replace with the following.

In July of 1985, during a visit to Washington, an Israeli diplomatic advised National Security Advisor, Robert McFarlane, that Israel had established a channel of communications with authoritative elements in Iran who were interested in determining whether the United States was open to a discreet, high level dialogue with them. The Iranians were described as comprising the principal figures of the government (i.e. Speaker of the Majlis Rafsanjani and Prime Minister Musavi) and as being devoted to a reorientation of Iranian policy.

At this first meeting, McFarlane went to great length to draw out the Israeli diplomat as to why he found the Iranian proposal credible, given the events of the past 6 years. He replied that their exhaustive analysis had gone beyond the surface logic deriving from the chaos and decline within Iran and the degenerative effects of the war, to more concrete tests of the willingness of the Iranians to take personal risks (i.e. by exposure of themselves in meetings with Israelis to compromise as well as by the transfer of extremely sensitive intelligence on the situation (and political lineup) within Iran; information which was proven valid).

The Israeli asked for our position on agreeing to open such a dialogue. No mention was made of any preconditions or Iranian priorities. McFarlane conveyed this proposal to the President (in the presence of the Chief of Staff). The President said that he believed such a dialogue would be worthwhile at least to the point of determining the validity of the interlocutors. This was conveyed back to the Israeli diplomat.

490

Within days the Israeli called again on McFarlane. This meeting, he stated that he had conveyed our position and that the Iranians had responded that recognizing the need for both sides to have tangible evidence of the bona fides of the other, that from their side they wanted us to know that they believed they could affect the release of the Americans held hostage in Lebanon.

As a separate matter the Iranians stated that they were vulnerable as a group and before having any prospect of being able to affect change within Iran they would need to be substantially strengthened. To do so, they would need to secure the cooperation of military and/or Revolutionary Guard leaders. Toward this end, they expressed the view that the most credible demonstration of their influence and abilities would be to secure limited amounts of US equipment. The Israeli asked for our position toward such actions.

Mr. McFarlane elevated this proposition to the President at a meeting within days that included the Secretaries of State and Defense and the Director of Central Intelligence. The President stated that while he could understand that, assuming the legitimacy of the interlocutors, they would be quite vulnerable and ultimately might deserve our support to include tangible material, that at the time, without any first hand experience in dealing with them, he could not authorize any transfers of military material. This was conveyed to the Israeli.

Within days (mid August) the Israeli diplomat called once more to report that the message had been conveyed and that an impasse of confidence existed. He asked what the position of the US Government would be to an Israeli transfer of modest quantities of material. McFarlane replied that to him, that would represent a distinction without a difference. The Israeli diplomat explained at great length that Israel had its own policy interests that would be served by fostering such a dialogue in behalf of the US but that a problem would arise when ultimately they needed to replace items shipped. He asked whether at that time Israel would be able to purchase replacement parts. McFarlane stated that again, the issue was not the ability of Israel to purchase military equipment from the US—they had done so for a generation and would do so in the future—but rather the issue was whether it was US policy to ship or allow others to ship military equipment to Iran. The Israeli asked for a position from our government. McFarlane elevated the question to the President (and to the Secretaries of State and Defense and the DCI). Again the President stated that while he could imagine the day coming when we might choose to support such elements with material, he could not approve any transfer of military material at that time. This position was conveyed to the Israeli diplomat.

On September 14, 1985, Reverend Benjamin Weir
* * *

(At end of para, insert the following) We subsequently learned that in late August the Israelis had transferred 508 TOW missiles to Iran. Later in the fall, other transfers of equipment were made between Israel and Iran although some of the items were returned to Israel. McFarlane conveyed these reports to the President who directed that we insist on a direct meeting with the Iranian interlocutors while expressing our position against further arms transfers. A meeting was arranged to take place in London in early December. The President instructed McFarlane to represent the US at the meeting and to make two basic points: 1. That the US was open to a political dialogue with Iran; but that no such dialogue could make progress for as long as groups seen as dominated by Iran held US hostages, and 2. That we could under no circumstances transfer arms to Iran in exchange for hostages. These points were made to the Iranian interlocutor. He replied that unless his circle of associates were strengthened they could not risk going ahead with the exchanges. Mr. McFarlane acknowledged the position but stated we could not change our position and returned to Washington. He debriefed the President and appropriate Cabinet officers, recommending that no further action be pursued. He then left the government.

(Note: Enter at the appropriate place the following account of RCM's involvement in the May meeting.)

In April, Mr. McFarlane was contacted and advised that further staff-level contacts had been pursued since he had left government that had led to an arrangement for the release of the remaining hostages. He was asked whether he would be prepared to meet with Iranian officials to open the political dialogue. He agreed to do so and traveled to Iran in late May to do so. (Then pick up with existing text.)

Returning to Mr. McFarlane's testimony:

And I think that is an accurate reflection of how that is cast. Now it was done as a briefing memo to be used by people who would brief the President prior to the next day's press conference, and in my judgment expected to go through a number of iterations before it reached that point. But that is my opinion of the climate in which that session occurred and the intent of its outcome.

\* \* \*

I think it was \* \* \* the 18th \* \* \* I believe it was actually North saying the Admiral had directed that he call me and ask my help in coming over that evening to scrub and finish a chronology that would be used in helping out in the prebrief of the President for the press conference. And he said we were under the gun to get it done, but we have it. And that was about 5:00, as I recall, or late in the day.

And so I cancelled a dinner I was supposed to go to and went over, but I didn't get there actually until about 8:00 and it was in Colonel North's office. It was kind of a feverish climate in which four or five officers —Colonel North, Mr. Teicher, Mr. Coy, Colonel Earle, a couple of secretaries——

Mr. Garment: Al Keel?

Mr. McFarlane: Periodically, but not originally. Cut and paste—some original, some typed, some handwritten documents, ones that had been prepared, I believe, in Mr. Buchanan's office to be used the next day. And separately a draft chronology, the so-called master of which had been done by the CIA, or so I was told by Colonel North.

Senator Muskie: Incidentally, do we have that?

Mr. Dawson: Yes, sir.

Mr. McFarlane: I started by looking at the opening statement and believed that it did not fully treat the political purpose at issue here of the longer-term relationship with Iran and other points that were less important. But I sat down and drafted a three-section note that went out in three separate messages by PROFs to Admiral Poindexter. He reacted to the first two by telephone after he got them, probably by 10:00 by this time, at night. Other people had been working on the chronology for the same two hours, while I'd been working on the opening statement. And at that point I finished and 10:30 or so turned my attention to the chronology and was given the master, which was a CIA product, and I think fairly it was understandably wrong because the officer tasked to prepare it had not been involved in many of the events.

But you could see several errors in it, and I pointed out perhaps a half dozen and got through it to about the middle of it, to where it treated the President's involvement in the original decision. The treatment that was there was ambiguous in a number of respects, but it said, for example, that he had aquiesced in the sale, as I recall, and it left out issues of timing.

And I sat down and, after looking through a separate stack of several pieces of paper, was given one that had two paragraphs on it on this issue. The first part of it treated the basic matter of the approval itself, and the second paragraph dealt with his reaction once he had learned about it in an ex post context.

And in looking at the first part of it it was not technically wrong. As I recall, it had words to the effect that the President did not approve, did not formally approve the September 2 shipment and then it went on in the second paragraph to say upon learning about it after Mr. Weir's release was upset and directed someone to have me—it didn't say—directed that Mr. McFarlane so advise the government of Israel.

Well, in looking at those, those were expressive to me, first of all, of a climate in which there was an obvious effort to, as I said, distance and to blur the President's role in the initial authorization, in both timing and substance.

General Scowcroft: Did you raise that point with anybody here? I mean, this is the first time you've seen this maneuvering.

Mr. McFarlane: Well, I did, and it was a little—it was very curious because in truth none of those officers there were involved at that point in time, and so they weren't in a position to say. They could have written this. No one owned up to it. Mr. Teicher said and has said since that he did not. Colonel North asked me. I said, well where does this come from? They said well, I don't know, but it's something I can't personally throw any light on.

And innocent shrugs from Mr. Coy and Colonel Earle. There was no one in the room that had written it.

Mr. Dawson: But these two conversations that you had with Admiral Poindexter, did they concern the President's involvement and his authorization?

Mr. McFarlane: His original call to me on November 3 had, and he recalled it the way that I have, and I have testified to that—that the President met in his pajamas in the residence and then subsequently approved it.

I recall having talked to him that night, Admiral Poindexter, that evening when I sent him the first two sections on the opening statement, and then later on when he came back on the third one and said yes, it is good too. Now I do remember very clearly talking to

495

him after I had finished all work that evening, and it is only unclear in my mind whether it was that night or the following day.

But I wrapped up what I had done for him and I said: John, there are at least a half dozen or more serious problems with this chronology. I have noted them. Colonel North believes that he can straighten out the ones that I have pointed out to him. And the portrayal of the President's role in this is directed toward, apparently, putting some distance and ambiguity around the timing and the substance of his approval—that is, was it before or after.

Now it isn't technically wrong the way somebody has written it down here, but we know that the President approved this before the Israelis did it. And I tend to think that that was exchanged with him in a stand-up conversation the next day—that is, the day of the press conference, Wednesday. And he acknowledged what I had said, and he said, yes, we are working on it still. Or we will continue to work on it after you have finished and thanks for your help.

I say that because just the memory of saying that I had pointed out the several mistakes is pretty vivid in my mind as a stand-up exchange between myself and him and Mr. Keel present as a witness, and his acknowledging, okay, we will get this straightened out.

But I said, and I had participated the night before in preparing it, I said: You know, it is technically not inaccurate to say that the President didn't formally approve the September 2 shipment discretely. But, of course, he approved it as an authority for it to be done. And, secondly, the part that I accepted and sent you in my note about his being upset about it, I can imagine maybe he was and so I can't disprove it, but he didn't say that to me.

\* \* \*

Mr. Garment: By the way, you said that John Poindexter was not there that night. Was he there at any point? Was he there when you came to the meeting?

Do you know why he went home? Do you know why he didn't attend the meeting? Can you shed any light on that?

Mr. McFarlane: He wasn't there and I don't know why. He had gone home, but he had gone perhaps to an outside obligation beforehand.

Mr. Garment: Well, he was at home?

Mr. McFarlane: He reached home, I would guess, no later than 10:00 or so, but I don't know why.

Mr. Garment: Did you speak to him before the meeting at any point after North asked you to come to that meeting—that is, from the time North called you until you appeared at the OEOB, speaking to Admiral Poindexter?

Mr. McFarlane: I remember speaking to him that night at least once, and perhaps twice, again after that session before the press conference, to make it emphatic that it was not an accurate chronology.

Mr. Garment: Rhett, do you intend to get into the business of the meeting with the Attorney General and that sequence of events? If not, I think it would be helpful for him to continue with that in the same vein.

Mr. Dawson: I think that's a good idea.

Mr. Garment: Discussing matters which he has now had an opportunity to refresh his recollection with documents on.

Mr. McFarlane: Well, the meeting was called at the Attorney General's initiative, and he called me. I was at home.

General Scowcroft: When was this?

Mr. McFarlane: This was the 21st, which would have been Friday. He called and I was at home working on a speech that I had to give and he asked me—well, he said, first of all, Bud, I have been tasked by the President to put together an accurate record of events in this matter and I would like to talk to you. When can you come in? I volunteered as soon as possible—driving time.

And within about an hour—it would have been 2:00 or 3:00—I was in his office, his inner office, and it was the Attorney General and an associate, Mr.—I assume, Charles Cooper. We were seated about like this, between the Attorney General and myself, and Mr. Cooper was sitting next to us taking notes.

And in the course of about an hour I went through my recollection really, because I hadn't referred to records still, what I remembered about the decision process and my account was essentially as I had acceded to it in the Tuesday night session. And Mr. Meese then had a number of questions about the President's involvement, other people's involvement, positions of various Cabinet officers.

And this was a back and forth that went for perhaps another half hour and he said okay, that's fine.

And we rose to break up. His secretary came in and gave me a message that had come in some time before and said your wife called with some urgency and you need to call her right away.

Mr. Cooper left the room and Ed began to leave the room. And I said: Ed, wait a minute. I want to talk to you about this. Now, I wanted to talk to him because it was very apparent. I'm talking to the chief law enforcement officer of the country. It is essential that there not be any ambiguity in what he is telling the President about the truth of the actions here. And so I told him, you know, as you may have seen in this morning's papers I gave a speech last night and I have taken on responsibility for every bit of this that I can, Ed, and I shall continue to do that.

And he interrupted and said yes, that's been noted. But I want you to know that from the very beginning of this, Ed, the President was four-square behind it, that he never had any reservations about approving anything that the Israelis wanted to do here. Ed said, Bud, I know that, and I can understand why. And, as a

498

practical matter, I'm glad you told me this because his legal position is far better the earlier that he made the decision.

And I said well, I don't have any knowledge of that, but there was no question about it, Ed. He said, okay. I may have to get back to you. Thanks a lot. And that was that.

And then, on Sunday night—no, Monday afternoon he called and asked me to come by again, and I went down to his office again, and by that time he had learned, I suppose from his associates turning up the evidence of the diversion of funds to the Contra business, about it and he asked me to come down and began to ask questions about that. I told him when I learned about it and my lack of knowledge on the antecedents to it and so forth.

And he said fine. And I said, Ed, you know, I think this has gone well beyond timewise what it should have and the President ought to get out the facts right away, and I think also that there are a number of other policy initiatives that ought to be taken if he's going to be able to show leadership in foreign policy at all. And if you think that it's of value I'd be glad to jot some of these down and send them to you.

And he said, yes, I'd appreciate that very much. So I went home—this is Monday afternoon—and in the space of about an hour put down about three or four pages of ideas.

\* \* \*

After his conversation with Mr. Meese, Mr. McFarlane sent another PROF note to VADM Poindexter at 21:01 on the 21st of November. A portion of this note follows.

\* \* \* I spent a couple of hours with Ed Meese today going over the record with him. The only blind spot on my part concerned a shipment in November '85 which still doesn't ring a bell with me.

But it appears that the matter of not notifying the

Israeli transfers can be covered if the President made a "mental finding" before the transfers took place. Well on that score we ought to be ok because he was all for letting the Israelis do anything they wanted at the very first briefing in the hospital. Ed seemed relieved at that.

Returning to Mr. McFarlane's testimony:

[Regarding the President's Approval in August 1985:]

Chairman Tower: Now, did you communicate the President's approval and inform anybody on your staff about it? Did you tell Poindexter? Who did you tell? Who did you contact to tell them the President had approved this on our side?

Mr. McFarlane: Admiral Poindexter is the short answer. In my recurring memory of how it took place—and I've asked my wife to try to recall this image—is that it occurred at home, and he called me from Camp David and that I then called Mr. Kimche and not until the next day, however, did I tell Admiral Poindexter.

There ought to be a record, although not on my record because I was at home, probably in the Camp David operators that a call took place.

General Scowcroft: Did you tell Mike Ledeen about the approval? Did you tell him to convey it?

Mr. McFarlane: I don't have any mental image of a meeting, but I expect that I did convey it to him, not for him to further carry it out but to inform him that that was the decision. [I've called that.] He came out to make a speech in Los Angeles at a moment when the Presidential party was there . . . And, if not before, surely then I would have told him about it.

Chairman Tower: Understanding that this was on a pretty closely held basis, was there anybody beside Poindexter that you would have told that the President communicated to you his approval?

Mr. McFarlane: Not on the NSC staff, no, sir.

Chairman Tower: And you did not inform the other NSC principals?

Mr. McFarlane: Within a day or so I did.

Chairman Tower: Which ones?

Mr. McFarlane: It would have been the Secretary of State, Defense, Mr. Regan and the Vice President.

Chairman Tower: That the President had given you the go-ahead on this?

Mr. McFarlane: That is correct.

Mr. McFadden: How about Mr. Casey?

Mr. McFarlane: And Mr. Casey, yes.

Chairman Tower: Bud, were you aware if there was ever a contingency plan to deal with this issue, a planned public diplomacy campaign of any kind to deal with it once it became public knowledge, whether by official release or by just simply being exposed?

Mr. McFarlane: I know of no such plan.

\* \* \*

# The White House Position Changed

In the first days after the disclosure, the President stood firmly with VADM Poindexter in support of protecting the channel and the operation. Mr. McDaniel noted that during VADM Poindexter's morning briefings the issue was discussed on November 6 and 7; in both discussions, the President apparently agreed to make no comment in hope that additional hostages would be freed and out of fear for the safety of the second channel.

The President met with the Vice President, Secretaries Shultz and Weinberger, Mr. Regan, Director Casey, Attorney General Meese, VADM Poindexter, and Dr. Alton Keel (Acting Deputy at NSC) on November 10 to discuss the initiative and possible government reactions. Notes of the meeting by Dr. Keel provide some insight into this meeting. The President felt a need for a statement of U.S. intentions in the initiative. VADM Poindexter offered a brief history of the initiative. Following questions by Secretaries Shultz and Weinberger, the President stated that rumors had endangered what they were doing. Dr. Keel's notes suggest that the President felt that we had not dealt with terrorists or paid ransom and that one of the purposes of government was to protect its citizens. The President felt that a basic statement had to come out but that we needed to avoid details and specifics of the operation; he urged that we could not engage in speculation because the lives of the hostages and the Iranians were at stake.

On November 13, Mr. McDaniel noted that the President decided to address the nation that evening. There appear to have been several drafts of the President's speech and a hectic struggle to produce the final product. That night, the President addressed the nation.

# The President's Address to the Nation

The President told the American people that they were "going to hear the facts from a White House source and you know my name."

The President stated that a diplomatic initiative had been underway for 18 months, for the following reasons:

—to renew relationship with Iran;

—to bring an honorable end to Iran-Iraq war;

—to eliminate state-sponsored terrorism;

—to attain the safe return of the hostages.

The President said, "The United States has not swapped boatloads or planeloads of American weapons for the return of the American hostages."

"I authorized the transfer of small amounts of defensive weapons and spare parts for defensive systems to Iran. . . . These modest deliveries, taken together, could easily

502

fit into a single cargo plane. They could not, taken together, affect the outcome of the . . . war . . . nor . . . the military balance."

The President noted that various countries had tried to broker a relationship between Iran and the United States since 1983. "With this history in mind, we were receptive last year when we were alerted to the possibility of establishing a direct dialogue with Iranian officials."

"It's because of Iran's strategic importance and its influence in the Islamic world that we chose to probe for a better relationship between our countries."

"Our discussions continued into the spring of this year. Based upon the progress we felt we had made, we sought to raise the diplomatic level of contacts. A meeting was arranged in Tehran. I then asked my former National Security Adviser, Robert McFarlane, to undertake a secret mission and gave him explicit instructions."

"There is ample precedent in our history for this kind of secret diplomacy. In 1971, then-President Nixon sent his national security adviser on a secret mission to China."

"Although the efforts we undertook were highly sensitive and involvement of government officials was limited to those with a strict need to know, all appropriate Cabinet Officers were fully consulted. The actions I authorized were and continue to be in full complance with federal law. And the relevant committees of Congress are being and will be fully informed."

"We did not—repeat—did not trade weapons or anything else for hostages—nor will we."

# VADM Poindexter Briefed Reporters

VADM Poindexter briefed reporters on background the same day. The following interchange between VADM Poindexter and reporters officially exposed a connection between Israel and the United States in the 1985 shipments.

Q. "—a few things on the shipments, just to clarify this. Any shipments that were made prior to January of 1986 you're saying the U.S. had no role in, either condoning, winking, encouraging, or anything of that nature? Is that correct?

VADM Poindexter: "That's correct."

\* \* \*

Q. "Could you say then what prompted the release of Benjamin Weir then in September of '85? What event do you think was related to his release?

VADM Poindexter: Well, I think that it was a matter of our talking to the contacts through our channel, making the case as to what our long-range objectives were, demonstrating our good faith——

Q. "How was that done?"

VADM Poindexter: "Well, that was one of the motivations behind the small amount of stuff that we transferred to them."

Q. "But that was done later?"

VADM Poindexter: "The problem is—and don't draw any inferences from this—but there are other countries involved, but I don't want to confirm what countries those are and—because I think that it is still important that that be protected. And going back to the question you asked me earlier, there was one shipment that was made not by us, but by a third country prior to the signing of that document."

Q. "This shipment to Israel?"

VADM Poindexter: "I'm not confirming that, George."

Q. "Was that on our behalf?"

VADM Poindexter: "It was done in our interests."

Q. "Was that before Weir was released?"

VADM Poindexter: "I honestly don't know. And if I knew, I don't think I would tell you precisely."

Q. "You just said previously that you did not condone any shipments?"

VADM Poindexter: "I went back and corrected—there was one exception and that was the one I just described."

# The President's News Conference

The speech did not stem the pressure mounting in Congress and the U.S. media. By November 19, the President decided to conduct a news conference; excerpts from the conference follow:

"Several top advisers opposed the sale of even modest shipment of defensive weapons and spare parts to Iran. Others felt no progress could be made without this sale. I weighed their views. I considered the risks of failure and the rewards of success, and I decided to proceed, and the responsibility for the decision and the operation is mine and mine alone."

"I was convinced then and I am convinced now that while the risks were great, so, too, was the potential reward. Bringing Iran back into the community of responsible nations, ending its participation in political terror, bringing an end to that terrible war, and bringing our hostages home—these are causes that justify taking risks."

On the Danish ships and the Danish sailors' union officials' stories the President commented, "we certainly never had any contact with anything of the kind."

On conflicts with established policy, the President responded, "I don't think it was duplicity, and as I say, the so-called 'violation' did not in any way alter the balance, military balance, between the two countries."

Q. "Mr. President, you say that the equipment which was shipped didn't alter the military balance. Yet, several things—we understand that there were 1,000 TOW anti-tank missiles shipped by the U.S. The U.S. apparently condoned shipments by Israel and other nations of other quantities of arms as an ancillary part of this deal—not directly connected, but had to condone it, or the shipments could not have gone forward, sir. So, how can you say that it cannot alter the military balance, and how can you say, sir, that it didn't break the law, when the National Security Act of 1977 plainly talks about timely notification of Congress and also, sir, stipulates that if the national security required secrecy, the President is still required to advise the leadership and the chairman of the intelligence committees?

The President: "Bill, everything you've said here is based on a supposition that is false. We did not condone, and do not condone the shipment of arms from other countries."

Q. "Is it possible that the Iraqis, sir, might think that

1,000 anti-tank missiles was enough to alter the balance of that war?"

The President: "This is a purely defensive weapon—it is a shoulder-carried weapon and we don't think that in this defensive thing—we didn't add to any offensive power on the part of Iran. . . . And, as I say, all of those weapons could be very easily carried in one mission."

"We, as I say, have had nothing to do with other countries or their shipment of arms or doing what they're doing."

Q. ". . . Are you telling us tonight that the only shipments with which we were involved were the one or two that followed your January 17th finding and that, whatever your aides have said on background or on the record, there are not other shipments with which the U.S. condoned?"

The President: "That's right. I'm saying nothing but the missiles that we sold—and remember, there are too many people that are saying 'gave.' They bought them."

Q. "Mr. President, to follow up on that, we've been told by the Chief of Staff Donald Regan that we condoned, this government condoned an Israeli shipment in September of 1985, shortly before the release of hostage Benjamin Weir. . . ."

The President: "No, that—I've never heard Mr. Regan say that and I'll ask him about that, because we believe in the embargo and, as I say, we waived it for a specific purpose . . ."

". . . To the best of our knowledge, Iran does not own or have authority over the Hezballah. They cannot order them to do something. It is apparent that they evidently have either some persuasion and they don't always succeed, but they can sometimes persuade or pressure the Hezbollah into doing what they did in this instance. And, as I say, the Iranian government had no hostages and they bought a shipment from us and we, in turn—I might as well tell you—that we, in turn, had said when they wanted to kind of know our position and whether we were trustworthy and all of this, we told them that we were—we did not want to do business with any nation that openly backed terrorism. And they gave us information that they did not and they said also that they had some evidence that there had been a lessening of this on the part of—Khomeini and the government and that they'd made some progress. As a matter of fact, some individuals associated with terrorist acts had been put in prison there. And so that was when we said well, there's a very easy way for you to verify that if that's the way you feel, and they're being held hostage in Lebanon."

On being corrected about a TOW missile, the President responded, ". . . if I have been misinformed, then I will yield on that, but it was my understanding that that is a man-carried weapon, and we have a number of other shoulder-borne weapons."

The President concluded, "I don't think a mistake was made. It was a high-risk gamble, and it was a gamble that, as I've said, I believe the circumstances warranted. And I don't see that it has been a fiasco or a great failure of any kind. We still have those contacts, we still have made some ground, we got our hostages back—three of them. And so I think that what we did was right, and we're going to continue on this path."

In the wake of the press response to the news conference, the President asked Attorney General Meese to come to the White House to straighten out what had happened over the course of the initiative. It was during these discussions on November 21–23 that the Attorney General discovered the possibility of diversion.

# Case Studies Prepared for the Board

These case studies were prepared, under the direction of the Board, by Graham Allison, John F. Kennedy School of Government; Michael Beschloss, Smithsonian Institution; MacGregor Knox, University of Rochester; Williamson Murray, Ohio State University; Albert Pierce, National Defense University; Gregory Treverton, John F. Kennedy School of Government.

The Board extends special thanks to Robert Murray of the John F. Kennedy School of Government who made a major contribution in the interpretation and preparation of these cases.

# President's Special Review Board Interviews*

(Covering the period 1 Dec 1986–26 Feb 1987)

| *Name* | *Date* |
| --- | --- |
| Abrams, Elliot | 19 Dec |
| Allen, Charles | 30 Dec/11 Feb |
| Allen, Richard V | 13 Jan |
| Armitage, Richard L | 18 Dec |
| Brown, Harold | 15 Jan |
| Brzezinski, Zbigniew | 19 Jan |
| Bush, George | 18 Dec |
| Carlucci, Frank C | 19 Dec/20 Feb |
| Carter, James E | 21 Jan |
| Cave, George | 5 Jan |
| Clarridge, Duane R | 18 Dec |
| Clifford, Clark | 22 Jan |
| Colby, William | 8 Jan |
| Coy, Craig | 2 Jan |
| Doherty, David P | 19 Dec |
| Ford, Gerald | 25 Jan |
| Fuller, Graham | 2 Jan |
| Furmark, Roy M | 15 Jan |
| Gates, Robert | 12 Jan |
| George, Clair | 14 Jan |
| Ghorbanifar, Manucher | 29 Jan |
| Haig, Alexander M., Jr | 18 Dec |
| Helms, Richard | 20 Jan |
| Jones, David C | 9 Feb |
| Khashoggi, Adnan | 29 Jan |
| Kimmitt, Robert | 12 Dec |

| Name | Date |
|------|------|
| Kissinger, Henry .............. | 23 Jan |
| Laird, Melvin ................. | 16 Jan |
| Ledeen, Michael .............. | 9 Jan/12 Feb |
| McFarlane, Robert C.......... | 11 Dec/19 Feb/21 Feb |
| McMahon, John N ............ | 6 Jan |
| McNamara, Robert............ | 19 Jan |
| Meese, Edwin ................. | 20 Jan |
| Mondale, Walter .............. | 4 Feb |
| Moorer, Thomas H............ | 11 Feb |
| Nixon, Richard................. | 23 Jan |
| Oakley, Robert................. | 17 Dec |
| Reagan, Ronald ............... | 26 Jan/11 Feb |
| Regan, Donald ................ | 7 Jan |
| Rogers, William ............... | 16 Jan |
| Rosenne, Meir ................. | 4 Feb |
| Rostow, Walt.................... | 7 Jan |
| Schlesinger, James ............ | 6 Feb |
| Shackley, Theodore G......... | 5 Feb |
| Shultz, George ................. | 22 Jan |
| Sporkin, Stanley .............. | 9 Jan |
| Teicher, Howard .............. | 19 Dec |
| Turner, Stansfield ............. | 24 Jan |
| Vance, Cyrus.................... | 19 Jan |
| Weinberger, Caspar ........... | 14 Jan |

The Board also interviewed the following officials:

Chief of the Near East and South Asian Division in the Operations Directorate, CIA —— 5 Jan

Chief of the Iran Branch, Operations Directorate, CIA —— 6 Feb

Director of the Central American Task Force, Operations Directorate, CIA —— 8 Jan

\* There were a substantial number of additional interviews conducted by the staff at the direction of the Board.

510

PRESIDENT'S SPECIAL REVIEW BOARD

December 12, 1986

Vice Admiral John Poindexter
10 Barrington Lane
Rockville, Maryland 20850

Dear Admiral Poindexter:

On behalf of the Special Review Board established by Executive Order No. 12575, I request that you appear before the Board, at 10:00 a.m., December 17, 1986, to discuss and respond to questions regarding the manner in which foreign and national security policies established by the President have been implemented by the NSC staff.

Should you have any questions regarding this request please contact me or Mr. Clark McFadden, General Counsel to the Board, at 456-2566.

The Board would appreciate a response to this request as soon as possible.

Sincerely,

John Tower, Chairman
President's Special Review Board

FULBRIGHT & JAWORSKI

1150 Connecticut Avenue, N.W.
Washington, D.C. 20036

Telephone: 202/452-6800
Telex: 89-2602

Houston
Washington, D.C.
Austin
San Antonio
Dallas
London
Zurich

December 16, 1986

<u>BY HAND</u>

Clark McFadden, Esq.
General Counsel to the President's
  Special Review Board
New Executive Office Building
Room 5221
Washington, D.C.

Dear Mr. McFadden:

        We represent Vice Admiral John M. Poindexter, and he
has provided us with Chairman Tower's letter, dated
December 12, 1986, requesting the Admiral's appearance before
the President's Special Review Board on December 17, 1986. At
the present time, Admiral Poindexter must respectfully decline
to appear before the Board. He has asked us, however, to
assure you that he would be pleased, at an appropriate time, to
discuss and respond to the Board's questions regarding the
manner in which foreign and national security policies
established by the President have been implemented by the NSC
staff.

                        Very truly yours,

                        Richard W. Beckler

cc:  Vice Admiral John M. Poindexter

PRESIDENT'S SPECIAL REVIEW BOARD

December 12, 1986

Lt Col Oliver North
Kentland Drive
Great Falls, Virginia  22066

Dear Colonel North:

On behalf of the Special Review Board established by
Executive Order No. 12575, I request that you appear before
the Board, at 2:30 p.m., December 17, 1986, to discuss and
respond to questions regarding the manner in which foreign
and national security policies established by the President
have been implemented by the NSC staff.

Should you have any questions regarding this request
please contact me or Mr. Clark McFadden, General Counsel to
the Board, at 456-2566.

The Board would appreciate a response to this request
as soon as possible.

Sincerely,

*signed*

John Tower, Chairman
President's Special Review Board

December 15, 1986

HAND DELIVER

John Tower, Chairman
President's Special Review Board
Room 5221
New Executive Office Building
Washington, D.C.  20506

Dear Mr. Tower:

    As you know, LtCol North has asserted his constitutional right not to answer questions with respect to the subject matter of your December 12, 1986 letter.  We regret we cannot be of assistance to you at this time.  LtCol North looks forward to the opportunity of answering all of your questions at the appropriate time.

    In view of the fact that LtCol North is represented by counsel, please direct all further correspondence to me directly.

Sincerely yours,

*Brendan V. Sullivan*

Brendan V. Sullivan, Jr.

BVS:lng

cc:  W. Clark McFadden, II
     General Counsel to the Board

## PRESIDENT'S SPECIAL REVIEW BOARD
New Executive Office Building - Room 5221
Washington, D.C. 20506
202-456-2566

JOHN TOWER
*Chairman*

EDMUND MUSKIE

BRENT SCOWCROFT
—————
RHETT DAWSON
*Director*

W. CLARK MCFADDEN II
*General Counsel*

February 4, 1987

The President
The White House
Washington, D.C. 20500

Dear Mr. President:

For the last several weeks, the President's Special Review Board has been studying the National Security Council process. Pursuant to your direction, a focus of the Board's attention has been the recent transfers of arms to Iran and the possible diversion of funds to the Contras. Establishing the essential facts surrounding these transactions has proven to be a difficult challenge.

Two individuals, Admiral John Poindexter and Lt. Col. Oliver North, played central roles in these transactions. The ability of the Board to make an informed and useful appraisal of the Iran-Contra matter would be greatly enhanced by the testimony of these individuals. To this end, the Board invited these individuals to appear before it, but through their attorneys, they declined.

Under these circumstances and consistent with the responsibility which the Board has accepted, the Board respectfully requests that in your capacity as Commander-in-Chief you order these individuals to appear before the Board and to cooperate in connection with its inquiry. In this way we believe the Board can most effectively accomplish its purpose.

Thank you for your cooperation.

Sincerely,

*John Tower*

John Tower

February 6, 1987

Dear Senator Tower:

Thank you for your letter to the President of February 4, 1987, requesting that he, as Commander in Chief, order Vice Admiral John Poindexter and Lt. Col. Oliver North to appear before and cooperate with the President's Special Review Board.

On numerous occasions, the President has made clear his desire that both Vice Admiral Poindexter and Lt. Col. North cooperate fully with all on-going inquiries into the Iran matter and the alleged diversion of funds to the anti-Sandinista forces in Nicaragua. In these statements, however, the President has recognized that Messrs. Poindexter and North have a constitutional right not to testify, and that this right must be respected even when its assertion unduly hinders the disclosure process the President himself has set in motion.

In response to your request, we have confirmed with the General Counsel of the Department of Defense what had been our previous advice to the President -- that the order you seek would conflict with the constitutional rights of Messrs. Poindexter and North, as well as their rights under Article 31 of the Uniform Code of Military Justice, and hence would not be a lawful order under the Manual for Courts-Martial, E.O. 12473 (1984). A copy of the opinion of the General Counsel of the Department of Defense is attached.

If you have any questions, or if I may be of further assistance, please contact me.

Very truly yours,

Peter J. Wallison
Counsel to the President

The Honorable John G. Tower
Chairman
President's Special Review Board
The White House
Washington, D.C. 20500

Attachment

February 5, 1987

MEMORANDUM FOR MR. PETER J. WALLISON, COUNSEL TO THE PRESIDENT

SUBJECT: Tower Commission Request Regarding Former NSC Personnel

In my opinion, the request by the Tower Commission that the President, as Commander-in-Chief, order Vice Admiral Poindexter and Lieutenant Colonel North to answer the Commission's questions should be denied. In the absence of a grant of testimonial immunity, the Commission's request asks the President to issue an order which would be clearly unlawful and, therefore, unenforceable through the provisions of the Uniform Code of Military Justice (UCMJ).

Military personnel are protected against compelled self-incrimination by both the Fifth Amendment and Article 31 of the UCMJ, 10 U.S.C. §831. Although Article 31 only applies to interrogations or investigations conducted by persons subject to the UCMJ, Fifth Amendment protections apply independently to both civilian and military investigations. United States v. Tempia, 37 C.M.R. 249 (C.M.A. 1967).

Military personnel may be prosecuted before courts-martial for willful violations of the lawful orders of their military superiors. Articles 90 and 92, UCMJ, 10 U.S.C. §§890, 892. As Commander-in-Chief of the armed forces, the President is the military superior of both individuals; willful failure to obey his lawful orders does violate Article 92. Violation of his lawful orders is sufficiently "service-connected" to support the exercise of military jurisdiction, regardless of where given or disobeyed. United States v. Fuller, 2 M.J. 702 (A.F.C.M.R. 1976).

However, to be lawful, an order "must not conflict with the statutory or constitutional rights of" the recipient. Part IV, Paragraph 14c(2)(a)(iv), Manual for Courts-Martial, E.O. 12473 (1984). An order which contravenes the recipient's rights under Article 31 and the Fifth Amendment is not a lawful order. United States v. Jordan, 22 C.M.R. 242 (C.M.A. 1957); United States v. Jackson, 1 M.J. 606 (A.C.M.R. 1975). To the extent an order requires the recipient to perform a self-incriminating act, it violates Article 31, and cannot serve as the basis of a conviction for violating Articles 90 or 92. United States v. Hay, 3 M.J. 654 (A.C.M.R. 1977).

517

Nor can servicemembers be administratively separated from the service or otherwise penalized for invoking their protection against self-incrimination. Lefkowitz v. Cunningham, 431 U.S. 801 (1977); Lefkowitz v. Turley, 414 U.S. 70 (1973); Sanitation Men v. Sanitation Commissioner, 392 U.S. 280 (1968); Gardner v. Broderick, 392 U.S. 273 (1968); Garrity v. New Jersey, 385 U.S. 493 (1967). Inasmuch as the Government is clearly on notice of the assertion of Fifth Amendment rights by both officers, they would almost surely obtain de facto immunity for their statements if they chose to obey rather than refuse the order.

If afforded testimonial immunity by the Attorney General under 18 U.S.C. §6002, Vice Admiral Poindexter and Lieutenant Colonel North may then be ordered to account for their official conduct. Refusal to do so might then provide a basis for prosecution under the UCMJ provisions discussed above, or adverse administrative action under service regulations. Gardner, 392 U.S. at 279. However, neither their statements nor any evidence derived therefrom may be used against them in a subsequent criminal prosecution or court-martial, except for perjury or other falsity arising out of their statements. Evidence independently derived would, of course, not be precluded from use by such immunity.

Statements made pursuant to a grant of immunity could be used to support any appropriate adverse administrative action, to include admonition, reprimand, determination of retired grade, or separation from the naval service. See United States v. Apfelbaum, 445 U.S. 124, 125 (1980) and cases cited therein.

Accordingly, I conclude that such an order from the President as is requested by the Tower Commission would not be lawful unless accompanied by a grant of immunity, and could not be enforced by threat of punishment under the UCMJ or other adverse action. Although the giving of such an order would not itself violate the law, it would set an extremely poor precedent within the military justice system by suggesting that commanders may, for reasons of command, confer de facto immunity to obtain information without adhering to established provisions of law governing grants of immunity.

I recommend the Tower Commission's request be rejected.

H. Lawrence Garrett, III

# Appendix H

18 February 1987

The Honorable John Tower
President's Special Review Board
New Executive Office Building, Room 5221
Washington, D.C. 20506

Dear Senator Tower:

In my appearance before the President's Special Review Board I was asked whether a finding under the Hughes-Ryan Amendment would have been necessary if it were found that the Central Intelligence Agency rendered certain kinds of assistance to a covert arms transfer to Iran prior to the President's authorizing such a transfer. The purpose of this letter is to respond to the Board's request for a considered, written answer to this question.

The Board's question assumed that the CIA, without prior presidential authorization, assisted in the November 1985 arms shipment to Iran by attempting to obtain flight clearances at a foreign airport and by arranging for a proprietary airline to carry the arms from Israel to Iran. The question further assumed that the objective of the transfer was to influence the policy and actions of a foreign government while not publicly disclosing the American role in exerting that influence. Under these assumed facts, I believe that a finding under the Hughes-Ryan Amendment would be required.

The so-called Hughes-Ryan Amendment, section 662 of the Foreign Assistance Act, (codified as amended at 22 U.S.C. 2422), provides in its present form:

> No funds appropriated under the authority of this chapter or any other Act may be expended by or on behalf of the Central Intelligence Agency for operations in foreign countries, other than activities intended solely for obtaining necessary intelligence, unless and until the President finds that each such operation is important to the national security of the United States. Each such operation shall be considered a significant anticipated intelligence activity for the purpose of section 413 of title 50 [i.e. section 501 of the National Security Act].

The arms transfer you describe would constitute an "operation in a foreign country," the kind of situation at which the Hughes-Ryan Amendment was apparently aimed. Assuming the accuracy of the facts outlined above, and assuming further that intelligence gathering was not the sole objective of the operation, I believe that such CIA assistance in transferring the arms would require a prior finding by the President that the operation was "important to the national security of the United States."

I am aware of statements that CIA personnel did not fully understand or did not have full information concerning the nature of the operation at the time the agency was asked for its assistance. If the operation was described to CIA personnel in terms that made Hughes-Ryan seem inapplicable, that would have a bearing on whether the CIA could be held responsible for the lack of a presidential finding. Moreover, nothing in this letter should be read as implying that a Hughes-Ryan finding would be required for every single foreign operation that is not strictly intended solely for obtaining necessary intelligence. Nor do I intend to imply that every form of CIA assistance to another agency, no matter how peripheral or indirect, would require a Hughes-Ryan finding merely because the other agency was engaged in a covert operation.

Please let me know if I can be of further assistance.

Sincerely yours,

*Edwin Meese III*

EDWIN MEESE III
Attorney General

## PRESIDENT'S SPECIAL REVIEW BOARD STAFF

BRAITHWAITE, Karl
Analyst

Executive Assistant Director,
Los Alamos National Laboratory

BOWEN, Patricia
Secretary

Department of Defense

BRUH, Brian M.
Chief Investigator

Director, Office of Criminal
Investigations, Internal Revenue Service

COON, Donna M.
Secretary

Department of Defense

DAWSON, Rhett
Director

Partner, McNair Law Firm

HADLEY, Stephen
Counsel

Partner, Shea & Gardner

HETU, Herbert E.
Counselor for Public Affairs

Senior Vice President,
Hill and Knowlton, Inc.

HOWLAND, Dorrance P.
Security Officer

Department of Defense

KEMPISTY, Raymond P.
Deputy Counselor for
Public Affairs

Navy Broadcasting Service

KOVAR, Jeffrey O.
Attorney

Office of the Legal Adviser,
Department of State

KOWAL, John F.
Administrative Officer

Army Protocol Office

KREUZER, Roger Lee
Investigator

Department of Defense

KREIG, Kenneth J.
Analyst

Office of the Secretary of Defense

MARKOFF, Michele G.
Analyst

Executive Secretary, Strategic Arms
Reduction Talks, Department of State

McFADDEN, W. Clark, II
General Counsel

Partner, Dewey, Ballantine, Bushby,
Palmer and Wood

NAGY, Helen S.
Secretary

Department of State

OLSZEWSKI, Margaret L.
Secretary

Department of Defense

ROSTOW, Nicholas
Counsel

Special Assistant to the Legal
Adviser, Department of State

RUSSELL, Michael S.
Investigator

Special Agent, Bureau of Alcohol,
Tobacco, and Firearms

ST. JOHN, Dennis M.
Analyst

Department of Defense

SWANSON, E. Jane
Executive Secretary

Central Intelligence Agency

WILKENS, Katherine
Analyst

Department of State

YANAGIDA, Joy
Attorney

Office of the Legal Adviser,
Department of State

### CONSULTANT TO THE BOARD

MURRAY, Robert J.

Harvard University

# Footnotes

## Part I

## Introduction

1. See Appendix A, Executive Order No. 12575.

2. A list of those case studies is contained in Appendix E.

3. A list of the witnesses interviewed by the Board is contained in Appendix F.

## Part III

## Arms Transfers to Iran, Diversion, and Support for the Contras

1. The correspondence to the President from the Board's Chairman and the reply, on his behalf, of White House Counsel Peter Wallison, are at Appendix G.

2. The "PROF" system, The Professional Office System, is an interoffice mail system run through an IBM main frame computer and managed by the White House Communications Agency for the NSC. All NSC officers have personal passwords which enable them to send and receive messages to each other from terminals at their desks.

3. On August 27, 1986, a new section was added to the Arms Export Control Act which prohibited the export of arms to countries which the Secretary of State has determined support acts of international terrorism. Such a determination was in effect at that time for Iran.

4. The acronym "TOW" stands for tube-launched, optically-tracked, wire-guided missile. It is a man-portable anti-tank missile. A "HAWK" is a type of ground-launched, anti-aircraft missile.

5. The financing of these and other arms transactions discussed in this

Part III is described in detail in the charts annexed to the end of Appendix B.

6. Section 662 of the Foreign Assistance Act, the so-called Hughes-Ryan Amendment, prohibits covert operations by the CIA unless and until the President "finds such operation is important to the national security of the United States."

7. In October, 1985, the United States obtained reliable evidence that William Buckley had died the preceding June.

8. This appears to be the plan discussed at the meeting on December 7, 1985.

9. The financing of this and the other transactions involved in the arms sale initiative is covered in the charts annexed to the end of Appendix B.

10. The Board has found no evidence that would give any credence to this assumption.

11. This memorandum also contained a reference to the diversion of funds to the Contras, discussed in Section B of this Part III.

12. Mr. McDaniel became Executive Secretary of the NSC in February, 1986. Though uninvolved in both the policy and implementation of the Iran initiative, Mr. McDaniel accompanied VADM Poindexter to his morning briefings of the President as a note taker.

13. This excludes two and possibly three dual-national U.S. citizens seized during this period.

14. Charts describing the various arms sales transactions involved in the initiative are annexed to Appendix B.

15. We have no information linking the activities described herein as "Project Democracy" with the National Endowment for Democracy (NED). The latter was created in 1983 by Congressional act and is funded by legislation. Its purpose is to strengthen democratic institutions around the world through private, non-governmental efforts. NED grew out of an earlier Administration public initiative to promote democracy around the world, which came to be known as "Project Democracy". It appears that North later adopted the term to refer to his own covert operations network. We believe this is the only link between the NED and North's activities.

## Part IV

# What Was Wrong

1. The issue of legal advice to the NSC staff is treated in more detail in Part V of this report.

2. It may be possible to authorize transfers by another country under the Arms Export Control Act without obtaining the President's consent. As a practical matter, however, the legal requirements may not differ significantly. For example, section 614(2) permits the President to waive the requirements of the Act. But this waiver authority may not be exercised unless it is determined that the international arms sales are "vital to the national security interests of the United States." Moreover, before granting a waiver, the President must consult with and provide written justification to the foreign affairs and appropriations committees of the Congress. 22 U.S.C. 2374(3).

3. A copy of the letter is set forth in Appendix H.

4. Apparently no determination was made at the time as to the legality of these activities even though serious concerns about legality were expressed by the Deputy Director of CIA, a Presidential finding was sought by CIA officials before any further CIA activities in support of the Iran initiative were undertaken, and the CIA counsel, Mr. Stanley Sporkin, advised that as a matter of prudence any new finding should seek to ratify the prior CIA activities.

5. See Appendix D.

## Part V

# Recommendations

1. As discussed in more detail in Part II, the statutory members of the National Security Council are the President, Vice President, Secretary of State, and Secretary of Defense. By the phrase "National Security Council principals" or "NSC principals," the Board generally means those four statutory members plus the Director of Central Intelligence and the Chairman of the Joint Chiefs of Staff.

# The Iran/Contra Affair: A Narrative

1. An unattributed and undated note analysed meetings involving Hashemi, Shackley, and Iranians at about this time and in March 1985, when the same topics noted by Shackley were discussed. This note added that "[w]e determined that the Iranan [sic] side was only interesed [sic] in money."

Ledeen told the Board that Ghorbanifar had tried for some time to establish contact with the United States. "[H]aving failed to reach us at the front door, he went around to the side door." Shackley transmitted his report to General Walters. (Ledeen (1) 41–42) Ledeen and Shackley separately told the Board that, in May 1985, Shackley told Ledeen that he had no response from Walters. In June 1985, he gave the report, together with an update, to Ledeen who, without reading it, he said, passed it to North with the report "that Shackley had had a contact with an Iranian who had said he thought he could ransom Buckley." (Ledeen (1) 43); Ledeen (2) 2–6; Shackley 13–24)

2. Ledeen told the Board that McFarlane approved all his trips, except for his vacation in Israel in July–August 1985, and the NSC paid his expenses. Ledeen said he considered himself an employee of the United States while on these trips, and made clear to his interlocutors that he had no authority to negotiate, but would "report fully and accurately everything that transpired in these discussions and that I would, if asked, report and communicate fully and accurately back to them whatever decisions were made in Washington." (Ledeen T-15)

3. Apparently Ledeen thought he could make the trip without Ambassador Lewis finding out about it. McFarlane doubted it was possible. (McFarlane PROF note to Fortier, 4/9/85, 12:45:22)

4. On May 13, 1985, Fortier informed Poindexter that "[w]e have a draft [of the NSDD?]. I asked Howard and Steve [Rosen] to rework it. I will give you a copy of what we have and of the suggestions I gave them on how it could [be] improved. . . . We have also done a lot of additional work on outlining requirements for the SNIE." (Fortier PROF note to Poindexter, 5/13/85, 18:12:20)

5. Roy Furmark, an associate of the Saudi businessman Adnan Khashoggi, told the Board that he met Ghorbanifar in January 1985, and subsequently introduced him to Khashoggi. He recalled that Ghorbanifar and Khashoggi had a number of conversations about Middle Eastern politics. (Furmark 3) Ghorbanifar and Khashoggi had a number of meetings starting in January 1985. Khashoggi reported Ghorbanifar's views on Iranian politics to McFarlane in a long memorandum on July 1. (*Id.;* Ghorbanifar 37–38)

6. Perhaps a reference to Ghorbanifar's suggestion that the hostages be ransomed for cash in a disguised transaction using himself as middleman. See *supra* p. B 3.

7. In his first interview, Ledeen told the Board that he made a second trip to Israel at the end of May to meet with Gazit to find out what the Israelis knew about the Iranian situation. (Ledeen (1) 13, 14–16) In his second interview, Ledeen reported that, although he thought he had made two trips to Israel in May, his passport and other records do not corroborate his memory. He concluded that he did not return to Israel until July 1985. (Ledeen (2) 15)

8. Documentary evidence suggests that the private source of these funds was H. Ross Perot. On August 6, North noted that Perot had called with the news that an NBC reporter had asked him to confirm that he had donated $2 million to obtain the release of hostages. ("6 Aug," note in North's handwriting)

9. In November 1986, the NSC staff prepared a number of chronologies. The two fullest, entitled "U.S./Iranian Contacts and the American Hostages," bear the designations "11/17/86 2000 (Maximum Version)" ("Maximum Version") and "11/20/86 2000 (Historical Chronology)" ("Historical Chronology"). The Maximum Version notes that "U.S. intelligence reports indicate that Majlis Speaker Rafsanjani, who was travelling in the mid-east at the time, and Iranian Foreign Minister Velayati both intervened with the captors [to secure the release]. Rafsanjani, in his speech on November 4, 1986, for the first time publicly acknowledged his role in this matter."

10. This "emissary" apparently was Schwimmer. A note from McFarlane's secretary, dated July 11, 1985, contained the following:

JMP [Poindexter] talked with Michael Ledeen this morning about an urgent message from Peres for McFarlane which Al Schwimmer, a Jewish-American who provides lots of money to Peres, wants to deliver to RCM [McFarlane].

McFarlane's secretary reported that Ledeen had lunch with Schwimmer on July 11 and left the following message for McFarlane:

"It is indeed a message from Prime Minister of Israel; it is a follow-on to the private conversation he had last week when David Kimche was here. It is extremely urgent and extremely sensitive and it regards the matter he told David he was going to raise with the President. The situation has fundamentally changed for the better and that I must explain to him because it will affect his decision. It is very important. It won't keep more than a day or two but could keep until Saturday morning. This is the real thing and it is just wonderful news."

McFarlane indicated on this note that he would see Ledeen Saturday, July 13. McFarlane's desk calendar confirms this meeting. McFarlane told the Board he supposed the "emissary" was Schwimmer, that he did not meet him, and that he probably received Schwimmer's message from Ledeen. (McFarlane (2) 4) On July 13, the President underwent his cancer operation.

11. This reference to political "lines" in Iran and to information from Iranians listing members of the "lines" with their political preferences is consistent with a document, dated February 5, 1985, prepared by, or with the assistance of, Ghorbanifar, (Ghorbanifar 52), which Khashoggi sent McFarlane on July 1, 1985.

12. In the course of a long description of the origins of the November 1986 chronologies, McFarlane said that motives for them changed during the process. He said that, at the beginning (November 3, 1986), Poindexter's actions reflected his concern for the hostages and hope that others than Jacobsen would be released. (McFarlane (3) 42) Later, around November 18 when McFarlane was asked to lend a hand, the drafting group's

> principal objective, probably the primary objective, was to describe a sequence of events that would distance the President from the initial approval of the Iran arms sale, distance him from it to blur his association with it.
>
> The November 18 chronology, which I indeed helped prepare, was not a full and completely accurate account of those events, but rather this effort to blur and leave ambiguous the President's role. The language was intended, I would say, to convey the impression that the United States had not expressly authorized the sale either [of] arms directly from the United States or by the Israelis on behalf of the United States, but, second, to preserve the ability to say that if Israel were to make such sales that they could expect to purchase replacement items from the United States.
>
> And I think that is an accurate reflection of how that is cast. Now it was done as a briefing memo to be used by people who would brief the President prior to the next day's press conference, and in my judgement expected to go through a number of iterations before it reached that point. But that is my opinion of the climate in which that session occurred and the intent of its outcome.
>
> General Scowcroft: To put it baldly, could one say that the intent of this was in a sense to put the burden on the Israelis? We didn't approve it, they went off and did it—to soften that by the comment about replenishment?
>
> In other words, if you're going to say that the President didn't authorize it, only two things can happen—that you told the Israelis to do it on their own, or that the Israelis did it on their own.
>
> Mr. McFarlane: Well, I think your portrayal of it as you originally cast it is an accurate description. It was an intent to give the impression that Israel had taken the action.
>
> Mr. Dawson: Why did Poindexter, though, at that point focus in on trying to distance the President from the prior approval in advance

of the Israeli shipments? Why was that, even at that juncture, so important an issue?

Mr. McFarlane: Well, bear in mind I think this is an important part of it, that before this ever occurred he had already himself on the record acknowledged that the President did approve in advance, and that is in the White House transcripts. Don Regan did, too.

Mr. Dawson: You're referring there to the backgrounders that Poindexter and Regan have in advance of the November 18——

Mr. McFarlane: I believe that's right.

Mr. Dawson: And would you also add to that that the President had already denied prior approval? I mean, was that also something else which you would put into the context of that?

Mr. McFarlane: Well, it is difficult to harmonize those positions. That is clear. But the President's position, which I think did misrepresent things—I'm not sure timing-wise which statement you are talking about.

Mr. Dawson: Well, you had said earlier——

Mr. McFarlane: Yes, and those remarks were cast at a time when they were still relying or mostly on the hope that there were still hostages that were going to come out.

Mr. Dawson: This is right after the public disclosure?

Mr. McFarlane: Yes.

(Historical Chronology 5. *Cf.* CIA/IG Chronology 3)

13. According to the "Maximum Version,"
[o]n August 22, 1985, the U.S., through the U.S. citizen intermediary [Ledeen, whom the Maximum Version identified by name and described as "a private American citizen"], acquiesced in an Israeli delivery of military supplies (508 TOWs) to Tehran. We were subsequently informed that the delivery had taken place at the end of August, though we were not aware of the shipment at the time it was made. U.S. acquiescence in this Israeli operation was based on a decision at the highest level to exploit existing Israeli channels with Tehran in an effort to establish an American strategic dialogue with the Iranian government.
(Maximum Version at 4)

14. Ledeen told the Board that he thought this episode marked the first time North heard about the program. (Ledeen (1) 46; Ledeen (2) 74)

15. The original distribution list provided included Vice Admiral Moreau of the JCS staff, not Secretary Weinberger. When the Secretary saw an intelligence report pertaining to this program in the fall of 1985, he insisted that he receive all such documents. His military assistant, General Powell, reported that "the White House told [the releasing agency] that those [reports] were not to be distributed to anybody except the White House." (Weinberger 8)

528

16. The Historical Chronology contains the following paragraph, not contained in the Maximum Version:

In late September, we learned that the Israelis had transferred 508 TOW missiles to Iran and that this shipment had taken place in late August. [Handwritten in the margin: "30 Aug?"] The Israelis told us that they undertook the action, despite our objections, because they believed it to be in their strategic interests. The Israelis managed this entire operation, to include delivery arrangements, funding, and transportation. After discussing this matter with the President, it was decided not to expose this Israeli delivery because we wanted to retain the option of exploiting the existing Israeli channel with Tehran in our own effort to establish a strategic dialogue with the Iranian government. The total value of the 508 TOWs shipped by Israel was estimated to be less than $2 million.

17. In a memorandum, dated December 5, 1985, North provided still a different account of the origins of Iran arms transactions. He wrote that "[s]everal months ago" an agent involved in shipping material to the Contras saw U.S. military equipment in a Lisbon warehouse, which inquiries identified as Israeli equipment being shipped to Iran by a private company.

A "high-level Israeli official" explained that the weapons were being sent to Iran in exchange for Iranian Jews, and that because private intermediaries were used, the transaction was not a technical violation of United States arms export control laws. The Israelis hoped the arms sales would enhance "the credibility of moderate elements in the Iranian army" who might become powerful enough to establish a more reasonable Iranian government than presently existed; prevent the collapse of Iran in the war with Iraq; and extricate Jews from Iran.

In early September, in order that we not take action to terminate the arms sales, the Israelis proposed that this process be used as leverage to recover the American citizens held hostage in Lebanon. It was decided to test the validity of this proposal and on September 14, the Israelis, using chartered aircraft, delivered 500 TOW missiles to Tabriz, Iran. Prior to commencing this operation, we committed to the Israelis that we would sell them replacements for the items they sold and delivered to Iran. Two days later Reverend Benjamin Weir was released.

("Special Project re Iran," 12/5/85)

18. Whereas Furmark told the Board that he introduced Ghorbanifar to Khashoggi in January 1985, (Furmark 3), George Cave, who had been stationed in Tehran before the overthrow of the Shah and who had been responsible for terminating the CIA's relationship with Ghorbanifar in 1983, told the Board that, contrary to reports he had seen, Ghorbanifar had known Khashoggi for years. (Cave 44)

19. Ledeen told the Board that McFarlane did not tell him that North was to be more involved. (Ledeen (1) 51) Bernard McMahon, Staff

Director of the Senate Select Committee on Intelligence, said that Ledeen testified that North told him in September 1985 that "McFarlane has told me I'm supposed to now handle all the operational aspects of this, and McFarlane has no knowledge, A, that Ledeen is doing anything, much less that North has taken over what he is doing." (B. McMahon 10)

20. According to both the Maximum Version and the Historical Chronology, this announcement was false. Iranians with whom CIA and NSC staff personnel met in the following months, and Jenco and Jacobsen, two hostages released later, reported that Buckley probably died on June 3, 1985, of "pneumonia-like symptoms." (Maximum Version 5; Historical Chronology 6)

21. According to North's office calendar, North, McFarlane, and Kimche met on November 9, 1985.

22. The Maximum Version and Historical Chronologies provide different accounts of the origins of the November 1985 HAWK shipment. According to the Maximum Version:

In late November 1985, the Israelis, responding to urgent entreaties from the Iranians, provided 18 basic HAWK missiles to Iran in order to improve the static defenses around Tehran. The Israeli delivery of HAWK missiles raised U.S. concerns that we could well be creating misunderstandings in Tehran and thereby jeopardizing our objective of arranging a direct meeting with high-level Iranian officials. These missiles were subsequently returned to Israel in February 1986, with U.S. assistance.
(Maximum Version 5)

The Historical Chronology states:

In mid-November, the Israelis, through a senior officer in the Foreign Minister's office (Kimche), indicated that the Government of Israel was convinced that they were nearing a breakthrough with Iran on a high-level dialogue. The Israeli contacted a U.S. official (North) and asked for the name of a European-based airline which could discreetly transit to Iran for the purpose of delivering passengers and cargo. He specifically noted that neither a U.S. carrier nor an Israeli affiliated carrier could be used. We were assured, at the time, that the Israelis were going to "try oil drilling spare parts as an incentive," since we had expressed so much displeasure over the earlier TOW shipment. The name of [a CIA proprietary airline] was passed to the Israeli, who subsequently had the aircraft chartered through normal commercial contract for a flight from Tel Aviv to Tabriz, Iran, on November 25, 1985. The Israelis were unwitting of the CIA's involvement in the airline and the airline was paid at the normal commercial charter rate (approximately $127,700). The airline personel [sic] were also unwitting of the cargo they carried.
(Historical Chronology 6)

23. On November 26, McFarlane wrote North that he was "inclined

530

to think that we should bring this operation into the NSC and take Mike [Ledeen] out of it but will await John's [Poindexter] thoughts. No further communications to Mike on this until I have thought it through. Just tell him that I am thinking about it." (McFarlane PROF note to North, 11/26/85, 12:57:29)

24. Secretary Shultz testified that, on December 6, Poindexter told him that the transfer " 'misfired' when Iran had rejected the shipment as 'too old—1979 markings'." (Shultz, 12/86, 15; 1/87, 26)

25. Ghorbanifar told the Board that this fiasco caused him to explode with rage and anxiety at what he and Ledeen agreed was an example of Israeli incompetence. (Ghorbanifar 117–21)

26. At this time, Major General Menachem Meron was Director General of the Israeli Ministry of Defense.

27. Armitage had lunch with North in late November, after seeing reports that someone in the White House was meeting with Iranians. North acknowledged meeting Iranians in Europe, and Armitage
said to him, I don't think my boss knows anything about this. I doubt that Secretary of State Shultz knows anything about [this]. I think your ass is way out on a limb and you best get all the elephants together to discuss the issue.
Ollie was, I think, a little shocked that I was so strong about the necessity of getting everybody together.
(Armitage 4–5) Ambassador Oakley, the Near East and South Asia bureau at the State Department, told the Board that he and Under Secretary of State for Political Affairs Michael Armacost forced an NSPG meeting to be held at this time. (Oakley 4)

28. The Maximum Version's account of this part of the conversation reads: "Mr. McFarlane made clear that a Western dialogue with Iran would be precluded unless Iran was willing to use its influence to achieve the release of Western hostages in Beirut. He also made clear that we could not and would not engage in trading arms for hostages." (Maximum Version at 5)
The Historical Chronology account reads: "At this meeting, Mr. McFarlane, as instructed by the President, stated that: . . . —the U.S. could under no circumstances transfer arms to Iran in exchange for hostages." (Historically Chronology at 7)
On November 23, 1986, North told the Attorney General, W. Bradford Reynolds, Charles J. Cooper, and John Richardson, that McFarlane told Kimche during these meetings that the transaction could not be seen to be an exchange of arms for hostages. (Reynolds notes) (McFarlane (1) 27–28)

29. According to the NSC "Chronology of Events: U.S.-Iran Dialogue," dated 11/20/86, Ghorbanifar came to the United States on December 22 for meetings with American officials. This date is consistent with a suggestion in a memorandum from the Chief of the CIA's

Near East Directorate to the Director of Central Intelligence. *See* pp. *et seq. infra.* Ghorbanifar told the Board only that he visited Washington in December 1985. (Ghorbanifar 127)

30. George Cave and C/NE/I told the Board that Cave prepared the questions for the examination. (Cave 3-5; C/NE (2) 76)

31. North told the Attorney General's team in November 1986 that, in January 1986, Nir suggested that the Israelis transfer funds from an account containing residual funds from the arms transfers to Iran and pay such funds into an account used by the Nicaraguan Contras. (Reynolds notes; Richardson notes)

32. North's first draft Finding was dated January 3, 1986. The accompanying memorandum is undated. The changes from the first drafts are indicated below by square brackets. When the changes were material, the original language is reproduced in footnotes.

33. The first draft read: "the U.S. and Israel."

34. The first draft contained the following sentence instead of the two sentences in this version: "The Israelis are obviously very concerned that the course of the Iran-Iraq war and the potential for further radicalization in Iran pose a significant threat to the security of Israel."

35. The first draft contained the following last sentence of this paragraph: "Since the Israeli sales are technically a violation of our Arms Export Control Act embargo for Iran, a Presidential Covert Action Finding is required in order for us to allow the Israeli sales to proceed and for our subsequent replenishment sales.

36. The original opening sentence read: "The Israelis and the Iranians with whom they are in contact agree that the continued holding of the five American hostages in Beirut will be immediately solved through commencement of this action."

37. The word "privately" appeared here in the first draft.

38. The original sentence read: "If, based on their input, you decide to proceed, the Finding should be signed and held."

39. Point (3) did not appear in the first draft. According to Sporkin this language was added after a meeting on January 5 between Sporkin, North, and Director Casey at the Director's house. (Sporkin 22–23)

40. In response to a question, Regan said that he, the President, the Vice President, Poindexter, and Rodney McDaniel, Executive Secretary of the NSC, attended this briefing. According to the Presidential Diary, Fortier, not McDaniel, attended. (Jones to Stephens, 1/24/87) Regan remembered this fact, and subsequently corrected himself. (Regan 42)

41. According to the CIA Inspector General, the Secretary of Defense, the Attorney General, the Director of Central Intelligence, and Poindexter met and discussed delaying Congressional notification. (CIA/IG Chronology 15) The Secretary of Defense did not remember the meeting. (Weinberger 56) The Attorney General recalled that Sporkin attended the January 16 meeting in Poindexter's office. Discussion focused on the law regarding arms exports and notice to Congress. (Meese 15-20)

Possibly in preparation for this meeting, the CIA General Counsel's Office prepared the following talking points for the Director of Central Intelligence:

"The Israelis are moving ahead on their Tow for Hostage deal with the Iranians. You recall that in Sporkin's legal analysis there were two options: One for DoD to do it directly with the Israelis, the other to do it through CIA. Sporkin feels that the most defensible way to do it from a legal standpoint is through CIA. We prefer keeping CIA out of the execution even though a Presidential Finding would authorize the way Defense would have to handle the transactions.

"Under this option the idea was that the Israelis would buy the improved version of the TOWs and ship the basic TOWs they now have to the Israelis [sic]. The Israelis would then replace those basic TOWs by buying the improved version. Unfortunately, there is not enough money available to do this. The Iranians have placed $22 million in an account in Switzerland. This is enough for the basic TOWs but for the Israelis to buy the improved version would cost about $44 million.

"Therefore, they want to use the second option under which CIA would buy 4,000 basic TOWs from DoD for $21 million. As far as Defense is concerned these purchases would be purchased in general for CIA uses for assistance in [country names deleted] and other purposes. The money for the Iranian account would be transferred to the Israelis. The Israelis would transfer that money to a CIA account to pay for this purchase, provide the TOWs from DoD, the shippers would move the TOWs to the Israelis who would then move them on to the Iranians. The Israelis would keep their basic TOWs and the problem of upgrading them to the new TOWs would be handled in the normal DoD Israeli relationship.

"I am told that time is of the essence in getting this done for two reasons: First, the situation in Lebanon is deteriorating so that any delay [sic] we can see in the prospects of getting the hostages out of Lebanon should be avoided. . . ."

42. Probably a reference to General Secord.

43. The CIA Inspector General dated this meeting January 25. (CIA/IG Chronology 18)

44. North's draft recommended that Poindexter privately discuss the subject with the President. There is no evidence that the Memoran-

dum was put into final form. It bears the caption *"PLEASE DESTROY AFTER READING".*

45. According to the Maximum Version and the Historical Chronology, C/NE attended this meeting. (Maximum Version at 5, Historical Chronology at 9) The CIA Inspector General notes that a meeting occurred, but does not mention C/NE. (CIA/IG Chronology 18) C/NE denied that there was a meeting with the Tehran contact on February 15. (C/NE (1) 14) The Maximum Version states that the meeting was in Germany; the Historical Chronology places the meeting in London. The accounts of what was discussed are similar:

—The Iranian intermediary (Ghorbanifar) would deposit funds in an Israeli account.

—The Israelis would transfer funds to a sterile U.S.-controlled account in an overseas bank.

—Using these funds, the CIA would covertly obtain materiel authorized for transfer from U.S. military stocks and transport this to Israel for onward movement to Iran.

Using the procedures stipulated above, funds were deposited in the CIA account in Geneva on February 11, 1986 and on February 14 1,000 TOWs were transported to Israel for prepositioning. The TOWs were off-loaded and placed in a covert Israeli facility. (Maximum Version 6. *Cf.* Historical Chronology 9)

46. This description might fit C/NE.

47. Possibly a reference to video and recording devices requested by C/NE on January 21. (CIA/IG Chronology 16)

48. The Secretary of State recalled that "[o]n January 22, my staff noted reports received about Lieutenant Colonel North. They speculated that perhaps the operation was alive again. But the reports seemed implausible, namely a proposal by Lieutenant Colonel North to seek the help of the Pope and Cardinal O'Connor, and to trade some Shia prisoners held by General Lahad in South Lebanon as Nir had earlier suggested.

"I heard nothing more until February 28, 1986." (Shultz, SRB, 50–51)

49. Ghorbanifar told the Board that one of the 18 HAWK missiles had been test-fired against an Iraqi fighter over Kharg Island. (Ghorbanifar 143)

50. In discussing what he insisted was a meeting in Frankfurt in the first week of February, but which he may have confused with the meeting February 20, Ghorbanifar told the Board that when he heard that Hakim was to attend the meeting, he successfully persuaded the Americans to change the delegation.

I said are you crazy? The Albert Hakim is known to all Iranian intelligence agencies and Iranian authorities, that he works, is operating for CIA. He was acting against Islamic Republic by CIA in

1980 and 1981, in Turkey, in the form of companies performing for making trouble for them in the Turkish border, and so on. They know him. If he comes in, they call this again another trick. So, I don't accept that such a man comes. They call me back in two days and say you are right.
(Ghorbanifar 133)

51. C/NE remembered who attended and that the meeting took place February 19. (C/NE (1) 14) According to the Maximum Version, the meeting occurred February 19–21.

> U.S. and Iranian officials (NSC and CIA) met again in Germany to discuss problems in arranging a meeting among higher-level officials. At this meeting, the U.S. side agreed to provide 1,000 TOWs to Iran as a clear signal of U.S. sincerity. This delivery was commenced on the morning of February 20 and completed in two transits to Tehran on February 21. (Maximum Version 6)

The Historical Chronology states:

> On February 19–21, U.S. (NSC and CIA), Israel; and Iranian officials met in Germany to discuss problems in arranging a meeting among higher-level officials. After coded authorization was received from Washington, the U.S. side agreed to provide 1,000 TOWs to Iran as a clear signal of U.S. sincerity. This delivery was commenced on the morning of February 20 and completed in two transits to Tehran on February 21. Transportation from Israel to Iran was aboard a false flag Israeli aircraft. On the return flight from Iran, these aircraft carried the 18 HAWK [sic] missiles which Israel had sent to Tehran in November 1985 with USG aforeknowledge. [sic] (Historical Chronology 10)

The CIA Inspector General's chronology states:

> *19 February 1986:* C/NE, North, Secord, and Nir meet with Ghorbanifar in Frankfurt. Iranian officials are expected, but do not show.

> *20 or 21 February 1986:* The delivery of 1,000 TOWs from Israel to Iran begins, using a false flag aircraft. (The backload on the return flight from Tehran was the HAWK missiles which had been shipped in November 1985. The Iranians returned them because they were outdated models. The delivery is completed 27 February.)

(CIA/IG Chronology 19)

52. An "old SAVAK-maintained island off the coast of Iran." (C. Allen 15)

53. McFarlane told the Board:

> I left the government and didn't hear anything more on the issue until I had a call from Admiral Poindexter in late April of this year, and he summarized that basically, that the program had been renewed and contacts re-established, and that the Presi-

dent had authorized quite an active dialogue and the transfer of weapons.

And to make a long story short, it wasn't a long conversation. He said: We believe we have an arrangement whereby they would release all of the remaining hostages, and they have agreed to start this exchange on political matters, and the President wants to know, will you undertake that political exchange.

\* \* \*

[Between the date that he reported on his December trip and Poindexter's call in April, McFarlane's contact with the Iranian question amounted to] one or two phone calls that dealt with other matters, either Lieutenant Colonel North, just kind of in a social context, but just by way of mentioning how things were going in life and professionally and so forth, I remember either it was him or it was Admiral Poindexter, I don't know saying: By the way, things aren't totally moribund on the Iranian connection; we have some promise there, but without any precision.

(McFarlane (1) 28–29)

54. On February 27, C/NE asked the CIA for alias passports for C/NE, Cave, Secord, and Hakim. On March 3, the passports were provided. Hakim never used his passport, which was returned on May 22. Secord's passport was returned on November 20, 1986. (CIA/IG Chronology 20).

55. In contrast, on February 20, 1986, after Ghorbanifar passed him information on preparations for a number of terrorist attacks, Charles Allen wrote that: "I believe we should move quickly to consolidate our relations with Subject [Ghorbanifar]. Although he exaggerates and manufactures some of his information, he has excellent contacts with Iranian officials in Tehran. He also has interesting contacts with Iranian nationals in Western Europe. I believe we would be remiss unless we begin to work with Subject and evaluate the potential of some of his associates, particularly [names deleted]. I have met [name deleted] and believe that he has excellent potential." (C. Allen, "Discussions with Subject," 2/20/86)

56. Probably a reference to Hakim. Ghorbanifar told the Board that Cave's Farsi was "very, very poor," probably due to disuse. (Ghorbanifar 159)

57. Attached to the copy of these talking points in North's file was the following note in North's handwriting:
   —Probing for foothold
   —access before transition
   —fear of Soviets—left inside
   —Anti Western terrorism
   —Tactical success in near-term could be to our advantage in that it offers opportunity for settlement.
   —People who know

—Shultz
—Weinberger
—Powell
—Koch
—Casey
·[C/NE]
·McMahon
·Allen
·Gates
—RR
—JMP
—Don R[egan].
—Don F [ortier]
—VP
—Peter [Rodman]
—Howard [Teicher].
(Handwritten note. Feb. 1986)

58. Cave said the meeting took place on March 7. (Cave 5) According to North's calendar, travel forms, and subsequent report to McFarlane, it took place on March 8.

59. According to Cave, Nir proposed the meeting "to see what we could salvage" after the meeting with the official from the Iranian PM's office in February. (Cave 5) On March 4, Ghorbanifar called Charles Allen, among other things, to suggest that he establish a " 'continuing relationship' " with Allen and the CIA. (C. Allen, "Conversation with Subject, 4 March 1986," 3/6/86. CIA Docs.)

60. In the same message, North asked McFarlane's advice about an opportunity to return to the Marine Corps. McFarlane replied that the two should discuss it. He added:

Frankly, I would expect the heat from the Hill to become immense on you by summer. Consequently, it strikes me as wise that you leave the White House. At the same time, there will be no one to do all (or even a small part of what) you have done. And if it isn't done, virtually all of the investment of the past five years will go down the drain.

How's this for a self-serving scenario: 1. North leaves the White House in May and takes 30 days leave. 2. July 1st North is assigned as a fellow at the CSIS and (lo and behold) is assigned to McFarlane's office. 3. McFarlane/North continue to work the Iran account as well as to build other clandestine capabilities so much in demand here and there. Just a knee jerk musing.

(McFarlane PROF note to North, 3/10/86, 22:14:24)

61. On March 9, Ghorbanifar called Charles Allen, reporting, among other things, that the Paris meetings had been successful, although additional effort remained. Allen thought Ghorbanifar "seemed un-

usually subdued and less sanguine than in previous conversations."
(C. Allen, "Conversation with Subject," 3/11/86. CIA Docs.)

62. Ghorbanifar went to Tehran on March 13, "at some personal
risk," returning to France on the 17th. (C. Allen, "Conversation with
Subject," 3/12/86. CIA Docs.) On March 20, Ghorbanifar told Allen
he had briefed Nir ("Adam") on his meetings with the Iranian Prime
Minister, Rafsanjani, and Ahmad Khomeini (the Ayatollah's son). He
reported that the Ayatollah remained "very ill"; that the Prime Minister had uncovered Soviet penetration of his office; that he was sending
a report to North, which would include some requirements from the
Iranian military; and that he hoped a meeting of principals could take
place soon. (C. Allen, "Conversation with Subject," 3/21/86)

63. In a series of telephone conversations with Ghorbanifar and Nir,
March 24–April 2, Charles Allen learned that Ghorbanifar was under
pressure in Tehran; that he was passing through a difficult period
financially, but that the Israelis were helping him; that an important
meeting would occur on March 29, at which Khomeini himself would
be informed of the state of play with the United States; and that, after
that meeting, Ghorbanifar had "excellent news" for North. An NSC
consultant reported to Allen that Ghorbanifar was upset in part because his California girlfriend's house had been entered, as had
Furmark's office in New York. Ghorbanifar blamed the CIA. (C. Allen,
Memoranda for the Record, 3/24, 3/28, 3/28, 3/31, 4/2/86)

64. Teicher prepared the draft terms of reference and submitted it to
North and Rodman, "and they worked on it." (Teicher 18) On April
22, a United States Customs operation resulted in the arrest of 17–18
arms dealers, including Ghorbanifar, allegedly violating the embargo
with Iran. Ghorbanifar was held only briefly. (CIA/IG Chronology 22)
On April 25, Charles Allen set forth his own views as to the parties'
desiderata. He thought the Iranians urgently needed weapons;
wanted a source of continuing supply; a favorable end to the Iraq war;
and "re-establishment of their 'rightful place' and spread of fundamentalism," in that order. He noted that the United States refused to
supply HAWK radars, which Iran has demanded, and had imposed a
termination date 2–3 weeks hence if the operation had not succeeded. He thought that, unless the United States were "willing to
sweeten the pot, we can only stand fast and present to them the
appearance that time is on our side and not on theirs. This would
require resolve on our part in the face of possible damage to one or
more hostages." The Israelis could solve the problem of continuing
supply to Iran by the United States committing a sin of omission.
(C. Allen, Working Paper, 4/25/86) Allen sent this paper to North on
April 26. (C. Allen 15; CIA/IG Chronology 22)

65. The NSC staff and CIA officers involved in the initiative learned
at this time that the Iranian official's instructions to Ghorbanifar were
that, if the U.S. did not deliver all the HAWK spares with the arrival of

the U.S. delegation, only one hostage would be released. It was presented to Ghorbanifar as a "take it or leave it" proposition to the U.S.

66. The transaction involving HAWK spare parts in May 1986 covered some 299 items worth $6.5 million. Iran was to have paid $15 million. The financial arrangements followed the pattern established for the February shipment of 1,000 TOWs. Khashoggi raised $15 million from various financiers and deposited the funds in the Lake Resources account on 14 May. CIA's Swiss account was credited with $6.5 million on 16 May to repay the Defense Department. The transaction was not completed. The United States failed to deliver all the spare parts because Iran failed to secure the release of all American hostages being held in Lebanon. In reviewing price lists for what had been provided, Iran discovered a substantial overcharge. By August, Tehran had provided Ghorbanifar with only $8 million to repay Khashoggi, leaving the Saudi $10 million in debt (the balance of the $15 million advanced plus a 20 per cent "costs and financing" markup —in this case $3 million). When the United States decided not to use Ghorbanifar as an intermediary, Khashoggi had little prospect to recover the rest of his money. All he held were unfunded drafts from Ghorbanifar. When Khashoggi attempted, through Roy Furmark, to obtain his money from Lake Resources, he discovered that only $30,000 remained in the Lake account. Another $8.5 million was unaccounted for, leaving the amount for diversion at somewhat just short of $15 million (including $6.3 million unaccounted for from the February transaction). An additional $2 million was unaccounted for after the November 1986 shipment of 500 TOWs.

67. At this time, Poindexter became concerned that North's "operational role" was becoming "too public. From now on," he wrote, "I don't want you to talk to anybody else, including Casey, except me about any of your operational roles. In fact you need to quietly generate a cover story that I have insisted that you stop." (Poindexter PROF note to North, 5/15/86, 21:21:58) North replied on May 15: "Done." (North PROF note to Poindexter, 5/15/86, 21:39:23)

68. An NSPG on aid to the Nicaraguan resistance was held on May 16. North attended.

69. According to both the Maximum Version and Historical Chronology, the President approved the trip on May 15. (Maximum Version 7; Historical Chronology 11) McFarlane told the Board that, in his view,

the President was very moved by the hostage captivity, and that is purely speculation. But I know that that was terribly important to him.
* * *
[The President met with the hostages' families] almost every time he took a trip. I remember one to Dallas, Indianapolis, Chicago, on separate occasions. And there would be a family or two, and they

would come in and he'd meet with them, and it would be a very anguishing kind of a thing.

70. Press guidance prepared covered the release of the hostages, the discovery of the mission to Tehran, and the holding of the delegation hostage. (North to Poindexter, "Hostage Recovery Plan," 5/22/86)

71. According to the CIA Inspector General, during the meetings Ghorbanifar told Cave the price of the weapons quoted to the Iranians was $24.5 million, and asked Cave to say "the price is right" if the Iranians asked. Cave informed North, and together they asked Nir about it. Nir told them "Don't worry, it involves other deals, and that there are enormous expenses in this operation. . . ." Cave had the impression that McFarlane could " 'care less about' the pricing discrepancy." (CIA/IG Chronology 26) (McFarlane (1) 42) C/NE recalled that the spare parts cost the Americans $6.5 million, but that the Iranians were charged between $21 and $24 million (C/NE (1) 10–11)

72. Burghardt wrote [Poindexter] at this time[?]:
I understand that Elliott [Abrams] briefed you today on where this stands ["aid for freedom fighters"]. If we do not get a positive response fairly soon from the Saudis or Brunei, I would advocate moving right away. . . . I can understand the reluctance to incur a debt, but it would be almost a sure thing and we will definately [sic] need the $10 M bridge money. With the House scheduled to take up the issue on the 24th, Senate approval would be after the July 4 recess and the date of delivery keeps fading into the distance.
(Burghardt PROF note to [?Poindexter], reply to note of 6/9/86)

73. Except as indicated, the material between square brackets is in the document as annotated by the CIA. The Board cannot verify the authenticity of the letter. According to the CIA Inspector General, Cave obtained this letter in late July 1986. (CIA/IG Chronology 27) Clair George told the Board that, while Cave began his involvement as an interpreter, he "became a player. . . . I'm afraid he got way out there somewhere and we didn't have a string on him every step of the way." (George 49–50)

74. Supplied.

75. Supplied.

76. Supplied.

77. On July 2, Ghorbanifar told his contact in the Prime Minister's office that the United States thought Iran used the pricing problem as an excuse to cover Iran's inability to obtain the release of another hostage. He said that United States suggested that, if another hostage were released, then the United States immediately would ship the remaining HAWK spare parts.

78. According to the CIA Inspector General:

"[July 7–26]: Allen remains in almost daily contact wit̲h̲ [̲...] telephone. (According to Allen, Nir is clearly alarmed at [̲.̲.̲] direct contact with North and appears to be working feverish̲l̲y̲ with Ghorbanifar and others to free an American hostage.) Nir tells Allen that, according to Ghorbanifar, I/1 is making an effort to secure the release of a hostage. He asks Allen to refrain from informing North since he does not want to raise North's "hopes too high." When Father Jenco is released, North again resumes direct contact with Nir."
(CIA/IG Chronology 27)

79. On June 29, 1986, a column by Jack Anderson and Dale Van Atta in the *Washington Post* stated: "We can reveal that the secret negotiations over arms supply and release of American hostages have involved members of the National Security Council and a former official of the CIA."

80. According to North's desk calendar, North met "Tabatabaie," possibly with Senator Helms, on June 27.

81. North apparently received a copy of this message. He wrote McFarlane: "[t]he bottom line is that this is the direct result of your mission and neither the Syrians nor a non-existent Casey trip had anything to do with it." (North PROF note to McFarlane, 7/29/86, 20:36:04 (reply to note of 7/26/86, 13:51))

82. According to the CIA Inspector General, Charles Allen prepared this memorandum. (CIA/IG Chronology 28)

83. The Maximum Version and the Historical Chronology both state: "On June 10, Majlis Speaker Rafsanjani, in a speech in Tehran made guarded reference to Iranian interest in improved relations with the U.S. On July 26, Father Lawrence Jenco was released in the Bekka Valley and found his way to a Syrian military checkpoint." (Maximum Version 8; Historical Chronology 13)

84. Charles Allen told the Board that he remembered the memorandum as reporting Nir to have talked about

the Israelis initiating, taking the initiative, proposing this, sort of directing this. I think probably overstated my understanding of the situation.

Indeed, I think they were proposing it and pressing it on the United States, but based on my understanding and all the memoranda that I have put together is that Mr. McFarlane saw a real strategic need to pursue this effort.

And also, an ancillary aspect was to solve the hostage problem in order to move to broader relationships.
(C. Allen (2) 13–14)

. The Historical Chronology contains the following summary of events in August:

On August 3, the remaining three pallets (less than 1/2 planeload) of electronic parts for Iranian anti-aircraft defenses (HAWK missile sub-components) arrived in Tehran. As in all flights to/from Iran this delivery was made with an Israeli Air Force aircraft (707) using false flag markings. Timing of the delivery was based on coordination among U.S., Israeli and Iranian officials.

In early August 1986, the contact with the Iranian expatriate [Ghorbanifar] began to focus exclusively on the willingness of the USG to provide military assistance to Iran in exchange for hostages and we sought to establish different channels of communication which would lead us more directly to pragmatic and moderate elements in the Iranian hierarchy. In mid-August, a private American citizen (MGEN Richard Secord, USAF [Ret.]) acting within the purview of the January Covert Action Finding, made contact in Europe with * * * a relative * * * of a senior Iranian official * * *. With the assistance of the CIA, this Iranian was brought covertly to Washington for detailed discussions. We judged this effort to be useful in establishing contact with a close confidant of the man judged to be the most influential and pragmatic political figure in Iran * * *). These discussions reaffirmed the basic objectives of the U.S. in seeking a political dialogue with Tehran. We also provided assessments designed to discourage an Iranian offensive and contribute to an Iranian decision to negotiate an end to the war.

(Historical Chronology 13) The Maximum Version of the delivery of spare parts omits the last two sentences in the first paragraph quoted above. (Maximum Version 8) The Historical Chronology added the following sentence to the second paragraph quoted above, from the Maximum Version (id. at 8–9): "The assessments also detailed the Soviet threat to Iran." (Historical Chronology 13)

Cave told the Board that "the decision to get rid of Ghorbanifar was on our part to clean this up operationally, so that we had better control." (Cave 25)

Furmark told the Board that, when he and Ghorbanifar discussed "the inflated pricing" in August, Ghorbanifar said the money may have gone to the Contras, or the Afghans, or someplace. And he even said—and he said that North told him that now they've passed this bill, if we don't complete this transaction we'll pay you the money back, the $10 million; they passed the Aid to the Contras bill —so Ghorbanifar said, if they never complete the deal we'll still get our money back because now they can, you know.

So that's an inference that the money was used and they'll repay it back.

(Furmark 17)

86. North requested travel orders to go to Frankfurt on August 6. According to the NSC staff Chronology of Events, dated 11/20/86,

the first American contact with [The] relative occurred in London and Madrid on August 10. North wrote McFarlane on October 3 that [the] relative came into contact with us through Dick Secord who met him in Brussels while arranging a pick-up for our friends in a certain resistance movement." (North PROF note to McFarlane, 10/03/86, 22:08:16) North was on leave when the Director of Central Intelligence briefed Poindexter on Cave's meeting, July 25, with Tabatabai in London. Vincent M. Cannistraro of the NSC staff wrote Poindexter that Tabatabai "claims to be a channel to Rasfanjani and has passed the usual message via Cave that the Iranian government wishes to establish a regular channel to the U.S. but is constrained until after the end of the war with Iraq. (We also know that Tabatabai has made contact with some of the Iranian exile groups in Paris—particularly the Ali Amini crowd. His bonafides [sic] as an authentic channel to Rasfanjani, however, have yet to be proven.)" (Cannistraro to Poindexter, 8/13/86)

87. An undated, unsigned note, adds a grace note to Secord's message:

> [The Relative] claims he can be of great assistance in establishing the right relation. The Hague, he claims, is the best avenue.
> NOTE: The report goes into detail regarding the above 3 items.
> E. [Secord's Iranian expatriate agent's] recommendations: Try everything not to lose this man *if* he can not be a representative of [Rafsanjani] he definitely is trainable to be an excellent source in country.
> P.S. [Rafsanjani] participated with Hafezalasad for release of Hostages. The release of the rest is possible.

88. At North's request, on September 2, Charles Allen tipped law enforcement officials of another possible arms transfer to Iran from Houston. Ghorbanifar and Khashoggi were thought to be involved. (C. Allen, Memorandum for the Record, 9/2/86; Earl PROF note to North, 8/28/86, 19:09)

89. In a number of telephone conversations taped by Cave early in September, Cave and the Iranian official talked about the problems associated with what the Iranian official said were 65 "broken" parts. (Transcripts of telephone calls) The confusion over the number of spare parts to be shipped apparently results from the fact that certain of the line items requested included multiple parts. (Army/IG Report)

90. On September 9, Cave informed [the official in the Prime Minister's office] by telephone. Cave informed [him] that Islamic Jihad had seized another hostage. [The Iranian office] said "I know nothing of this. I have no news." (Transcript, 9/10/86) Cave explained that the kidnapping had been undertaken by "Mugniyyah's group." On September 8, Allen had written Poindexter that

[n]o threat from Mughniyah should be considered idle. He is a violent extremist capable of impetuously killing the hostages. Yet he does not operate without constraints, among them:

—*Iran*, which certainly has significant influence over the captors, including Mughniyah. We doubt that Iran wants the hostages disposed of without recompense,

—*other Hezballah leaders*, who probably see in the hostages a valuable lever over the US and France, and an indirect means of deterring the Israeli Defense Forces from air attacks on Hezballah facilities in the Biqa', and

—*his own assessment of his self-interest*, which would likely reflect that the cost of holding the hostages is minimal whereas killing them would run a serious risk US or French retaliation. As for conducting terrorist efforts against the Gulf states, Mughniyah could certainly do that without killing the hostages.

(Allen to Poindexter, 9/8/86, Tab II to North to Poindexter, 9/8/86) Cave told [the Iranian official] that

this matter (Reed) has got to be settled as soon as possible. Please look into it and settle as soon as possible because our boss is very very mad. The boss called me at seven and asked me what was going on, then about an hour ago the islamic jihad [sic] announced that they had taken him hostage. He lkthe [sic] head of a college in Beirut, his name is Reed.

[The Iranian official]. Yes.

S[am O'neil]. You look into this matter, and I will call you this afternoon at about 8 your time, okay? Will you be at home?

[The Iranian officials]. Yes, yes, yes. (very dejected).

(Transcript, 9/9/86) Mughniyah's brother-in-law was one of the Da' Wa prisoners in Kuwait.

91. On September 25, after Craig Coy, a member of the NSC staff and former executive assistant to Admiral Holloway, Executive Director of the Vice President's Task Force on Terrorism, spoke to Ambassador Bremer about the editorial, North sent the editorial to Bremer with instructions to broadcast it on September 26 and 27. (North to Bremer, 9/25/86 Coy 3–4)

92. "'And the Scripture, forseeing that God would justify the Gentiles by faith, preached the gospel beforehand to Abraham, saying, 'All the nations shall be blessed in you.' Galatians 3:8' Ronald Reagan Oct. 3, 1986" The President told the Board that he did inscribe the Bible because VADM Poindexter told him this was a favorite passage with one of the people with whom the U.S. was dealing in Iran. The President said he made the inscription to show the recipient that he was "getting through."

93. The day North left, an aircraft with Eugene Hasenfus aboard, crashed in Nicaragua. Robert Earl, who shared an office with North, reported to Poindexter:

"[O]ne of the Democracy Inc aircraft apparently went down on a resupply mission to FDN forces in the north. It is overdue from its mission, and no radio contact was received. It is currently unknown where or why the aircraft went down, but [third country] assets are discreetly organizing a SAR effort over international waters & friendly territory portions of the route. Three Americans and one Nicaraguan national aboard. I will keep you advised of details as I get them."

(Earl PROF note to Poindexter, 10/06/86, 11:49:16)

William Perry, an NSC staff member who worked on Latin America, wrote Poindexter on October 7:

Plane down in Nicaragua and survivor of crash had no USG connection according to CIA and DIA. This tracks with Elliott's denial and has been passed on to Dan Howard.

FYI, and not for release, the flight originated in El Salvador and is probably tied in with present U.S. assistance to the Contras. Survivor could testify to this type of connection. . . .

(Perry PROF note to Poindexter, 10/7/86, 12:42)

North wrote McFarlane on October 12:

We urgently need to find a high powered lawyer and benefactor who can raise a legal defense for Hassenfus [sic] in Managua. If we can find such persons we can not only hold Gene and Sally Hassenfus together (i.e., on our side, not pawns of the Sandinista propaganda machine) but can make some significant headway of our own in counter-attacking in the media. Obviously, there is the added benefit of being able to do something substantive in the legal system to defend this young man. I know that this is a tall order and that many U.S. lawyers will not want to step up to this task, but for the man (or woman) who does, there will be a fair bite of history made in the next few weeks. There will, no doubt, be a show trial of some kind launched and unless we have an overt, competent legal defense, Hassenfus will become nothing but a tool in their hands—none of which is in our interests, or his. By Tuesday, a Swiss lawyer, retained by Corporate Air Services, should be in Managua. We should not rely on this person to represent the whole case since he is supported by covert means. We would be far better off if we had an overt mechanism here in the States which represented USG/Hassenfus' interests, and who would not have to respond to questions regarding the origins of Corporate Air Services, Inc. (CASI), or its other ongoing activities. The CASI lawyer is being instructed to cooperate fully w/ this U.S. Attorney, whoever he/she may be. Have also located approx. $100K from a donor who does not care if this contribution becomes known (though the donor has done things in the past to keep CASI in operation—a fact which need not become known). Can you help? If need be, I can meet w/ you/others tomorrow or Tues. [October 13 or 14] Believe this to be a matter of great urgency to hold things together. Unfortunately RR

was briefed that this plan was being contemplated before he left for Iceland and am concerned that along about Wednesday when people begin to think of things other than meetings in cold places, he will remember this and nothing will have been done. Any thoughts wd be much appreciated. Elliott Abrams willing to sit-in any time after Yom Kippur fast is finished tomorrow night. Pls Advise.
(North PROF note to McFarlane, 10/12/86, 16:33:11)

94. The NSC staff chronologies tell the following tale for the summer and fall of 1986 (Maximum Version 9; Historical Chronology 13–14. Where the Historical Chronology differs from the Maximum Version, this fact is indicated by square brackets.):

Through August, September, and October 1986, numerous additional meetings were held in Europe between U.S. representatives and the new and Iranian contacts [sic]. During the October 26, 1986 meeting in Frankfurt, Germany, the U.S. side, as in the past, insisted that the release of the hostages was a prerequisite to any progress. [The Relative] urged that we take a more active role in support for the Afghan resistance . . . The Iranians also proffered, and the U.S. accepted, the offer of a Soviet T-72 tank captured from Iraq. [The Iranians have also offered to provide a copy of the 400 page interrogation of William Buckley.] At this meeting, [the Relative] stated that there was a "very good chance that another American or two would be [f]reed soon." On October 29, with U.S. acquiescence, Israel provided Iran with an additional increment (500 TOW missiles) of these defensive weapons. [On October 29, with U.S. acquiescence, Israel provided Iran with an additional increment of defensive weapons (500 TOW missiles).]

Late on October 31, [the Relative] called the U.S. citizen (Hakim) tasked to maintain contact and advised that Iran had "exercised its influence with the Lebanese" in order to obtain the release of American—David Jacobsen—and an uncertain number of French hostages. He further noted that this was part of the purpose of the Iranian Foreign Minister's visit to Syria. [The Relative] stated that the situation in Tehran, as well as Iranian influence over Hezballah were both deteriorating; . . . On November 2, David Jacobsen was driven to a point near the old American Embassy compound in West Beirut. The U.S. Embassy in East Beirut immediately dispatched an embassy officer to West Beirut to pick up Mr. Jacobsen. This operation is about to spin out of control from an operational security point of view, and I will say right now—and I've said it to the Congress in depth—my concerns were not on illegal diversion of funds to the contras. That was about the farthest from my mind. Here was an intiative that had been going on for about 14 months and was about to spin out of control, and no one seemed to be realizing what was occurring.

95. McFarlane again expressed concern about North. He wrote Poin-

dexter on October 10: "At some point I would like to raise Ollie's situation with you. I really think he has become every Democrat's best target and as hard as it would be to lose him, it will serve your and his long term interest to send him back to the Corps". (McFarlane PROF note to Poindexter, 10/10/86, 15:10:42)

96. North also expressed frustration over the investigation of Secord's air line, Southern Air Transport. *(Id.)*

# Charts and Narratives

1. Monies are actually transferred to an Iranian Government account prior to release to Ghorbanifar. This intermediate step has been dropped for purposes of simplification.

2. Two deposits were made to the same Iranian account at Credit Suisse used to finance the two earlier TOW purchases. The third deposit was to an Iranian account at a different Swiss bank. The $24.72 million transfer apparently was to cover the purchase of 120 HAWK missiles. The Board has no evidence to conclude for what purpose the other two deposits were intended.

3. The eighteenth missile was test-fired without success at an Iraqi fighter over Kharg Island.

4. The Board concludes that the difference between this transfer and the $12 million repaid Khashoggi was covered by the $5 million withheld by Israel pending return of the HAWK missiles.

5. There is some discrepency surrounding these dates. The September 26, 1986, date is contained in a PROF note from North to Poindexter which also contains the $7 million figure. The CIA I/G report, relying on George Cave, states that the relative brought a check for $4 million with him to the late October meetings in Frankfurt. Confronted with this inconsistency, the Board has chosen to rely on the contemporaneous account of LtCol North.

547

## Appendix C

# The NSC Staff and the Contras

1. A narrower but substantively similar provision was incorporated the next day into the Intelligence Authorization Act for Fiscal Year 1985. A series of continuing resolutions extended the prohibition through December 19, 1985.

2. The IOB did not provide a copy of this document in response to the Board's request for all memoranda "providing legal advice to the NSC staff in 1985 and 1986." The IOB did provide two other memoranda to the Board dated May 19, 1986 and May 29, 1986, respectively, that address allegations: (a) that North and CIA employees made statements to overthrow the government in Nicaragua; and (b) that the CIA prepared an "assassination manual" contrary to law. In both cases, the IOB found the allegations unfounded. A third IOB memorandum provided in response to the Board's request is discussed *infra*.

3. The IOB cited three points to establish that section 8066 did not apply to the NSC and, presumably, its staff. First, the IOB looked to Congressional intent, which it asserted was demonstrated by the parallel but narrower provisions of the FY 1985 Intelligence Authorization Act. That Act, passed by Congress the day after section 8066, was narrower in two respects: (a) it omitted the reference to "any agency or entity involved in intelligence activity"; and (b) it was limited to "funds authorized to be appropriated by this Act or by the Intelligence Authorization Act for Fiscal Year 1984." Legal intent as evinced by this narrower statute was deemed to govern interpretation of the DOD Appropriations Act.

Second, the IOB noted that E.O. 12333, which designates the NSC as the "highest Executive Branch entity" responsible for the conduct of foreign intelligence, does not include the NSC among the agencies comprising "the Intelligence Community."

Finally, the IOB argued that the exclusion of the NSC Staff was intended by Congress because the prescribed role of the NSC was to coordinate rather than implement covert action.

4. Section 8050 of P.L. 99–190 provided:
None of the funds available to the Central Intelligence Agency, the Department of Defense, or any other agency or entity of the United States involved in intelligence activities may be obligated or expended during fiscal year 1986 to provide funds, material, or other assistance to the Nicaraguan democratic resistance unless in accordance with the terms and conditions specified by section 105 of the Intelligence Authorization Act (Public Law 99–169) for fiscal year 1986.

5. On December 4, 1985, the date the provision passed, Lee Hamilton, Chairman of the House Permanent Select Committee on Intelligence, wrote to CIA Director Casey on the statute:

[I]ntelligence personnel are not to act as military advisors to the contras. This certainly includes advising them on logistical operations upon which military or paramilitary operations depend for their effectiveness.

David Durenberger, then Chairman of the Senate Select Committee on Intelligence, offered a different view, forwarding CIA Director Casey a copy of his letter to Congressman Hamilton of December 5:

[A]dvice on logistics activities integral to the effectiveness of *particular* military and paramilitary operations is precluded if it would 'amount to' participation in such activities, even if there is no *physical* participation. At the same time . . . the conferees did not mean to place the entire subject of logistics off limits. We certainly would, for example, want to encourage advice on logistics related to the effective distribution of humanitarian and communications assistance.

Congressman Hamilton countered by letter of December 9:

[T]he Act makes clear direct CIA logistical advice on the effective distribution of humanitarian assistance is not appropriate.

6. The IOB memorandum addressed the question, "Can the Central Intelligence Agency or any other agency of the U.S. Government legally provide generic military training to the Nicaraguan democratic resistance?"

It concluded:

[T]he Intelligence Authorization Act for FY 1986 does authorize the obligation or expenditure of funds by the Central Intelligence Agency, the Department of Defense or other intelligence-related agencies of the U.S. Government to provide basic military training for the Nicaraguan democratic resistance so long as such training does not amount to the participation in the planning or execution of military or paramilitary operations in Nicaragua.

7. Even before the CIA field officer made his disclosures to the Board, his activities had triggered a legal debate within the CIA. In a memorandum dated December 5, 1986 to the Deputy Director for Operations, CIA Associate General Counsel Jameson stated that "contacts with the benefactors, although contrary to policy, were not contrary to law." Flight vectors, Sandanista anti-aircraft positions, and other similar information needed to carry out safe aerial deliveries fell within the terms of the "advice" authorized in December, 1985 by the Intelligence Authorization Act.

By memorandum to the CIA General Counsel of January 22, 1987, the CIA Inspector General's office questioned Jameson's interpretation. The Inspector General maintained, among other things, that the field officer's activities could be characterized as planning for a paramilitary operation, expressly barred in the Joint Explanatory Statement accompanying the Conference Committee Report to H.R. 2419.

8. We have no information linking the activities described herein as "Project Democracy" with the National Endowment for Democracy. The latter was created in 1983 by Congress and is funded by legislation. Its purpose is to strengthen democratic institutions around the world through private, non-governmental efforts. NED grew out of an earlier Administration public initiative to promote democracy around the world, which came to be known as "Project Democracy." It appears that LtCol North later adopted the term to refer to his own covert operations network. We believe this is the only link between the NED and LtCol North's activities.

9. President Arias learned of the existence of the airport shortly after he came to office in May 1986. He felt the airstrip compromised Costa Rican neutrality and informed Ambassador Tambs that it was not to be used.